Electronic Financial Services: Technology and Management

HAKMAN A. WAN

CP

Chandos Publishing
Oxford · England

Chandos Publishing (Oxford) Limited
Chandos House
5 & 6 Steadys Lane
Stanton Harcourt
Oxford OX29 5RL
UK
Tel: +44 (0) 1865 884447 Fax: +44 (0) 1865 884448
Email: info@chandospublishing.com
www.chandospublishing.com

First published in Great Britain in 2006

ISBN:
1 84334 132 8 (paperback)
1 84334 190 5 (hardback)

British Library Cataloguing-in-Publication Data.
A catalogue record for this book is available from the British Library.

Typeset by Domex e-Data Pvt. Ltd.
Printed in the UK and USA.

Contents

List of figures

List of tables

Preface

Unlike the tidal wave of e-commerce that hit (and left?) the retail market at the turn of the century, the financial services industry has been quietly revolutionised by information and communication technology (ICT). We have seen more and more financial services institutions and their consumers making transactions online. To the industry, corporate websites and Web-based applications are a means to cut cost, to get more customers, and to retain competitiveness in the increasingly hazardous business environment. A better understanding of the ICT infrastructure on which those applications depend can certainly support better management of their strategic use, as well as supporting the daily operations of those systems that are unique in the financial services industry.

This book is written to fill the gap between a generalist's view on information system management and the almost unreadable techies' manuals. It introduces the contemporary concepts of ICT – hardware, software, communication and information management – in the first two chapters. Most of the technical jargon used in the book is explained in Chapter 2. The next five chapters are dedicated to the discussion of the ICT applications developed for various sectors of the financial services industry – banking, payment, insurance, stock brokerage and fundraising. The book also offers a rather comprehensive review of risk management, which is divided into three areas: security management, regulatory compliance, and financial risk management – the three topics of the last three chapters. These three areas are definitely the major concern of today's financial services institutions, whether they operate on- or offline.

Descriptions of ICT applications are given at both a high-level perspective (which shows the functionality of the applications) as well as a lower-level view (which reveals the applications' capacity, limitations, scalability and maintainability). The book does not intend to explain technicality in great detail. It only mentions a few technological developments that are commonly found in the vocabulary of systems analysts and consultants when they deal with ICT applications in the financial services sector. The jargon selected, especially in Chapter 2, represents those terms needed in the descriptions of systems at the higher level.

Besides descriptions of technological and management issues, a number of small cases are collected in various places throughout the book. These are real-life examples of application developments that have been put into practical use. A few questions are attached at the end of each chapter to let readers recap some of the topics in the chapter or begin a more in-depth discussion of them. Besides being an information source for management, the book could be used as a textbook for courses in relation to modern financial services.

This book is prepared at the time when both ICT products and the financial services market are rapidly changing. The information it captures reflects the contemporary development of ICT applications in the e-financial services sector as well as the regulatory landscape of 2006. This is the time when the effects of several new laws and regulations (such as the Sarbanes-Oxley Act and Patriot Act in the USA) have just begun to emerge; these effects will surely affect the next generation of ICT applications that are designed for the financial services sector. However, it is believed that the basic infrastructure for ICT applications will not deviate too widely from the ones described in this book.

The author is indebted to Dr Glyn Jones and Dr Rex Sharman for their generous advice in relation to the completion of the book.

Disclaimer

This book aims to provide up-to-date information on e-financial services and the information and communication technologies deployed in the finance sector. Any theory, opinion, report, or recommendation in it cannot be deemed to engage the author, any contributor, or the publisher. Thus, neither the author nor the publisher shall: provide any warranty, expressed or implied, as to the accuracy, timeliness, completeness, merchantability or fitness for any purpose of any information contained in the book; assume any liability for any damage or loss, in contract, warranty, tort or otherwise, incurred in connection with any information contained in this book; or endorse or accept any liability for the content or use of linked websites. The URLs mentioned in this book are for information purposes only and are subject to change without notice.

Moreover, mentioning of commercial products is also for illustration only. The author has no intention to recommend or endorse those products, and mentioning them does not imply that they are the best available products in the market.

About the author

Hakman A. Wan is an assistant professor in the School of Business and Administration of the Open University of Hong Kong. Besides teaching and researching subjects related to ICT usage in e-business for many years, Dr Wan is also the designer of several study programmes offered by the university and is an experienced writer of cases and teaching materials at both under- and postgraduate levels.

The author may be contacted at:

E-mail: *hmwan@ouhk.edu.hk* or *haman838@hotmail.com*

1

The new age of financial services

Impact of technology

All the turmoil and instability experienced by the financial services sector in the last decade or so can be attributed, either directly or indirectly, to the advance in information and communication technology (ICT), among which the Internet has triggered the greatest change. It is the new frontier for business opportunity, but also the treacherous waters where people and businesses have drowned. The e-commerce hype that turned into the dot.com bubble a few years ago still haunts our memory today.

Similar bubbles occurred in the financial services sector. Having been optimistic about the potential of the Internet, Wells Fargo Bank, the Security First Network Bank (SFNB), NetBank (Nasdaq: NTBK; formerly NetB@nk) and some others corporations (mostly in the USA) began Internet banking in 1995 and 1996. Only NetBank managed any profit[1] and when SFNB was sold to Royal Bank of Canada in 1998, the deal could still have included a handsome amount of assets,[2] however, many other Internet banks were simply being shut down within one or two years.

Failure stories in e-commerce are lessons to learn from, but they do not make the Internet less attractive. The growth in e-commerce continues and has even been praised as one of the few high points in the otherwise flat economic landscape in the new millennium (Hansen, 2003). The US Department of Commerce released figures of retail e-commerce sales on 19 August, 2005, showing an upward trend of sales (Figure 1.1). Similarly encouraging figures can be found in other parts of the world. In the UK, for example, the Interactive Media in Retail Group reported a 44 per cent growth rate for the online retail sector in 2003, and Forrester Research predicted that the growth rate in 2004 would increase slightly to 46 per cent. In the Far East, iNAGO, the inventor of

Figure 1.1 **Estimated quarterly US retail e-commerce sales from Q4 1999 to Q2 2005**

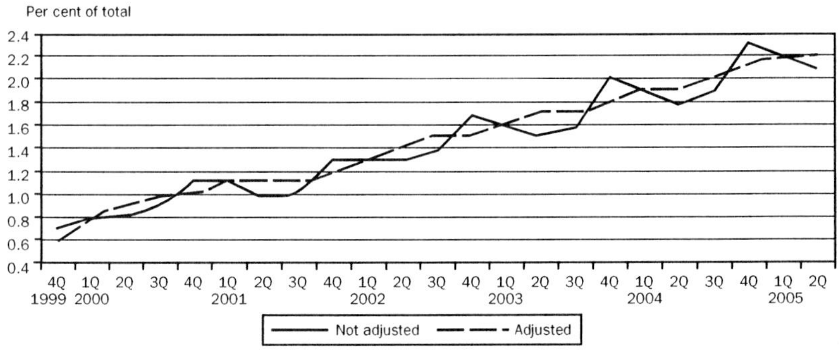

Source: US Department of Commerce (2005)

digital pets and a provider of e-service solutions, maintains its positive perspective towards the development of e-business in Japan.

The optimism is unmistakable. This time, every country is more ready to accept the Internet as a new battleground for business. In the Economist Intelligence Unit[3] (EIU) white paper 'The 2004 e-readiness rankings', researchers measured different countries' e-business environments by assessing their technology infrastructure; general business environment; degree to which e-business was adopted by consumers and companies; social and cultural conditions that influenced Internet usage; and the availability of services to support e-business. The EIU concluded that governments could influence the rate and nature of adoption of technology and applications. Success in the Scandinavian countries was attributed to the formal coordination between government agencies and the IT industry, so was the rapid acceptance rate of broadband technology in Asia (in particular, South Korea, Hong Kong, Taiwan and Singapore). Governments in these countries played a major role in three areas: being an early adopter (e-government), promoting education programmes and enacting new legislation.

Figure 1.2 shows how the ranking of e-readiness changed from 2003 to 2004; it also reflects how much some of these countries have done to improve their rankings. Denmark, for example, moved up one step, largely due to the Danish government's efforts in promoting B2B e-commerce, with a number of Danish companies making themselves global leaders in the use of B2B applications (Andersen et al., 2003). These efforts gave Denmark the largest relative population of online shoppers (36 per cent).

Figure 1.2 **The change in e-reading rankings**

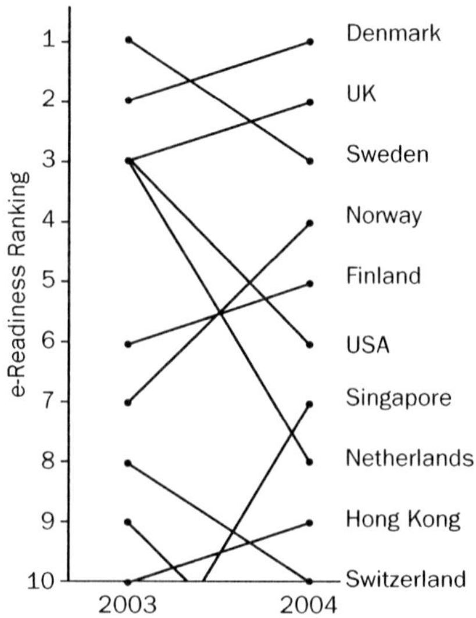

Data source: EIU (2004)

Andersen et al. (2001) analysed the changes that had occurred in Denmark and drew a conceptual framework for the growth of e-commerce in the country. The framework divided changes into three layers: demand drivers, enablers/inhibitors and social/economic impacts. Without loss of generality, the same framework is applicable to the analysis of the changes in the financial services sector.

The top of Figure 1.3 illustrates four demand drivers: industry and organisational structure; information infrastructure; financial and human resources; and consumer and social factors. The finance market began its process of change only when the financial services industry had gathered sufficient momentum. This was attained by increased competitiveness, sound ICT infrastructure and availability of financial and human resource support. Only then did the financial services community begin to accept the idea of electronic finance; and its market – the e-finance market – could then take shape quickly. In responding to industry demand, governments might give their blessing to the e-finance market by establishing laws and policy to regulate it. That is to say, those governments who are slow in responding to the demand may inhibit the development of the e-finance market in their respective countries.

The e-finance market might then take a few years to diffuse and, in turn, to impact on the socio-economic structure of the country. Figure 1.3 shows three areas where further change is possible. Traditional businesses

Figure 1.3 Conceptual framework of e-finance development

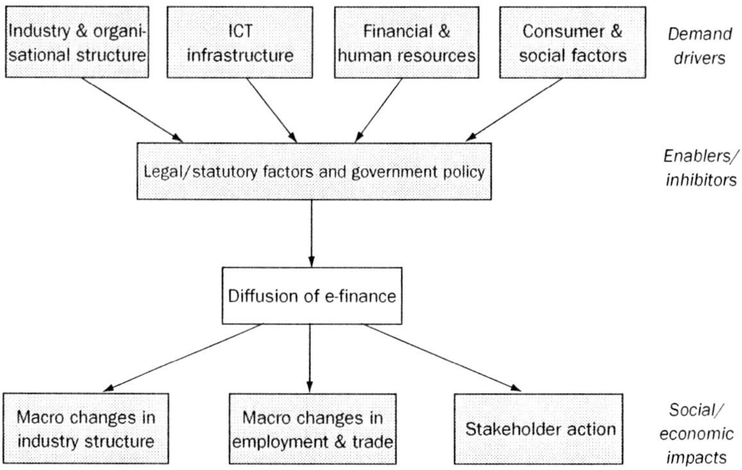

Adapted from: Andersen et al. (2001)

might need to reconsider their strategy, or to change the industry structure in order to cope with challenges from the Internet. The human resource market and the education systems might respond to the predictable shortage of qualified people in the e-finance sector. Last but not least, stakeholders might adjust their expectations and investment strategy.

This is the big picture of the development of the e-financial services sector. However, this book focuses on just one of the demand drivers – ICT. As Allen (2002) defined e-finance as 'the provision of financial services and markets using electronic communication and computation', it is certain that ICT is one of the critical factors for success in this new breed of financial services. The industry and organisational structure must be ready for e-finance development; the market should not be short of financial and human resources; and finally, consumers should learn to accept the new products and services that are offered. However, if these products and services are to be successfully offered in the e-financial services sector, they must be the result of collaboration between managers who know the business and ICT applications. Indeed, ICT stands out as the main catalyst that triggers all the action among the other demand drivers in Figure 1.3.

As an introduction to the importance of ICT in the finance service sector, this chapter examines two issues on ICT management – *infrastructure* management and *information* management.

ICT management in e-financial services

Computer Associates (NYSE: CA), one of the leading providers of e-business software, classifies its products into three levels: infrastructure management, information management and business process management. Similarly, the management of ICT in the field of e-finance can also be divided, as follows:

- *Business process management*: To take care of various stakeholders and those business processes that are integrated to form a value chain.
- *Information management*: To enable the management of a massive volume of information that comes from various sources and diversified applications.
- *Infrastructure management*: To manage networks, systems, databases and applications (including security mechanisms).

At the lowest level, the management must be able to provide a faultless and secure environment for data to be transmitted, controlled, stored and processed. At the highest level, the management must monitor key processes to see if they are supported by appropriate ICT to guarantee effective and efficient operations, which can then be seamlessly integrated into the value chain of the e-finance institution. At the middle level, proper management of the information flow between the other two levels is essential to channel the business-critical information from multiple sources to support their destined e-finance processes.

On the other hand, the three levels of ICT management can also be regarded as a portfolio of ICT installation. The base of the installation is to guarantee security at the data level; the network structure (internal and external to the institution) provides the information flow; and the strategic applications are implemented to gain competitive advantage in the market. The management of each level requires a different set of know-how – for the lower-level structure, management is more technology-oriented.

The stratification of ICT also implies that each level should be working independently so that a modification at one level does not mandate changes at the other levels. A high proportion of reusable parts is necessary if the ICT structure was designed for constant upgrading. From a technical point of view, these parts are implemented in the form of 'components', each of which has a specific function, which can be brought together to build applications at higher levels. This component-oriented architecture depends on the reusability of components and provides the maintainability and scalability that many e-financial systems require. There could be thousands of components in an e-financial system, each supporting the functions of other components. Hence, a layered structure is a common scene in ICT systems.

The two lower levels of ICT management are discussed in the rest of this chapter. The e-finance applications level is left to later chapters.

ICT infrastructure management

The infrastructure of most information systems installed in an e-finance institution is influenced by the technology of client-server architecture. This is a two-layered structure where *clients* are applications or devices that make requests and receive information over the network. *Servers*, however, are applications or devices that host databases and websites, and often respond to the requests of the clients. The management of such an infrastructure involves at least the control of the clients, servers and the network in between.

The idea of client and server originates from a database server, a device dedicated to run a database management system (DBMS) and to respond to user queries directly. As SQL is the standard language to compose queries, SQL is a form of communication between database servers and client applications. For those applications in a *distributed* client-server system, they could also adopt a technology known as 'remote procedure calls' (RPC) to invoke a server.

Today, the client-server architecture is less popular than other architectures. The terms 'client' and 'server' could refer to any applications or devices. The only difference between the two is that the client applications request services or data from the servers, which respond to clients' requests. For example, a web server returns an HTML page when it receives a HTTP request. But if the same web server requests information from a database server, the former becomes a client during this session.

There are three-tiered and multi-tiered structures in today's e-financial systems. These are the subjects of the next chapter. To focus on ICT infrastructure, we will examine several technologies that are commonly found in the servers of those e-financial systems, including storage devices, servers, hosting and network management.

Storage device

The storage server (database server or file server) is vital to the operation of an e-financial system, as all transactions, records, messages, reports, web contents and security log files are stored in it. Storage management is concerned with the following tasks:

- *Configuration of the storage server*: Each server must comply with the hardware requirement. If there are several servers (and they are probably from different vendors), the configuration must include a unified interface so that users don't need to know the uniqueness of each server.
- *Data management*: Some applications doing the job of data management must be able to guarantee easy storage and retrieval of data. For backup purposes, they are also responsible for the production of shadow copies for various applications and the automation of file backup and disaster recovery. For security reasons, they should retain transaction logs and handle encryption and decryption processes.
- *Device monitoring*: The performance, capacity and utilisation attributes of the multi-vendor storage devices must be monitored at all times. When requested by applications, the monitor should respond and allocate storage resources if available.
- *Compliance with regulations*: Laws concerning data storage must be observed. For example, in the USA, these laws include data retention laws (including the Sarbanes-Oxley Act 2002 for all public corporations, the Health Insurance Portability and Accountability Act 1996 (HIPAA) for corporations in the healthcare industry and SEC regulations for retention of all electronic correspondence with clients). Legal issues will be discussed further in Chapter 9.

In the networked environment, two different technologies are available for the implementation of storage devices: network attached storage (NAS) and storage area network (SAN). NAS is a computer and a large storage device (a box called a 'storage appliance') that connects directly to the local area network (LAN). It acts like a file server, but works much faster and is more fault-tolerant. It provides a centralised point of data storage, especially favouring the situation in which many users simultaneously access a single file (e.g. a website). SAN, however, is a network of storage devices interconnected by fibre channels and each server on a LAN is connected to the SAN by a fibre channel. With a network structure, SAN is more scalable and performs better than traditional storage servers; however, it suffers from interoperability problems[4] and high implementation costs.

Although NAS and SAN were developed from different concepts, the storage market shows signs that these two technologies are converging. Management of NAS or SAN is thus concerned with similar problems such as:

- *Virtualisation*: This is a method mapping all disks that are connected to a server as a single resource. With virtualisation, storage administrators need not know the infrastructure (physical location, disk structure and the like) of each storage device, but they are still able to control files and data on multi-disk storage as if they come from a single logical entity. There are two kinds of virtualisation: in-band virtualisation and out-of-band virtualisation. In the former case, a virtualisation appliance (e.g. a router or any device with virtualisation software) is placed between the servers and the storage devices. If a server makes a request for data (by sending some control data, such as I/O addresses) it reaches the virtualisation appliance, which reads the control data and physically locates the required data and sends it to the server. In the latter case, an appliance adopting the out-of-band approach lies outside the data path. Receiving control data from the requesting server on one path, the appliance finds the data that are then returned to the server via another path (see Figure 1.4.)
- *Snapshot*: This is a way to speed up data access and recovery. There are two kinds of snapshot approaches: copy-on-write snapshot and

Figure 1.4 In-band virtualisation (left) and out-of-band virtualisation (right)

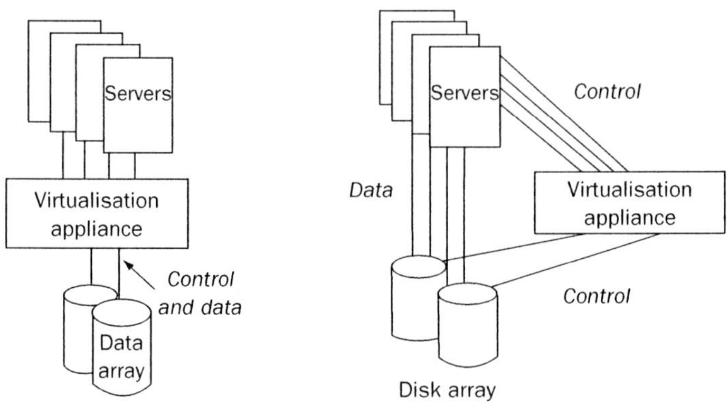

split-mirror snapshot. Using the former approach, utility software makes a snapshot (record) of changes to stored data whenever new data are entered or existing data are updated. If stored data are corrupted, recovery is possible with the present and all previous snapshots. Using the latter approach, the utility using a split-mirror approach creates a mirror copy of the entire volume of data periodically.

- *Provisioning*: This is the process to determine the exact type and quality of storage required by a new application (or when an existing application exceeds the current storage allocation), to locate the storage device within the NAS or SAN, and if SAN is used, to identify a path between the storage device and the application. The task is so time-consuming that administrators typically provide more storage than is needed. Recently, software tools for storage resource management have become available and provisioning has become an automated process. Moreover, the advent in provisioning combines virtualisation technology to provision a smaller storage than what has been requested. This method, called 'thin provisioning', can utilise storage space better without deteriorating the performance of the storage device.

There are storage service providers (SSPs) in the market. They offer a variety of storage-related services, including solutions to the aforementioned problems. The financial services are particularly attracted to SSPs because of their promises of uninterrupted access to data, unlimited storage and qualified (expert) management. Some SSPs also offer hosting services, which will be discussed later.

Case: AOK (Hitachi Data Systems, 2003)

AOK is the largest health insurance company in Germany and takes 37 per cent of the country's health insurance market. One of its branches, AOK Baden-Wuerttemberg insures about 4.2 million people, which is equivalent to almost 50 per cent of the population in the state of Baden-Wuerttemberg.

Historically, the IT structure of the branch office was divided into 13 production areas which could be run in parallel. For the sake of integration, these 13 areas were consolidated into a master data file for better customer coverage in 2001. The problem of capacity and performance was solved by using eight StorageTek SVA 9500 virtual disk systems, and the production of backup copies was taken care of by

StorageTek Virtual Snapshot. In the following year, four additional StorageTek V2X virtual disk arrays were installed, providing another 20 Tb of storage. StorageTek Snapshot worked well with both types of virtual disk systems. It could provide backup copies in the nightly batch processing. If an error was found in the process, restoration work could be carried out in seconds.

Hubertus Weilandt, project manager at AOK Baden-Wuerttemberg, said of the project:

> StorageTek Virtual Snapshot brought us many advantages in batch processing. We process not only our data in a time window. We make up to six backup copies at the same time in the same period. These backup copies are our guarantee of smooth and, above all, timely processing of our batches. Further copies are produced analogously for test data files. All of this is an enormous security advantage for our data processing.

Server management

To e-financial services institutions, network downtime can be devastating; yet institutions are unable to avoid errors or attacks that could bring their systems down. To reduce downtime, institutions need to invest in network fault tolerance – that is, the provision of duplicates to key components of their networked systems. Following this philosophy, fault tolerance on a network is created by load balancing and device failover (explained below). The former provides scalability to the network while the latter ensures reliability and recoverability.

Load balancing is the process of spreading requests across multiple devices in order to keep each device's load at a safer level. For example, if it is impossible to predict the visit rate to the website of a stockbroker, load balancing is implemented to house the corporate website in two or more web servers. If traffic to one server is too congested, requests are forwarded to another server. There are a number of algorithms by which a hardware- or software-based load balancer can determine which server to forward to.

The principle of load balancing implies that two or more devices of the same nature exist on the network. Many vendors implement load balancing by aggregating several identical servers into a 'server cluster'. For example, Microsoft 2000 Server may contain as many as 32 servers. They are connected together but appear to the network manager as one logical device. Moreover, the mechanism can detect the failure of any one of these servers, and quickly reallocate its load to another server in the cluster. To the users, the network system works continuously without the users knowing about any interruptions.

Failover is the process of moving services offered on one device to another when the device fails. This approach again relies on the existence of a device cluster. For example, two servers that share the same external storage device form a failover cluster. They are interconnected and constantly monitoring each other by using a 'heartbeat' mechanism. When one fails to send a heartbeat message, the other can immediately take up the storage of the failed server, resume its IP address, all network services and re-run any necessary applications. The shifting is usually carried out by a load balancer.

As several servers can respond to a request because of load balancing, it is often desirable to have the same server chosen to remain attached to the same client. This feature, called 'persistence', is essential in a transaction – like filling out a form or giving information on a credit card – when data are exchanged through a series of connections.

Case: Lehman Brothers (Hochmuth, 2001)

Lehman Brothers had a data centre and its IT department at the World Trade Financial Centre, but it was linked using four Cisco ONS 15000 optical transport system boxes to another data centre in Jersey City, New Jersey. The firm's trove of data was kept in EMC Corporation's storage arrays in both data centres. EMC's Symmetrix Remote Data Facility (SRDF), a data replication software, also provided backup for each array in case of an equipment failure in one of the two centres.

The September 11 attack destroyed 5,000 desktops and the entire data centre of the firm. However, its New Jersey data centre was able to increase the amount of bandwidth, allowing the firm to keep all of its offices up and running that very afternoon. The firm had 400 traders online to handle equities when the New York Stock Exchange reopened the next Monday. Surviving the attack, Bob Schwartz, managing director and CTO said, 'The network was the hero. No information was lost. I'm sure there were a couple of little things here and there, but nothing that interfered with our ability to provide service to our customers.'

Disaster recovery was soon on its way. Vendors such as Compaq quickly shipped and installed 2,500 PCs and a trading facility was created in the New Jersey data centre. The firm took over the Sheraton Manhattan Hotel and turned it into a new office. The hotel's ballroom became an IT hub and virtual private network connectivity was restored to the New Jersey data centre. One of its first activities was to declare a new failover site in London.

Enterprise hosting

For the sake of total cost of ownership (TCO), many e-financial institutions rely on external hosting providers to operate their online storefront. Not only do they supply sufficient storage for housing web pages and other applications, enterprise hosting companies offer value-added services such as domain name registration, e-mail account management, security management, traffic monitoring, disaster recovery (business continuity), server backup and provisioning, among other services.

In general, hosting providers offer two principal services: dedicated hosting and complex hosting.

- *Dedicated hosting*: Renting a dedicated server from the provider, the client corporation can have full control of the computer, which usually resides in the provider's data centre, allowing faster access, tighter security and greater scalability. If the client who owns the dedicated server takes up the work of hardware configuration, administration and maintenance, the provider is only responsible for supplying power, network bandwidth and data centre space. This is called a 'colocation' service.
- *Complex hosting*: Corporations that run large and complex online services may need a complex hosting solution, which involves multiple servers (e.g. multiple application servers and database servers). The highest level of service that a hosting provider can offer is to allow and assist custom configuration. A corporate customer can negotiate a favourable contract with the hosting providers, but many functionalities and services that could be contracted are fee-based. The corporate customer should consider whether these services are all necessary and cost-effective.

Enterprise hosting is outsourcing part of the management work of an online storefront to an external party. For a financial institution, conducting a due diligence on the hosting provider is necessary to ensure that the technical know-how and financial viability of the provider is sufficient to guarantee the same level of service in the future. For this matter, analysts of the hosting industry, hosting brokers and other intermediaries can offer benchmarking information.

Network management

The LAN used in an e-financial institution could have a number of storage servers and many other devices (such as routers, PCs, print servers and so on) that support day-to-day operations. Network management is a rather tedious job as most networks today are heterogeneous – that is, different manufacturers make the hardware and software that compose a network – which usually leads to compatibility problems. Network management becomes even more difficult if the LAN is connected to the Internet, which is so large that many problems occurring somewhere else on the Internet are not traceable. However, ISO developed a network management model that divides the activities of network management into the following five areas (Cisco, 2002: Chapter 6)

- *Performance management*: Performance parameters are monitored and compared with user-defined thresholds.
- *Configuration management*: The network and system configuration must be constantly under surveillance. Particular attention must be paid to assigning an IP address to every machine on the network, IP routing tables, different protocols used on the network and the counts of packets handled by each protocol.
- *Accounting management*: Utilisation by individual or group users is measured and recorded. This provides data to study capacity and maximises fairness of network access across all users.
- *Fault management*: Network problems, when detected, are logged and signalled to stakeholders. If possible, the network management system should initiate recovery processes to ensure minimal disruption of normal operations.
- *Security management*: To provide access control to the network as well as to individual resources (including systems, databases and other entities).

E-financial systems that run on the Internet rely on a common protocol for data transmission – TCP/IP. There is a subset of the TCP/IP protocol called 'Simple Network Management Protocol' (SNMP) that offers some tools for the management of devices on a network. Using SNMP, each device on the network has an application that collects and returns information on the device to a central manager. In SNMP terminology, those devices to be monitored are called 'agents' (such as network servers, bridges, hubs, routers and the like) and the 'manager' is a console through which the network administrator performs network management activities.

SNMP defines the format and meaning of messages that are exchanged between the manager and an agent. By sending a message with a special code, the manager can request an agent to return performance and state information. By using another code on the message, the manager can also control the agent. More importantly, the manager can use another code to 'trap' the agent; i.e. to require the agent to notify the manager about a certain incident, as determined by the code. The five areas of network management mentioned above can be accomplished by using SNMP.

All applications that constitute an e-financial system are implemented on top of the previously discussed infrastructure. The quality of the information output from these applications depends on how data are received by the storefront, processed by the application, stored and transmitted across the network. The ICT infrastructure of an e-financial system is not just any other ICT infrastructure. It must be capable of handling data of diversified origins, from distributed sources, and at a volume that fluctuates significantly on a minute-to-minute basis. Only when the infrastructure works well can information management be performed effectively.

Information management

Information management has a different meaning for the financial services sector, which has a wide range of information sources, such as customer transactions, public records, breaking news, market research, credit reports and bulletins from supervisory bodies. All information must be loaded, cleaned, reconciled, consolidated and delivered to the right applications in the system, and stored in a way that is safe and compliant with local laws and regulations.

The following sections cover four issues: data warehousing, information integration, business intelligence and knowledge management. Data warehousing is important to information management as it is a common technology for information storage; information integration is the process of consolidating information from various sources; e-business intelligence explores the practical use of data warehousing and other technologies; and knowledge management aims to elicit and maintain knowledge in the organisation so that information can be used effectively. Even if they are not found in some e-financial systems, these issues will have popped up at some time during the design and implementation stages of the systems.

Data warehouse management

To cater for the diversified sources and variety of data, financial institutions look to data warehousing technology for the storage, management and exploitation of these data. A data warehouse is an advanced form of database, constructed to supply an integrated, company-wide view of high-quality information to decision-support systems (DSS). Many data warehousing solutions in the market are associated with data-mining tools, which can be used alone or by a DSS on a data warehouse. Common data-mining tools include statistical and heuristic algorithms, the details of which are beyond the scope of this book.

The installation of an advanced storage device is not enough to integrate data from disparate sources. The mass of data could be incomplete, self-contradictory, duplicated and in different formats, and would need to be consolidated (i.e. combined into matching records) before being put into practical use. There are service providers that are expert in data extraction, cleansing and loading, in a process known as 'extraction, transformation and loading' (ETL). All a client corporation needs to do is to weigh between cost and benefit. To reduce the cost, the corporation should determine what sort of applications, including DSS, are supported by the data warehouse and what data should be supplied.

The banking industry has quickly accepted the advantages of data warehousing. Either using an all-inclusive approach or a selective approach, banks build up their data warehouse for their DSS or for gathering business intelligence. One highly publicised DSS works for customer relationship management (CRM), which is no stranger to many financial institutions. In the last decade, the market has seen institutions using CRM and data-mining techniques to discover trends and behaviours. To financial services, CRM is inseparable from knowing customer preferences, promoting new products and retaining valued customers. With the right sort of information in data warehouses, financial institutions can use data-mining tools in credit risk assessment, forensic accounting, financial engineering and related situations (see Figure 1.5).[5]

Figure 1.5 Data mining can solve problems in customer relationship management

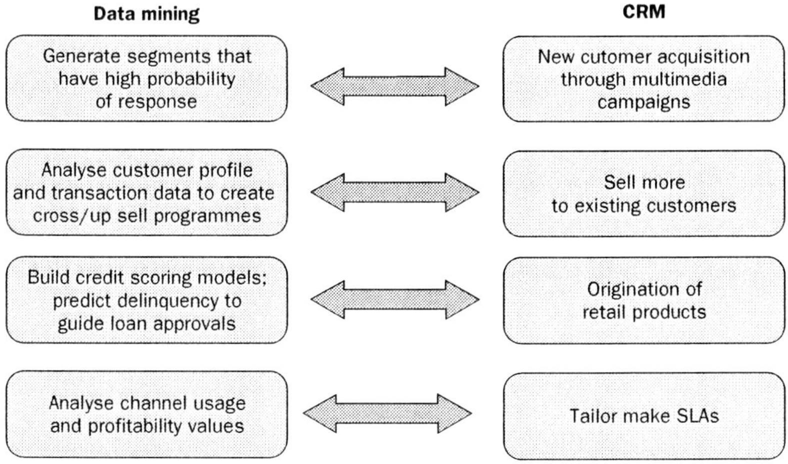

CRM: customer relationship management; SLA: service level agreement
Source: Vaidya (2003)

Enterprise information integration

Data integration using ETL tools is a process to present users with a unified and consistent view of the data aggregated in a corporation's data warehouses. This is particularly important to financial institutions that receive information from a variety of sources. Moreover, data can come in different formats and media. Without information integration, a manager cannot compile a risk report, for example, with financial data that come from different data sources (they could be corporate databases, data warehouses, data marts and even Internet portals). For the sake of simplicity, these data resources are called 'data silos' in this book.

A technique known as 'enterprise information integration' (EII) is available to deal with this diversity problem. It provides information integration at the data level and delivers aggregated data to external applications (e.g. an online storefront). From the user's perspective, EII is a network of data silos where the user may query without needing to know precisely how data are retrieved from each data silo. Upon request, the EII can produce real-time aggregated information and allow data updating. To the e-financial institution, EII does more than data-level integration. It can be used to support the value chain by integrating data silos and applications, including operational systems and DSS, with the efficiency that meets customers' expectation.

The technology of EII supports the implementation of straight-through processing (STP) – a dream that is shared among consumers, financial traders, insurers and other parties in the finance industry. STP is the ultimate purpose of integration. It is an automation of the end-to-end processing of transactions to allow maximum efficiency and minimum TCO. To achieve STP, an institution needs to streamline back-office activities, integrate all applications involved and rationalise all business processes.

STP in the financial services sector also means interorganisational integration. As shown in Figure 1.6,[6] the process of making an investment involves a number of steps and a number of parties. From initiation to completion, the investment transaction may involve fund managers, Global Straight Through Processing Association's Transaction Flow Manager,[7] brokers, custodians and the Depository Trust Company.[8] Each party runs its own management process such as tracking and reporting, and generates data that would be entered to the process of another party. With STP, data and all these processes are integrated into a continuous workflow that can be run automatically without re-keying any data in between.

STP requires (1) integration of data silos; (2) integration of applications (including web portals, transaction processing, CRM and other back-end systems); as well as (3) integration of business processes of all parties involved in the STP. Data integration is made possible by EII and sometimes data warehousing; application integration is accomplished by a technology known as 'enterprise application integration' (EAI). EAI aggregates enterprise information by using a messaging system, which is a system of message standards; middleware for routing messages; and adapters for interfacing applications and data silos. EAI and messaging systems are discussed in greater detail in Chapter 2.

Figure 1.6 **An end-to-end investment process**

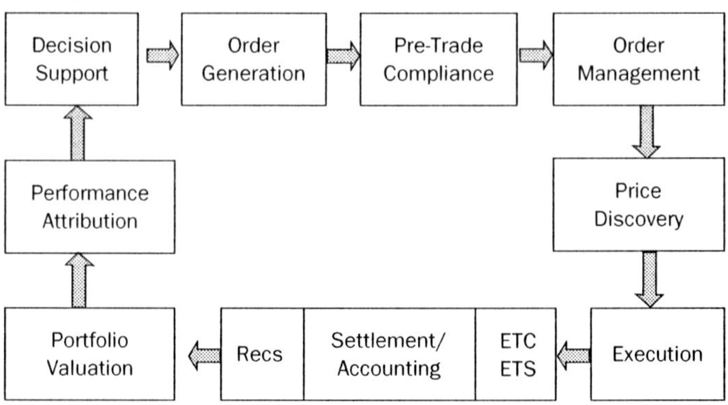

ETC/ETS: electronic trade confirmation/settlement
Source: Wraith (2001)

E-business intelligence

The term 'business intelligence' is almost a synonym of 'decision-support system' but it has become more popular lately. In the broad sense, business intelligence is a collection of applications and technologies for gathering, storing, analysing and providing access to data to support decision making. Thus, a business intelligence system usually includes a data warehouse, in which data have gone through ETL and are ready for flexible drill-down and roll-up analyses.[9] Many enterprise resource planning solutions incorporate data warehouses as well as business intelligence tools, and are capable of providing information for decision making in all levels of management. Some corporations integrate their business intelligence systems with their business processes in a way that decisions made by the business intelligence systems can be applied directly. For example, a credit assessment operation can be linked up to a business intelligence system that gathers information including credit bureau and scoring services. This tight integration is known as 'closed-loop decision-making'.

If seen in the whole picture of ICT framework (Figure 1.7), a business intelligence solution lies as a middle layer between the layers of data silos and applications. Through the enterprise portal, external and internal users may get access to the business intelligence tools. Not only does the portal act as an interface between the corporate ICT structure and the

Figure 1.7 **A general ICT framework showing business intelligence system**

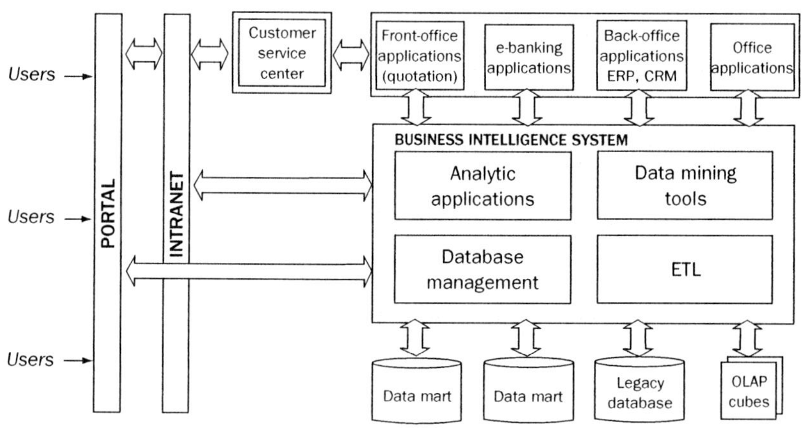

CRM: customer relationship management; ERP: enterprise resource planning; ETL: extraction, transformation and loading; OLAP: online analytical processing

users, it also needs to show an integrated view of the data repositories as well as applications available to the users.

From the management's perspective, business intelligence tools are used to find means to reduce costs, to search for new business opportunities and to optimise pricing. To discover intelligence from data silos, a business intelligence system has a large arsenal of techniques, including SQL for database queries, OnLine Analytical Processing (OLAP) tools, data-mining tools, and special purpose tools such as activity-based costing, supply chain analytics, customer analytics, balanced scorecards, optimisation models and simulation. Depending on the available data, these tools are capable of analysing correlations, causes and effects, trends and patterns, or to test hypotheses with the data. Findings in the discovery-based or hypothesis-based tests could give an edge to the financial institution.

CRM, as one of the applications of business intelligence, has become fashionable in recent years. A CRM system provides business intelligence techniques to identify value customers, to discover customer demands and to foster a stronger tie with customers. For e-financial services institutions, business intelligence techniques can be linked to corporate portals (that convert business intelligence into e-business intelligence). It explains the business intelligence tools found on the websites of many mortgage banks or insurance companies. Through these tools, customers can get an instant quotation of mortgage rates or policy prices. Some business intelligence CRM tools can also be integrated into corporate portals for management purposes, such as to monitor online transactions and customer click-through.

Business intelligence tools can be used for management at the strategic level. For example, the balanced scorecard is a common tool for corporate management. Developed by Robert Kaplan and David Norton in 1992, the balanced scorecard measures a selected set of key performance indicators (KPIs) in order to give a 'balanced' view of an organisation. Kaplan and Norton suggested that the performance of an organisation should be assessed from four perspectives: financial, customer, learning and growth, and internal process. Figure 1.8 shows the perspectives as well as relevant KPIs in the bancassurance industry. Notice that financial measure is not the only measure as in traditional accounting. The scorecard method takes both quantitative and qualitative measures into account; it also considers internal and external factors – past, current and future.

From each of the perspectives, an organisation must define its objectives, measures, targets and initiatives, such that each perspective

Figure 1.8 Balanced scorecard framework of the bancassurance industry

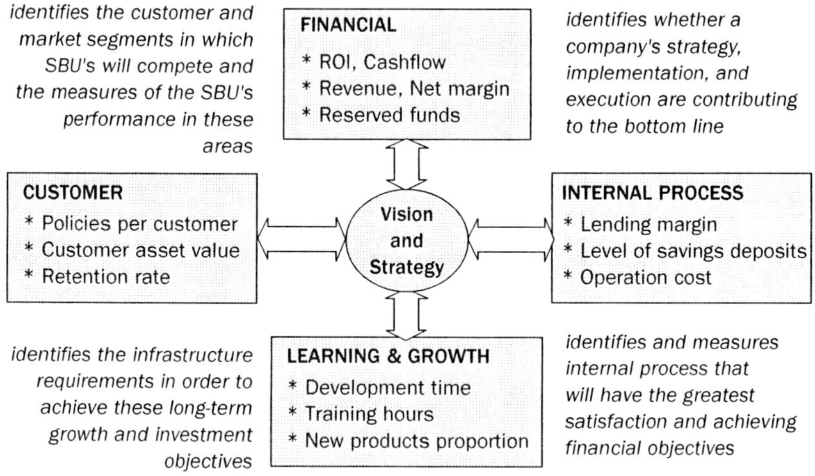

has its objectives, each objective has its measures, each measure has its targets, and each target has its initiatives. These initiatives are action programmes that drive performance. As business intelligence solutions collect continual streams of data from the initiatives, the corporate data warehouse can supply real-time data to compare with KPI targets and to generate immediate exception reports if necessary. The method is popular among banks, including Chemical Bank, Citibank, HSBC, NatWest (Anand, 2003).

Knowledge management

While business intelligence systems cater for the structured information in the data silos, knowledge management systems glean business knowledge from the mass of unstructured information (often much knowledge is found in unstructured data). Knowledge management is important for corporations that wish to be sensitive to the market, quick to respond and bold to innovate. These are the critical success factors for financial services institutions that extend their operations online. Their management needs the mindset of an entrepreneur and cherishes all skills and knowledge within their reach. Using knowledge management solutions, they are able to elicit knowledge from pilot work teams, communities of practice and other knowledge sources internal or external to the institutions. The system could codify elicited knowledge, package it and let it be shared among employees, customers and/or business partners. For example, Skandia regards intellectual capital as important as financial capital to the corporation (Earl, 2001) and invests in knowledge management initiatives. Many credit unions offer their automated advice and knowledge-based solutions online to let customers search for loan information that suits their needs.

Knowledge management is a process, and business organisations should be concerned with encouraging company-wide participation and communication, and developing a self-questioning approach to knowledge management. They should organise large and small communities of practice (CoPs) for this purpose. First coined by Lave and Wenger (1991), the term 'CoP' now refers to a cross-organisational group of people who share common skills and practices in selected business processes. Three features characterise a CoP that distinguish it from a taskforce or project team (Wenger, 1998):

- It is focused on a particular area of activity or body of knowledge. The understanding of the focus is continually re-negotiated among members in the community.
- People join a CoP because they are involved in some common activities. Very often they act as the champion, facilitator, practice leader, sponsor and members in the group. They are bound together by their interest in the shared focus, mutual exchange and learning.
- A CoP produces a 'shared repertoire' of communal resources, which includes written procedures, policies, rules, vocabularies, styles and other codified knowledge.

Kimble et al. (2001) differentiate between 'hard' and 'soft' knowledge, although they assert that the two are not mutually exclusive. As hard knowledge is more formalised and can be structured and articulated much easier, management feels soft knowledge is elusive. Soft knowledge often tangles with the social and cultural environment that affects human cognition. It is more subtle, implicit and difficult to capture. Describing the function of a CoP, Kimble et al. discern three methods that CoPs may use to construct soft knowledge:

- gathering of domain knowledge – for example, how to solve a tricky problem;
- construction of knowledge of work practices specific to the community – for example, knowledge of the idiosyncrasies of a special system;
- construction of knowledge about the competencies of some people.

As more and more organisations are adopting an international strategy, the Internet or intranet provides an easy means for communications, for sharing information, and for participation in a CoP, which can now have members geographically distributed, and may even include people outside the organisation. The community is configured as a network and is re-named a 'network of practice' (NoP). This concept of 'virtual CoP' was once believed to be a natural outcome of the marriage of CoP and the Internet; but many researchers (including Kimble et al., 2001) find face-to-face communication is still essential for building trust among members in a CoP.

A CoP could be a self-directed and self-motivated group that can build commitment, ownership, engagement and focus without much interference from managerial control. However, management may doubt if a CoP has ever performed. It has been suggested that an organisation needs to foster a culture of knowledge management such that CoPs may work under peer pressure.

Knowledge captured into various kinds of documents is stored in the knowledge management system where proper directories and pointers are set up. However, it takes more than technology to promote a knowledge management culture that encourages sharing of knowledge. The corporation may need to organise learning events periodically and gradually adopt a strategy of being a learning organisation, when its CoPs are capable of learning from external experts.

Case: Communities of practice at the Inter-American Development Bank (Moreno, 2001)

The Inter-American Development Bank (IDB) is a multilateral development institution established to help accelerate economic and social development in Latin America and the Caribbean. It has 46 national memberships and includes the Inter-American Investment Corporation and the Multilateral Investment Fund. Headquartered in Washington, DC, IDB has country offices in each of its borrowing member countries and in Paris and Tokyo; its annual lending reached $5.2 billion in the year 2000.

In 1999, IDB established an interdepartmental coordinating group, the Knowledge Exchange Network Steering Committee (KENSTEER), to explore the potential of knowledge exchange and leveraging institutional knowledge principles. In particular, KENSTEER was asked to study those informal interest groups in IDB. Called by the names *clusters*, *networks*, *communities of practice*, or *thematic groups*, these groups appeared to be forums for professional staff to promote knowledge generation and dissemination, and had become a way to connect those staff from various departments in the bank who were working or interested in similar issues.

KENSTEER found that ICT was acting as an enabler for the proliferation of the activities of these groups. Face-to-face interactions were considered very important, but group members also used e-mail, distribution lists, and electronic public folders as a virtual forum space for professional staff and as aids to discussion and members' communication. Content in the public folders indicated a modest level conversion of tacit knowledge into explicit knowledge and there were some efforts at collaboration among the groups.

As CoPs are also established in other institutions (e.g. World Bank, BP Amoco and the United Nations Development Programme), KENSTEER is positive towards the various groups in IDB. Knowing that many of these groups are in the early stages of development, KENSTEER recommended giving these groups some kind of support and recognition. However, the management is cautious in maintaining the natural dynamism and necessary autonomy of these groups.

Summary

As an introduction to the e-financial services industry from a technology management angle, this chapter underlines the impact of the Internet and the importance of ICT deployment in the industry. Our attention rests on two levels of ICT management – ICT infrastructure management and information management.

Technologies were described in this chapter as they are basic components of the ICT infrastructure of e-financial systems. They are imperative to management in e-financial services because they represent the contemporary technologies that are being deployed in almost all Web-based systems. Theories on information management reviewed in this chapter are equally important because they are being implemented in e-financial systems and make a difference from traditional business. In Chapter 2, we will recap some of the technologies and more technical details will be examined.

Questions for discussion

1. What is the implication of the layered structure of Computer Associates' products; i.e. does it matter about putting business process management in the middle layer?
2. Investigate how a storage service provider is assessed.
3. What is the difference between a business intelligence and a knowledge management system?

Notes

1. Source: *http://www.ababj.com/feature1_0799.html* (accessed: 20 October 2004).
2. The deal included $5.4 million in deposits, $14.3 million in loans, $46.5 million in securities and $10 million in capital; see: *http://www.ababj.com/webnotes_0598.html.*
3. The Economist Group's EIU is a leading provider of global business intelligence.
4. In the context of data storage, interoperability of different storage device refers to compatibility of data structure, format and interface.
5. See presentation at: *www.ficci.com/ficci/media-room/speeches-presentations/2003/sep/session5-g-vaidya.ppt.*
6. From Wraith (2001) 'Leveraging XML for STP', Conf. on Wall Street, NY; see presentation at: *http://lighthouse-partners.com/xml/presentations/James%20Wraith.ppt* (Last accessed: 4 January 2006).
7. Transaction Flow Manager (TFM) is a platform offered by Global Straight Through Processing Association, an association of the securities industry. TFM can track and route global trades and is the manager of the STP transaction.
8. Depository Trust Company is the central securities depository of the global market. It is owned by most of the major banks, broker-dealers and exchanges on Wall Street.
9. Techniques used in data analysis. Applications with drill-down tools are able to show data at a lower (in-depth) level if it is desired and with roll-up tools, data at a more generalised level is shown.

2

Information technology and the Internet

Fundamentals of information and communication technology

Information and communication technology (ICT) is described in Chapter 1 as the infrastructure that integrates data silos and applications in e-business systems. From the management's perspective, ICT can cause problems at two levels: infrastructure management and information management, where theories, rules, techniques and tools are changing rapidly. If their knowledge of computer literacy is too general, business managers simply do not have the training to understand what has happened in ICT in relation to infrastructure and information management. To make matters worse, few books and magazines in the market are published to bridge the gap between the level of freshman computer literacy and that of formal technology training. This leaves little choice for business managers but to turn a deaf ear to any jargon emerging in their daily managerial work.

However, the speed of evolution and revolution in the ICT industry has never slowed down. If technical people need to be informed of the latest development, so do business managers. Managers in various functional areas, such as strategic planning, risk management, marketing and customer relationship, are frequent end-users of the information systems in the organisation. Their performance is related to how much they know about the usage, structure, technology and possible advancement of those systems. They would find information of the latest development and deployment of ICT interesting and helpful. This book is written for this purpose. Here, jargon is introduced on a need-to-know basis; using this jargon, ICT deployments in the e-finance sector can be described in more precise terminology. With some understanding of ICT infrastructure, managers may contribute more to the determination of rules, restrictions, potentials, advantages and evolution of their e-financial system.

The purpose of this chapter is to explain recent technological developments that are the foundation to ICT deployment in the e-finance service industry. The chapter is divided into three main topics, dedicated respectively to three major areas: communications and Internet technology, server technology and XML.

Communications and Internet technology

In the new millennium, every organisation clings to the Internet as a convenient, inexpensive and ubiquitous network to communicate with its clients, staff, suppliers and regulatory bodies. Some organisations might have a lingering memory of their networks as being dedicated LANs or WANs, but now these private networks have become parts of the Internet and their LAN and WAN are subsumed by intranet and virtual private networks (VPNs). It is the Internet technology that adds the letter 'e' to a financial system and converts an institution to an e-financial services institution.

To let every computer on the Internet talk with each other, the connection between computers is established by a collection of standard protocols known as TCP/IP (Transmission Control Protocol/Internet Protocol). These protocols enable data transmission on the Internet in the form of packets, which are small pieces of data sent from the sender along different routes to a destination. This method of transmission is known as 'packet-switching' and is considered an advanced form of communication (for example, packet switching is impossible for a telephone connection because a telephone conversation requires a fixed line to be established linking two talkers). TCP/IP is a low-level protocol as it treats data at the level of packets. There are higher-level protocols for larger or more formatted pieces of data. Two of them are prevalent:

- HTTP (HyperText Transfer Protocol) for transferring World Wide Web documents (web pages); and
- FTP (File Transfer Protocol) for downloading or uploading files from one computer to another via the Internet.

One of the features of TCP/IP is to give each computer on the Internet an identity, known as an 'IP address'. As the IP address is a string of 32 binary bits and is difficult to remember, it is associated with a domain name (e.g. www.chandospublishing.com), which is text-based and relatively meaningful. To have a domain name of its choice, an organisation needs to register the domain name with local Internet registries, which are non-profit organisations sharing the burden of distributing domain names on a regional level. The domain name system (DNS) is managed by The Internet Corporation for Assigned Names and Numbers (ICANN).

The largest portion of the Internet is the World Wide Web, where computers are connected by HTTP. Web pages displayed on the Web are written in a special coding system, HTML (HyperText Markup Language), which is made up of simple text and special tags. The text is the information content of a web page and the tags control its format, such as layout, structure, links to other web pages, and graphics and multimedia clips embedded in it. Using a browser, a text file in HTML can be converted to a stylish web page according to the formatting of the tags.

Even with its style tags and multimedia clips, a web page in HTML is usually static – that is, it only shows on a browser the information content that is defined in its text portion. If a customer wants to search for a share price on an e-stock system, they might expect the system to return a web page filled with the appropriate information. This is called a 'dynamic' web page, as it shows different content tailored for the viewer. It is made up of HTML with special elements embedded, for example, small pieces of program written in languages such as Java or more complex elements such as servlets.

The development of Java

Since Java was first offered by Sun Microsystems, Inc. (Nasdaq: SUNW) in the mid-1990s, it has become the most general language to construct business information systems. The language is designed to work in a 'virtual machine' (VM), which is an add-on to an Internet browser. Whenever a browser receives a Java program, it is activated in the VM regardless of the underlying machine or the operating system. This makes programs written in Java particularly suitable to work on the Internet. Many tools for Java application development can also be found from third-party vendors.

Another property that distinguishes Java from most third-generation languages ('3GLs', such as COBOL, Pascal and C) is that it is object-oriented' (OO). That is, programs written in Java adopt a principle to pack data entities together with specific procedures by which the entities are manipulated. These objects are self-contained, re-usable building blocks that enable quick program development and easy maintenance. The idea of objects later evolved into 'components'. In Java terminology, these application building blocks are called 'beans' and they are used to build up small applications called 'JavaBeans'. For example, if a JavaBean for calculating portfolio performance is available, it is relatively easy to plug into a Java-based investment management system so that the latter is capable of calculating portfolio performance.

Technically speaking, JavaBeans are constructed by application programming interfaces (APIs), which are sets of routines published by a particular operating system or application. By invoking these APIs in a program, a programmer can make requests to (i.e. interface with) the corresponding operating system or application. Four types of APIs are commonly used (Bray, 2004) by networked systems in a financial services institution. These are:

- *Remote procedure calls (RPCs)*: Embedded in the client, RPCs are used to invoke applications on remote servers.
- *Messaging APIs*: A client sends a message to a server that returns another message, usually in an asynchronous mode. Messaging APIs are responsible for ensuring the messages are delivered to the destination. They are sometimes called 'message-oriented middleware' (MOM) and will be examined later in this chapter.
- *Structured query language (SQL)*: SQL APIs allow applications to share data retrieved from common databases.
- *File transfer*: These APIs exchange data in the file format.

Note that the first two types of APIs help communications among applications but the last two types are for communications between applications and databases.

The financial services industry is not a novice in the use of Java. Charles Schwab implemented a Java-based system called 'Velocity' in August 1999. Using JavaBean components, Velocity is able to provide balance, trading history and quotes to Schwab's active traders. On the other hand, Wells Fargo Bank (one of the pioneers in e-banking) had the experience of using a Java-based enterprise model to integrate 25 disparate systems. The availability of Java tools and easy development of Java applications enabled the bank to complete the project well before the scheduled time (Rommel, 1999).

Web-database integration

An e-financial system requires TCP/IP to communicate with outside systems, Java language to implement internal logics and a database for the storage of data. The database is normally a relational database controlled by a database management system (DBMS). If a Java program is to get access to a database, it needs to specify how data are input, edited, or searched for by proper SQL statements embedded in the program. However, SQL is a vendor-specific language. For an e-financial system with multiple and diversified databases, identifying the right dialect of SQL before contacting any individual database is an essential but tedious job. Sun Microsystems thus developed their own API known as 'Java Database Connectivity' (JDBC) to convert general query statements to the special dialect that the DBMS can understand. With the JDBC lying in the middle, the Java application is said to be 'loosely coupled' with the databases. (In two later sections, the term 'loose coupling' might have other meanings in different circumstances.)

JDBC is an extension of ODBC (Open Database Connectivity) – Microsoft's attempt to link applications to MS Access, Excel and a few other databases (including dBase and DB2). ODBC is less favourable than JDBC for several reasons. First, ODBC is less portable, as it is not designed to work with Java programs. Second, ODBC is installed in the client's side and each of the client machines needs to be configured before they can be connected to the database. This implies that each time a new version of the ODBC is released, the process of re-configuring each client machine must be repeated. On the other hand, the JDBC driver rests with the server and benefits from the 'thin client' approach, i.e. it saves the client from bearing too many processes. However, ODBC is sometimes essential to a web-database connection, for example, in cases where an ODBC driver for a database exists but not JDBC. It is therefore not surprising to have both JDBC and ODBC in a system. Figure 2.1 shows a software driver known as 'JDBC-ODBC bridge', which is used to connect a Java program to any database that recognises ODBC.

Web application development and integration

As more and more applications are connected to the Internet, it is logical to speculate whether they could function as a whole – for example, to operate in a predefined workflow, to share the same data silos, or to hide behind the same firewall – in order to achieve the strategic goals of the

Figure 2.1 JDBC interfacing Java programs and databases

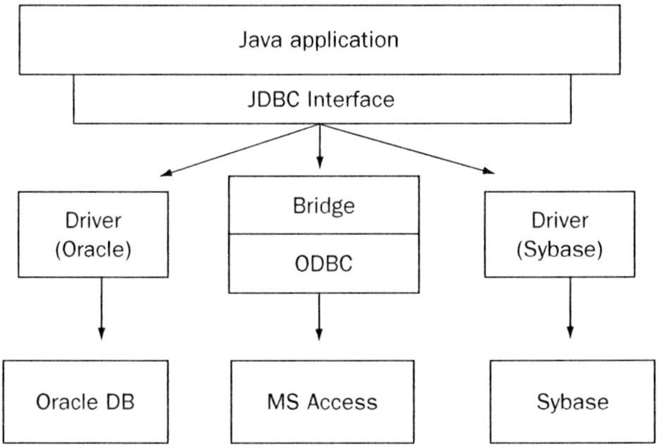

institution. Integration has therefore become an objective in application development because any new application must integrate with the existing applications. However, integration is not easy in reality. Applications in an organisational information system could be extremely heterogeneous. There could be legacy systems written in 3GLs and newer applications that are based on standards such as Java, XML and web services. Each of them could be designed for a different reason and on a different platform; and each is running towards the end of its lifecycle at a different speed. Thus, integrating these applications – i.e. making them talk to each other, share the same resources and work under the same principle – is difficult.

At the technical level, a clue is found in the 'component' structure of most applications developed in the last decade. A component is a small software piece that is implemented to process specific data entities in certain specific ways. Like an object, a component is self-contained and encapsulated; this means it has all the data resources and functions necessary to produce the desired result. As the working inside a component is isolated from the outside, a component can easily be replaced and re-used. Components are also designed to conform to a certain standard (e.g. CORBA[1] or Microsoft COM[2]); they can be assembled into some larger software modules or even applications. To these applications, integration begins at the component level.

From the management's perspective, an application is a business process. Thus in the technical sense, components are also building blocks of a business process. This gives birth to a term 'service' that has recently become very fashionable. At a higher level, a service is a unit of work done by a service provider to satisfy a particular need of the service consumer (i.e. any application that invokes a service). At a lower level, the term 'service' refers to a group of components that are brought together in a logical way to satisfy a business requirement.

Closely related to services are two new developments that have changed the course of application development methodologies: service-oriented architecture (SOA) and web services.

Service-oriented architecture and web services

For example, the withdrawal operation from a bank account can be implemented as a service. The operation may consist of several business processes, such as receiving a request, checking funds, verifying withdrawal limits, creating a log, calculating current balance, approving money discharge. Because each of these processes can be a service in its own right, the entire operation can thus be regarded as a network of services. By using SOA, a business application can be developed as a defined sequence of deployment of application-neutral services. This minimises the amount of custom coding and shortens return on investment (ROI). Structurally speaking, SOA provides the flexibility and adaptability to enterprise systems that the financial services industry needs.

The concept of SOA arises as one of the popular models of software engineering today. This is a generalisation of the earlier 'object-oriented methodology' (or the more current 'component-based' methodology) because the 'services' are encapsulated as the objects (or components). Encapsulation supports the 'loose coupling' principle of SOA, which does not require the consumer to have detailed knowledge of a service before invoking it. When business processes in the SOA are loosely coupled, their integration requires less programming and implementation effort. In the SOA framework, all applications are integrated at the level of services.

The SOA framework contains a particular 'directory service', to which service providers (i.e. the network addressable entities that provide the service) must register their services by publishing their interface contracts, which specify the format of messages received (requests) and messages from the services (responses). The directory service acts as the yellow pages and allows applications and services (as service consumers) to search – perhaps at runtime – through the contracts for a suitable service or a service provider where the desired service can be found. Figure 2.2 shows the relationship between the three main players in the SOA framework.

The 'loose' coupling is made by contracts and bindings. When the service consumer finds a service in the directory, it receives an interface contract and reference to the service. The service consumer can invoke the service by sending it a message according to the contract and the service will act as the contract specifies. This means that the consumer is only coupled to the contract but not the service. Communications between all parties are in the form of messages. As SOA is platform- and language-independent, the messages must also be implemented according to an open standard. In practice, these messages are composed in XML.

Rudiments of the SOA concepts existed when components led the trend of application development. For example, CORBA is one of the prototypes of SOA. It uses a non-XML based language, Interface Definition Language (IDL), to compose interface contracts. IBM's MQSeries and Microsoft's DCOM follow the same trait. However, these early implementations are regarded as tightly coupled object models and are not accepted in modern SOA.

One of the modern implementations of SOA is the environment given by web services. The three players in SOA (provider, directory service and consumer) are now renamed as publisher, broker and subscriber; all of them are active on a network or the Web. The interface contract is written in Web Services Definition Language (WSDL), describing the

Figure 2.2 **Directory service**

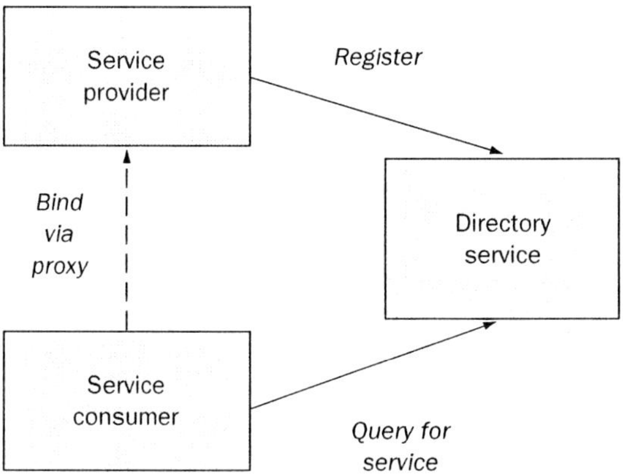

Source: Hashimi (2003)

methods provided, the input and output parameters and the instructions for connection of the web service. The broker makes use of universal description discovery and integration (UDDI), the *de facto* standard web services yellow pages. Subscribers send Simple Object Access Protocol (SOAP)[3] messages to invoke web services. WSDL, UDDI and SOAP are all XML-based standards.

Case: Danske Bank's SOA project (Sliwa, 2004; IBM, 2004a)

Danske Bank is the largest bank in Denmark. Its SOA project to develop and integrate its information systems provides the bank with a single view of the customers across its many product lines including traditional banking services for individuals, corporations and other institutions, life insurance and pension products, asset management, mortgage finance, brokerage, real estate and leasing services.

However, Danske Bank's SOA project ran into trouble when it realised that services could not be identified. This left no choice to the bank but to revise its concept of a service, to refine its repository and to establish a governance process to enforce best practices. For example, the bank previously defined a service as 'one function' but now a service is viewed at a higher level, as a logic grouping of functionality and data, such as 'customer' or 'account'. Analysts learned to figure out which business processes could be turned into services, which were carefully designed, defined and distinguished from components. The result discovered more

Figure 2.3 **The operation of web services**

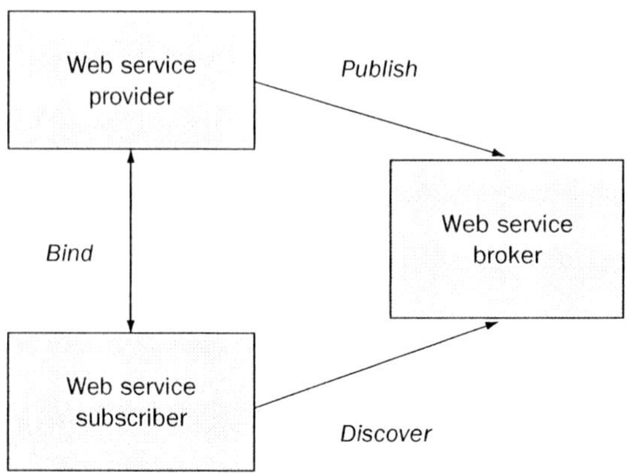

than 1,000 services from its legacy programs in mainframes and application servers.

The bank uses modelling tools to develop logical maps of the functional building blocks and business processes. Then it matches the business processes to the services to make sure it has solved the right problem.

Separate repositories are maintained for components from its mainframes and J2EE- and Microsoft.NET-based application servers. Identified services and their corresponding interfaces are recorded in a structured library, which also houses information about the relationships between the bank's functional and process models.

To help the bank stick to its SOA principles, steering committees are established across the bank in 18 different business areas for product, process and IT development. But when business managers are anxious to beat the competition, they are sometimes tempted to forgo the generic SOA approach if it takes longer to complete.

Server technology

The client-server architecture described in Chapter 1 is the rudiment of server technology. Although servers have now become the indispensable part of most information systems in the business sector, there remains some confusion in the definition of 'server'. A server could be both hardware and software. As a hardware device, a server is often implemented by a high-speed processor or even a mainframe computer. As a software component, a server contains various applications that provide the functionality of the information system.

The client-server architecture is a two-tiered structure which usually consists of a database server responding to queries from the client applications. When a large business application is implemented in this structure, it is found that the two layers are tightly coupled, that is, it is difficult to separate the presentation applications, data model and business logic from the database. As there is a general belief that the separation could make development and maintenance easier, a three-tiered structure is proposed. It consists of a general framework of the following three levels of applications:

- *Presentation layer*: usually contained in the user's PC (i.e. the client), the presentation application interacts with the user via a graphical user interface (GUI).

- *Business logic layer*: applications for handling business transactions and other workflows are held together with other functionality, such as database manipulation and security.
- *Database layer*: this server supplies data to other layers of the structure and handles lower levels of database management, such as data definition, views and query processing.

Today, the presentation application may be replaced by a web browser on a PC or other devices such as PDA, cell phone and the like. This client level is called a 'thin client' because it leaves most of the processing (particularly those processes related to business logic) to the other levels. The middle business logic layer consists of objects (e.g. in SOA or CORBA standards) that perform business functions such as account administration, loan application and user authentication. Often the functionality of the middle layer is further differentiated into multiple layers and the structure becomes very complex. Objects in the middle layer would be connected to databases at the bottom layer. They could be configured in a diversified data model and stored in different media.

A special kind of application known as 'middleware' enables communications among applications on the three levels. Technically speaking, middleware uses APIs to exchange messages or data with applications (Figure 2.4). Thus, one may say that the API provides a low-level integration of multiple software products. Recall the common APIs that were discussed earlier – these are the RPCs and messaging APIs that people often refer to as middleware. Confusion of naming APIs and

Figure 2.4 **Middleware and application programming interfaces**

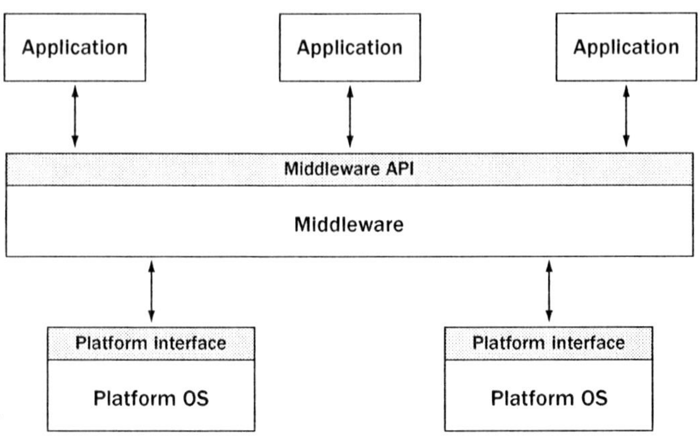

API: application programming interface; OS: operating system

middleware highlights the anarchy and severe competition in the middleware market. The classification of middleware is shown in the next section when two types of servers are examined. In the three-tier structure, these appear in the middle tier.

Application server and middleware

The middle layer of a three-tiered architecture is generally called an 'application server' (or app server) as it houses all major applications of the entire system. These applications are mainly component-based, which means that they are formed by small building blocks called 'components' (or 'objects', though the two terms differ slightly in meaning). Each component is responsible for a clearly defined task. For example, a credit card transaction application may have a component that verifies credit limit.

The application server also makes use of middleware to handle communications among applications (and components). Middleware can roughly be classified according to its functions (Boucher, 1999):

- *Database middleware*: Also known as 'SQL-oriented database access middleware', data access middleware provides the ability to read from (or write to) different types of relational and non-relational databases. It can also integrate data retrieved from diverged data silos into a single image. For data backup purposes, database replication middleware can replicate or update one or more remote mirrors of the master database. To let other applications at the middle tier get access to the database in a standard manner, the database access middleware usually complies with a connectivity standard such as ODBC or JDBC.
- *Transaction processing monitors (TP monitors)*: Their main function is to coordinate and monitor transactions across multiple data resources (as in Figure 2.5). When a transaction is received, the monitor puts it in a queue and looks after it through to completion. By doing so, the monitor establishes a framework of the server-side applications. (In fact, some systems use TP monitors to build the middle tier.) On Unix systems, BEA's Tuxedo and Top End and IBM's Encina are the most widely known TP monitors.
- *Message-oriented middleware (MOM)*: This middleware is for passing, queuing, switching and replication of messages. MOMs provide reliable message transmission from one application to

Figure 2.5 **Transaction processing monitor as a multiplexor**

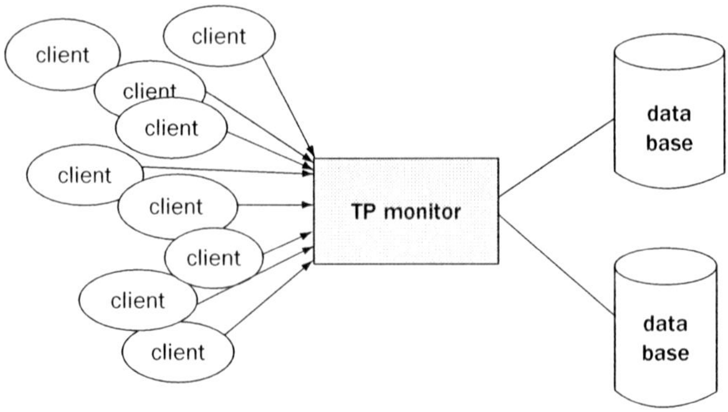

TP: transaction processing

another, regardless of the differences in network protocols, computer systems and software in the sender and recipient. Unlike RPCs, MOMs are used in asynchronous communications. Often a message is sent to a queue if the target application is busy. For example, IBM MQSeries, Microsoft Message Queue Server (MSMQ) and TIBCO RV are well known message-queuing products. In some implementations, the message queue is extended into a message switch, which intercepts messages sent by client devices, parses the messages and reformats them before they are re-routed to their destined applications. That is to say, some MOMs have the logic to route these messages and perform processes as instructed. To enhance business continuity, some systems use message replication middleware that can replicate messages and continue operating in the event of a failure.

- *Publish/subscribe middleware*: This allows sending applications (i.e. publishers) to label a message with only the name of the topic without a destination address. The publish/subscribe middleware then sends the message to all applications that are eligible subscribers. To be a subscriber, an application must have registered its interest in a certain topic. Messages are broadcast by user type, subject and other types of selection criteria. Publish/subscribe can also guarantee message delivery in asynchronous communication. It is a much more loosely coupled method than message queuing.
- *Enterprise application integration (EAI) middleware*: This is event-based middleware that starts operating when an event occurs. For

example, on receiving a policy enquiry, the EAI middleware puts the information from this event into a message queue and makes it available to other applications. While the enquiry is processed, the middleware acts as a hub that connects to those applications concerned. Using messaging middleware, transaction managers, database middleware and others, EAI middleware connects all applications that take part in the event and returns data in an integrated format.

- *Remote procedure call (RPC)*: This consists of low-level procedures that enable an application to call a routine that executes on a local or remote server(s). While there is still a connection the server returns output; if the connection is broken, however, the RPC guarantees that the whole process starts from the first invocation again. The RPC middleware is best used for non-transaction services such as batch and print processing. Originally RPCs were developed for synchronous communication but asynchronous RPCs also appear in the recent market.
- *Object request broker (ORB)*: This provides interoperability in a network by allowing both object and non-object resources to send (or receive) requests (or responses) transparently. The ORB keeps track of all the differences in language, operating system and location of each resource by using standard interfaces and service APIs. The most popular classes of ORB are based on either the CORBA architecture or the COM/DCOM architecture.
- *Transaction managers*: These are middleware controlling transactions and communication among distributed heterogeneous resource managers. Modern transaction managers use the Open Group's XA (eXtended Architecture) protocol to specify how transaction managers control resource managers. Like TP monitors, transaction managers should be incorporated into the application at the time of development.

There has, however, never been a clear-cut demarcation between different types of middleware. The boundary became even more unclear in the last decade when new vendors entered the market and new functionality was being added to existing middleware. For example, contemporary ORBs may also provide services for transactions, queuing and messaging and asynchronous RPCs have started to appear. To know which middleware to use, a system development manager should have professional advice from solution providers.

Case: FundServ (Johnson et al., 2001)

FundServ is a Toronto-based service provider for mutual funds. Because mutual fund manufacturers in Canada cannot directly sell their products to investors, FundServ takes orders from mutual fund sellers and distributors and sends them to the mutual fund manufacturers for execution. The organisation has had a long-term relationship with BEA Systems Inc. The latter, a San Jose-based IT expert, offered its Tuxedo platform that has been executing trades very well. In 2001, FundServ planned to develop a message system for the communication of non-transaction items from the distributors to the manufacturers. As the messaging system would receive messages from multiple companies, it needed to be non-intrusive but still easily configurable. Moreover, the system needed to be prepared for very high speed messaging performance during peak periods.

FundServ chose SmartSockets from Talarian Corp. for this project. (Talarian was acquired by TIBCO in 2002). SmartSockets adopts a central message broker approach and takes requests from multiple sources without the need for complicated methods such as intrusive queues. The SmartSockets MOM enables remote checking of customer references and retrieving information in various stock-trading accounts. In addition, FundServ was confident that SmartSockets would have no difficulty in handling 1,300 messages per second – the peak load expected.

Web server

Web server technology emerged when vendors discovered that TCP/IP protocol could be used to link up machines in a network so that workstations on a LAN can exchange information as web pages. A web server is the place where a website resides. It stands between browsers and a database, but has many supports, such as business objects, applications, operating system resources, authentication services, data access objects[4] (DAOs) and the like. In the simplest case, when a HTTP request is received, a web server identifies the SQL scripts inside the request and sends them to the database server. When the latter retrieves information, it requires web-to-database middleware to dress up the message as an HTML page, which is then returned to the calling browser (Figure 2.6).

Common web servers in the market include the freeware Apache (market share 69 per cent in November 2005),[5] MS IIS and Netscape

Figure 2.6 Web-database middleware connecting web server and data storage

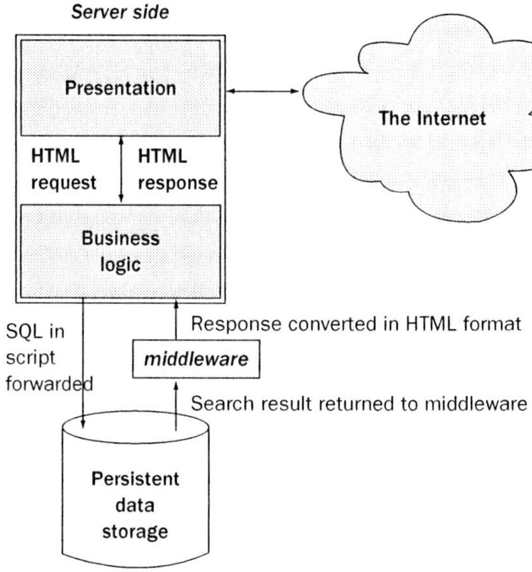

Enterprise Server. In these servers, requests are passed to appropriate applications (probably on an application server) without bothering with database connectivity and messaging between applications and database. There are two types of applications in web servers (also known as 'web applications'):

- *Presentation-oriented web applications*, which generate dynamic web pages in response to requests.
- *Service-oriented web applications*, which are supportive services that are made available to other applications that include presentation-oriented web applications.

Web applications return data in the form of HTML. To put dynamic content on an HTML page, the applications are constructed by many kinds of server-side programming technologies, which include CGI scripts, servlets, JSPs and ASPs, as described below:

- *CGI (Common Gateway Interface)* is a 'traditional' way of creating dynamic content on a web server. Using CGI scripts (or programs, which can be in C, C++, Perl, VB and others) as middleware, a web server can interact with content-generating programs on a remote machine. However, CGI is criticised as being platform-dependent.

- *Servlets*, which are written in Java, are small and platform-independent programs placed on the server side. They can also produce dynamic web pages and have access to all Java APIs, including JDBC API. They are widely supported by vendors like Sun, Apache, Oracle, IBM and BEA.
- *JSP (JavaServer Pages)* is an extension of servlet technology. A JSP page embeds the application logic within an HTML or XML template. While the page is shown on a browser, the JSP is automatically compiled and activated, giving dynamic web content to HTML pages together with data from the database layer.
- *ASP (Active Server Page)* is the Microsoft version of JSP. Using VB, ASPs provide processing capability on the server side, but they are designed for Microsoft products only.

Although application server and web server can be distinguished functionally as two separate layers, application servers available in the market are often combined into one. They are indistinguishably called 'enterprise servers', as they are capable of providing EAI. A typical example is found in Sun's J2EE architecture.

J2EE connector architecture

In 1999, Sun Microsystems created Java 2 Platform Enterprise Edition (J2EE), a platform-independent, Java-centric environment for businesses to develop their Web-based application servers. The J2EE architecture has guided the development of Sun's application server series, which include the Sun Java System Application Server and its former version, Sun ONE Application Server. J2EE has also become the basic architecture of many application servers. Its success may partly be explained by its adoption of open standards, but the collaboration of various vendors that participate in the development process is equally critical.

Consisting of standardised services, APIs and protocols, the J2EE platform supports a three-tier application architecture called 'J2EE Connector Architecture'. The structure can be divided into three layers: a client tier (typically of web applications), a middle tier (the J2EE platform) and an EIS (enterprise information system) tier, as depicted in Figure 2.7.

Figure 2.7 Three-tier J2EE connector architecture

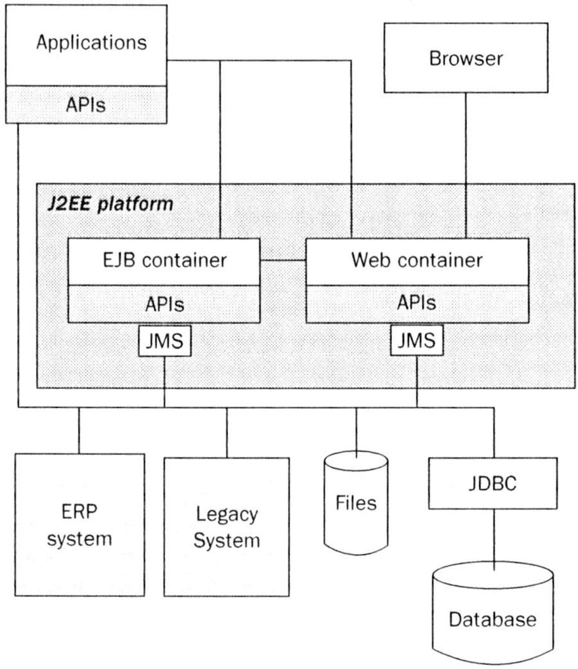

ERP: enterprise resource planning; EJB: enterprise JavaBeans; JDBC: Java database connectivity; JMS: Java message service

Unique in the J2EE middle tier are two servers known as 'web container' and 'EJB container'. These are standardised runtime environments that provide specific services to support the software units (components) inside them. The web container provides a runtime environment for web applications, whih are made up of servlets, HTML pages and other resources that respond to a client's HTTP request; performs the necessary processing (e.g. invoking relevant web applications); and returns the result in HTML or XML to the client. It is the 'presentation logic' of the server. As web applications are built upon servlets, JSPs and HTML, the web container is also responsible for managing and dispatching those components that support the web applications while they are active.

On the other hand, the Enterprise JavaBeans (EJB) container is the runtime environment that supports the transaction, security, persistence and lifecycle management of those beans. Also known as 'enterprise beans', these EJB components are small software modules that developers can use and re-use to implement business processes. This is why the tier of EJB containers is also known as 'business logic'. In the J2EE environment, there are three types of enterprise beans:

- *Session beans*: business entities (objects, in OO terminology) created and used by the client. They are relatively short-lived (e.g. interest calculation) and can either be 'stateless' (no client-related data are involved) or otherwise 'stateful'.
- *Entity beans*: each of these represents a business object (e.g. a customer account, a catalogue item) stored in a persistent storage or an application. Each has a unique identity and can be used by multiple clients.
- *Message-driven beans*: special components that contain business logic to handle asynchronous messages delivered via the Java Message Service (JMS). The latter is the MOM that provides standard Java API for applications (especially those in the EIS layer) to communicate among themselves, for example, by accessing an asynchronous messaging service (a queue-based or publish/subscribe messaging system).

The first two types of beans execute, when invoked, synchronously. That is, when a client requests a session or entity bean, the EJB container is responsible for dispatching a synchronous invocation to the bean. The client has to wait until the bean returns some values. However, if the client requests a message-driven bean, it sends a message to the JMS. The latter notifies the EJB container, which then invokes the required message-driven bean asynchronously. In the meantime, the client can continue its sequence of work without idling for the execution of the bean.

The J2EE platform supports a board spectrum of clients. According to how they interact with the platform, clients are classified into three categories:

- *Web clients*: These get access to the web container by using HTML pages, dynamically generated JSPs, the HTTP transport protocol, XML, Java applications, or Java applets (small applications hosted by a client). A web client could be a browser, a Java applet, a browser plug-in, or even non-Java clients. They can connect to the J2EE platform from across the Web or the institution's intranet.
- *EJB clients*: These could be servlets, JSPs, or other Java applications that connect to the EJB container.
- *EIS clients*: Mostly related to the administrative and management functions of the system, EIS clients get access to the EIS layer of the

architecture. For example, they may use JDBC to access any type of database that has a JDBC driver without prior knowledge of the database implementation.

The EIS tier lies at the bottom of the J2EE platform. It consists of back-end systems (including ERP systems) which are integrated with databases. Connecting with the web and EJB containers via JMS, the EIS tier provides a web-based enterprise application integration (EAI).

J2EE architecture has guided the development of many third-party servers. For example, BEA WebLogic Server, IBM WebSphere and Oracle App Server 10g are popular J2EE servers among finance and insurance industries. However, Microsoft offered its counterpart, .NET platform, in 2001 to compete in the market and has won over the market share in the manufacturing, retail and wholesales sectors. We examine BEA WebLogic Server as an example of J2EE implementation.

BEA WebLogic server

The application server offered by BEA is one of the most favoured J2EE-compliant servers that support e-financial systems. It is integrated with other BEA products in an environment known as 'BEA WebLogic Platform'. The platform (Figure 2.8) supports the building, extension, integration, deployment and management of enterprise applications and business processes.

Figure 2.8 **BEA WebLogic platform 8.1 is an integrated environment**

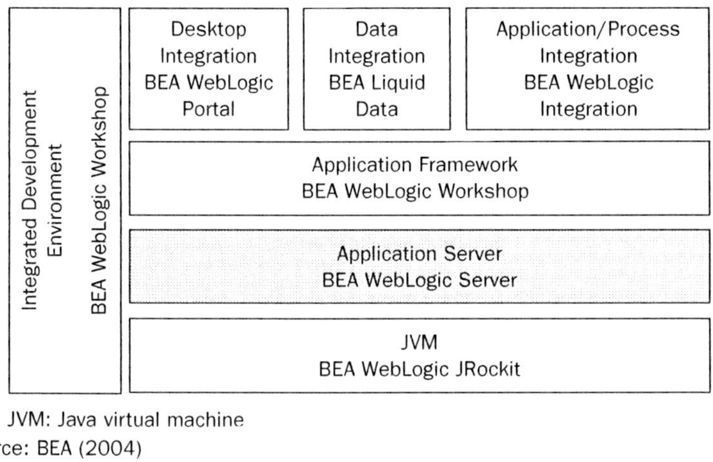

JVM: Java virtual machine
Source: BEA (2004)

The BEA WebLogic Platform 8.1 is basically a virtual working space for Java application development. Within the BEA WebLogic Workshop 8.1 environment, developers are provided with visual models for the development of J2EE or even non-J2EE web services, web applications, portals and integration projects. Adopting the SOA approach, the Workshop enables developers to assemble JSPs, EJBs, web services and applications to build applications.

The Workshop also provides a runtime 'application framework' that runs on top of the WebLogic Server. With this framework, developers need only to annotate where and what components should be deployed in Java code. The framework can automatically generate standard EJB components, message queues and database connectivity. It also saves the developers the trouble of finding the details of individual components that are deployed and compiling the components into an application.

The top three boxes in Figure 2.8 are also environments that help web portal development, data source sharing and application development and integration. These three boxes are sometimes called 'user, data and process integration' respectively, as BEA pays much attention to integration. The lower side shows the JRockit, which is the VM environment for Java programs' development and running.

Figure 2.9 **Three layers of the WebLogic server**

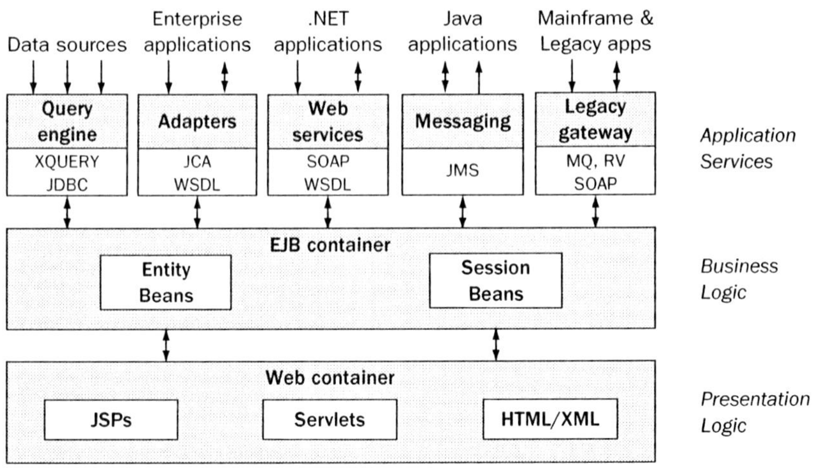

JCA: J2EE connector architecture; JDBC: Java database connectivity; JMS: Java message service; JSP: JavaServer page; HTML: HyperText Markup Language; MQ: message queue; RV: a Tibco MQ product named after 'rendezvous'; SOAP: Simple Object Access Protocol; WSDL: Web Services Definition Language; XML: Extensible Markup Language; XQUERY: a query language for extracting information from XML files.

Central to the WebLogic Platform, WebLogic Server is a three-tiered structure like the J2EE platform. BEA engineers refer to these three layers as the 'presentation logic, business logic and application services' as shown in Figure 2.9.

The names of presentation logic and business logic follow the J2EE nomenclature. BEA server also has web container and EJB container. The former is particularly designed for the 'web services application model'. When it receives a client's request (in HTTP), it responds with HTML or XML pages that may be static or contain applets that execute in a web browser. If the client requests a servlet, the small application executes in the server and the result is returned in HTML or XML. But if a JSP is requested, it would be transformed by the WebLogic JSP compiler into a servlet before it is returned in HTML.

The EJB container caters for the 'Web-based component application model', which is an extension of the web services application model. Here the client is allowed to access servlets and JSPs that request EJB components or other services on the WebLogic Server. The EJB container has only two types of EJBs: session beans and entity beans. The entity beans (each representing a business object) are connected to a database via a JDBC, which is a standard interface enabling SQL command execution and data processing in Java programs.

The application services layer implements J2EE services such as JDBC, JNDI, JMS and JTA to enable web and EJB containers to integrate with back-end databases and applications. This layer acts as a hub to many enterprise information systems (EISs) such as ERP, SCM, CRM and other legacy systems. Some of the APIs and components used in the application services layer are described in Table 2.1.

J2EE is an open standard and a server like BEA WebLogic, and is basically an environment where any e-business system can be built. However, many financial services institutions often include one more server in their Web-based financial system. For example, they may install an enterprise-class server like BEA WebLogic and IBM WebSphere together with Financial Fusion Server, with special features not found in more general-purpose servers.

Architecture of Financial Fusion Server

Financial Fusion Server is regarded as the basic platform for building enterprise-class e-financial systems for more than 200 leading financial institutions in the world. Offered by Financial Fusion, Inc., a subsidiary

Table 2.1 **APIs and components deployed in application services of BEA WebLogic**

APIs and components	Application
J2EE connector architecture (JCA)	Defines a standard architecture for connecting the J2EE platform to heterogenous EIS
Java naming and directory services (JNDI)	Provides a standard mechanism for locating resources, including remote objects, environment properties and directory services
Java database connectivity (JDBC)	Provides vendor-neutral access to enterprise relational database management systems
Java message service (JMS)	Provides reliable point-to-point and publish/subscribe messaging for J2EE components
Java transaction API (JTA)	Provides mechanisms for declaring, accessing and coordinating transaction processing
JavaMail	Provides support for sending Internet email from J2EE applications
Remote method invocation (RMI)	Allows developers to build distributed applications in the Java environment
RMI-IIOP	RMI API implemented over the Internet Inter-ORB Protocol (IIOP), which allows developers to write remote interfaces in Java
WebLogic enterprise connectivity (WLEC)	Components to allow servlet, EJB, JSP, RMI to get access to BEA Tuxedo CORBA objects
Secure sockets layer (SSL)	A protocol that uses public key encryption to protect data transferred over TCP/IP

of Sybase, Inc., the server supports a wide range of financial processes such as retail and business banking, bill presentment, global straight through processing (GSTP)[6] and cross-border trading.

The name of the server implies that integration is being taken one step further – 'fusion' should be the main objective of an e-financial system. To the finance sector, fusion could refer to the vertical integration across applications for different services like banking, brokerage and institutional trading as well as the horizontal integration across legacy, web and wireless applications. Two versions of Financial Fusion Server are available; they are:

- *Financial Fusion Server Capital Markets e-Trading Suite*: for brokers, dealers and institutional traders. It can handle message standards such as SWIFT, FIX, FIXML and FpML.

Figure 2.10 **Building blocks of the Financial Fusion solution**

Financial Services Applications (STP)	
STP Message Formats and Adapters: FIX, OFX, SWIFT, HTML, XML, Omgeo, GSTP, ...	
Extended Financial Service Platform: Financial Fusion Server	EAI Infrastructure: IBM WMQI
Application Services: Sybase EA Server, IBM WebSphere, BEA WebLogic, SUN's iPlanet, ...	
Operating Systems: SUN Solaris, IBM AIX, MS Windows NT, IBM S/390, ...	

WMQI: WebSphere MQ Integrator

- *Financial Fusion Banking Suite*: for consumers, small businesses and large corporate banks. It supports banking functionalities including account and payment management, bill payment and presentment, alerts and entitlements. It handles standards such as SWIFT, FIX and OFX.

The implementation of Financial Fusion Server assumes that the entire e-financial system is composed of the following servers (Figure 2.10):

- *Application servers*: These are Java-based servers housing business applications (such as those for trade order management, market feeds, brokerage, position keeping and compliance). These applications get access to databases.
- *Financial Fusion Server*: This provides support to messages of various standards and formats used in the financial services industry. Alongside EAI infrastructure, the Financial Fusion Server integrates target applications (e.g. brokerage, trade order management and compliance) with XML rules-based routing and transformation.
- *EAI*: An IBM WMQI (WebSphere MQ Integrator, formerly known as MQ Series Integrator or MQSI) or Sybase e-Biz Integrator which contains:
  - formatters – APIs for parsing and reformating messages to suit the requirement of the receiving application;

- rules – APIs for evaluating messages by routing them through (usually thousands of) rules and reacting to the results; and
- middleware for handling various message standards.

EAI in the Financial Fusion solution relies on message brokering services provided by the integrator. For example, formats defined by SWIFT include those for securities settlement and reconciliation, foreign exchange, interest rate swaps, forward rate agreements (FRAs), precious metals, among others.

Message passing is the major function of a Financial Fusion Server. The server is supported by several adapters for message standards that are adopted in financial applications. Communication between different message formats and applications is controlled by a tool kit called 'Message Broker'. It allows institutions to specify message standards, define validation and transformation rules and store this information in a special Message Broker Database. To a Financial Fusion Server with a GlobalFIX adapter, the Message Broker parses and validates messages received from back-office applications or remote FIX servers using the formats and rules in the database. It can also transform these messages (e.g. from FIX to SWIFT or any proprietary message standard) and route these messages to target applications.

The distinctive role played by the Financial Fusion Server reveals problems emerging from the message standards adopted in the finance industry. These standards are examined in the following section.

Message standards

The financial services industry learned the benefits of message standards long ago. As far back as 1973, banks were already used to the SWIFT standard mandated by the Society for the Worldwide Interbank Financial Telecommunication. With financial systems moving to the Internet, many new message standards are being developed to meet new challenges, such as the TCP/IP communication protocols, the quest for straight-through processing (STP), shortened settlement dates and security risk. This section reviews how SWIFT and some other standard (or protocol) organisations have been leading the development of message standards, for the purpose of communication and automation. These standards might have started as independent projects with different objectives and approaches, but over the years, they have shown a tendency of learning from each other and there are some signs of converging under the roof of XML.

There are multiple benefits in using eXtensible Markup Language (XML) for the representation of business data in e-financial systems. The language is text-based and is self-describing, i.e. the meaning of its content is delineated. When an XML message is received, it can be parsed and validated by a common XML parser. But most importantly, XML is extensible and any format can be added to it if necessary. Extensibility is essential to any message standard if it is to be adopted by the ever-changing financial services industry.

The convergence of standards is believed to be one big effort to achieve STP in the financial services industry. As STP is about interoperability and interoperability requires open or common standards, all the discrepancies in communication protocols, database access methods, operating systems, applications and networks are factors that undermine STP. When the industry calls for STP, message standard convergence should be a logical move.

SWIFT

Formed in 1973, the Society for Worldwide Interbank Financial Telecommunications (SWIFT) is an industry-owned cooperative that created an electronic messaging system that is also known as SWIFT. The system is used by over 7,000 financial institutions in almost 200 countries. Lying at the centre of the system is a set of standards for financial messages, such as letters of credit, payments and securities transactions. To use this system, a financial institution should have a dedicated terminal and proprietary software from the Society.

In the 1980s, the Society adopted ISO7775, a standard for electronic messages exchange in the securities sector. ISO7775 marked the first generation of message standards, which was designed by the so-called 'message centric approach'. Besides specifications to data fields, formats and usage rules, the standard was supplied with validation rules and usage guidance. The standard was deployed during the period 1984–1997. However, when the Society terminated its support in November 2002 many institutions were forced to migrate their systems to SWIFT ISO15022.

ISO15022 was released in 2000 as an enhanced set of message standards for the securities sector. The standard includes rules of syntax and message design, but it is also attached to a 'data field dictionary' (DFD) and a 'catalogue of messages'. ISO15022 is the first attempt to separate the definition of data items and formats from the message standard. For example, in this standard, the process 'place an order' is defined as a logical workflow that involves several data items such as 'trade date' and 'exchange rate'. The syntax of those definitions aligns with ISO15022. But if the process is defined in another standard, say, FIX, both data elements and logical workflow should remain unchanged. By using the catalogue of messages (that registers defined messages) and the DFD (that holds the metadata of data elements in defined messages), a business process defined in ISO15022 can be easily redefined in another message standard.

With the second edition of ISO15022, the shift of focus from message to business process is obvious. The new edition extends its scope from securities to all financial messages. WG10, the working group that developed ISO15022, has even used reverse engineering to turn existing industry messages to message standards. The most innovative change in the new ISO15022 – which was renamed ISO20022 in 2004 – is to abstract a complete business process into a business model in which business processes, actors and interactions are all defined. The society now plays the role of a registration authority. Any organisation involved in financial message development may register their business requirement with SWIFT and define message sets according to ISO20022.

ISO15022 has three layers:

- *Business layer*: business domain and business requirements, including processes and actors.
- *Logical layer*: definition of syntax-independent standard solution for the identified business requirements, including message structure and system interaction.
- *Technical layer*: the physical representation of the standard solution including the messaging and relevant software, including format transformation rules (DTDs, schemas).

The business model is the top layer of ISO20022. Usually depicted by using UML (a modelling language), this layer details the context of the business process, including the business domain, actors and messages involved. The process is described as a means to meet the business requirements. The model spells out what is being done but not how. The middle layer is the abstract and technology-independent solution of the business process. In particular, it specifies how business data can be exchanged in a structured way following a number of rules. A set of mapping specifications links the logical layer to the actual implementation (in XML) of the messages, which lies in the physical layer at the bottom. In that layer, the grammar of the XML messages (e.g. how a message is coded in XML) is defined in a specification called 'data type definition' (DTD) or XML schema.

The ISO20022 standard, which is now called UNIFI (UNIversal Financial Industry message scheme), is expected to become a uniform message standard for all financial services in the future. Any existing non-20022 message can be reverse engineered to capture its underlying logical structure and business process; and a business model can also be reverse engineered from the business logic. We may appreciate the ambition of WG10 but the full benefits of ISO20022 can only be expected to appear after some more years.

FIX

The Financial Information eXchange (FIX) message standard was initiated in 1992 as a mutual communication framework for equity trading between two large financial firms: Fidelity Investments and Salomon Brothers. The FIX Protocol Ltd. (FPL) was formed three years later by a group of banking and financial institutions, including Fidelity and Salomon Brothers, to make FIX a public-domain protocol for the real-time electronic communications of pre-trade and trade messages between financial institutions. Since then, many investment mangers, broker/dealers, ECNs and stock exchanges have adopted FIX. Even

Figure 2.11 FIX system connectivity

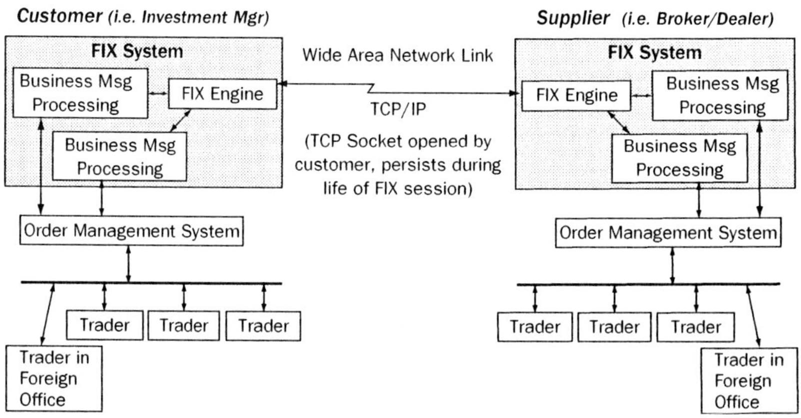

Source: Atwell (1998)

when XML-based standards have been considered in many other sectors of the financial services industry, FIX is still being used by 82 per cent of the brokers in the USA (Malik, 2003). Their counterparts in Europe and Asia are also interested in using it.

To use the FIX protocol, a securities firm needs to install a FIX engine, such as those offered by vendors like Financial Fusion and Javelin Technologies. A FIX engine is a software application that handles low-level communications (e.g. handshaking, getting IP address, de/encryption, message storing and the like) and binds the protocol to the applications that process business messages. The protocol is thus platform-independent.

FIX differs from other protocols in its layered structure, which consists of a session layer and an application layer. The session layer specifies how the communication session is established, including logon/logout, heartbeat, test and resend request, reject, authentication, data integrity

Figure 2.12 **An example of a quote for single security message in FIX**

FIX Message	Remark
8 = FIX.4.2	8 means Begin String; 4.2 is the version
9 = 24	9 means Body Length
35 = S	35 means Message Type; S is field value
49 = Broker	49 means sender ID; the sender is Broker
56 = Institution	56 means target ID; it is called Institution
34 = 251	34 means Message Sequence Number
52 = 20051208-13:57:22	52 means Sending Time; it was 13:57 on Dec 8, 2005
117 = Q7	117 means Quote ID
131 = R72	131 means Quote Request ID
55 = AA	55 is a Symbol
200 = 200510	200 means Mature Year Month
202 = 25.00	202 means Strike Price; at $25.00
201 = 1	Put or Call is 1
132 = 5.00	132 means Bid Price
133 = 5.25	133 means Offer Price
134 = 10	134 means Bid Size
135 = 10	135 means Offer Size
10 = 174	Checksum is 174

and message sequencing. The application layer contains the business-related data such as indications of interest, quotes, orders, execution reports, etc. All information in the message is written in a so-called 'tag=value' syntax, which implies that information can be written in any order. It is illustrated in the message in Figure 2.12.

FIX is a popular standard for ECNs and exchanges for communication among standards themselves and with their clients. Clearing firms use the protocol to report completed trades to settlement providers and regulatory agencies. FIX covers many types of messages in the securities business. For institutions, there are standards for quote requests, orders/modifications/cancels, allocations, basket trading, security status request, trading session status request. Brokers may use FIX protocols to send messages of indications of interests, post trade advertisements, quote, order acknowledgment, fills, or mass quote. However, FIX applies mostly to pre-trade and trade messaging. It covers a different area from ISO15022 (Figure 2.13).

FPL is trying to extend the functionality of FIX. A recent version of FIX (version 4.4) has been extended to cover fixed income and derivatives. FPL plan to expand their support to FIX up to even listed derivatives and foreign exchange products. In addition, several leading buy- and sell-side firms, exchanges, ECNs, clearing corporations and technology vendors also work together to promote the FIX protocol as a major component in the building of the electronic trade cycle and STP.

FIXML

As early as in 1998, FIX Protocol Ltd. formed the FIXML Working Group to investigate the migrating of FIX to XML format. A FIXML

Figure 2.13 FIX and SWIFT differ in coverage

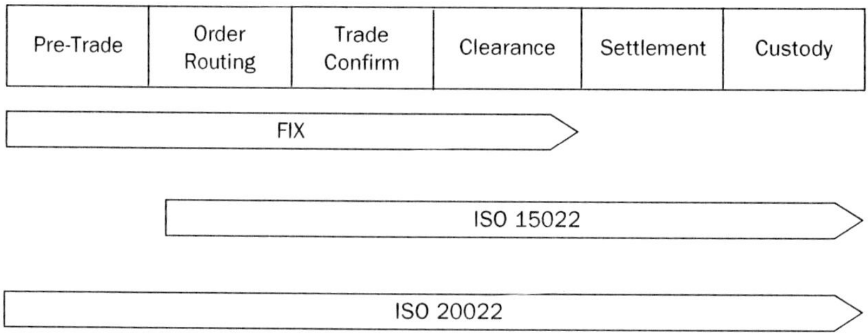

Figure 2.14 A message in FIXML

```
49=BROKER                         SenderCompID
56=HUB                            TargetCompID
128=INST                          DeliverToCompID
212=245                           FIXML Data Length
213=<FIXML>                       FIXMLData
       <Header>
       ....
       </Header>
       <Indication>
       ....
       </Indication>
    </FIXML>
```

Source: Lynn & Northey (2002)

DTD was released in the next year. When FIX version 4.4 was released, it was soon converted into an XML schema and a new FIXML was made available in January 2004. The Options Clearing Corporation (OCC) and Chicago Mercantile Exchange Inc. (CME) in the USA were the first to adopt the standard.

Messages written in FIXML have the benefits of both FIX and XML. They leave their FIX session layer intact and connection can be established as simply as in FIX. (Note the FIX session layer wraps around FIXML code in Figure 2.14). Moreover, FIXML messages isolate the security mechanism in their session layer. The separation leaves the application layer undistributed if a new security model is deployed. In addition, the XML-based messages can be parsed by a common XML parser and take advantage of the flexible XML message structure.

FIXML has been used to support trading and execution for US cash equities. Merrill Lynch's Corporate and Institutional Client Group's e-commerce Direct Markets are also using FIXML. The standard has been criticised for only being targeted at institutional business, thus some communities (e.g. the retail market) opt for another standard, OFX.

With the collaboration of SWIFT and ISDA (the owner of another standard, FpML), FIXML also adopts ISO15022 and FpML to provide a link between front- and back-office operations of securities institutions and extends to cover post-trade operations. However, whether FIXML will be amalgamated into UNIFI remains uncertain.

Case: Chicago Mercantile Exchange using XML (Northey, 2002)

Chicago Mercantile Exchange (CME) is the largest futures exchange in the USA. It offers futures and options primarily in the areas of interest rates, stock indexes, foreign exchange and commodities. The management was interested in FIX as early as in 2002. Because FIX lacked the standard for position management messages, CME made a few contacts with the FIX Global Derivatives Committee.

CME has been using XML internally for quite some time. The management believed the highly nested and complex messages found in trade reporting, position reporting and give-up processing could be greatly simplified by using XML. With that experience, CME worked with FIX in the development of FIXML.

The Futures Industry Association (FIA) was also selling the idea of FIXML to all US futures exchanges in June 2002. FIA found that many firms and clearinghouses were concerned about the change. In particular, they wanted the introduction to a new standard to include three issues:

- commitment from all US futures exchanges;
- continued use of MQSeries as the message transport; and
- added business value in terms of improved processing efficiencies must be the basis for the change.

Their dependence on IBM's MQSeries is based on its extensive use in the derivatives back-office space. As FIXML was machine-independent, honouring the tradition was not a problem to FIA and its member organisations.

To ease implementation, FIA emphasised that the introduction of FIXML was not just a modernisation in message formats. It provides firms with automation opportunities to improve their back-office workflows, so as to add business value. CME posts the FIXML users' guide and specification documents on its website and holds developers' training sessions in Chicago and New York. Pilot tests with Midday and EOD files were conducted. CME also guaranteed the continued use of MQSeries.

CME currently provides support for FIXML in the following services: position change submission, position maintenance requests, request for positions (with or without trade detail) and future spreads trade reporting.

FpML

The Financial Products Markup Language (FpML) is specially designed for transactions of over-the-counter (OTC) financial instruments, such as the direct transactions between banks. Traditionally, the trading parties require private negotiation over the details of transactions because they are trading complex financial products such as derivatives and swaps without the presence of an exchange.

FpML was offered by the International Swaps and Derivatives Association (ISDA). The standard was supported by JP Morgan & Co., Inc., PriceWaterhouseCoopers LLP, IBM, WebMethods, Inc. and Forecross Corp. It is now used in interest rate products (caps, floors, swaptions and cancellable and extendible swaps), forward rate agreements (FRAs), foreign exchange (FX) and derivatives (equity, credit).

Unlike FIXML, FpML was developed from scratch to take advantage of the XML format. It is structured in three parts: trade, party and portfolio (Figure 2.15).

Version 4.0 of FpML is defined in an XML schema. It is freely available under public licence. It is machine-independent and vendor-neutral. Users are free to create private extensions for product or workflow description. In February 2004, ISDA announced that it would

Figure 2.15 **Format of an FpML message**

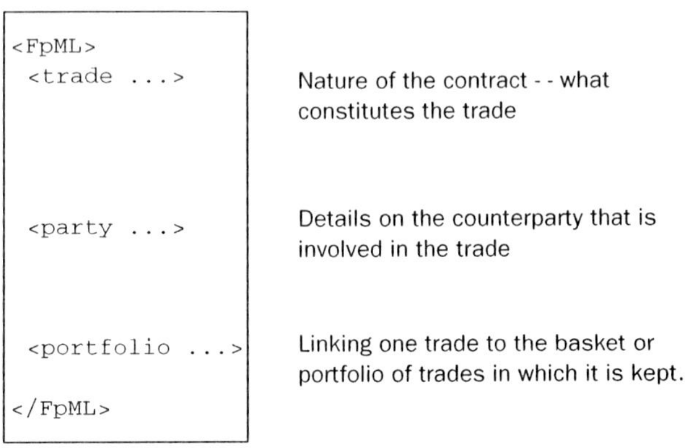

Source: Malik (2003)

create a joint working group with FPL and commit to the collaboration agreement between FIX, FpML, MDDL and ISO20022.

Other languages

The aforementioned message standards serve most parts of the financial services sector. With their convergence on the way, anyone outside their coverage would think twice about adopting a different message standard. However, due to historical, geographical, or other reasons, other message standards are still being used. Some of them are already XML-compliant. The following is part of the list:

- *Interactive Financial eXchange (IFX)*: Specially designed for electronic bill presentment and payment, B2B payments, B2B banking (balance and transaction reporting, remittance information), ATM communications, C2B payments and C2B banking.
- *Market Data Definition Language (MDDL)*: Proposed by the Financial Information Services Division (FISD) of the Software & Information Industry Association (SIIA), MDDL is another XML-based standard to enable interchange of data of the world's financial markets. MDDL was first released in November 2001. It was initially focused on end-of-day and snap information for financial instruments like share prices.
- *Open Financial eXchange (OFX)*: OFX was created by a joint venture of CheckFree, Intuit and Microsoft. It was released in the USA in 1997 to support a wide range of financial activities, including consumer and small business banking, consumer and small business bill payment, bill presentment and investments tracking including stocks, bonds, mutual funds and 401(k) account details. OFX 2.0 became XML-compliant in 2000. It is publicly available and by March 2004, it is used by over 200 banks, brokerages and many major payroll processing companies. E-financial systems such as Intuit's Quicken and Microsoft's Money have adopted OFX.
- *eXtensible Business Reporting Language (XBRL)*: Used in specifications for corporate business reporting, i.e. financial information written on annual reports, general ledgers and other filings. It has been strongly supported by international accounting authorities.

Their applicability is summarised in Table 2.2.

Table 2.2 The current message landscape

	Pre-trade	Trade	Post-trade/Pre-settlement	Settlement	Post-settlement
OTC derivatives			FpML, SWIFT		
Mutual funds/Unit trusts		FIX		SWIFT	SWIFT
Foreign exchange	FIX	FIX, SWIFT	SWIFT	SWIFT	SWIFT
Exchange traded derivatives	FIX	FIX, SWIFT		SWIFT	SWIFT
Fixed income	FIX	FIX, SWIFT	FIX, SWIFT	SWIFT	SWIFT
Equities	FIX	FIX, SWIFT	FIX, SWIFT	SWIFT	SWIFT
Retail banking	FIX OFX IFX	FIX OFX IFX	FIX OFX IFX	FIX OFX IFX	FIX OFX IFX
Market data	MDDL	MDDL	MDDL	MDDL	MDDL
Payment	SWIFT	SWIFT	SWIFT	SWIFT	SWIFT

Summary

This chapter serves as the foundation for the study of technology management that will be examined in the following chapters. It did not cover all the advancements in ITC; instead it focused on three areas – application development, server technology and message standards – all of which are common hurdles in the implementation and management of Internet-based information systems in the financial services sector.

To operate on the Internet, an e-financial system needs to be able to exploit the related technologies (including the protocols, client-side browsers, Java languages, databases and legacy systems). In this chapter, the section on Java language and service-oriented architecture described the emergence of a general architecture for e-financial systems. It is a layered structure made up by components and middleware and is central to the server technology that we will examine in the next section. Today's e-financial system is the result of the integration effort. To build the system, developers and managers needed to find the right components or middleware to link an application server to client applications, databases, legacy systems and others. While middleware provides the technical linkage between applications, it is the message standard that ensures linkages between institutions. This was the final type of technology discussed in this chapter. Message standards were initially being developed separately, but newer versions are now converging to the XML-based ISO20022.

Technology is only an enabler for financial institutions to meet market demands and to explore new opportunities. Management needs much more business incentive and management skills to turn technological advantage into profit. But if the hurdles of technology are not overcome, e-financial systems will not function, and will not enhance competitiveness.

Questions for discussion

1. What are the advantages of a three-tier architecture over a client-server architecture? Why is a multi-tier structure preferred to a three-tier structure in some cases?
2. ISO15022 decouples the creation of messages and the message standard. What good does it bring to a common user?

Notes

1. A standard (common object request broker architecture) developed by the Object Management Group, which is a consortium of almost all the major software vendors.
2. The component object model was developed by Microsoft in the 1990s.
3. The name is a bit misleading because subscribers may ask for non-object services.
4. DAOs are objects that allow Visual Basic applications to access Microsoft's databases via an ODBC. They are now being replaced by ADO (ActiveX Data Objects).
5. From a survey by Netscraft, available at: *http://news.netcraft.com/archives/web_server_survey.html* (last accessed: 30 November 2005).
6. GSTP protocol, was offered by the GSTP AG. The latter promoted GSTP by building multilateral interconnectivity among investment managers, broker/dealers, and global custodians involved in post-trade, pre-settlement securities processing. However, GSTP AG closed down at the end of 2002.

3

E-banking: technology and design

E-banking services

Since the end of the last millennium, the banking industry has evolved to a new stage of electronic banking (or e-banking) where banking services are delivered on the Internet (thus its alias 'Internet banking'), a far more competent channel than the traditional electronic means, such as the automatic teller machine (ATM) and telephone. Over the past few years, this concept has lured huge amounts of investments to offer new banking services through the new channel. Although a few of the virtual banking services[1] closed down after the 2000 e-commerce bubble, the impact of the Internet on the banking industry is not to be overlooked.

To banks with long traditions, the Internet channel was first seen only as an inexpensive means to distribute corporate information. They built websites for the sake of web presence but maintained their usual business in 'bricks-and-mortar' status. But later, when the Internet's potential in cost reduction was realised, many banks did not hesitate to add 'brick-to-click' business processes and to revise their marketing strategies to attract customers to their virtual branches. They developed e-banking systems that served their customers as well as their managers and staff. The capacity of their systems has surpassed being just Web presence, they can now deliver the following services online:

- *Information dissemination*: The Internet is used for static information displays, for example, information of IPOs, new products, marketing and contacts to branches or personnel.
- *Transactions*: Portals allow interactive enquiries and customer transactions, such as funds transfer and bill payment. These transactions include account enquiry, transfer between accounts, local and utility

bill payment, opening accounts, credit or loan applications, interbank transfers, foreign currency transfers, electronic bill presentment and payment (EBPP), account aggregation, financial advice, online brokerage, insurance and cash management. To enable secure transactions over the Internet, e-banking systems are protected by sophisticated security mechanisms for user verification and authentication.

- *Customisation*: The Internet is used to build a closer relationship with customers, who may receive selected information, such as market news, ads and gifts and/or services tailored for their needs, such as software planners.
- *Wealth management*: New services can be offered on the Internet. For example, many banks that have turned to the insurance and investment business are offering online wealth management service packages.

The sequence of these services also represents a general trend in e-banking development. The financial industry progresses by exploring new applications and new business opportunities. For example, many banks are now offering their insurance and/or stockbrokerage services (topics that belong to a later chapter) as new transaction processing applications added into their e-banking systems. While banks are expanding their business and adding more capabilities to their systems, the boundaries between different sectors of banking are becoming blurred. It is not unsurprising to find retail banks offering services that used to be the speciality of corporate or investment banks, while corporate banks are now offering personal banking services. However, as the web-based information systems being used in the banking industry can still be divided according to the major business they serve, the discussion below is separated into three subsections: retail banking, corporate banking and investment banking.

Retail banking

To prepare for the fierce competition in the retailing market, banks have no alternatives but to adopt the following strategies that are common for businesses in the Internet era:

- *Multi-channel*: From the 'brick-to-click' to 'm-banking', the Internet is one of the channels through which products and services can be delivered. The speed of putting more weight on their Internet portals varies between countries and banks. But even if business is limited to the simplest brick-to-click operations, operating banking services on multiple channels is still very expensive.

- *New products and services*: Many banks rely on innovative products and services to remain competitive. As they are eager to know how customers perceive their new endeavours, retail banks have been investing heavily in customer relationship management (CRM) solutions.

Electronic retail banking is accepted because customers see the convenience of online transactions, which include account enquiry, fund transfer, bill delivery and payment. To promote their online services and to alleviate customers' worries concerning Internet security, e-banks provide their systems with the highest level of security.

The customers, who are now enjoying more services from the bank (possibly from multiple channels), are likely to have their personal data recorded in various data silos across the bank. Data for the same customer may come from daily transactions at a teller's counter or the bank's portal, enquiries at the call centre and interviews with an asset manager or investment consultant. To provide persistent services to the customers, it is necessary to aggregate all of the disparate customer data and provide a single view of each customer throughout the entire system. Thus, although data integration is a major challenge for a multi-channel banking system, the bottom line is simply that the bank must provide adequate protection of customer data.

Innovative products and services are developed with the help of CRM, which provides data to help the bank determine product variety and customisation. For example, Oracle's Product Life Management suite uses customer data to understand their life stages so that new products can be bundled to meet their needs at each of their life stages. The suite can also identify the optimal channel to sell and deliver service and share product knowledge across sales, marketing, service and transaction processing functions of the bank.

Besides processing speed and capacity, legal compliance is also a necessary feature of e-banking systems. For example, many e-banking systems are claimed to be Check 21 compliant.

Check 21

Effective in 2004, the US Check Clearing for the 21st Century Act (Check 21) requires banks to create a substitute cheque called an 'image replacement document' (IRD) for each cheque received. The IRD contains images of both sides of the original cheque – including signature(s), any endorsements, additional printed information added during the clearing process and merchant-written information (such as phone number) added at the time of acceptance. Under the new law, the IRD can be stored and transferred electronically and is used for cheque truncation. This relieves banks from the burden of exchanging physical cheques and greatly reduces float time. It is expected that the new environment will yield more bounced or cancelled cheques as well as new flaws. Banks must therefore invest in a new cheque processing system that is Check 21 compliant, i.e. that the system:

- is able to capture images and has image-survivable security features at the teller window and ATMs;
- is able to redirect imaging to back-office operations in order to achieve next-day posting, returns and exceptions;
- caters for many presentment, posting and return processing scenarios.

To facilitate transactions from other parts of the world, some banks are establishing strategic hubs in, for example, Europe and Asia for remote cheque capture, processing and imaging. These banks, including Deutsche Bank and JP Morgan Chase, plan to transfer the electronic cheque images to the US correspondent banks through the SWIFT network. However, the enactment of Check 21 in 2004 is not entirely free from criticism. While critics in the USA warn the general public of the lessening of float time, Lipis (2004) asserts that the existing cheque image clearing infrastructure in the USA is capable of handling the huge volume of cheques in the country.

Corporate banking

If compared with retail banks, corporate banks were slow in developing their Internet banking alternatives.[2] They were attracted to this new frontier when proven security measures became available to corporate e-banking solutions. Their systems could have the following functions:

- *Informational*: for example, account advising (cash position, transaction and balance reporting), receivable and payable advising and corporate limits.
- *Transactional*: for example, electronic fund transfer, automated clearinghouse (ACH) payment, remittance, tax payment (e.g. EFTPS),[3]

trade finance services (including letters of credit (LC), bank guarantees), autopay (e.g. payroll) and time deposits.

- *Wealth management*: for example, fund and FX management, cash planning, securities custody, investment portfolio management, capital and risk management, liability insurance, estate planning and retirement savings.

Electronic corporate banking systems are characterised by their reporting capability as their corporate clients require extensive reports on their accounts, transactions and investments. These reports might be needed for general decision making or for auditing. They could contain daily details or summarised information. For example, Financial Fusion's Corporate Banking Solution includes an operational reporting module, which generates transactional reports to itemise daily details and a summary for wires, ACH, tax, child support and bill payments. To provide the bank with a more comprehensive view of the customers, the module also produces detailed exception reports and positive pay reports.

Bank of America and JP Morgan Chase teamed up with several vendors (Wachovia, Sun, NEC/Niteo Partners) to work on the Financial Services Technology Consortium[4] to develop a multi-bank reporting system using web services for corporate cash management. The first phase of the project was completed in 2003 but the next phase is still being planned. Niteo Partners wants to add web service monitoring/management functions and security features to the cash management system in this next phase (FSTC report, at *http://fstc.org/projects/web-services/index.cfm*).

Many corporate banking services can be migrated to the Internet if the related back-office workflows can be accelerated to cope with the speed attained on the Internet. To customers, a bank portal is only a convenient channel to submit their requests, but the bank requires some back-office applications to process requests, such as the following transactional services:

- *Commercial lending*: On receiving a client's lending application, a corporate bank may consider multiple factors that are commonly aggregated to the 4Cs – capacity, credit, capital and collateral. The reviewing process is complex and slow, as illustrated in Figure 3.1. There are commercial lending applications to manage the 4Cs and other factors to speed up the review and decision-making process. For example, Fidelity Information Services' ACBS commercial lending and trading system focuses on optimising workflow from deal building through servicing and trading. The UK-based solution provider

Figure 3.1 **High-level workflow of commercial lending origination**

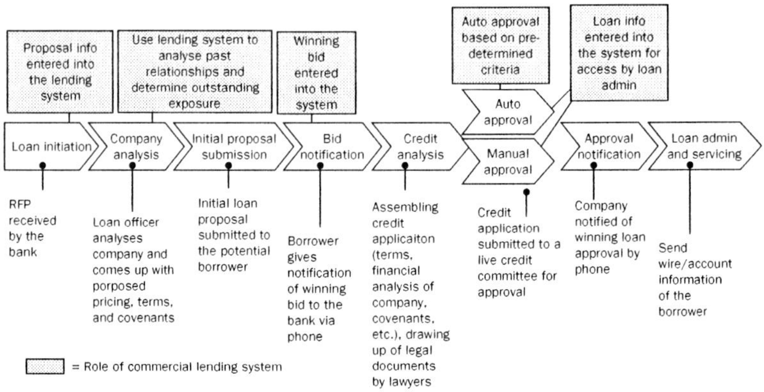

Source: Celent (2002)

Xbridge's commercial mortgage platform has an underwriting filter to supply data for mortgage decisions. The system can return a commercial mortgage quote tailored to the individual needs of each customer.

- *Trade finance*: Bolero[5] (the UK-based Bill of Lading Electronic Registry Organisation) initiated in 1999 is a model that turns all documents (e.g. BL) accompanying the existing LC transactions into electronic documents. Trading parties subscribing to the web-based system can exchange electronic documents through a core messaging platform. The latter is connected to the Title Registry database, which facilitates online transfer of ownership of goods (Figure 3.2). Other similar systems exist. For example, Standard Federal Bank (a subsidiary of ABN AMRO) developed the MaxTrad Online system[6] that allows online LC application and amendment requests. The system also stores information to prepare for repetitive applications.

Figure 3.2 **Bolero.net**

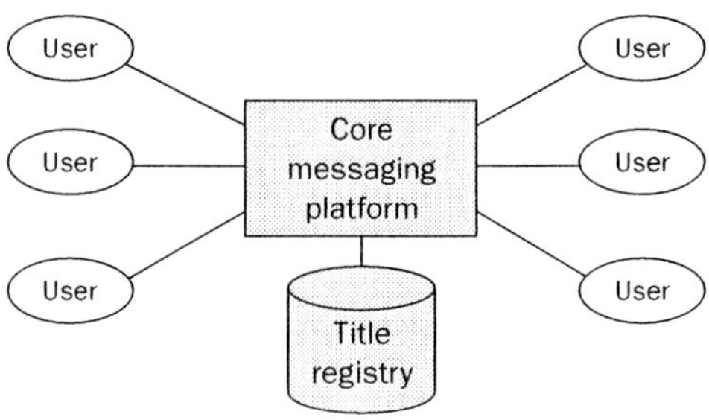

Figure 3.3 TradeCard payment settlement system

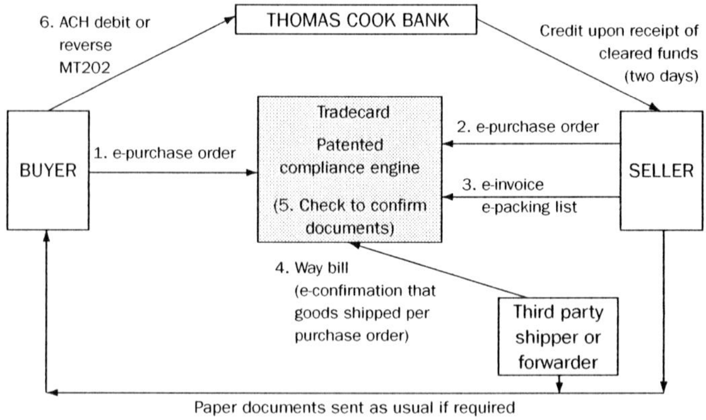

Source: Well (2001)

- *Payments*: The US company TradeCard also provides solutions to trade finance problems, but it focuses more on cross-border payment settlement. Buyers wanting to use the system must first be qualified by Coface (a credit insurer) and give Thomas Cook (an authorised bank) a mandate to debit their bank accounts. The payment transaction is illustrated in Figure 3.3.

Clearing a settlement

On receiving payment orders, such as cheques and funds transfers, the bank sends the information to an ACH for clearing and settlement. The ACH stores and forwards the payment orders in a batch process, which is usually settled on a daily basis. Today's ACHs deploy a real-time gross settlement (RTGS) system, in which processing and settlement take place simultaneously and continuously – the gross feature of the system refers to the fact that each transaction is settled separately (Murphy, 2004). In the USA and the UK, clearing and settlement systems include the following:

- *Fedwire Funds Service*: This is the largest RTGS in the world and it is operated by the Federal Reserve Banks.[7] Their chief responsibilities are to regulate the banking industry and to control money supply in the USA – the total quantity of money in the country, including cash and bank deposits. Fedwire is implemented to provide interbank payment services, safekeeping and transfer services for US government and agency securities and mortgage-backed securities. A financial institution having an account with a Federal Reserve Bank is able to send Fedwire an irrevocable payment order to authorise its bank to debit their account for the transfer amount and to give credit in the same amount to the payee. These banks also perform a variety of services for other banks, e.g. they make emergency loans to banks that are short of cash and clear cheques that are drawn and paid out by different banks.

- *Clearing House Interbank Payments System (CHIPS)* is often used by US banks for large payments related to international interbank transactions. Participants are able to settle end-of-day balances between each other. Its latest enhancements include online cash management tools to allow CHIPS customers to request real-time position information, current status of payment messages and status of unresolved payment messages from anywhere in the world.
- Other US ACHs include National Settlement Service (NSS), SWIFT and CLS bank.[8]
- *Clearing House Automated Payment System (CHAPS)*: a UK system that operates in partnership with the Bank of England in providing a payment and settlement service for banks to transfer money electronically between accounts so that the payee's account is cleared on the same working day. It is the second largest RTGS in the world and is expanding its services to Europe in its CHAPS Euro Project.
- *Bankers Automated Clearing System (BACS)*: maintained by BACS Payment Schemes Ltd. but owned by Voca Ltd., the BACS is an electronic clearing system for direct debits, such as payment of wages, salaries, pensions, utility billing and life and other insurance premiums. A new set of Internet protocols for file transmission was scheduled to roll out in 2005, called BACSTEL-IP, for customers to connect to the BACS.
- *Pan-European ACH* (or PE-ACH): member countries in the European Community have their domestic ACHs but the European Banking Association (EBA) proposed a pan-European ACH platform (originally called EBA STEP2) in 2003 as a first step toward the Single European Payment Arena (SEPA), a project to eliminate the cost of cross-border payments within the eurozone. The SWIFT-based STEP2 has become a *de facto* standard for mass intra-EU payment (Figure 3.4). As the European Payments Council is trying to unify all national and pan-European payments organisations in the SEPA by

Figure 3.4 **Architecture of EBA STEP2 solution**

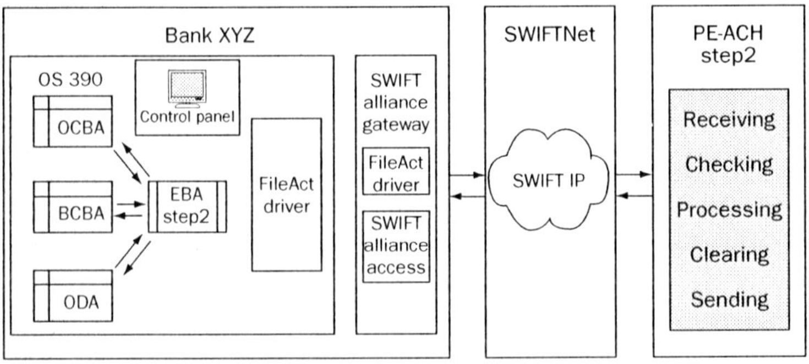

BCBA: Batch Cross Border Application; OCBA: Online Cross Border Applicaton; ODA: Online Domestic Application

Source: CSK (2003)

2010, it is planned to have concrete procedures to simplify transaction capture and initiation in 2006.

- *Trans-European Automated Real-time Gross settlement Express Transfer system (TARGET)*: the Eurosystem[9] offered a RTGS system, called TARGET for euro settlement of central bank operations, large-value euro interbank transfers and the like. Starting from 1999, TARGET connects national euro RTGS systems and the European Central Bank (ECB) payment mechanism. However, the Governing Council of the ECB is not satisfied with the heterogeneous technical design of TARGET and is now planning to upgrade TARGET to TARGET2 as a next generation of RTGS in eurozone.

To settle a transaction with a foreign bank, it is often necessary to send electronic payment messages over a secure communication network. Most banks would select the SWIFT network for this purpose. In 2003, Microsoft offered its BizTalk Server Accelerator for SWIFT (A4SWIFT) as an off-the-shelf solution to set up an infrastructure (including SWIFT ISO15022 messaging and middleware integration tools) for payment settlement, capital markets trading and securities trade settlement with overseas institutions. The solution competes with IBM's Middleware Solution for Banking Wholesale Payments, which was launched in 2004 and the market of payment solutions has been highly competitive ever since.

Financial supply chain

When more and more enterprises are involved in supply chains that support agile manufacturing or JIT methodology, their treasurers need to integrate cash flow with the flow of physical materials. Modern supply chains are characterised by a high level of automation and flexibility, which is supported by efficient financial procedures, such as quick reconciliation of invoices to purchase orders and precise payment timing. These procedures should be integrated with the web-based supply chain management (SCM) system to obtain real-time information and operational transparency. To optimise their procurement and expense management on the supply chain further, these enterprises might consider building a closer financial relationship, i.e. in a financial supply chain.

Banks contribute to financial supply chains by enhancing their services to payables and receivables that impact the cash flow of their client enterprises. Helping enterprises to move away from LC and towards faster payment is one of the results. Bank of America, for example, has developed a financial supply chain management service (FSCMS) which extends its invoice presentment and payment (IPP) services for importers to include the management and presentment of purchase orders. The FSCMS also reconciles payment conditions from the purchase order with invoice data presented by the exporters and triggers payment either under an LC or open account.

Figure 3.5 illustrates the role played by FSCMS in the activities of a purchasing process. Note that the FSCMS is regarded as an extension of traditional working capital management.

A financial supply chain may involve more than one bank, especially when the chain is made up of enterprises from all over the world. The information system managing the financial procedures should then be able to support the legal infrastructure and standards used by different parties. For example, the Bolero financial supply chain solution includes an open account suite, which takes care of order collaboration of importers and exporters in an open account environment, and a document credit suite, which comprises LC collaboration, document preparation, automated compliance checking and credit management.

Case: Basell polyolefins (ABN AMRO, 2004)

Basell is the world's largest producer of polypropylene and advanced polyolefin products. With annual net sales exceeding €5 billion, the

Figure 3.5 Bank of America's view on FSCMS

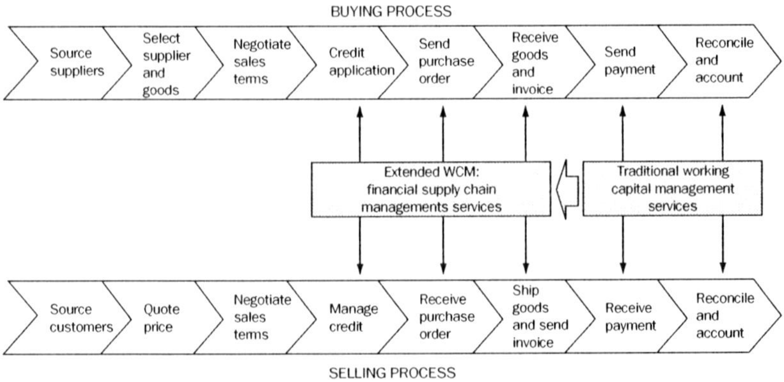

WCM: working capital management

Source: Scanlan (2004)

Dutch enterprise has manufacturing facilities in 18 countries on five continents and suppliers in more than 120 countries. Its Hong Kong regional office coordinates and processes international traded sales in Asia-Pacific, which reaches 400,000 metric tons (representing 600–700 export transactions) per month.

Basell outsources all of its international documentary collections business to ABN AMRO. Says Adrian Reincke, Manager of the Commercial Services at Basell Asia Pacific Ltd.:

> By concentrating our business through ABN AMRO, we gain better control over our trade activities ... MaxTrad helps improve processing through standardisation, with one reference point for information reporting that monitors country and bank exposures, paid and outstanding items and all bank fees.

MaxTrad is the global trade portal of ABN AMRO. It provides Basell online initiation and monitoring of export LC and export documentary draft collections; online access to reports on all export activities such as bills of lading, inspection certificates and packing lists; images of advised export LC and related payment advice notes; and the ability to link all counterparties to an export transaction.

ABN AMRO helped Basell re-engineer its processes, formulate controls and institute a monitoring policy to accelerate the payment cycle. The bank's trade system is also integrated with Basell's ERP system.

Investment banking

Investment banks, such as Merrill Lynch and JP Morgan Chase have developed a limited range of Web-based applications for communication with their corporate clients, financial institutions, governments and institutional investors worldwide. The Internet does not influence their usual business[10] as much as the other banking sectors. However, there are still some e-banking systems specially designed for investment banking.

Information integration and delivery is a primary reason for installing such a system. For example, one framework for investment banking available in the market is Thomson's ONE Banker. It integrates multiple information sources (including quotes, earning estimates, financial fundamentals, market moving news, transaction data, corporate filings, ownership profiles and research and other third-party content) to display as a customisable web page. Figure 3.6 illustrates the architecture of ONE Banker.

The information gathered needs to be organised and stored in a data warehouse, which is often associated with a business intelligence application and/or a knowledge management system. For example, top investment banks, such as Merrill Lynch & Co., Credit Suisse First Boston and FleetBoston Financial Corp. have installed Capital IQ's business intelligence software. The software combines research databases that are compiled on subjects including venture capital and buyout firms and allows quick research into potential buyers or backers for a client.

Investment banks also need to maintain a wide network of connectivity with their corporate clients, which include intermediaries, commercial

Figure 3.6 **Thomson ONE Banker framework**

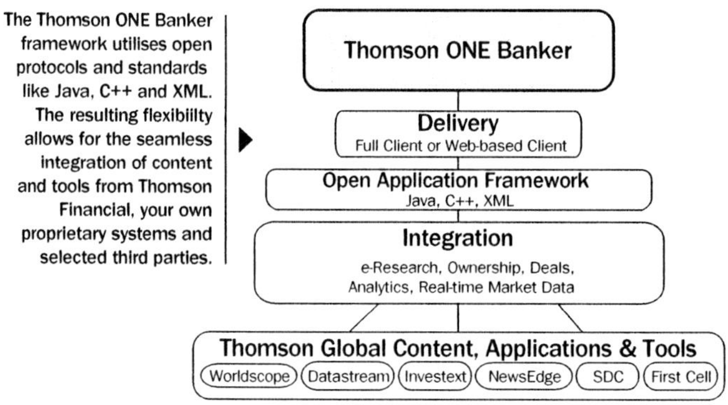

SDC: securities data company; a database of historical details of company IPOs, and related information

Source: Thomson Financial (2003)

lenders, advisers, selected partners and other private equity firms. A Web-based information system is thus valuable to the management of the relationship with these clients. Unlike the CRM system of a retail bank, an investment bank's CRM system is capable of the following tasks:

- generating relationship reports;
- helping to manage transactions for clients, e.g. to staff deal teams, to maintain investor records and to track progress;
- publishing custom web pages to communicate with selected partners and co-investors;
- creating 'watch-lists' to monitor the economics of any industry, sector, company, person, or transaction relevant to a project.

For example, the Chicago-based investment bank Lincoln Partners has installed a web-enabled CRM application, InterAction, for the management of the strategic and tactical business development initiatives aimed at clients and prospects in selected markets. The application also enables Lincoln Partners to track deals and manage its internal experience and expertise (Haimila, 2003).

The banking industry is promoting the efficiency and convenience of e-banking. However, the investment banking sector is reluctant to replace the tradition of face-to-face contact with portals on the Internet, as the sector relies on the personal contact to build up trust with their clients. To investment banks, e-banking systems, such as the CRM system mentioned earlier are mostly developed for the purpose of information dissemination and decision support.

E-banking systems in use

TowerGroup, a research and advisory group for the global financial services industry, studied the e-banking market and found investment in e-banking systems is still generous. Banks spend one-quarter of their technology budgets – approximately $37.5 billion on a global basis – on core banking software, hardware and services (Singer, 2002). The e-banking system market is as competitive as other business sectors. A bank may choose an off-the-shelf solution to set up an e-banking portal in a short time, a product specially designed for a particular function or service offered by the bank, or a system developed in-house – like HSBC, which insists that the in-house approach is more cost-effective and more value-added compared with packaged software (MIS 100, 2003).

Management is particularly interested in assessing the capability of an e-banking system in the following areas:

- *Integration with legacy systems*: Driven by both business needs and enabling technologies, the system could be developed to integrate with other systems at five levels: data, network, application, communication and business (see Table 3.1).
- *Business process provision*: To deliver the services or products as specified in the design, the system is usually component-oriented and allows easy maintenance and enhancement with new functionalities. For example, other than basic e-banking transaction functionalities (e.g. account administration, fund transfer and bill payment), an electronic retail banking system may have other value-added capabilities, such as business intelligence and CRM that can be added when needed.
- *Security*: To provide a secure environment for information exchange, the e-banking system is protected by a firewall and a user account security mechanism. Often banks are required to use secure sockets layer (SSL) protocol to transfer confidential information.
- *Compliance*: Regulations and legislation in different jurisdictions require e-banking systems to follow special procedures for the capture, storage, management and retrieval of electronic communication and documents (e.g. the Check 21 Act in the USA requires banks to modify their cheque-processing systems). Moreover, these systems should have control and risk self-assessment tools and loss events databases as required by Basel II regulations. Chapters 8–10 discuss security technology and legal issues in the financial sector.

Table 3.1 **Five levels of integration**

Data level	Consolidation of data from various sources to provide a single composite view of a client
Network level	Standardisation of communication hardware, such as IP, ethernet and optics
Application level	Interoperability between Web-based applications and legacy systems
Communication level	Inter-personal interaction through mobility, personalisation and rich media
Business level	To bring front- and back-office functions together (sometimes from external parties), irrespective of their platforms, databases and infrastructures

Several e-banking platforms described in the following sections show various levels of capability.

Flexcube

Flexcube is the application suite for the banking industry developed by i-flex Solutions, a Mumbai-based software company. Since its first emergence in the market in 1997, it has won nearly 200 customers in more than 88 countries. Its clients include big names, such as Citibank, the International Monetary Fund (IMF),[11] DBS Bank and American Stock Exchange, to name a few. It is renowned for its ability to capture and process banking transactions for various sectors in the banking industry and in laboratory testing it set a record of efficiently handling transaction loads of 3,000 branches and 20 million customer accounts.

Flexcube is an open architecture (Figure 3.7) that can be implemented by using J2EE servers, such as HP servers and IBM WebSphere servers. It can also be easily integrated with legacy systems for straight through processing (STP) as well as automation of back-office workflow. It has a modular structure, organised in an *n*-tier distributed architecture that supports customer interaction technologies, such as ATM, PDA, POS and interactive voice response.

The Flexcube system is capable of serving different banking sectors and in its business application suite offers several e-banking solutions that can be selected to compose the e-banking system.

Figure 3.7 General architecture of Flexcube

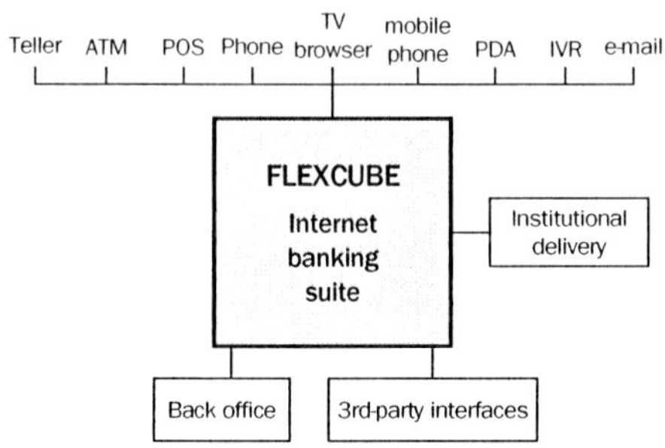

ATM: automatic teller machine; IVR: interactive voice response; PDA: personal digital assistant; POS: point of sale

Figure 3.8 Flexcube software architecture

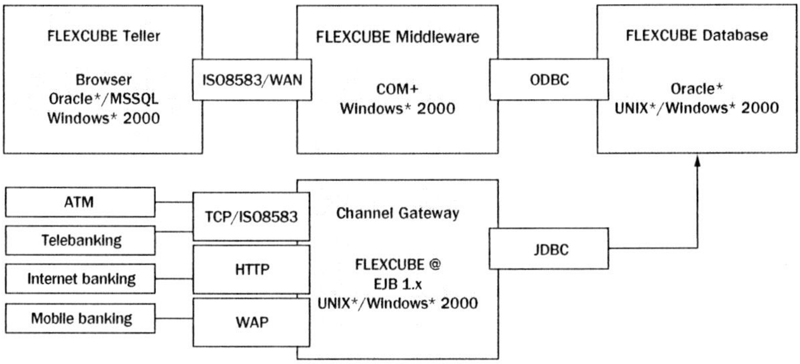

JDBC: Java database connectivity; ODBC: open database connetivity; ORACLE/MSSQL: Oracle or Microsoft's structured query language; TCP: Transmission control protocol; WAN: wide area network; WAP: wireless application protocol

Source: i-flex, HP and Intel (2002)

- *Flexcube Retail Banking*: supporting browser-based retail banking services (e.g. accessing accounts, fund transfers between accounts, opening deposits, mortgages, loan repayments) and customer service transactions (e.g. stopping cheques, requesting direct debits and statements).
- *Flexcube Corporate Banking*: global payments over SWIFT and Telex networks, execution and reporting of complex trade finance transactions, management of FX contracts and customer services, such as limits query.
- *Flexcube Investor Services*: mutual fund transactions (buy, sell, switch), portfolio management, standing instructions.
- *Flexcube Broker*: brokerage services, such as client management, order management, risk management, revenue management, settlement processing and reconciliation and electronic messaging to support cash and margin trading in exchange listed equities, futures, options and bonds.

The selected e-banking solution(s) can be displayed on a Flexcube portal, which is a set of HTML screens allowing direct contact between customers and the bank and a repository of many financial services. The core modules and functional modules of the system provide a variety of functions for banking operations. Flexcube is particularly proud of its modules in its application packs, such as:

- *Flexcube Pay*: for the bank to build a hosted payment and settlement system.
- *Flexcube EBPP*: supports e-billing, bill presentment and ACH as well as Electronic Clearing Services (ECS) provision of electronic cheque services networks.
- *Flexcube PKI*: offers public key infrastructure (PKI) as a cryptographic service to Flexcube and other applications in the system.
- *Flexcube Connect and Flexcube Intelligence e-Finance Middleware*: interfaces to integrate disparate applications and multiple channels.

The Flexcube e-banking system also exchanges information with external institutions, such as ACHs, SWIFT and GIRO. It has a report generator to interface with S1's FiRE regulatory reporting system, which is almost a *de facto* standard for central bank reporting for over 20 countries. Reuters, Dealing 2000, Telerate and other information sources can also send information on stock prices and rates to the Flexcube system. Figure 3.8 illustrates a variety of information sources feeding to the database of the system.

The success of Flexcube has not stopped its vendor from expanding its functionality. Besides teaming up with IBM to have the J2EE-based WebSphere server supporting Flexcube, i-flex also proposed a core systems transformation solution with IBM's backing. The solution offers a better environment for Flexcube by making use of IBM's middleware and database technologies. In 2004, i-flex allied with PeopleSoft (a legendary ERP vendor that was acquired by Oracle in mid-2005) to enhance Flexcube with CRM capabilities.

HP banking solutions

HP has been providing standard software solutions for the banking industry for a long time. As early as 1999, HP offered Nimius solution – a three-tier architecture – to the banking industry (Figure 3.9). The three tiers are as follows.

- *Xframework*: a web application framework that supports the development of servlets and JSPs. The latter converts response data to HTML pages.
- *E3 (enterprise e-services engine)*: is the container for business specific e-services. It houses the middleware components for the framework

Figure 3.9 Architecture of HP Nimius solution

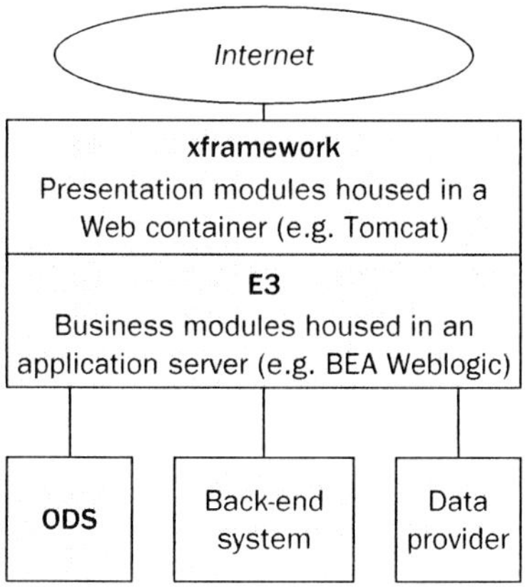

ODS: operational data store

and can run on any J2EE application server. It provides the basis for building e-financial applications, such as e-brokerage, e-payment, e-asset information, e-customer care and e-contact management.

- *ODS (operational data store)*: holds the business specific data. The architecture builds in a data model for the storage of user information (e.g. login data) and basic data. Some 'transit tables' are included in the ODS to strengthen the integration with legacy data. The Nimius solution for financial services comes with a specialised data model for e-banking.

Nimius solution is a generic framework on which to build an e-financial system. It emphasises its open architecture and security mechanism – two essential features of today's e-banking systems. It has a number of business modules and functions that can be used by different sectors in the financial services industry.

HP OpenBank architecture

In 2004, HP launched OpenBank.NET as an architecture designed in partnership with Microsoft. It is an infrastructure where mid- and back-office software and banking services can be integrated with channel applications. It is a framework including platforms, technologies, common data models, third-party solutions and other services.

One of the objectives of the OpenBank framework is to provide a consolidated view of total customer relationship. It requires integrated information across enterprise applications and consistent treatment of customers across different channels. Customer data and transaction data are stored in a data warehouse system, which supports CRM and integrated marketing. The architecture also facilitates compliance with open reporting and risk management regulations, including Basel II, US Check 21 and Patriot Act.

Figure 3.10 shows the layered structure of the functionalities of OpenBank. The layers roughly follow the *n*-tier system structure that was discussed in Chapter 2.

- *Channel messaging/connectivity*: Implemented by Microsoft BizTalk 2004, this layer performs message transformation, validation, routing and guaranteed delivery of messages to the target. It also provides integration between channel applications and back-end systems
- *Business activity manager (BAM)*: This orchestrates actions to process events. It may use the business rules in the next layer to apply pre-processing or configure the actions.
- *Common business processes/business rules*: This implements business logic, policy management, orchestrates business processes and workflow.
- *Application/service integration*: This leverages existing application integration infrastructure within the bank and provides integration of multiple data sources across the channels.

HP Real Time Financial Services (RTFS) is a pre-integrated, packaged set of software components, architecture and services based on adaptive infrastructure and OpenBank architecture.

Figure 3.10 **OpenBank functional view**

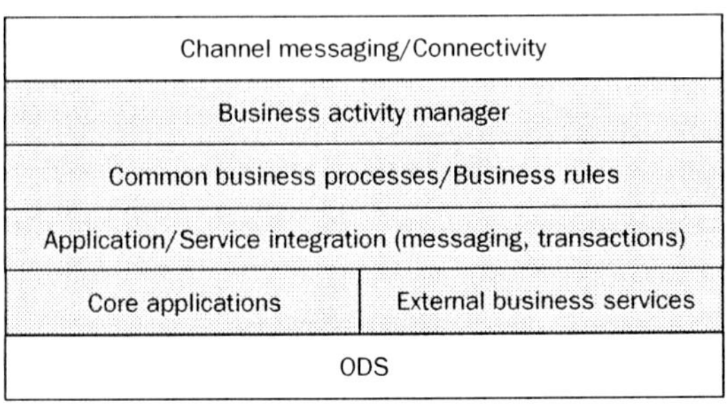

ODS: operational data store

Adapted from: HP (2004a)

Figure 3.11 **Functional view of the real-time financial services hub**

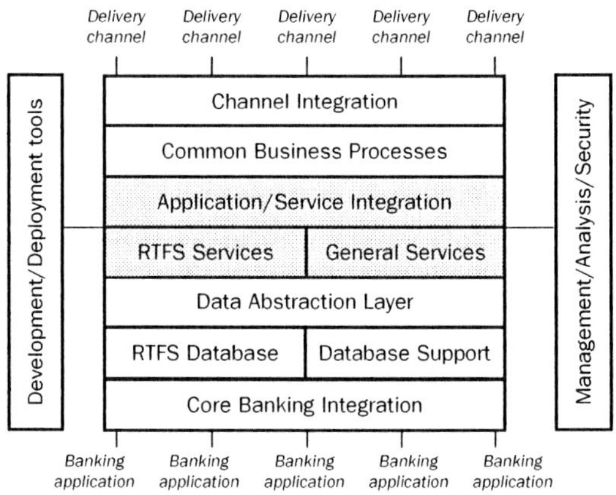

RTFS: real-time financial services

Adapted from: HP (2004c)

Unlike other e-banking systems, RTFS is a central hub that provides a single point of control for multi-application customer interactions and data points. Many features in OpenBank's functional architecture remain equally important in RTFS. For example, channel integration, optional BAM, common business processes and ODS exist in a RTFS hub (see Figure 3.11). Banking applications that can be enhanced by the RTFS include those for payments, billing, fraud and money laundering detection, CRM and exception management.

HP's RTFS is targeted at two segments of the finance industry: retail banking and wholesale banking. However, its retail banking solution is part of the OpenBank initiative but the wholesale banking solution is part of the initiative known as HP OpenPayments. The OpenPayments solution is a framework of platforms, technologies, common data models, partner solutions and professional services that can be integrated at enterprise level. The hub is connected to back-office applications, such as card/risk management system, legacy demand deposit accounts[12] and loan accounting systems and customer information system. More will be discussed in Chapter 4.

Finacle's e-banking solutions

Infosys Technologies Ltd. is one of the giant software vendors in India. Its flagship product, Finacle Universal Banking solution, has won the UK

Financial Times' 'Banker Technology Awards 2004'. The solution has been helping many banks, including American Express, Bank of America, ABN AMRO, Citi Group, Goldman Sachs and Bank Boston to implement their e-banking platforms.

Finacle's Universal Banking suite includes eight units: core banking, consumer e-banking, corporate e-banking, CRM, treasury, wealth management, mobile and alerts and Web-based cash management. They can be configured to be a vertically integrated and modular enterprise banking solution. All applications are integrated in an *n*-tier, thin-client architecture, which allows SWIFT messaging through multiple channels, such as ATMs, POS, telephone, the Internet and wireless devices (WAP or SMS).

The foundation of the Universal Banking solution is the core banking solution, as shown in Figure 3.12. Finacle's core banking solution supports several modules that are essential to run e-banking operations.

- *Finacle eChannels* delivers retail banking services across multiple channels. It also delivers the electronic bill presentment and payment (EBPP) module to support online retail payments. Functions include account management, fund transfers and requests, and management to support retail banking services.
- *Finacle eCorporate* addresses corporate banking requirements. Its functions are three-fold:
  - Corporate banking services, including trade finance functions like LC, bank guarantees and enquiry and monitoring of corporate limits.

Figure 3.12 Deployment architecture of Finacle's solution in ABN AMRO

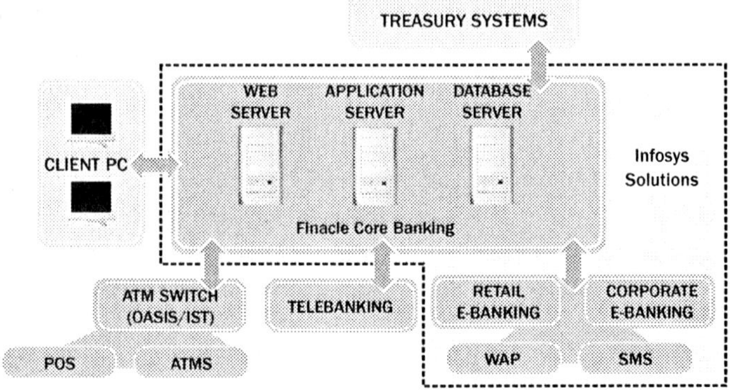

Source: Finacle (2004)

  - Electronic invoice presentment and payment (EIPP) for corporate payments. This module is believed to be a strategic tool for banks to enhance their services to corporate customers.
  - B2B payments, which is an escrow account mechanism to let customers track the status of multiple deals, and enable payments and receipts through various mechanisms, such as direct debit and credit.
- *Customer Management Module* is common for eChannels and eCorporate, handling cross-channel account maintenance, including customer creation, password, transaction limits and business rules. It is essential to manage bank products through multiple channels.
- *Personalisation and content management modules* are also common for eChannels and eCorporate, they are tools to deliver mass customised products and services to retail and corporate customers.

Finacle's solution can be implemented on servers like J2EE and .NET. It is thus easy to team up with other vendors, such as HP and IBM in e-banking system development projects. A remarkable venture between Sun and Infosys is their joint effort – Retail Banking Reference Architecture. It set a record of processing 5,200 transactions per second online by having Infosys' Finacle Core Banking software and Sun's Solaris 8 operating system implemented on a set of Sun's servers and storage arrays.

Proposed in 2002, the retail banking reference architecture is one of the reference architectures designed by Sun's iForce Solutions Centre (Menlo Park, California). Like the other reference architectures, which are claimed by iForce to be repeatable business models built and tested by implementations in live customer sites worldwide, the retail banking reference architecture should be able to reduce the start-up cost of an e-banking solution. The architecture is a combination of Sun's Fire servers, StorEdge arrays, Open Net Environment (ONE) and Finacle's core banking solution. It provides STP workflow automation for Web-based banking systems.

The examples described above depict the composition of e-banking systems that are available in the market. The following case illustrates the implementation of such a system in a 'cyberbank'.

Case: NetBank.com

Founded in 1996, NetBank, Inc. (Nasdaq: NTBK) is now being accepted as the first commercially successful e-bank in the USA. Although it is 'branchless', the Atlanta-based, 'totally virtual', e-bank spreads its business across the retail and corporate banking sectors and serves 270,000 customers in the USA and, by 2004, more than another 20 countries. By giving higher deposit rates and free account services, such as online payment, NetBank has been able to attract $2.5 billion in deposits.

At the end of 2003, NetBank migrated its e-banking system from S1's Edify platform to a NCR solution, which consists of the Corillian's Voyager Internet Banking and Teknowledge solutions on top of Sun's platform. The Voyager solution is a collection of applications to handle the banking activities, such as transaction processing, management of e-statements, e-notices and cheque imaging. The Teknowledge's software, TekPortal, is used to provide customers with a consolidated view of their financial information online. Lying at the centre to the system is the NCR Logical Data Model, which is a database connected to various third-party applications (shown as NCR LDM in Figure 3.13).

To maintain a good relationship with its customers, NetBank employs a team of relationship managers who are reachable via phone or e-mail. The virtual bank also has a dedicated customer-care unit to deal with personal enquiries from customers. NetBank's director of Small Business Banking, Bert Davis, says:

Figure 3.13 NCR LDM/Corillian Voyager e-banking suite

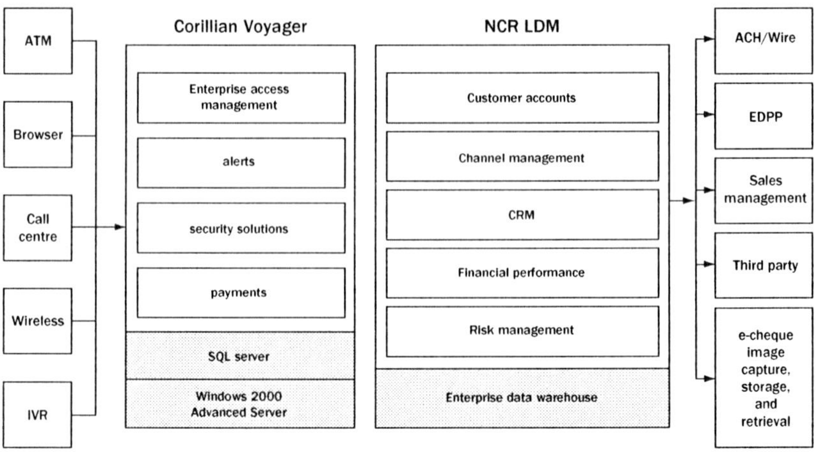

ATM: automatic teller machine; CRM: customer relationship management; EBPP: electronic bill presentment and payment; IVR: interactive voice response

Source: Solution Sheet NCR Corporation and Sun (year unknown)

> There were opportunities for companies that wanted the convenience and the technological advantages that they can get from banking over the Internet, but they didn't want to give up the personal relationship that they might have with a local branch officer ... You didn't have the choice to have the relationship advantages and maintain the technological edge that you get with our type of delivery channels. (Ramsaran, 2003)

Management issues of e-banking

The establishment of e-banking channels must influence the branching strategy of a bank. However, whether the replacement of 'bricks-and-mortar' branches by an Internet portal can bring in more revenue is controversial (Hirtle and Metli, 2004). When e-banking has become popular, the benefits of the first-movers vanish and management has to confront other strategic problems, such as service differentiation, price competition and increased risk. To promote safety and soundness of e-banking activities, the Electronic Banking Group (EBG), a study group sponsored by the Basel Committee,[13] proposed 14 risk management principles for e-banking (BIS, 2001). The authority did not put forth these principles as absolute requirements, but they suggested that each bank should tailor a risk mitigation approach for its scale of e-banking operations. The risk management principles were:

- Board and management oversight:
  - effective management oversight of e-banking activities;
  - establishment of a comprehensive security control process;
  - comprehensive due diligence and management oversight process for outsourcing relationships and other third-party dependencies.
- Security controls:
  - authentication of e-banking customers;
  - non-repudiation and accountability for e-banking transactions;
  - appropriate measures to ensure segregation of duties;
  - proper authorisation controls within e-banking systems, databases and applications;
  - data integrity of e-banking transactions, records and information;

  - establishment of clear audit trails for e-banking transaction;
  - confidentiality of key bank information.
- Legal and reputational risk management:
  - appropriate disclosures for e-banking services;
  - privacy of customer information;
  - capacity, business continuity and contingency planning to ensure availability of e-banking systems and services;
  - incident response planning.

Those principles proposed by the Basel Committee are concerned with management, security and legal risks. For the operation of e-banking, some other areas of risk are equally dangerous. Perumal and Shanmugam (2004) raise the following issues as the 'bane' of e-banking, where the first three are also known as market risks:

- *Credit risk*: E-banking reduces personal contact and the bank is less able to verify the bona fides of their customers who, if they apply for credit, give rise to credit risk. The bank needs specially designed policies, processes and practices to control the risk associated with those customers.
- *Interest rate risk*: Web-based applications deployed in e-banking could exacerbate the impact of illiquid hedging strategies or products.
- *Liquidity risk*: E-banking increases deposit volatility from customers who maintain accounts solely on the basis of rates or terms. As the Internet allows real-time transactions, the bank must be prepared for immediate changes and consequent liquidity risk.
- *Transaction risk*: This is risk associated with fraud, error and the inability to deliver products or services on the Internet.
- *Total reliability risk*: Not all products and services can be delivered online. It therefore bears some risk to move a transaction to the Internet.

EBG discussed with the bank supervisory community and concluded that the Internet delivery channel for e-banking products and services does increase some of the risks that exist in traditional banking practice. The management of banks engaged in e-banking should know the difference in the overall risk profile. To implement the risk management principles, the Basel Committee suggested that banks should develop four functions (BIS, 2001):

- Incident response plans to address recovery of e-banking systems and services under various business scenarios and geographic locations.
- Mechanisms to identify a crisis as soon as it occurs, assess its materiality and control the reputation risk associated with any disruption in service.
- Incident response teams with the authority to act in an emergency and sufficiently trained in analysing incident detection/response systems and interpreting the significance of related output.
- A process for collecting and preserving forensic evidence to facilitate appropriate post-mortem reviews of any e-banking incidents as well as to assist in the prosecution of attackers.

Risk management and regulatory compliance are issues that every financial services institution needs to address and will be discussed in detail in Chapters 8, 9 and 10. This chapter focuses on two related topics in e-banking management: cross-border e-banking and Basel II compliance.

Cross-border e-banking

In view of the expansion of e-banking and its capability to reach customers all over the world, many national authorities and supervisors are consciously trying to find a method to monitor or control e-banking activities that are offered, either by local banks to overseas customers, or by foreign banks to local customers. As such monitoring and control would be impossible without cross-border cooperation, the EBG particularly emphasises two more risk management principles to address the importance of risk assessment, due diligence, ongoing risk management and transparency for banks that consider cross-border e-banking services (BIS, 2003c):

- Prior to engaging in cross-border e-banking activities, a banking institution should conduct appropriate risk assessment and due diligence and establish an effective risk management programme for such activities.
- A banking institution intending to engage in cross-border e-banking activities should provide sufficient disclosure on its website to allow potential customers to determine the bank's identity, home country and regulatory licence(s).

A closer examination of these two principles reveals that they are refinements of Principles 1 and 11 of Basel's original risk management principles. The EBG asserts that banks considering cross-border e-banking activities should take the responsibility to implement these principles and authorities should take the supervisory modes and collaborate with foreign authorities. However, the collaboration is impossible in a country with no authority. McDowall (2002) refers to the following situations as 'country risk':

- *Non-compliance with different national laws*: including applicable consumer protection laws, advertising and disclosure laws, record keeping and reporting requirements, privacy and money laundering laws.
- *Legal uncertainties*: which foreign laws apply to cross-border e-banking activities.
- *Roles and responsibilities of local authorities*: home country supervisory bodies may have not yet provided adequate supervision of cross-border e-banking activities.

Vendors may offer information system solutions to assist with compliance to foreign laws and regulations. For example, netNumina promotes a global compliance system that allows end-users to set compliance limits and to monitor non-compliant trades globally (Figure 3.14).

The EBG discovered that cross-border activities have not been developing as rapidly as domestic e-banking and explained that customers may not trust the safety and security of cross-border transactions and are concerned

Figure 3.14 High-level architecture of a global compliance system

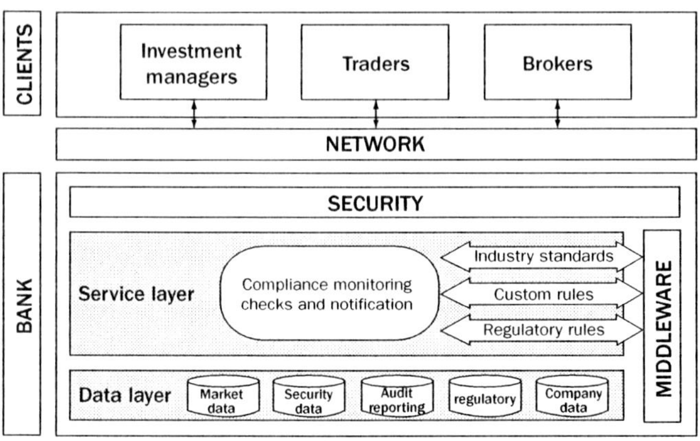

Source: netNumina (2002)

with national jurisdiction, choice of law and consumer protection requirements for these kinds of activities. To attract customers, the US depository institutions are required by laws to assure customers that:[14]

- interest rates charged for loans or paid on deposits are explained truthfully and clearly;
- bank deposits are insured;
- personal and confidential information is used and handled appropriately; and
- depository institutions are managed in a safe and sound manner and in full compliance with applicable federal and state laws and regulations.

Case: Cross-border payment (Anonymous, 2004)

Cross-border payment has been a challenge to many banks in the European Union. They need to consider whether to spend large sums of money on turning themselves into a payment hub or to partner with others to build an infrastructure for euro and dollar payments. The question of how to construct an EU payments infrastructure remains a central focus for the payments industry in the continent.

Even now, the banks are compelled to re-engineer their back-offices and payment processes to prepare for pan-European direct debits in 2010. The industry has to upgrade the in-country legacy payment systems that still exist all over Europe in order to reach the target. The process has become more urgent recently. According to EC Regulation 2560, payment companies were required to use payment orders for cross-border payments of up to €12,500 in July 2003.

Ed Glassman, managing director of global product delivery at ABN AMRO, remarks that although banks are complying with the requirement, their existing infrastructure may not be sufficient to let them run payments as a profitable business line. He believes that a shakeout is inevitable:

> With the first requirement to use payment orders for payments up to €12,500, a bank could change its pricing but still have its old, now unprofitable, infrastructure. Banks will be making very hard decisions in the next few years as to whether they continue to invest or choose a different business model as the reality of implementation hits home. We think that many other banks will be choosing to outsource their cross-border payments.

The threshold of high-value intra-EU payments is extended to €50,000 in January 2006. This is an effort contributing to the construction of the single European payments area (SEPA). But banks would most likely be affected as revenues would be reduced. As Glassman comments, banks finding their payments business unprofitable might outsource euro payments to larger players such as ABN AMRO, which has been quite successful in the market.

Payments business is evolving to a point at which the digitisation of operations has blurred the distinction between high and low value, domestic or cross-border payments. Banks' services and systems that have been built on these segmentations are becoming obsolete. The European Commission confirmed that domestic and cross-border payments in the EU are no longer treated differently. It is also expected that the threshold of high-value payment will vanish soon. Glassman says, 'For many banks, pricing convergence will come before capability. To mask the complexity of today's disparate pan-European payments systems, ABN AMRO delivers a harmonised, integrated cross-border payments service through a single window for its customers'.

Basel II compliance

To direct financial institutions to effective risk management, the Basel Committee on Banking Supervision published the Capital Adequacy Accord (also known as the Basel Accord) in 1988. It was accepted by the central banks of more than 100 countries as the basis of risk management within their banking systems.

In January 2001 the Basel Committee issued a proposal for a new Basel Capital Accord (Basel II) which will be mandatory for all banks and supervisors starting from 2007. The proposal is based on three mutually reinforcing pillars which allow banks and supervisors to evaluate properly the various risks that banks face. These three pillars are:

1. *Minimum capital requirement*: defines what capital is and sets out the minimum capital requirement, letting banks develop strategies to deal with credit, market and operational risk.
2. *Supervisory and review process*: creates a framework to encourage best risk practices and defines the structure to be adapted by banks for reporting to regulators. The bank is expected to implement processes to assess capital adequacy and the supervisory power to evaluate this assessment.

3. *Market discipline*: defines requirements to disclose capital structure, risk exposures and capital adequacy in detail, leading to greater transparency and accountability from bank management.

In particular, Basel II requires banks to quantify their credit risk, operational risk and market risk. Several methods have been suggested (Nayak, 2003), which include:

- *Credit risk*: minimum capital required to cover exposure to customers and counterparties. There are two measuring methods.
  - Standardised approach – a risk-weight is allocated to each asset and the weights are based on assessment by external credit rating institutions.
  - Internal ratings-based (IRB) approach – a borrower's credit risk is assessed by an internal evaluation system, using methods, such as probability of default (PD), loss given default (LGD), credit conversion factor (CCF) and exposure at default (EAD) to calculate the risk weights for exposure classes. Basel II divides these methods into two categories: *foundation* (using PD) and *advanced* (using all three). The IRB approach brings greater risk sensitivity.
- *Operational risk*: a certain percentage (say, 20 per cent) of the internal capital of a bank is usually allocated for operational risk, which includes failure of internal processes and natural or man-made disasters. Three measuring methods are available.
  - Basic indicator approach – a fixed percentage (called alpha factor) of the bank's gross annual revenue (or another operational parameter) is used to determine the capital charge for operational risk.
  - Standardised approach – different fixed percentages (called beta factors) are set for different business lines of the bank; thus, each business line can determine its capital charge. The capital charge for operational risk is the sum of all capital charges for individual business lines.
  - Internal measurement (IM) approach – a fixed percentage (known as gamma factor), determined by the Basel Committee, is used to determine the capital charge of a business line. The total capital charge is the sum of all capital charges for individual business lines.
- *Market risks*: capital set aside to cover exposure to changes in market conditions, such as fluctuations in interest rates, foreign exchange rates, equity prices and commodity prices.

Table 3.2 **Impact of Basel II on ICT deployment**

Category	Requirement	Impact
Design and architecture of the system	Integration with other technology programs across the enterprise	Ensure data quality and integrity
Information availability	Raw and enriched data from multiple systems	Use of high quality data for processes
Audit	Credit risk systems to support overall credit risk framework across the enterprise	Minimisation of risk
Performance	Accuracy and easy availability of data	Enhanced performance of processes
Security	Monitoring of risks	Minimisation of risks thus leading to security

Source: Nayak (2003)

The Basel Committee is still seeking comments from the industry and several consultative papers have been released since Basel II was first proposed. The Accord is in the process of fine-tuning, but institutions need to prepare for it. For example, if a bank opts for the IRB approach to assess credit risk, it needs to maintain a history of vital data prior to the implementation of Basel II for the calculation of capital reserve. Furthermore, Pillars 2 and 3 in Basel II suggest to business and IT management there is an immediate need to review their aging practices. As the Accord requires ongoing and progressive evidence of effective risk management practices, whatever practice of compliance that a bank wants to implement must be implemented prior to the effective date. Areas where Basel II has changed the use of ICT are summarised in Table 3.2.

Basel II presents a complex standard for banks to measure and manage risk. Software vendors do not hesitate to offer their solutions to seize the profit of the compliance market. For example, Accenture has a comprehensive framework to implement a system that is compliant with Basel II (Figure 3.15).

IBM and other business consultants indicate that data management is a key factor in Basel II compliance technology. They argue (Datamonitor, 2003) that processes for the collection and cleansing of data must be standardised. IBM also provides a risk and compliance solution – Basel II Information Management Offering – which is a combination of software,

Figure 3.15 Basel II framework pyramid

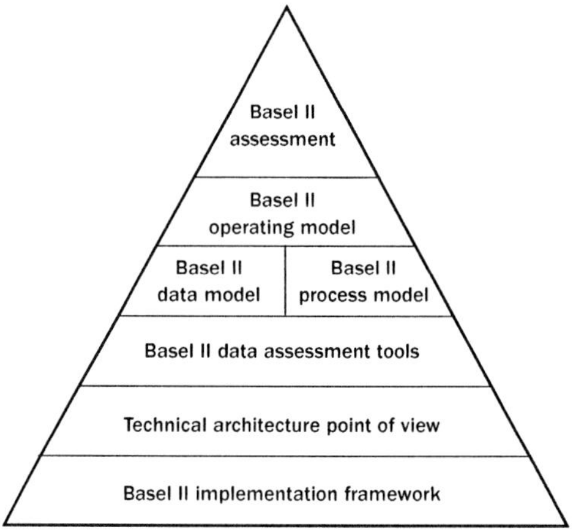

Source: Accenture (2005)

hardware and consulting services for banks to comply with the Accord.

Data are stored in the DB2 Universal Database or/and the banking data warehouse (BDW), which are central to the offering. The former is used together with DB2 Information Integrator and DB2 Cube Views to integrate information from across the bank. The latter, besides its capability of reporting, data mining and decision making, contains business solution templates which are datamart structures to provide reports required by the pillars of Basel II.

The BDW, however, also has a set of application solution templates to help capital reserve calculation using those approaches (e.g. LGD, EAD) suggested in Basel II. A standard six-tiered architecture suggested by IBM is illustrated in Figure 3.16. The functions of these six tiers are as follows (IBM, 2003):

1. *data sources*: sources of data (internal and external) required for Basel II;
2. *extraction*: process and technology to extract data from the diverse sources;
3. *enterprise data store*: to store all detailed data needed for Basel II;
4. *transformation and calculation*: where risk calculations are made;
5. *data marts*: where the aggregated data are stored to support the next tier; and
6. *reporting*: production and delivery of Basel II reports.

Figure 3.16 **Six tiers of the standard Basel II architecture as defined by IBM (2003)**

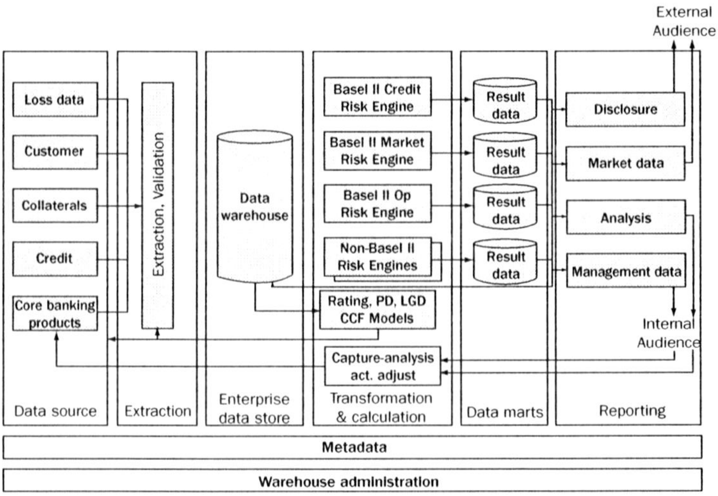

CCF: credit conversion factor; LGD: loss given default; PD: probability of default

Source: IBM (2003)

IBM's Risk and Compliance – Basel II Information Management Offering is a general framework that can be used to adopt other solutions that are compliant with other laws and regulations, such as the Sarbanes-Oxley Act and anti-money laundering.

Besides the banking sector, Basel II also applies to other financial services. We will discuss the Basel regulations of financial risk management in Chapter 10.

Summary

The retail banks, corporate banks and investment banks have their own set of problems, some of which emerge as a result of the banks' endeavours in e-banking. These problems are commonly dealt with by ICT applications. Those banking solutions described in this chapter are well-known systems in the banking industry. They also exemplify the *n*-tiered architecture of e-financial systems that were described in the last chapter. In the final section, this chapter brought up two other problems that management has to deal with, especially in the environment of e-banking: cross-border e-banking and Basel II compliance.

This chapter also represents the beginning of a series of discussions on the development of ICT applications in various fields of the financial services sector. Banking is certainly the largest and the most important sector in the entire financial services industry. Although the banking sector is seen expanding its business to other areas, we will see more focused discussion of those areas in the following chapters. For example, the use of ICT in e-payment and e-money will be examined in the next chapter.

Questions for discussion

1. Why is a single view of a customer important in the banking sector?
2. What is the difference between the function of a retail payment system and that of a corporate payment system?
3. Basel II requires banks to elicit a large amount of information. What opportunities could this information bring to banks, for example, in their pricing risk strategy?

Notes

1. That is, they ran purely online business, e.g. Wingspanbank and Citifi in the USA and Mbanx in Canada.
2. A survey in the first quarter of 1998 (by ABA Future Banker) revealed that Chase Manhattan Bank was the only corporate bank claiming to have an e-banking system on the Internet. See *http://www.jpmorgan.com/cm/cs?pagename=Templates/InfoCtrArticle/TSInfoArticle&cid=3333117433&c=InfoCtrArticle*.
3. The Electronic Federal Tax Payment System (EFTPS) is a service offered by the US Department of the Treasury to help business and individual taxpayers pay their federal taxes online.
4. The FSTC is made up of major US banks and technology companies (*www.fstc.org*).
5. Bolero.net is a service offered by SWIFT and TTC (Through Transport Club), a mutual marine insurer in 1999. The project is funded by the European Commission. Its customers include JP Morgan Chase, HSBC and BNP.
6. MaxTrad.com is a website developed by ABN AMRO in partnership with the Economist Intelligence Unit (EIU), Reuters, and the International Chamber of Commerce.
7. Federal Reserve Banks are US Government agencies that perform many financial services for the Government.

8. Continuous Linked Settlement bank is a special-purpose bank that provides organisations a way to settle international payments requiring foreign exchange services. The service offers a means for organisations to process both sides of the exchange simultaneously, so that the risk of suffering in fluctuating exchange rate can be eliminated.
9. Eurosystem is the collective name of European Central Bank and the national central banks of the EU member states.
10. Usual businesses of an investment bank include IPO, mergers and acquisitions, securitisation, capital raising, private equity placements, debt capital issuance, risk management, and corporate restructuring.
11. The IMF is an international organisation of 184 member countries. Headquartered in the USA, the IMF helps promote the health of the world economy. Its main activities involve surveillance of economic and financial policies of members, and offering financial and technical assistance to those in need.
12. A checking or share draft account from which funds (cheques or cash) can be drawn on demand.
13. Basel Committee on Banking Supervision is a banking supervisory authority established by the central bank governors of several European countries, Japan and the USA.
14. See: *http://www.newyorkfed.org/education/ebanking/border.html.*

4

E-payment

Introduction

The process of e-payment is indispensable for the completion of a business transaction on the Internet. It offers a convenient means to relieve buyers from the burden of writing cheques or mailing or delivering any cash in physical form. Businesses adopting e-payment systems wish to stay at the frontier of technology and enhance their competitiveness. By integrating an e-payment system with their management information systems, e-businesses would expect more operational efficiency and better financial management.

Practices of e-payment are divided into three types: credit/debit card, e-cheque and e-money. Very often, e-businesses partner with financial services institutions of their choice (probably banks) to offer e-payment services. Besides the customers (payers) and merchants (payees), an e-payment system (Figure 4.1) generally includes at least three players from the financial services sector: the issuer and acquirer banks, the payment gateway (an intermediary) and the clearinghouse. The technological infrastructure of the system is usually supported by a network operator.

The process of a credit/debit card payment over the Internet typifies the scenario of Figure 4.1; the card issuer often partners with the payment gateway. Operations and processing of credit/debit card transactions do not differ very much from their original design – the system now depends on the Internet for communications and thus requires special security measures, such as secure sockets layer (SSL)/Transport Layer Security (TLS).[1] Credit/debit card payment may be convenient for some buyers on the Internet, but it suffers from high processing cost (which makes it unsuitable for payments of small amounts) and non-anonymity (i.e. the identity of the buyer is recorded,

Figure 4.1 Major players in a generic e-payment scenario

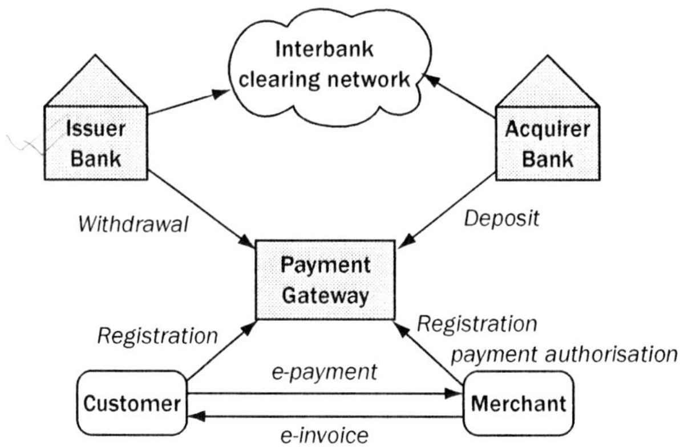

Source: Kasun (2003)

thus their buying habits can be traced and exploited by the credit/debit card company).

Unlike credit/debit cards, e-cheque and e-money are new inventions for business transactions on the Internet. They are designed to substitute for conventional paper-based cheques and money and to support transactions on the Internet. There are various schemes of e-cheque and e-money. They are normally provided by large financial institutions, which play the role of the gateway in Figure 4.1. For example, the payer would receive an e-cheque directly from the bank and send the e-cheque to the payee. To protect the payment information transmitted over the Internet, these systems include sophisticated security mechanisms. E-cheque and e-money are convenient to use and easy to process, but the intention to substitute for conventional cheques and money is possible only if they can get sufficient acceptance from the general public.

For obscure reasons, we do not see conventional cheques and money being replaced – neither at present nor in the near future. The only reason that may explain the general public's indifference to the new payment methods is their resistance to change. Figure 4.2 compares people's attitudes towards innovative financial services versus their age groups. Before making their promotion plan for their innovative e-cheque or e-money schemes it is a common strategy among financial institutions to identify a target group (such as the younger generation) from comparison studies, such as shown in Figure 4.2, In spite of the low acceptance rate in the past, the advisory firm, Celent, predicted (Tsai, 2004) e-cheque transactions would rise from $7.3 billion in 2003 to $17.9 billion in 2005 (or from 6 per cent to 9 per cent of e-commerce

Figure 4.2 Customer typologies concerning financial services

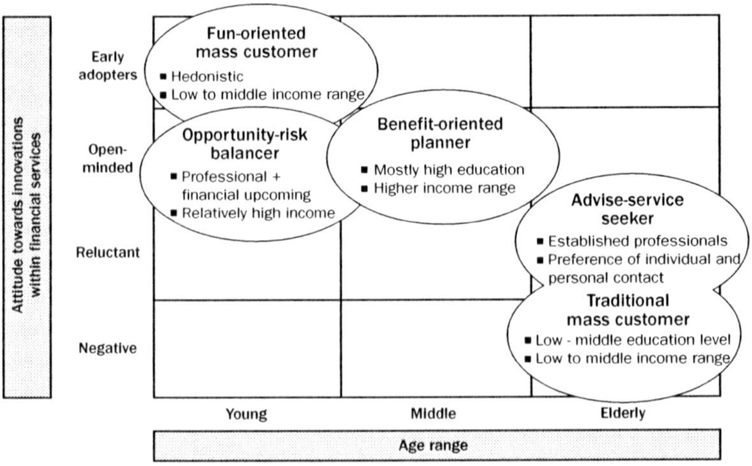

Source: BBDO Consulting (2004)

transactions). The growth is not significantly fast; yet the figure reflects that the number of retailers who accept e-payments is on the rise. The Federal Reserve of the USA confirmed that e-payment transactions in the country exceeded cheque payments for the first time in 2003 (Fettig, 2004). In particular, over 1.3 billion e-cheque payments were made in 2003, representing a 154 per cent increase over such payments in 2002 (NACHA, 2004).

With respect to the growth of e-payments, the government and utilities companies constitute a major driving force. E-payment is promoted as an efficient way to pay tax, licence fees, utility bills and the like. It saves people's time in lining up or mailing; it also reduces processing time and administrative work. As e-payment in this aspect is related to billing and/or invoicing, these processes are combined to give electronic bill presentment and payment (EBPP) and/or electronic invoice presentment and payment (EIPP). These are subjects for discussion in this chapter.

The impact of m-payment is presented as the last section of this chapter. The term 'm-payment' refers to payments carried out through a wireless device, such as a mobile phone. But the idea of using the telephone for payments is not new. Even before the Internet era, payments or other kinds of fund transfer instructions could be given by telephone. Being collectively known as mail order/telephone order (MOTO) transactions, these instructions are delivered together with credit card information. However, this kind of payment is not popular because providing protective measures to deliver credit card information through the insecure telephone channel is very expensive. The situation did not improve until the initiation of m-commerce in the new millennium where business is done by wireless data communication methods, such as short message service (SMS) and wireless application protocol (WAP). This is the time when telephone payment has been revived as m-payment. The e-financial sector perceives payment by using mobile phones as a prospective niche which could attract an increasingly large number of businesses and individuals who would like to do transactions on their phone.

Classification of e-payment schemes

E-payment schemes differ by the time of actual transfer of money. In this aspect, they are divided into three categories:

- *Pre-paid schemes*: The customer's account is debited before they make the payment. Most e-payment schemes today belong to this category; they include those that require consumers to buy a debit card, stored-value card, e-coins, or scrip. Anybody using gift certificates (e.g. amazon.com) to purchase online has experienced this.
- *Pay-now schemes*: The customer's account is debited at the time of the payment. They are rare in the market. Debit cards used at petrol stations belong to this category.
- *Post-pay schemes*: The merchant's account is credited before the customer's account is debited. A system in this category may be supported by a bank that, on the merchant's request, provides the verification that there are enough funds in the customer's account. E-cheque schemes and credit card-based systems belong to this category.

From the technological perspective, e-payment schemes available in the market (excluding the conventional credit/debit card) can be roughly divided into the following two categories:

- *Token-based*: A string of data is used to represent a certain monetary value and it can be used to exchange with some product or service of equal value. The string is commonly called an 'electronic coin' or 'e-coin' and the payment system based on e-coin is called 'e-cash'.
- *Notation-based*: Both payer and payee maintain their accounts in the system. The payer may store value in their account and transfer value to the payee's account in return for some product or service. Schemes of 'e-cheque' and 'e-purse' belong to this category.

The notation-based schemes are supported by banks and can be offered as a service to their clients; these schemes may reach a critical mass relatively easier. Token-based methods, however, rely on innovative technologies that are usually developed by non-bank institutions. Attracting consumers to an e-cash system is difficult.

Problems with e-payment

One of the hurdles of e-payment acceptance is security. Without the physical appearance of cards, cheques or money, transactions are recorded only by simple strings of digits. Thus, the processing of an e-payment requires extra work in registration, endorsement, authorisation, validation, encryption and decryption to make sure the right amount of money is transferred from the correct account to another (correct) account. There are many ways that the process can become faulty, including deliberate attempts to tamper with the record or through accidental mistakes. To build confidence in an e-payment scheme, each transaction is carefully logged along with information, such as the order description, merchant's account, amount transferred and timestamp – and the information is protected by security measures.

Security problems can be divided into three areas: authentication, confidentiality and integrity. Security measures are needed to assure that an authorised person or company is able to alter information correctly without interference from other persons. A comprehensive solution is provided by a combination of hardware and software methods; for example, e-payment schemes often require that the information stored and transmitted in the system is encrypted – usually by a public key infrastructure (PKI) system. The US Financial Services Technology Consortium (FSTC) has been researching many ways for secure payment technologies, such as the digital certificates for e-cheques.

To assess the applicability and sustainability of an e-payment scheme, management should also consider difficulties other than security. A sound e-payment scheme must be able to deal with some of these difficulties, if not all. Three of these difficulties, double spending, repudiation and micropayment, are discussed below.

Double spending

Conventional money is characterised by its effort to deter forgery. Digital money, however, is weak in preventing replication. Double spending, that is, when a person authorised to have money in digital form, uses it more than once, is a potential problem.

A famous solution to this problem is attributed to a pioneer in e-money, the founder of DigiCash Company, David Chaum (www.chaum.com). Chaum gives each electronic coin (an entity in his system that is called eCash) a serial number. The number is randomly generated and has 64 bits (thus, randomly generating two identical numbers is close to impossible). No one knows the serial number until the e-coin is presented to an eCash bank, which verifies whether its database has such a serial number. The e-coin will be cashed only if there is no record of its serial number. When it is cashed, the serial number will be recorded.

It can be anticipated that the size of the database storing all the serial numbers will expand rapidly. Thus, each coin has an expiry date and the serial numbers of expired coins can then be re-used.

Chaum's solution is ingenious but his e-money system, DigiCash, was a market failure (his story is discussed later). Later, when smartcard (e-purse) emerged in the market, the double spending problem found an easier solution. (A smartcard is also known as 'chip card' or 'stored value card' (SVC); but the term *smartcard* is used throughout this book.) People can install a program (called 'observer') on the microchip of the smartcard; it records every spending transaction in a small database. When the smartcard is connected to the issuer's system, any attempt at double spending is detected and disabled.

Repudiation

To discourage cardholders repudiating (denying) their transactions, e-payment systems are required to identify and authenticate the signature on a purchase order. MasterCard and Visa first relied on the secure electronic transaction (SET) protocol in 1997. SET offered a comprehensive solution to the problem by using special software 'wallets' and the SSL encryption technique to provide data confidentiality and integrity. However, the complexity and high cost of the scheme prevented it from gaining much ground in the market.

The two giants in the credit card business soon began their own projects on credit card payment security. MasterCard's SPA-UCAF (universal cardholder authentication field) and Visa's 3-D Secure were launched in 2001. Both of them rely on username and password/PIN to identify consumers. From April 2003, all Visa card issuers are mandated to support 3-D Secure.

SPA-UCAF is the combination of a secure payments application and a universal cardholder authentication field; the latter refers to a 32-byte field containing some authentication data of the cardholder and is hidden on the website of the merchant together with other hidden data fields. Using the SPA, a cardholder is required to download a tiny piece of software (called 'wallet') on their PC. When used to purchase online, the wallet detects the hidden UCAF on the merchant's website so that it can redirect the browser to the issuer's website. After the cardholder enters the password/PIN, the issuer validates the cardholder and returns a transaction token value. The wallet then includes the authentication data and transaction code to the UCAF (a process called 'populating the hidden fields') and returning it to the issuer via the acquirer. The issuer establishes an undeniable proof (non-repudiation) of the cardholder's transaction (see Figure 4.3).

Figure 4.3 **How SPA-UCAF works**

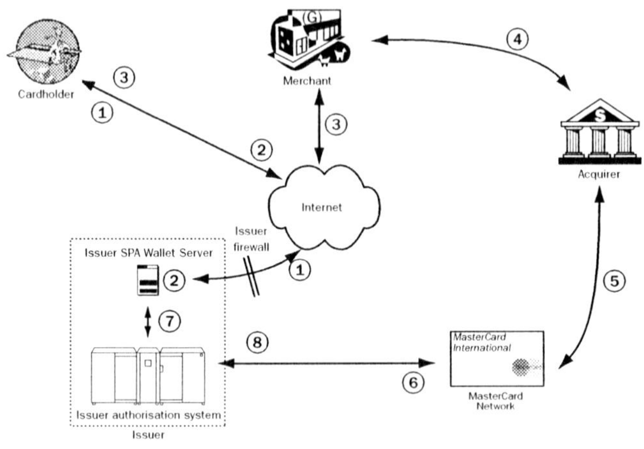

1: Cardholder visits merchant site and selects 'Buy'
2: Merchant plug-in Queries Directory for account participation
3: Issuer prompts for password or smart Visa card insertion, validates password, calculates cardholder authentication verification value (CAVV), digitally signs response for merchant, and transmits copy to authentication history server
4: Merchant verifies signature and sends authorisation request with authentication data (e-commerce indicator or ECI, CAVV and transaction identifier or XID) to acquirer
5: Acquirer confirms message with ECI value, CAVV and XID
6: Mastercard verifies cardholder authentication verification value (CAW), sets codes and forwards to issuer
7: Issuer authorises transaction and returns response
8: Issuer notifies Mastercard

Adapted from: Steeley (2001)

Instead of requiring the cardholder to download a wallet application as in SPA-UCAF, Visa requires the merchant to install a 'plug-in' at their site(s). This plug-in will redirect the cardholder's browser to a central directory operated by Visa. The directory identifies the issuing bank and asks the issuers to authenticate the cardholder. Probably using password/PIN, the issuer validates the cardholder and generates an authentication code. The latter is digitally signed and returned to the merchant, who passes the information to the acquirer and Visa for the non-repudiation of the transaction (see Figure 4.4).

Other e-payment schemes rely on digital signature technology. this is a string of data encrypted by using PKI, a sophisticated encryption method developed by the US Department of Defense that is widely applied in e-commerce security. (Further discussion on PKI will be found in Chapter 8.) In this chapter, PKI is interpreted as a system in which each user installs a special software package on their PC that can be used to generate a private key and to obtain a digital certificate from a certificate authority (CA). Based on the private key, the CA computes a public key and publishes it on the digital certificate. This is called an 'asymmetric key encryption system', which supplies each user with a pair of keys – a private and a public key. The public key of a user is published to anyone who might receive messages from the user but the private key is known to no one else. A message encrypted by a given public key can only be decrypted by the corresponding private key and vice versa.

Non-repudiation is provided as only the consumer is able to use their private key to encrypt a digital signature. Any authority holding the

Figure 4.4 How 3-D Secure works

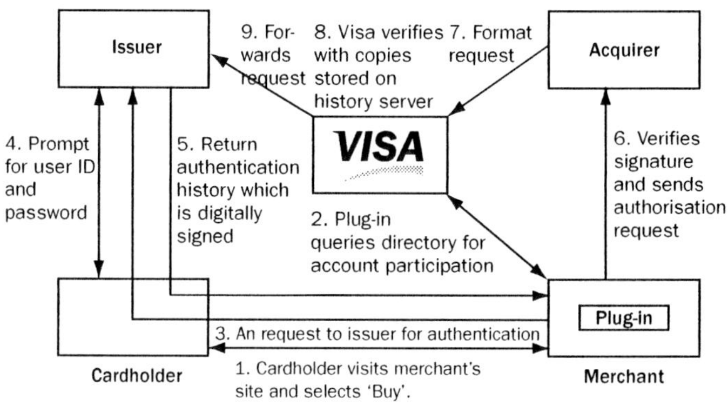

corresponding public key can then authenticate the signature. Not only does PKI support non-repudiation, it also fulfils the other three basic requirements of secure business on the Internet: authentication, confidentiality and data integrity. That is, the recipient of a digitally signed message is able to verify the identity of the sender and the integrity of the message.

Although the theory is technically sound, it is still vulnerable if the situation is placed under legal interrogation. The PKI system can prove a transaction is made by an authentic digital signature that is created by a device, but it cannot prove who ordered the device to create the digital signature. To fill this gap, the relevant law in many countries is enforced with an additional but rather vague requirement, such as 'the signature must be created under the direction of the signatory'.

Micropayment

An e-payment scheme needs to be protected by hardware and software devices and complicated computations for authentication and verification. An e-payment scheme for payments in small amounts would not be a profitable business if used by consumers to pay for low-priced items, such as downloading a piece of clipart or listening to an audio file, which usually cost less than a dollar. This specialised payment is called 'micropayment'. This payment scheme still has to face issues of forgery, double spending, repudiation and other problems, just like e-payment schemes designed for larger amounts (macropayment). However, the central problem in micropayment is how much should be charged for the process of payment if the price of the commodity is low.

Methods of micropayment are essential to small business on the Internet. They encourage the purchase of small and low-price items, to which most contents on the Internet belong. Without micropayment, a content provider might need to rely on subscription or aggregation to charge its customers. Although some micropayment schemes have emerged, they are far from successful. People have also considered special arrangements, so that macropayment schemes can be used for micropayments. For example, Lipton and Ostrovsky (1998) propose a so-called coin-flipping method which requires consumers to pay according to a probability rate (e.g. if the rate is 1/200, a consumer should pay with a chance of 1/200). If a consumer is to pay, they should pay an amount at a price higher than the listed price of the item but otherwise the item is free. While there are payment schemes particularly designed for the micropayment market (e.g. PepperCoin), some macropayment schemes are now allowing their customers to use them for micropayment (e.g. PayPal). These will be discussed later in this chapter.

E-cheque

An e-cheque is the electronic equivalent of the paper cheque, only it is written and signed in digital form. It can be transmitted across the Internet and processed directly, such as with a direct debit from the customer's account. Additionally, it has the same benefits of legal protection as a paper cheque.

In the USA, the feasibility and technology of e-cheques have been studied since the mid-1990s. For example, the NetCheque system of the Information Sciences Institute of the University of Southern California and the NetBill project of Carnegie Mellon University succeeded in producing e-cheque prototypes. About the same time, the Financial Services Technology Consortium (FSTC) delegated an e-cheque project steering committee to launch a pilot trial of e-cheques.

The idea of e-cheques does not arouse the same kind of interest in Europe as in the USA. Although cheque payments accounted for 14.8 per cent of all payments effected in the European Union in 2002, (conventional) cheque transactions are relatively scarce in many European countries, likewise the development of e-cheques. PayPal, an e-cash company, offers a partial form of e-cheque service to some countries like the UK. FSTC's patented model has intrigued many countries around the world (banks in Australia, India, New Zealand and Singapore are beginning to offer their own e-cheque services).

FSTC's echeck model

The FSTC's echeck[2] project produces a *de facto* standard for e-cheque schemes throughout the world. On a PC screen, an echeck looks like a paper cheque. A payer using the system has to fill in the amount and supply a digital signature before it can be passed to the recipient. The core technology of echeck consists of several security techniques (e.g. PKI and certificate authority) to protect and verify the information exchanged.

Figure 4.5 illustrates a generic processing cycle of an echeck. When the merchant receives an echeck, it is endorsed and sent to the payee's bank

Figure 4.5 FSTC's echeck model (deposit-and-clear scenario)

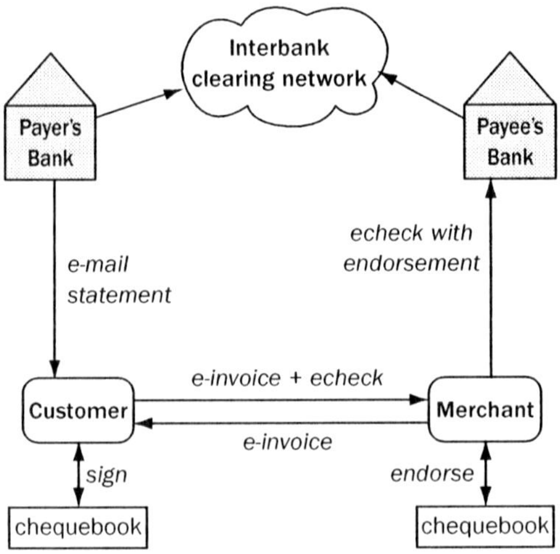

with additional encryption information. FTSC considers four scenarios in using its echeck. Figure 4.5 illustrates only the most common scenario – deposit-and-clear – i.e. clearing is done soon after the echeck is received by the payee's bank.

In the cash-and-transfer scenario where the payee's bank is not able to accept the echeck, it needs to present the echeck to the payer's bank directly. The payer's bank credits the payee's account by transferring electronic funds to the payee's bank and notifies the payee. The third scenario is called 'lockbox', which is a special-purpose account maintained by the payee's bank on behalf of the payee. Instead of e-mailing the echeck to the payee, the echeck is now sent directly to the payee's bank, which updates the lockbox account and notifies the payee after the echeck is cleared with the payer's bank. 'Fund transfer' is the final scenario in which the payer forwards the echeck to the payer's bank, which debits and credits the payer and payee's accounts respectively using the conventional interbank electronic fund transfer.

Electronic chequebook

In FSTC's echeck model, a user must have an electronic chequebook to keep their private key. The chequebook is a hardware device and is believed to be a safer repository for the private key because it is separated from the user's computer and is inaccessible to hackers via the Internet. The software part of the chequebook is implemented on a smartcard. The echeck issuing bank registers the cheque account and the chequebook of each user, while the bank's certificate authority stores the public key of the chequebook.

The functions of the electronic chequebook include the following:

- to generate a private-public key pair for the user;
- to export the public key in a digital certificate signed by the CA;
- to create a digital signature on the echeck using the private key and a signing algorithm;
- to attach the signer's personal information on the echeck, if appropriate;
- to number each echeck consecutively to ensure the uniqueness of each echeck;
- to keep a log in a cheque register of each echeck signed, endorsed and deposited; and
- to control access to the chequebook through the user's PIN and the CA's PIN.

Note that payer and payee have their own electronic chequebook. In Figure 4.6, in the middle of the echeck system, is the software installed

Figure 4.6 **Software infrastructure of the e-cheque system: (a) payer's echeck system; (b) payee's echeck system**

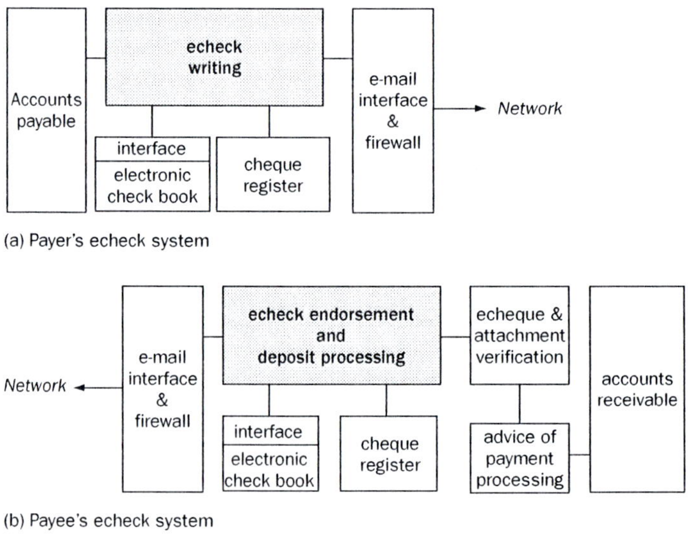

on the user's computer interfaces with the electronic chequebook, a browser to see the echeck onscreen (not shown), e-mail and applications for accounting and verification.

From echeck to accounts receivable cheque

Phase 1 of FSTC's echeck market trial ended in 2000 and the echeck model is now being incorporated in various other payment systems. As echeck is regarded as an electronic equivalent of the conventional paper cheque, a paper cheque can easily be transformed into an echeck. The only difference is the procedure in the automated clearinghouse (ACH), which generates an electronic debit for each cheque received.

The National Automated Clearing House Association (NACHA) introduced the idea of the accounts receivable cheque (ARC) in 2002. It published operating rules and guidelines to ACHs for the conversion of consumer cheques into ACH debits.

The operating rules and guidelines in ARC conversion can be summarised as follows (C.J. & Tuck Consulting, year unknown):

- Only consumer cheques, drawn from a US bank account qualify. Corporate cheques, government cheques, credit card cheques and the like do not qualify.
- The cheque writer cannot be present. Cheques must be received through a lockbox, through the mail or at a dropbox location.
- You must provide advanced written notice to your customers that you will convert their cheques electronically; notice can be included in your statements or invoices.
- Magnetic ink character recognition (MICR)[3] information must be captured with a scanner: it cannot be manually entered or keyed.

ACH applications, which are specifically designed for cheque-to-ACH conversion, are now available and can be integrated with information systems for payment processing in large organisations, such as universities. The process begins when the payee notifies the payer that the cheque will be processed electronically. On receiving the paper cheque, the data on the MICR on the cheque is scanned and the dollar value and the payer's information are entered into the payment system, which presents the information to an ACH debit. According to the Check Truncation Act 2003, an electronic image of the original paper cheque should be captured and kept for seven years while the paper cheque is destroyed within 14 days of settlement.

Also called an ARC, the ACH debit is then sent to the payee's bank (or originating depository financial institution). Communications with the payer's bank (or receiving depository financial institution) and the clearing and settlement of the ARC are accomplished through an ACH operator (which is either the Electronic Payments Network[4] or Federal Reserve). Figure 4.7 illustrates the ARC process.

Besides ARC, ACH debits may take other forms. A brief discussion on each of the common ACH debits is given below. The three-letter acronyms are standard entry class (SEC) codes designed to identify different ACH entries.

- *Point-of-purchase (POP)*: Cheque payments at a cash register, for example, can be scanned and transformed into ACH debits. The original paper cheque can be returned to the consumer with a receipt.
- *Re-presented cheque (RCK)*: A cheque with a face value of $2,500 or less if bounced for non-sufficient funds (NSF) or uncollected funds (UCF)[5] can be transmitted electronically through the ACH network as a debit entry within 180 days.
- *Accounts receivable cheque (ARC)*: Sending a cheque through mail (by courier, at a dropbox and the like) is regarded as an authorisation to convert the cheque to an ACH debit.
- *WEB*: This is an Internet-initiated ACH entry. When a consumer opts for a debit to their cheque account when they are purchasing on a

Figure 4.7 **Accounts receivable cheques and automated clearinghouse processing**

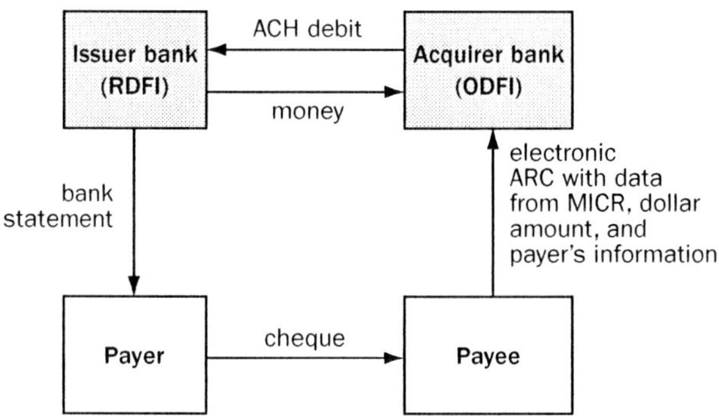

ARC: accounts receivable cheque; ODFI: originating depository financial institution; MICR: magnetic ink character recognition; RDFI: receiving depository financial institution

merchant's website, the consumer provides authorisation, including account number, to the merchant who sends a debit through the ACH network to debit the consumer's account.

- *TEL*: This works like the WEB transactions except that the consumer provides their information on the telephone.

The ARC is the modern form of echeck. The aforementioned regulations and procedures bring cheque conversion and processing under the jurisdiction of the Electronic Fund Transfer Act 1978 (EFTA), Federal Reserve Regulation E, NACHA Rules ('EFT law') and electronic banking law, as the paper cheque is now regarded as a 'source document' (not a cheque) that is no longer protected by the conventional cheque law. NACHA reported (McEntee, 2005) that 27 billion of these echecks were processed in 2004 and the trend of echecks replacing paper cheques is on the rise.

Clareon's PayMode

FTSC's echeck obtained a patent (US05677955) in October 1997 and ran a pilot trial with BankBoston and NationsBank in the market. The pilot concluded in 2000 and the commercialisation of the model was taken over by two companies: Clareon Corp. and Xign Corp. Organisations using the echeck system include banks, government agencies, technology vendors and many Fortune 500 enterprises.

Clareon Corp. was a joint venture of FleetBoston Financial and Morgan Stanley in mid-2001 and it was later acquired by the Bank of America. Clareon offers a secure e-payment engine called PayMode, in which the digital signature technology is used to support echeck and some other B2B e-payment methods. PayMode can be used in e-commerce and can be integrated with ERP systems.

As shown in Figure 4.8, PayMode is capable of handling remittance and payment information at the same time; it makes use of the XML protocol for the transmission of remittance information. Putting the two kinds of information together fastens the process of reconciliation and provides better integration with the accounting applications and other functions in an ERP system. The transfer of information does not involve banks; thus the system works regardless of the banks of the buyer and seller. Bank of America has high hopes for the system and hopes that more payment methods can be added to the engine in the future.

Figure 4.8 Operation of PayMode engine

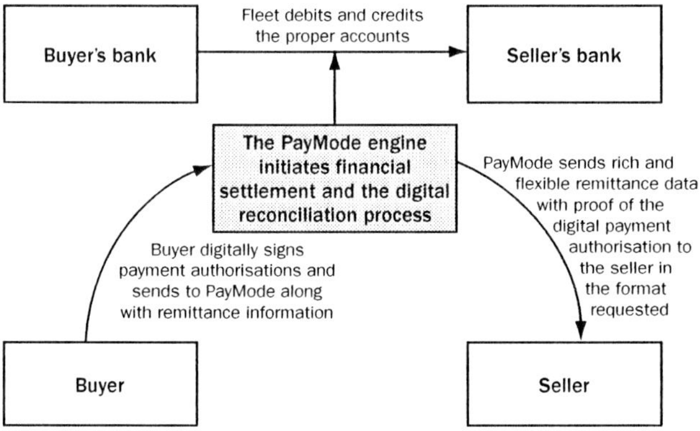

Adapted from: McCormick & Litchfield (2004)

IBM's WebSphere commerce payments

IBM's Check Processing Control System (CPCS) has long been a common installation in most large banks in North America. With the company's experience in cheque processing, IBM was consulted by the FSTC when the echeck project was conducted. To help test the feasibility of the FSTC's model, the company designed an echeck bank server based on FSTC's standard. The company also played an important role in the design of the financial services markup language (FSML), which was chosen to be the language used in formatting the information on an echeck (including the data arrangement and the cryptographic signature).

Another of the IBM's products, WebSphere Payment Manager (formerly called IBM Payment Server, whose ancestor was IBM CommercePOINT eTill), was originally an electronic cash register for merchants. Its functions could be extended to allow multiple payment methods by adding specific payment 'cassettes'.[6] Since 2002, IBM WebSphere Payment Manager has been collected under a large family of IBM products known as IBM WebSphere Commerce Suite. The WebSphere Payment Manager is a component of the WebSphere Commerce Payments solution and is made up of a payment engine and a database, wherein cassettes of protocols, security and message format functions can be added when needed (Figure 4.9).

Payment Servlet is the centre of WebSphere Commerce Payments. When it receives a request from the user interface or other merchant

Figure 4.9 Components in IBM WebSphere Payment Manager

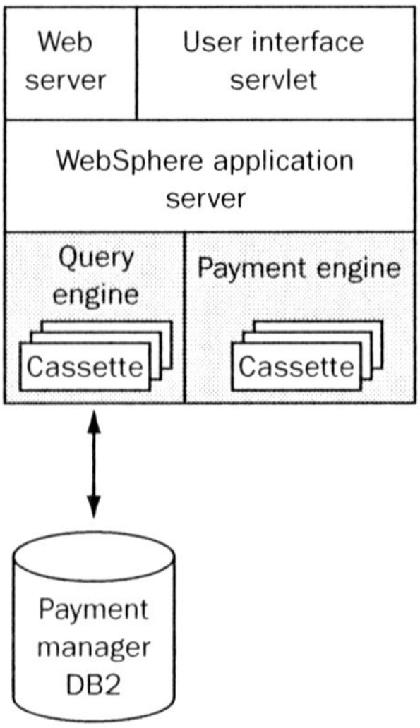

Adapted from: Moore et al. (2001)

applications, it performs a security check and invokes a payment cassette to process the request. The response from the cassette is then returned to the calling application.

IBM's WebSphere Commerce Payments is a merchant's solution. It provides a generic framework for multiple payment models. Besides SET, the system supports other payment protocols, including third-party payment cassettes written for WebSphere Commerce Payments.

Retail e-payment

Retail payments are consumer-oriented. They are confined to the following methods: cheque, ACH, credit/debit cards and EBT.[7] They are relatively small in value per transaction but large in transaction volume. Although digitisation and automation of the processing of these payment methods has been promoted for decades, a high volume of conventional cheques are processed every year. The dominance of cheque payments remained unchallenged until 2000, after which a relatively sizable increase in e-payments has been recorded. In the USA, 30.6 billion e-payments were originated with a value of $20.2 trillion in 2000 but the figures changed to $44.5 billion and $27.4 trillion in 2003 (Federal Reserve System, 2004).

The retail payment market has been greatly affected by the emergence of e-payment methods and the urge to optimise the processes of existing payment instruments. Furst and Nolle (2004) studied the implications on the practices and regulatory and supervisory policies in the banking industry. Besides new challenges in risk management and security problems, the researchers urged some serious consideration of the following changes:

- continual shift toward e-payments favours larger banks and lowers the competitive advantage of community banks;
- suitable regulations and supervision of e-payment services offered by large banks that operate on a global scale, because e-payments are less constrained by geographical and political boundaries;
- non-bank payment system service providers and other third parties raise issues of competition, pricing, supervision and risk management for the banking industry.

Challenges not only exist in domestic markets – cross-border retail payments pose additional problems to the financial services industry. A 2002 study by the Payments System Development Committee of the Federal Reserve reported concerns about standardisation, particularly in payment-message formats, which may reduce costs of correspondent banks, enhance straight-through processing (STP) and improve quality of services (Federal Reserve System, 2002). For example, countries in the euro area generally use the SWIFT standard while the USA uses proprietary standards for wire transfers and NACHA standards for the ACH – a clear case of differing standards.

In Europe, clearing methods differ among nations. They are also striving to remove political and legal obstacles in the building of the single euro payment area (SEPA). It was still unclear in 2002 whether the European countries had a consistent view on digital signatures and electronic certifications (EBA, 2002). The European Payments Council (EPC) is a pan-European banking organisation that aims at bringing about SEPA by 2010. However, the pan-European strategy (ECB, 2004) needs collaboration from various parties in the industry. For example, the EPC established the European Committee for Banking Standards (ECBS) to work on common decisions on standards, and the European Banking Association (EBA) established the STEP1 system for cross-border retail payment processing. STEP1 was created for European retail banks to handle retail credit transfers, direct debits and interbank

Figure 4.10 Workflow of settlement via STEP2

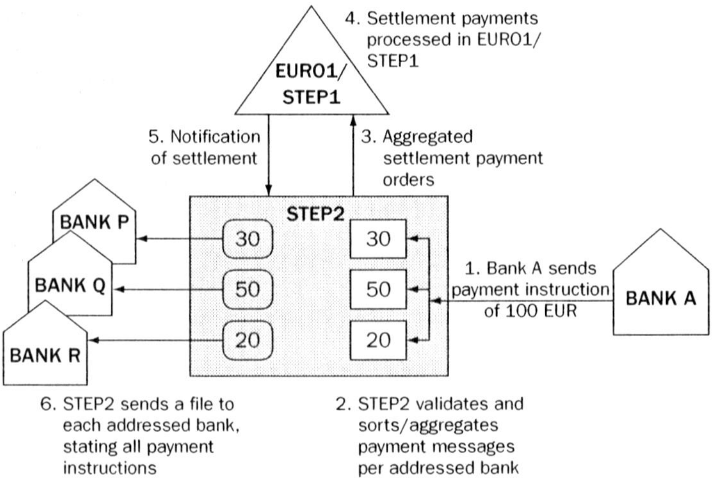

Adapted from: EBA (2003)

transfers. It also promotes the use of industry standards to enable STP in financial institutions.

STEP2 began operation on 28 April, 2003. It is a pan-European automated clearing house (PE-ACH) that enables banks to automate bulk payments of low value (between €12,500–50,000 in 2006) and high volume. It handles commercial and retail cross-border credit transfer and distributes payment instructions to almost all banks in the EU and some banks that have a registered office or branch within the EU. The system uses SWIFT as its message standard and by May 2004 was processing an average of 125,000 payments per day.

Both STEP1 and STEP2 are connected to EURO1, a large-value payment platform managed by the EBA. The relationship between these three platforms is shown in Figure 4.10. Unlike EURO1, STEP1 and STEP2 admit only payment orders whose payer and payee have their domicile in the EU. The function of EURO1 will be discussed further in the section on wholesale payment.

Nonetheless, each national market in Europe differs slightly in its favourite means of payment. As retail payments are mostly domestic, the European retail payment market remains heterogeneous in spite of the standardisation effort made by EBA and other EU authorities.

To illustrate the technology that is used in retail e-payment systems, the PayHound platform is described below.

Case: PayHound's enterprise payment platform (Microsoft, 2003a)

The Way2Pay system, offered by Amsterdam-based global bank and insurance company ING (a former investor in PayPal until the latter was acquired by eBay), is built on a PayHound platform and was launched in May 2003. PayHound Ltd. also runs its own e-payment business in the EU. In the UK, *www.payhound.com* has been known since 2001 and has attracted over 100,000 account holders. With a PayHound account, a consumer can transfer money over to another account or to online stores and auction sites on the Internet. The consumer's account is connected to their bank or credit/debit card account. The cleared funds are lodged at NatWest Bank Plc.

Consumers are allowed to transfer funds using PayHound up to a maximum limit of £90. Any transfer larger than £90 has to use STP. The transfer is totally free for an amount within £25–90. Any amount less than £25 is charged a fee of 25 pence. All recipients are charged 3 per cent of the amount received.

PayHound's e-payment platform is known as Enterprise Payment Platform 3 (EPP3) but when it is offered to banks, it is a 'white-label' service that allows individual banks to name their services. For example, ING calls its e-payment service Way2Pay. The infrastructure of EPP3 is built on a Microsoft Windows 2003 Server, using .NET architecture to take advantage of XML SOAP web services and Microsoft's COM+ technology.

Wholesale e-payment

Wholesale payments transactions are involved in commercial loan, real estate transactions and financial market-related activities. In addition, a wholesale payment system may also provide final clearing and settlement for some retail payment systems. It is thus common knowledge that optimising wholesale payment systems would have tremendous effects on the efficiency of the global financial system. Authorities in the financial sector are studying the effects of digitisation and automation on wholesale payment systems, which are characterised by large value, possibly interbank and/or cross-border transactions. An immediate concern is to upgrade the clearing and settlement systems so that interbank payment activities can be automated.

In the USA, the primary domestic funds transfer systems involving large values are handled by two networks – Fedwire Funds Service and CHIPS. Together with ACH networks, these payment networks are the three electronic funds clearing systems in the USA:

1. *The Fedwire Funds Service* is a real-time gross settlement (RTGS) system operated by the Federal Reserve Banks. Anyone who wants to use Fedwire must maintain a reserve or securities account with a Federal Reserve Bank: this regulation excludes non-financial organisations from the list of direct users.
2. *Clearing House Interbank Payments System* (CHIPS) is a privately operated multilateral settlement system. It clears and settles large-value final payments (including international interbank transactions) in US dollars and in real-time. It handles over 250,000 payments per day; the figure includes 95 per cent of all US dollar foreign exchange payments. Figure 4.11 shows how CHIPS works with Federal Reserve in an international interbank transaction.

Additionally, there are other clearinghouse, settlement and messaging systems, such as the following:

- *National Settlement Service (NSS)*: Operated by the Federal Reserve Banks, it only serves organisations participating in private-sector clearing arrangements. These organisations are, for example,

Figure 4.11 **Workflow of CHIPS**

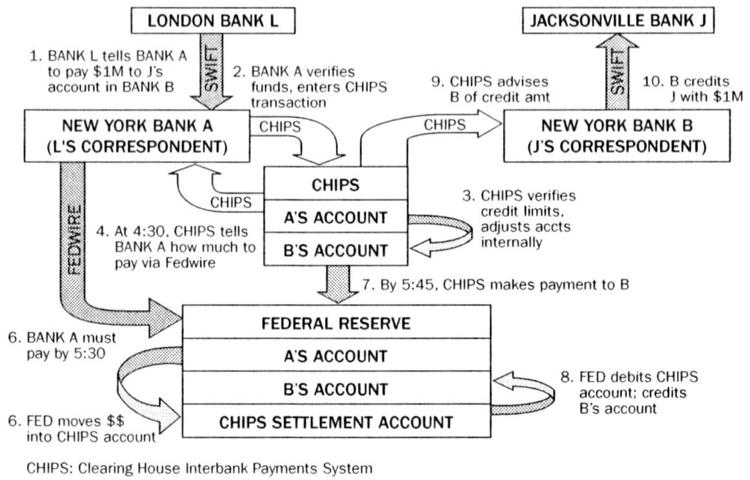

Source: Shamos (2004)

automated clearinghouse networks, credit card processors, ATM networks and national and regional funds-transfer and securities-transfer networks.

- *SWIFT*: This organisation provides standard messages for the transmission of payment instructions for domestic or international transactions. Financial institutions can establish direct SWIFT connectivity with their internal funds transfer system for the transmission of payment instructions.
- *Telex-based messaging systems*: These are offered by telecommunications companies to financial institutions if the latter do not have access to the SWIFT system. However, telex systems do not have built-in security features.
- *Continuous Linked Settlement (CLS) Bank*: Offers the business sector a payment settlement system if foreign exchange transactions are required. The bank welcomes customers joining their services as settlement members or user members. Both may submit payment instructions but a settlement member, as a shareholder of CLS Group Holdings, has an account in the CLS Bank and may control and approve instructions submitted by its sponsored user members.

Note the difference between payment systems and messaging systems. The former transmits actual debit and credit entries, but the latter is responsible for the processing of administrative messages and instructions to move funds. These messages initiate debit and credit entries if a transaction involves two companies. The actual movement of funds is accomplished by the Fedwire Funds Service or CHIPS.

In Europe, each national central bank has its own wholesale RTGS system, which is interfaced to the Trans-European Automated Real-time Gross settlement Express Transfer (TARGET) system. TARGET is thus able to provide a uniform platform for processing domestic and cross-border payments within the euro area. It allows interbank and customer payments without upper or lower value limits. At present, there are more than 40,000 banks worldwide that are addressable in TARGET and the system is used by CLS Bank and EURO1, another clearing system operated by the EBA.

Although TARGET transactions can be processed within minutes, if not seconds, the system is accused of being too expensive – twice as expensive as Fedwire (Godeffroy, 2000). A new phase of the TARGET project (TARGET2) was initiated in 2002 to enhance the system and to solve the problems of heterogeneity of the present TARGET.

Moreover, the EBA established the EBA Clearing Company to operate STEP2 and EURO1 – the two important clearing and settlement platforms in Europe. EURO1 is an EBA system for the exchange of high-value payment instructions among participating banks in the EU. The messages are transmitted via SWIFT and the settlement balances are provided at the end of each clearing day in the European Central Bank. EURO1 has established itself as a processor of commercial payment orders.

Below we examine two ICT solutions for wholesale e-payment: HP's OpenPayments and Oracle's iPayment.

HP's OpenPayments

As the payment process is regarded as a strong source of revenue for wholesale banking institutions, HP developed its wholesale banking solution towards a highly efficient payment process system – OpenPayments – released in October 2004.

OpenPayments is built on HP's Real Time Financial Services (RTFS) platform, which supports a hub architecture. Figure 4.12 illustrates the RTFS hub as a middle-office system whereas applications in the front- and back-offices are represented on the left and right sides. The hub draws together a number of HP software applications, which are divided into three portions: multi-channel integration (MCI) layer, wholesale

Figure 4.12 Application architecture of HP's OpenPayments

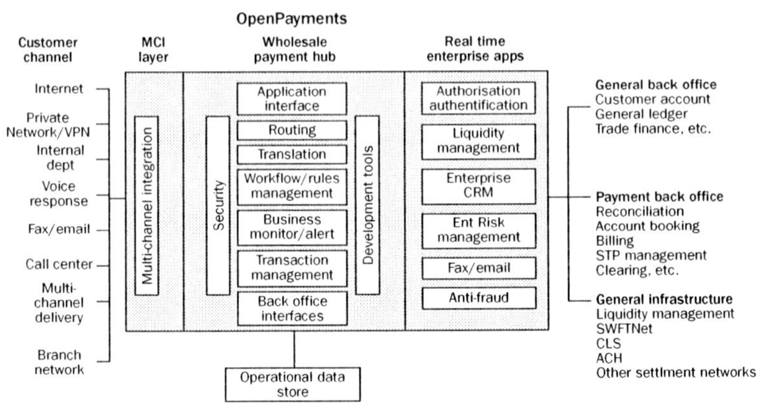

ACH: automated clearinghouse; CLS: continuous linked settlement; MCI layer: multi-channel integration; STP: straight-through processing

Adapted from: HP (year unknown)

payment hub and real-time enterprise applications. An operational data store (ODS) is connected to the hub; it hosts the data model and provides an integrated view of a common customer across the channels in real-time. Although no conspicuous layer-structure is drawn in the diagram (as with the horizontal layers described in Chapter 3), functionalities in the hub can still be divided into three layers: business process control, enterprise applications and database management.

HP's RTFS can easily be integrated with other applications, including solutions from other parties, such as LogicaCMG, Dovetail and Gresham.

Note that HP's RTFS excels in its capability of providing an integrated and up-to-the-second view of customer and business. The OpenPayments application aims to foster better customer relationships. If it is to provide payment channels for special e-payment schemes, it must be interfaced with relevant software applications.

Oracle's iPayment

Oracle's iPayment module is a component in the iStore application within the sales solution of Oracle's E-Business Suite. As iStore is the tool to build an Internet store site, iPayment is a module to add multiple payment systems to the store. It supports two electronic payment methods: credit card payments and bank account transfers. It also supports some third-party payment schemes ('field installable payment systems'), such as CheckFree and CyberCash. Figure 4.13 shows the

Figure 4.13 Relationship between iStore and iPayment

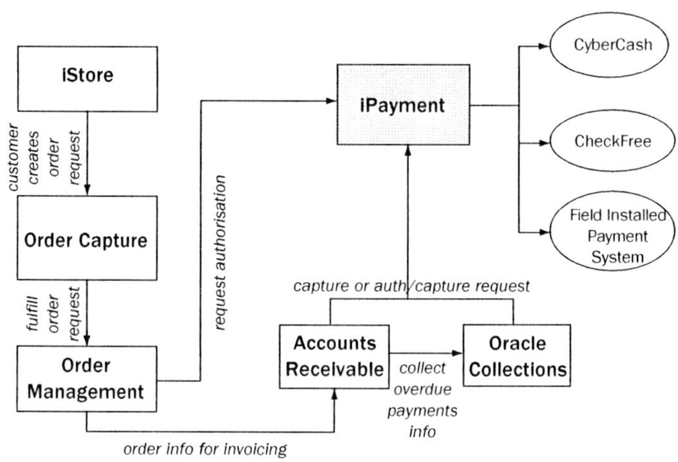

Source: Oracle (2001)

information flow from iStore to iPayment and how modules in iStore are connected. The 'field installable payment systems' branch in the system increases the flexibility of the architecture.

Lying at the centre of iPayment is the iPayment engine. This contains the logic for multi-payment method support, routing and risk management. When a consumer buys at the store site (iStore), the order is captured and the information on the consumer's credit card is entered in the order request. The order is routed through the processes of authorisation, settlement and reconciliation. If the payment is found overdue, iPayment can authorise and capture the credit card transaction from 'collections', special data types in Oracle terminology. These are commonly implemented as PL/SQL[8] tables.

The iPayment engine works with various APIs and servlets for functionality including risk management, credit validation, status update and interfacing with payment schemes, such as CheckFree and CyberCash. Sometimes back-end payment (BEP) APIs and account transfer (AcctXfer) APIs are needed to work with appropriate servlets when the system is linked to these payment schemes. As Figure 4.14 depicts, AcctXfer APIs do not connect to 'field installed payment scheme' because iPayment only supports offline payments for bank account transfers.

iPayment supports both online and offline payment processing. In online processing, the payment processing request is immediately forwarded to the BEP processor for processing; in offline processing,

Figure 4.14 Architecture of Oracle iPayment

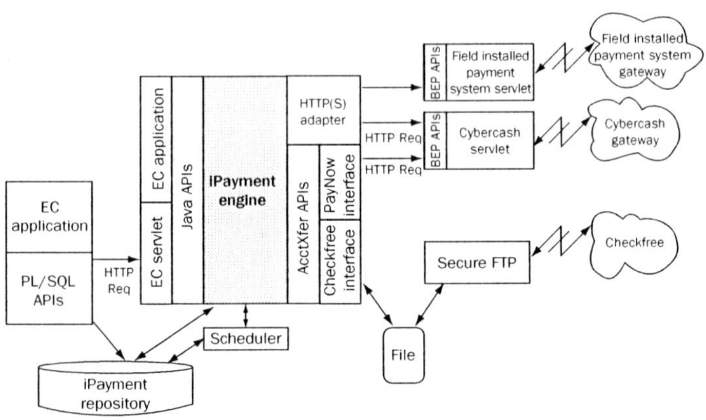

API: application programming interface; BEP: back-end payment; EC: e-commerce;
FTP: file transfer protocol; PL/SQL: (Oracle): procedural language/structured query language
Adapted from: Oracle (2001)

however, the payment request is saved in the iPayment database. At regular intervals, the scheduler browses the stored requests and sends those requests to the BEP systems and the updates are sent to the EC applications.

Electronic bill presentment and payment

Today's technology allows billers (the merchants) to present their bills electronically (e.g. through e-mailing) to customers and receive payments from them electronically. This is particularly suitable for recurring bills and pre-authorised debits to cheque accounts (e.g. utility, insurance and credit card bills) and is believed to be a driver of the financial supply chain, which has become popular lately (Atkinson, 2004). The entire EBPP process requires the collaboration among customers, billers, financial institutions (customer's and biller's), bill consolidators and customer service providers.

Andreeff et al. (2003) describe two primary EBPP models: biller-direct model and the consolidation (aggregation) model:

- *Biller direct model*: The biller notifies its customers of pending bills via e-mail and customers find the respective e-bills when they log on to the biller's website. Sometimes, a bill service provider (BSP) acts on behalf of the biller in electronic bill presentment and even hosts the biller's website. The biller (or the BSP) holds the full control over the relationship with its customers.
- *Consolidation model*: Several billers send their customer's billing information to a third party called a 'bill consolidator' (sometimes a customer service provider). The latter combines data from the billers and aggregates the information into a single e-bill to each customer. There are two kinds of consolidators: thick and thin:
  - *Thick consolidation* – the consolidator maintains both the summary and details of the customers' billing information.
  - *Thin consolidation* – billers only give summaries of customer information to consolidators. Thus, a customer can only find summaries on the consolidator's sites and needs to contact the biller for more details. Thin consolidation may suit bill presentment on a WAP phone, for example, where consumers will not want to download the full details of their bills.

The variety of EBPP models is illustrated in Figure 4.15.

Figure 4.15 Different models of electronic bill presentment and payment

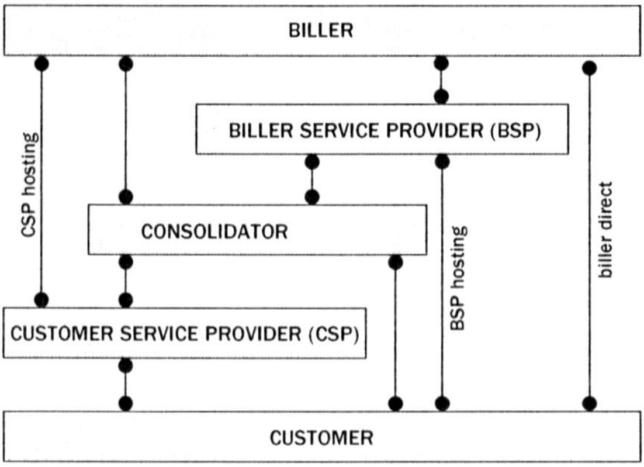

Modified from: LogicaCMG (year unknown)

At present, the banking industry and utility billers are leading the development of the EBPP market. They offer EBPP and EIPP services to their corporate customers and individual customers. Notice that the term EBPP is sometimes interchangeable with EIPP (electronic invoice presentment and payment) although the latter generally applies to B2B transactions while EBPP often refers to B2C e-billing and payments. In EBPP, the bill presentment may involve a series of work phases including electronic bill translation, formatting and data parsing.

In spite of the promised convenience and cost efficiency, EBPP is being accepted at a relatively slow speed throughout the world and the biller-direct model has been relatively more successful than the other two. Many of the pioneers in the market are engaging in fierce competition within a small circle of users. There are mixed feelings towards the prospect of the EBPP market; for example, Bank of International Settlements (BIS, 2004) comments that service providers in Canada have no extensive reach, but Sem (2004) reports over 10,000 European companies participate in an EBPP network and expects the volume of e-invoices will rise from 190 million in 2004 to 280 million in 2005.

The cases below describe two prominent figures in the US and UK EBPP markets. They are considered successful payment service providers (PSPs) in the business and they are striving to enlarge their market share.

Case: BillDirect (USA)

BillDirect was a joint venture of edocs, Inc. and Net Perceptions (NASDAQ: NETP). Launched in 1999, the EBPP application was used by many large corporations in the USA (including American Express, GE Capital and CheckFree). At the end of 2004, Siebel acquired edocs and the scheme is now promoted by Yodlee, Inc., which claims to have aggregated almost 2 million bills per month from nearly 2,500 billers through its OnCentre service. These billers mainly include lenders, credit card and mortgage companies and non-financial billers, such as mobile-phone companies – one of its latest users is America Online (AOL).

BillDirect can be implemented as a fully-hosted ASP solution or purchased as an off-the-shelf software product. It can be installed on a server with a RDBMS, which stores the locations of billing data and summary data. The application can also be integrated with customer care, e-mail servers, legacy billing, as well as financial and accounting systems. BillDirect supports standards including SSL, HTTP, HTML, POP3, Java, OFX, XML and MIME. Billers may also partner with e-payment schemes, such as CyberCash and CheckFree so that customers can choose their payment methods.

BillDirect is renowned for its functionalities of parsing and presentment. Its workflow roughly follows the biller-direct EBPP model. BillDirect allows billers to select appropriate text and associate it with an extraction rule. The system comes with tools for billers to define and test rules for parsing and extracting legacy data. Data extracted can be encrypted and saved in a database. Thus, billing data can be transformed into Internet-friendly e-bills.

In the hands of Yodlee, BillDirect is implemented on Yodlee's iFinity platform, which is patented as an 'account aggregation' by Yodlee. This is a technology to consolidate personal account data for customers and let them track expenses and transactions from the same interface. Hence, merchants (the billers) can integrate billing, accounting and CRM into a single system.

Case: Global electronic invoice delivery by OB^{10}

OB^{10} was developed by Open Business Exchange (OBE) in the UK. Since 2002, it has been offered to suppliers in the UK, the Netherlands, Germany and the USA and is now open to global suppliers. In the UK, OBE worked closely with the tax authorities to ensure that its e-invoice presentment (delivery) service meets the government tax standards. In other words, the company can assure its clients to dispose of paper invoices without fear of violating Customs & Excise requirements.

The infrastructure of the OB^{10} network includes several Sun servers with Sun storage arrays and a BEA WebLogic application server with an Oracle database. The basic software application is Oasis Technology's IST/Switch, a transaction processing platform. OB^{10} implements a central datacentre with a large data warehouse and a data translation engine. The data warehouse allows remote audits of supplier and purchaser tax accounting records when required. The data translation engine is able to integrate with the client's invoicing processing applications. The integration ends up as a complex system because of the variety of these applications, which range from ERP platforms, such as SAP and Oracle to mid-range systems, such as Sun Accounting, Sage and Pegasus. The system can handle some 10,000 invoices per hour. Security is provided by PKI encryption.

The electronic invoice delivery service is targeted at the B2B market where suppliers send invoices (by e-mail) to OB^{10}, which delivers them to purchasers on the Internet. OBE provides the OB^{10} network as a service that acts as a bridge between the client and its suppliers, but does not require the client to buy and install OB^{10} on the client's machine. Clients joining the system can just send invoice details electronically to the system, which automates reconciliation of invoices with matching purchase order numbers. They do not need to change the format of the invoices or the workflow of their accounting systems. Since mid-2004, it has recruited over 4,000 users worldwide, of which about half were in the UK and Europe.

Electronic bill presentment and payment in the future

People have not seen fast growth of EBPP as predicted by Gartner (Litan, 2003),[9] but some service providers are still striving to increase the popularity of e-billing and e-payment. Sanders (2004) observes that corporate customers are particularly slow in adopting the idea, but they are more attracted to the facilities of e-billing as offered by PSPs. Telephone and credit card companies are the leading business segments offering B2C e-billing services. Over the last few years, more and more individual customers are getting used to the e-payment web pages, which may also incorporate value-added features, such as clicking on an item to view a deeper level of details.

The business strategies of PSP and billers no longer repeat the benefits of EBPP, which has already been well understood. The only problem, like many kinds of e-businesses, is attaining a critical mass. Adding more value-added features to the EBPP websites is perhaps a way to boost the customer numbers. Table 4.1 gives a few value components that EBPP participants might include in their business strategy.

Some PSPs provide value-added features while others reconsider their business model. For example, the hybrid approach by BillDirect is praised (Star Systems, 2005) as a possibility for increasing market share. Lange (2005) proposes three success factors as follows:

- *Transparent and reliable security mechanisms*: To enhance the customers' trust in using the system.
- *Control collection of accounts*: To enforce claims for outstanding payments and to minimise the abuse of e-transaction relationships and e-payment mechanisms.
- *Spread*: To guarantee availability and to promote acceptance of the payment mechanisms in the target market.

Table 4.1 **Customer value framework**

Role of bank	Value improvement	Value components – content	Infrastructure
Network enabler	Quality enhancement	Content quality – Richness Accuracy, timeliness and relevance Detail and accuracy of informational content	Quality – Transaction security reassurance Reduction of economic, privacy, performance risk Degree of easiness in the process of transaction
Processor	Cost reduction	Content cost reduction – in transaction uncertainty in agency costs in asset specificity	Cost – Transaction infrastructural cost efficiencies due to volume
Advisor	Custom-isation	Content customisation – Differentiating the complexity of content of the transaction to the needs of the customer Creates "stickiness" of EBPP website for return visits	Customisation – Utilising establishing infrastructure to provide a personalised transaction environment Provides alternative channel for cross-selling activities

Source: Fairchild (2003)

E-money

The electronic form of money is not the electronic equivalent of the money we use daily. Its definition and characteristics vary according to its technical implementation and the purposes decided by its issuer. There are a number of e-money schemes, each differing slightly from the others in the way its value is transferred, transaction is recorded and currency of denomination.

In the E-money Directive published by European Commission, e-money is defined as:

> monetary value as represented by a claim on the issuer which is: (i) stored on an electronic device; (ii) stored on receipt of funds of an amount not less in value than the monetary value issued; (iii) accepted as means of payment by undertakings other than the issuer. (European Commission, 2000)

Thus, e-money is identified as a scheme of storing monetary values on some electronic devices. This is the pre-paid nature that distinguishes e-money from a credit card. BIS (1998) further divides e-money into e-purse and e-cash. The former consists of some hardware (e.g. chip card, such as the Mondex card) from which an account balance can be subtracted from or added to. E-cash is software-based and the monetary value stored inside can be used for purchasing on the Internet. However, the money that is transferred through an e-purse is also referred to as e-cash.

The 'pre-paid' nature of these e-purse and e-cash schemes freezes up some cash. In spite of their advantages of being paperless, most e-money schemes fail to reach a critical mass. Many of them are now used within small communities and very few are designed for purchasing online. If these schemes are compared among themselves, people in Europe and Asia are more used to e-purses (in the form of smartcards) while e-money is less accepted in the USA, without a clear reason.

E-purses

E-purses (or e-wallets) are e-payment systems that emerged in the early 1990s. They are implemented on a hardware device, such as a smartcard and are commonly issued by banks.

A smartcard is an advanced form of credit/debit card, replacing the magnetic strip with a microchip. With the microchip, a smartcard is equivalent to a small computer that can hold small programs (usually in Java) and a small amount of memory. The card is also capable of communicating with an external device through the gold contacts or a wireless device on it.

In 1998, Europay,[10] MasterCard and Visa published the EMV[11] specifications for the interface between a smartcard and the card reader/terminal for credit/debit payments. The specifications are compatible with the ISO7816 standard (ISO7816 defines the physical characteristics, dimensions and contact locations (points), electronic signals, transmission protocols, application identifiers, inter-industry commands for interchange, SCQL commands and data elements of a smartcard; see Figure 4.16) for smartcards – including contactless cards. At about the same time, Visa, American Express and ERG Ltd. (an Australian fare management and smartcard services company) also published the Common Electronic Purse Specifications (CEPS) for stored value/e-purse applications. CEPS is EMV compatible.

EMV has become an industrial standard and card associations in many parts of the world are mandating members to comply with EMV, although the USA is not one of these places. To become EMV compliant, a smartcard must get approval through a third-party test house and the corresponding POS terminals also need a certification test. The specifications were revised in 2000 to become EMV 2000 version 4.0. There are two levels of approval for a terminal:

- Level 1 specifies the physical characteristics of the card reader, including the physical and electrical parameters and the protocol between the smartcard and the interface module.

Figure 4.16 **ISO7816 defines the physical layout of a chip**

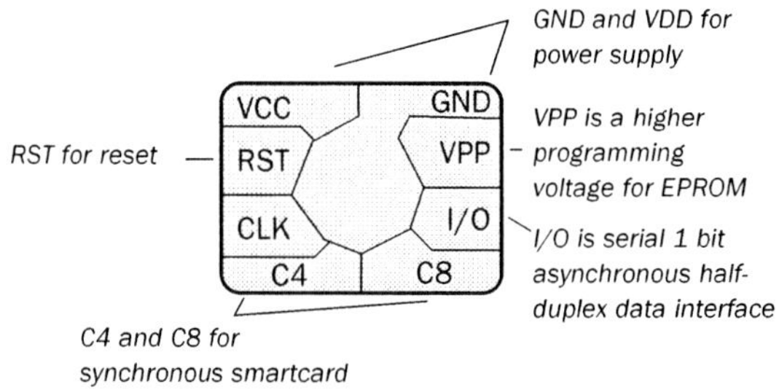

CLK: clock; GND: ground; I/O: input/output; RST: reset; VCC: power supply voltage; VPP: programming voltage

- Level 2 specifies the core software (often called the 'kernel') and the credit/debit card application. There could be other applications, such as those for loyalty and membership administration that are not controlled by EMV.

However, the EMV specifications presume face-to-face transactions and do not cover the operations of contactless cards.

As far as the operation is concerned, smartcards can be divided into 'accounted' and 'unaccounted' ones. They differ by whether or not the transactions are recorded by back-office systems. The unaccounted smartcards keep no records on their chips except audit trails. From an applicability perspective, smartcards can also be divided into 'open' and 'closed' where the latter have only limited use, such as paying for school meals or on a campus. But the widest differentiation is made by wireless technology as smartcards nowadays diverge to contact and contactless smartcards.

The technology of contactless smartcards is based on ISO14443 and ISO15693 standards. The ISO14443 standard presumes a system of a device in a smartcard (called a 'proximity integrated circuit card' or PICC) and a device in a card reader (called a 'proximity coupling device' or PCD). The PICC is equipped with an antenna that can communicate with the PCD if its antenna is within 10 cm issuing a radio frequency of 13.56 MHz. Smartcards compliant with ISO15693 can even be detected at 50–70 cm distance.

ISO14443 consists of four parts:

- Part 1 defines the size and physical characteristics of the card.
- Part 2 describes the characteristics of power transfer and communication between the PICC and PCD. There are two types of communication signal interface: Type A (bit modulation) and Type B (coding).
- Part 3 describes how the PCD talks first (polling for PICCs) and how to deal with situations when several cards are presented to the same reader (anti-collision methods).
- Part 4 publishes the half-duplex block transmission protocols for Type A and Type B.

The ISO standards do not specify operating systems, which are proprietary to the vendors. Their only concerns are the radio frequency identification (RFID) properties of the cards, such as effective distance, frequency and transmission speed. Surprisingly, one famous well-established standard is not accepted by ISO. The contactless IC card format, FeliCa, developed by Sony, is widely used in Japan and other parts of Asia. The microchip has an 8-bit CPU and 1–4 Mb of memory. It has the same operating range as ISO14443 Type B under the same frequency, but is twice as fast, with a transmission rate of 212 Kbps. This speed is ideal for transport cards as all operations from detection, authentication, reading and writing data can be completed within 0.1 to 0.2 seconds.

Operating systems for smartcards

The chip on a smartcard is a tiny processor that is controlled by an operating system (OS). Multos (or 'Mult-OS') and JavaCard are the two most popular operating systems for smartcards. Both are open systems because they allow anyone to write applications on their bases to promote the usage of the cards; thus, these operating systems presume a secure environment where multiple applications can be added to a smartcard during its lifetime to change its functionality. They are also compatible with existing standards like ISO7816 and EMV.

Multos was developed by Mondex International and is now owned by the Multos Consortium (also known as Maosco Ltd.), which is a group of international blue-chip organisations. The Multos specifications define the Multos Application Abstract Machine (AAM), which is a virtual machine, APIs and operating systems that accept applications written in a variety of languages, including C, Java and an assembly language known as 'Multos Executable Language' (MEL). However, the availability of an appropriate compiler determines which higher-level language can be accepted.

JavaCard is the OS developed by Sun Microsystems in 1996. It is specified together with JavaCard virtual machine and the open API for smartcards. However, the first edition was not welcomed by the market and the smartcard industry soon developed an enhanced version of API to support OO features of the Java language. In 1998, Visa introduced the Visa OpenPlatform (VOP), another smartcard specification, to standardise secure downloading and installing new applications on multi-application smartcards. Since then, VOP has become inseparable from JavaCard. The latest version of JavaCard builds in a software firewall and is capable of running Java programs.

As illustrated in Figure 4.17, the JavaCard virtual machine is positioned at a higher level than the specific integrated circuit and native functions of the microchip. Thus, the VM layer hides the low-level technology from the Java programs. The JavaCard framework defines a

Figure 4.17 JavaCard system architecture

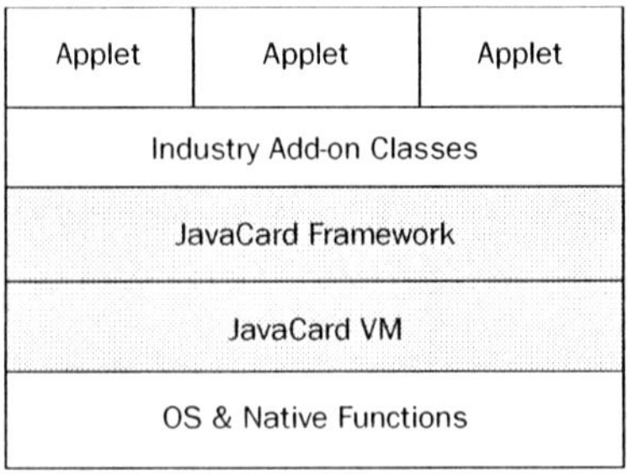

Source: Chan and Chan (1998)

set of API classes for application development and the business or industry may also supply more services as add-on libraries.

The Multos platform is widely used for financial smartcards in Asia and Latin America, although the Mondex card is fading away from the market. JavaCard is widely adopted for global system for mobile (GSM) communication and m-commerce applications.

Case: GeldKarte

GeldKarte was developed by Gieseke and Devrient in 1996. It is popular in Europe (Germany, Austria, France and Iceland) and by February 2005 has issued over 63 million cards in Germany. It claims to be the biggest e-purse scheme in the world.

Consumers can get a debit (Maestro) card from their banks with a GeldKarte chip on it or a preloaded 'Weisse Karte' ('white card') that is not linked to an account. Up to €200 (the ceiling is set to limit risk) can be uploaded at an ATM to a GeldKarte card, which can then be used for small payments on POS or on the Internet – in the latter case, an EUR-60 special card reader is needed. The card works for the consumer-to-merchant (C2M) payment systems but P2P (person-to-person or peer-to-peer) payment is not possible. All credit and debit transactions are logged at 'Börsenevidenzzentrale' (shadow account), which renders anonymous transactions impossible. Figure 4.18 shows the workflow of GeldKarte.

The card runs SECCOS (SEcure Chip Card Operating System) that supports the PKI and complies with the CEPS and EMV standards. Each card has a unique ID and uses DES encryption to secure a digital signature.

Figure 4.18 GeldKarte operations

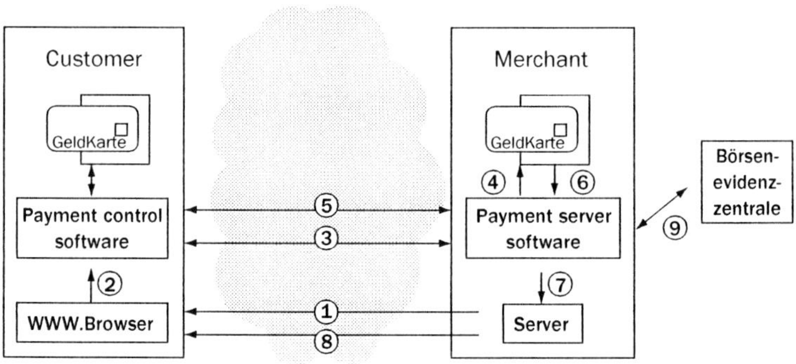

GeldKarte payment transaction for Internet:
1. Electronic invoice
2. Confirmation of invoice
3. Initiation of payment
4. Transfer of payment details to merchant GeldKarte
5. Authentication of customer and merchant Geldkarte, payment
6–8. Confirmation of payment
9. Recording of payment data at Börsenevidenzzentrale (offline)

Source: Schwiderski-Grosche (2003)

Case: Mondex

The Mondex card was developed by MasterCard International and initiated with Midland Bank in Swindon (UK) in 1995. Pilot schemes were soon introduced to other parts of the world, including the USA, Japan and Hong Kong, when Midland merged with HSBC. In 1997, MasterCard International acquired 51 per cent of Mondex International and began a long but insignificant process to promote Mondex's capacity to become a globally interoperable, multi-currency and highly secure e-purse system. However, Mondex has never been able to win the general public's attention and its usage remains confined to small communities like university campuses.

Consumers registered as Mondex users are given a smartcard (the Mondex card) and a special card reader, Mondex wallet. The chip on the smartcard is capable of holding the records of the last ten transactions. As depicted in Figure 4.19, money can be transferred from one card to another card or to a merchant's POS device with the proper device.

The smartcard was invented by Tim Jones and Graham Higgins of NatWest. It is a smartcard with five pockets to hold five currencies simultaneously. The value of each pocket can be varied by special devices, such as Mondex-compatible phones, Mondex wallets, balance

Figure 4.19 Mondex operations

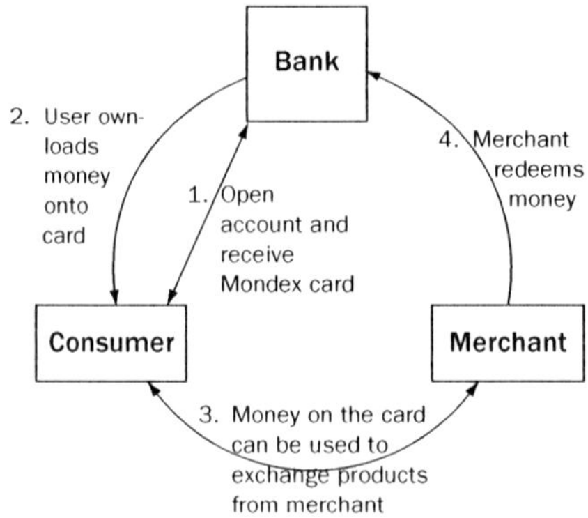

readers and the POS terminals, which may be used to load value onto the card. The value of each pocket can be locked on the card with a four-digit number.

The value on a Mondex card can be moved directly from one card to another without third-party (e.g. a bank) intervention. Such transactions mimic cash payments as money transfers without a clearing and settlement process. The identity of the cardholder is checked before money transfer by a 16-digit number. Additional security is provided by PKI cryptography and digital signature. For security reasons, the chip uses public key encryption and can automatically shut down if unusual transaction behaviour is detected. The security mechanism is installed on the Multos operating system of the Mondex card. However, if the card wants to increase its functionality by adding more applications, its actual capacity is limited by the memory size (16K or 32K) on the chip, although Multos is suitable for multi-applications.

Case: Octopus (Hong Kong)

The Octopus card was developed by several major transportation companies in Hong Kong. It was welcomed by the citizens as its stored value could be used for public transport payments, usually at a small discount. Soon the system was extended to other petty transactions and it is now used by photo booths, parking meters, fast food restaurants, convenience stores and supermarket chains and offers functions of a credit/debit card with banks. The Octopus chip is now incorporated into other appliances (e.g. wristwatch, mobile phone) so that these appliances can function as a contactless card. By the end of 2004, over 11 million Octopus cards have been in circulation – the figure exceeds the population of Hong Kong – and 150,000 Octopus watches. The total value of transactions through the system is US$2.2 billion each year and 25 per cent of them are not for transportation.

The technology of the card was designed and built by ERG. The company also provided support to the operator, Octopus Cards Limited (formerly known as Creative Star Ltd). The company chose the FeliCa format of Sony in 1997. Although it is not ISO14443 compliant, the card is also sensitive to 13.56 MHz radio frequency. Mutual authentication between the card and the reader is based on the DES technology.

The card is designed for transactions at the entry/exit point of a vehicle/station. By using a reader/writer device (which is a low-range radio transmitter), value can be subtracted from or added to an Octopus card and the transaction data are then sent to the company's central computer. The Octopus central clearinghouse system validates each transaction before it authorises the settlement.

The success of Octopus has attracted many cities and countries to follow its business model. Contactless smartcard systems have been developed for transit applications in cities like Kobe (Japan), Seoul (Korea), Singapore and London. Similar systems like ExxonMobil Speedpass and MasterCard PayPass have also been introduced in some cities in the USA for retailing purposes.

Chip-and-PIN cards

To reduce card fraud, the EU has mandated chip-and-PIN technology in credit and debit cards in 2005. That is, the retailers become financially responsible for fraudulent transactions if they do not have chip-and-PIN acceptance in place by January 2005 (EU) and January 2006 (Asia Pacific). The card is a simple form of smartcard, on which the chip stores a four-digit personal identification number (PIN). It is used to replace the signature of the cardholder. Authentication begins when the cardholder enters the PIN on a numeric keypad, which is installed with the POS equipment, for example, and is EMV-compliant.

However, to avoid disclosing the PIN to a third party, the present chip-and-PIN cards should not be used on the Internet or over the telephone. Some e-retailers accept payment by chip-and-PIN cards as if they were credit card payments. To provide a more secure way to use the card online, several innovative studies are underway; for example, it has been recommended to use another security code system for this purpose.

E-cash

The first generation of e-cash is the software-based e-money that requires special software to be installed at the user's local computer. As no hardware is involved, it has a low setup cost. However, the market has not been kind to these e-cash schemes and most of them have been relatively short-lived.

The next generation of e-cash schemes stores values and manages accounts at a central server rather than the PCs of individual users. These systems are promoted by merchants, who wish to alleviate their customers' difficulties in making payments. For those systems that are hosted by a merchant, the system keeps a database of customer accounts. For those that are offered to merchants, the systems keep both merchant and customers' accounts. Services to customers are normally offered for free, but a management fee is charged to merchants.

Case: Chaum's eCash

David Chaum developed his idea of eCash in 1994, and it was put on the market in 1995 by Mark Twain Bank, Missouri under a scheme called DigiCash. On joining the scheme, a consumer was given an eCash wallet, which was a software package installed on the consumer's PC. The wallet was able to create electronic coins of specified denomination, say, one hundred $5 coins. Each of them had a randomly selected 64-bit serial number and a specified value, but its validity needed to be checked by the issuing bank. The bank would deduct the amount from the consumer's account and return the e-coins to the consumer. The flow of operation is illustrated in Figure 4.20.

In order to accept the e-coins, the merchant needed an account with the issuing bank (i.e. acquirer bank is the same as the issuing bank). Anonymous payment was one of the characteristics of eCash, so Chaum developed a 'blind signature' technology that made the serial number of each coin invisible to the issuing bank even when it was being validated.

Each coin could, however, only be used once as there was a 'double spending test' each time the coin was spent. That is, when the coin was cashed, the issuing bank recorded its serial number and credits only when its serial number had not previously been recorded. Then the corresponding amount was credited to the merchant's DigiCash account.

However, DigiCash ran into bankruptcy in 1998, probably due to low acceptance. It was re-launched as 'eCash Technologies' until 2002. The

Figure 4.20 DigiCash e-coins operations

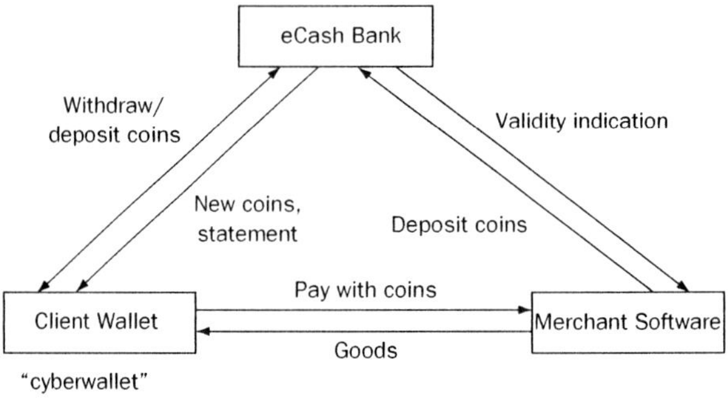

Source: O'Mahony et al. (2001)

business was acquired by InfoSpace, largely because the latter was interested in acquiring the valuable patents of Chaum's eCash concept.

P2P payment and PayPal

The ultimate form of e-money is a scheme that can be used in P2P payment. There have been a number of issuers since the mid-1990s but few survive today. They differ slightly in building their mechanisms of customer accounting and charging.

PayPal is perhaps the best-known e-payment service of its kind. Founded in 1998, PayPal is now a subsidiary of eBay Co. and has gathered 56 million account members worldwide, each of whom is able to send and receive funds online provided that the sender has a large enough credit line or amount in their bank account.

This implies that every buyer needs a credit card or a bank account to become a PayPal account holder. It is easy for a merchant to get a PayPal account. When the merchant sells a product online, an e-mail message notifies the merchant of the customer's payment so that shipment can proceed.

PayPal charges personal recipients or sellers a flat fee, depending on their nationality. Business sellers are charged a certain percentage of the transaction price (Figure 4.21).

However, the privacy and security problem in PayPal has been a controversial matter for a long time. There are numerous anti-PayPal websites where one can find cases of lawsuits and complaints against PayPal services. The company has also had problems in attending to data privacy over their member accounts, as members receive spam messages in their e-mail boxes from time to time.

Figure 4.21 How PayPal works

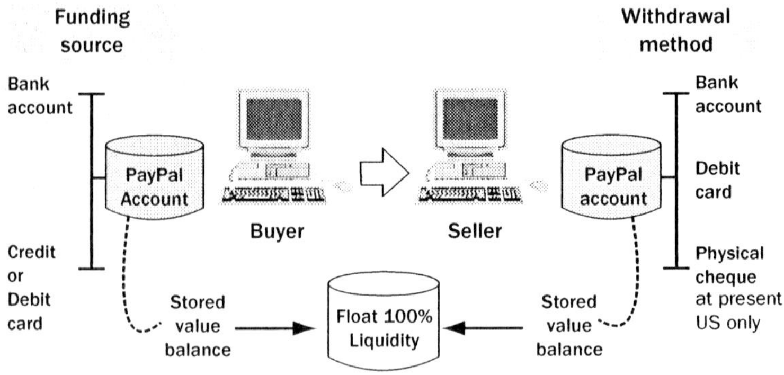

Source: Caplehorn (2004)

Payments in m-commerce

M-commerce is in its infancy, but payment schemes based on mobile phone or PDA technology continue to push onto the market. Most of these m-payment systems, including Paybox and Click&Buy, operate on pre-paid consumer accounts. As mobile devices are generally small in size and less powerful than a PC, they have limited computational capacity. M-payment transactions tend to be small in value and thus the capability of making micropayments becomes an essential feature of m-payment schemes.

Case: Paybox

The most popular m-payment scheme in Europe is Paybox, with 100,000 registered consumers and 3,000 acceptance points by September 2004. Paybox relies on the credit card network and interactive voice response (IVR) technology. To register as a user, the person has to pay Paybox an annual fee. At time of purchase, a consumer can call a service number, authenticate themselves with a PIN and enter the amount and the phone number of the merchant using a mobile phone. When the identities of both parties are validated, the money transfer is processed via the MasterCard and Maestro network and the Paybox system will notify the merchant about the fund transfer within a few seconds. As a PIN is used, no credit card information is transmitted on the mobile phone. In spite of the expansion policy of Paybox, business in some countries is not entirely satisfactory. In January 2003, Paybox terminated its service in the UK.

Micropayment

Although the costs of producing and storing e-cash are low, the cost of making an exchange is high because of the expensive protection mechanism. Thus, using e-cash for small payment amounts is not economical. Two micropayment schemes, Millicent and PepperCoin, are introduced below. The two schemes are totally different.

Case: Millicent

The pioneer – Millicent – was initiated by Digital Equipment Corporation in 1995 (DEC was later acquired by Compaq, which in turn was acquired by HP). Millicent is represented by a 'scrip', which is prepaid and verifiable cash (similar to an e-coin) issued by a merchant (merchant scrip) and a broker (broker scrip). A consumer joining the scheme can purchase a scrip from a broker. When the consumer wants to buy from a merchant, they can exchange a merchant scrip for their broker scrip. The consumer can then use the merchant scrip for micropayments (even for payments of 0.5 cents, maximum value is €10) of small denominations. The merchant scrip is sold to the broker. The operations of Millicent in terms of scrip movements are illustrated in Figure 4.22.

Figure 4.22 **MilliCent operations**

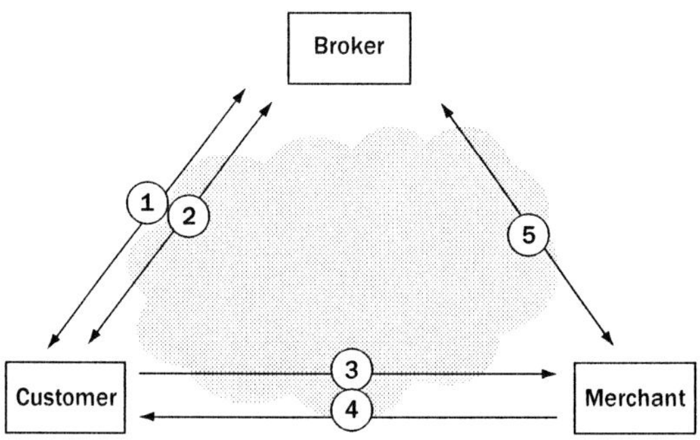

1. Purchase of broker scrip
2. Exchange of broker scrip to merchant scrip
5. Caching in of merchant scrip

Payment transaction:

3. Payment of goods with merchant scrip
4. Change given in form of change scrip

Source: Schwiderski-Grosche (2003)

The MilliCent system allows multiple brokers. It helps promote the system and fasten the validation process. To avoid the complicated computation, MilliCent uses a hash function instead of PKI for security. The double spending problem is tackled by looking for valid scrip in the merchant's database. The process is fast as it can be carried out in the broker's site.

Case: PepperCoin

Another micropayment scheme, PepperCoin, was created by two MIT professors, Silvio Micali and Ronald Rivest. Content providers joining the scheme are given a PepperMill application to encrypt their digital content for sale together with information of the price, merchant ID and content description. The resulting file of encrypted content is called a PepperBox. Consumers may acquire their e-cheques (known as PepperCoins) by opening a pre-paid or post-paid account with the PepperCoin Payment Service and install a small PepperPanel software package on their computers.

Having downloaded content (the PepperBox) from a merchant, the PepperPanel displays its price. The PepperPanel also creates PepperCoins with the user's information and sends them to the merchant and the PepperCoin Payment Service. If the PepperCoins are validated and accepted, the decryption key for the PepperBox will be created and sent to the user's PepperPanel. The user will receive bills from the PepperCoin Payment Service periodically.

The content provider does not receive payment each time a PepperBox is sold. The PepperCoin Payment Service determines whether to complete the PepperCoins processing cycle when they are received. This is a 'cryptographically secure selection' process that selects PepperCoins on a probabilistic basis. For example, if 1/10 of the PepperCoins from a user are selected to be processed completely, the value of the selected transaction will be multiplied by a factor of 10.

A new PepperCoin 2.0 scheme proposed in 2004 allows multi-merchant aggregation. That is, a user can use PepperCoins for small-value purchases across a wider range of content providers. Once the aggregate purchase reaches a predefined level, PepperCoin Payment Service will ask the issuer for authorisation and settlement processing on the aggregated transactions. After the payment is received and the processing fee is deducted, it will be disaggregated and sent to relevant merchants.

Magex platform and digital rights management

A New York-based payment technology company is behind some of the biggest e-payment schemes in the world. Originally headquartered in London, Magex offers a payment platform, the Magex Managed Payments Platform, which allows IVR, SMS and WAP access to its e-wallet application. Its clients include:

- *MasterCard's MoneySend*: To expand MasterCard's network and processing capability by providing member banks with a cost-efficient card-to-card money transfer service.
- *E-retailers*: For example, Universal Music Group allows customers to download its premium digital music format by using Magex as a clearinghouse.
- *Large retail banks worldwide*: Among them the Royal Bank of Scotland (which owns a third of Magex) delegated Magex to host its NatWest (the creator of Mondex in 1990) FastPay P2P payment service. *www.fastpay.com* is targeted at the youth market and at anyone with a bank account (whatever bank). It is replacing the role of cheques in auctions and small businesses. Consumers can pay by using the system on the Internet or over mobile phones and send 20 pence to make each payment.

The Magex platform is built with the J2EE architecture, which generally has three layers (Figure 4.23). The presentation layer interfaces with both Web and WAP. It also allows third-party services to integrate with mobile networks for SMS. The middle layer is a BEA WebLogic server, which houses business applications.

Figure 4.23 **The J2EE architecture of a Magex platform**

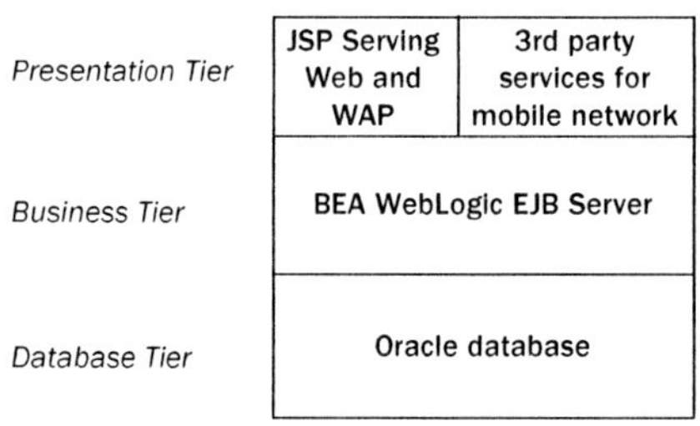

EJB: enterprise JavaBeans; JSP: JavaServer page

A well-known application of the Magex platform is the MetaTrust Utility, which is provided by Sunnyvale (California)-based InterTrust Technologies Corp. The MetaTrust Utility is also known as a digital rights management[12] (DRM) system, which offers protection to digital content delivered over the Internet and the management of subscriptions and memberships; for example, the DRM is capable of usage-administration and tracking. The system is particularly suitable for distribution of intellectual property over the Web. Transactions of intellectual properties require a trusted payment process and a financial clearinghouse.

Successful E/M-business models

E-payment schemes are slow in gaining customers' acceptance, especially in developed countries like the USA. Being aware of the significant developments in Asia (like Octopus in Hong Kong), critics (such as Vartanian et al., 2004) explain that the pervasiveness of existing payment methods – in particular, credit card, ATM and paper-based cheque systems as in the USA – is the reason behind the stagnant growth of e-payment systems.

In B2B trading environments, there are other hurdles for adopting e-payment. JP Morgan surveyed business organisations in the USA in 2003 and found four major barriers for them to migrate to e-payments (JP Morgan's Industry Issue Report, 2005). These are:

- accounting systems that are not integrated with e-payment systems;
- shortage of IT resources;
- lack of a single standard format for remittance information; and
- trading partners who cannot send or receive e-payments with sufficient remittance information.

An e-payment (including EBPP) scheme that has taken these problems into consideration would surely be an advantage in the market.

For providers of e-payment systems, Keeling (2002) suggests that choosing a successful business model is more important. The model could be built on the following:

- *A good understanding of consumer reactions*: including online trust, security and accountability of payment card services.

- *Completeness of service*: the possibility to conduct the entire transaction over the Internet or mobile communication channel from negotiation through ordering to payment.
- *Multi-channelling approach*: more than one channel is offered to customers who have the discretion to choose the preferred channel for each step of a transaction. For example, user authentication can be conducted over a mobile channel while the rest of the transaction could be performed over the Internet.
- *Image dimensions for the virtual store* (where relevant): maintain the physical product and consumer related services.
- *Focus on consumer-virtual store interface (where relevant) and boost the consumer experience*: the service is a key focus in e/m-commerce for the consumer.

Table 4.2 **Functional requirements in m-commerce**

Consumer requirements	Merchant requirements	Financial institutions requirements

▪ Ease of use
▪ High security (including transaction tracking and prevention of fraud)
▪ Free selection of payment instrument
▪ Broad acceptance by merchants
▪ Financial services accessible via all mobile equipment and operators
	▪ Availability with different payment instruments
	▪ Guarantee of payment and/or non-repudiation
	▪ Minimal integration and management costs
	▪ Broad acceptance by consumer
	▪ Financial service accessible via all mobile equipment and operators
	  ▪ Universality and openness
	  ▪ Fast efficient payment completion
		▪ Service and relationship management with consumer, including the ability to fund purchases with branded products
		▪ Control of transaction risk and security
		▪ Independence of the financial services from the operator services
		▪ Interoperability
		▪ High security
		  – Integration with existing infrastructure
		  – Universality and openness, including no proprietary solutions

Source: Keeling (2002: 33)

These are general principles for a sound business model. For the m-payment business, Keeling (2002) indicates the functional requirements as in Table 4.2.

No matter what the business model is, the truism seems to be that the model needs to attain critical mass and economies of scale in a short time. Many schemes fail because of their limited scope of applicability – and the consumers' lack incentive to use them. For this reason, consumers may not be satisfied just with sophisticated security protection and user-friendly devices. Siegel (2004) of Click&Buy suggests three principles or success factors to achieve critical mass:

- the payment scheme needs to be easy, convenient and secure to use for the consumer;
- it is efficient and cost-effective for the merchant;
- it is fully integrated into today's payment industry with no dependencies on new technologies or legislation.

Of course, Siegel is addressing the strategy of Click&Buy – the e-cash scheme similar to PayPal. For other classes of e-payment schemes, these principles might be different.

Summary

Since the last decade, e-payment systems have emerged to replace payments by conventional cheques or cash. Most of these schemes could not survive the e-commerce bubble, but those remaining in business can now see a brighter future as consumers and merchants gradually become used to transactions on the Internet. Industry authorities of various countries have also offered their help in establishing regulations and improving clearing and settlement procedures. Recent developments in e-payment systems have also been associated with the issues of obtaining intellectual properties online. Magex's investment on digital rights management and micropayment may have profound effects on consumers' behaviour on the Internet in the long term.

This chapter presented a rudimentary division of e-payment systems into credit/debit cards, e-cheque and e-money. E-cheque and e-money were the main focus of this chapter as they represent innovative payment methods designed by the e-financial services industry. Various ICT applications and systems have been developed to assist the launching of new e-cheque and e-money schemes.

Questions for discussion

1. How do merchants and customers differ in their expectations of an e-payment system?
2. Why do you think e-payment systems have never been really popular?
3. What can the financial industry do to make consumers feel secure about e-payment?

Notes

1. When one enters the credit card number and personal information to a retailer's website, SSL/TLS provides the protocol and encryption to protect the data from any eavesdropping between their PC and the website.
2. The term *echeck* is reserved for the FSTC's model while *e-cheque* refers to electronic cheques in general.
3. MICR is the characters printed on a cheque. Using magnetic ink, these characters carry information, such as the account number and the cheque number.
4. The Electronic Payments Network (*www.epaynetwork.com*) is a private e-payment processor that operates about 30 per cent of the domestic market in 2002.
5. UCF does not include stop payments or closed accounts and the like.
6. In IBM terminology, the term 'cassette' refers to the software component consisting of Java classes and interfaces that are written by IBM or third-party vendors and that can be easily installed into the WebSphere Commerce Payments framework to support different payment protocols (such as SET and CyberCash).
7. Electronic Benefits Transfer (EBT) is a replacement of food stamps and other subsidiaries issued by some state governments to people in need. When the card is run through an e-payment system, it authorises the transfer of the cardholder's government benefits to the retailer for payment of products received.
8. PL/SQL is Oracle's procedural extension of SQL.
9. Litan (2003) predicted that online bill payment in the USA would increase to 40 million users in 2003. Forrester Research (2005) estimates that a population of 47 million US households will pay bills online by 2010. (*http://www.internetadsales.com/modules/news/article.php?storyid=6530*; last accessed 2 December 2005).

10. Europay merged with MasterCard in 2002.
11. An abbreviation made up of its creators, Europay, MasterCard and Visa.
12. DRM defines rights to content through a 'rights model,' which controls the granting of rights through (1) legal tools, such as agreement, copyright notices, registration, and EU and international copyright laws; (2) audit trails, including IP address tracking and watermarking; and (3) technological measures including encryption, user authentication, and conditional access.

5

E-insurance

The insurance marketspace

The insurance industry is one of the best-known business sectors to take full advantage of the Internet. Clarke (1997) asserts that the majority of financial services are digital in nature and are therefore capable of being fully supported by e-commerce. In particular, he argues that when buyers know how to seek for the optimal price and other information on home and contents insurance policies on the Internet, the conventional intermediaries in the industry will be replaced by 'marketspace intermediation'.[1]

Not only are the intermediary players of the insurance market changed by the Internet, the insurance market has also seen increasing competition among insurance companies. This is partly due to the deregulation that has drawn international carriers to local markets, but in addition, the seemingly easy way of opening an insurance business by setting up a website has also drawn new entrants to the insurance market, including banks and non-financial services businesses. One such example is the UK retailer Marks & Spencer, which started selling car insurance policies on its website from 2004.

The marketspace is now full of insurers and their associates, each of which is trying to raise the hit rate to its website by providing more products, more customisation and more information. Products today are no longer restricted to property and casualty (P&C) and life insurance[2] – the industry's two traditional major product lines. There are proliferations of new breeds of products, including those linked to stock and bond investments, and innovations targeted at specific customer segments, such as insurance for weddings and pets.

Operations in the insurance companies are modelled from product-centric to customer-centric. Insurers' websites are designed to satisfy a wide range of visitors, who could be prospective customers, policyholders, agents, group benefits managers, healthcare providers and other intermediaries. Whether their policies are issued online or via a personal contact, insurers are supported by ICT for the management of business processes, such as channel management, actuarial services, underwriting, policy management and claims management. These processes form the primary activities in the insurance value chain as illustrated in Figure 5.1.

It is common for insurers to reduce the overall risk they bear by sharing it across a large number of independent insurers. The key players in the insurance market are insurers and reinsurers, who cooperate to diversify risks and provide services that no single insurer can provide. In recent years, reinsurers have found risk securitisation (e.g. investing in catastrophe bonds)[3] an effective means to raise capital to cover catastrophic claims. Securitisation further promotes the convergence of the insurance sector and other financial sectors. It also adds one more dimension to the functionality of an insurer's website.

However, many studies (e.g. Dumm and Hoyt, 2003) find only a small portion of insurance products are purchased via the Internet. An article written jointly by the Economist Intelligence Unit and PricewaterhouseCoopers (2001) reveals that only a few traditional insurers are prepared to explore the full potential of e-business, but many are prepared to increase their annual spending on e-business technology in the coming years so that more advanced customer services can be offered through the Web and other channels. The e-insurance marketspace grows slowly. In a Celent survey in 2004 (Josefowicz, 2004), 36 per cent of the P&C respondents and 16 per cent of the life respondents said that more than half of their new business is submitted online.

To describe the insurance marketspace, the first section in this chapter reviews the development of the two major products, P&C insurance and

Figure 5.1 Insurance value chain

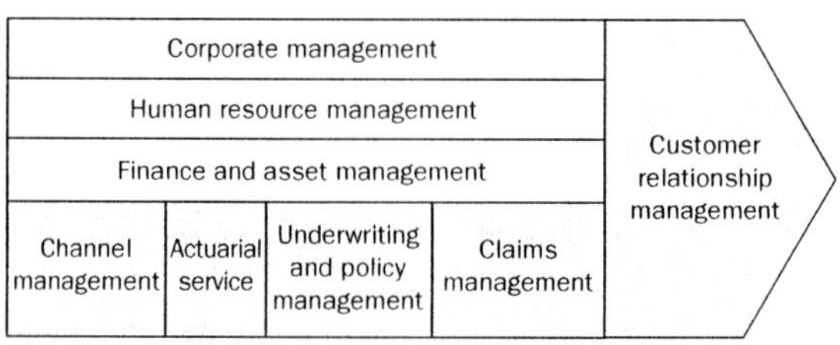

Source: Kumar and Swarup (2001)

life insurance. This is followed by discussing ICT deployment and the development of e-insurance in the subsequent two sections.

Property and casualty insurance

Property and casualty insurance covers the property and liability losses of businesses and individuals. Business organisations need property insurance to cover damage or loss to their machinery, equipment, tools or supplies, and liability insurance to prepare for loss arising out of their responsibility to others imposed by law or assumed by contract. Individuals may also need insurance policies for automobile, fire, theft, homeowner and other liabilities. P&C insurance is a volatile market. Its profitability is subject to recent incidents of terrorist attacks, natural disasters and political/economic changes.

Clemons et al. (2001) argue that P&C policyholders are interested in news of insurance products when their policies are due to be renewed, while life insurance policyholders are less likely to change their policies once they have made their purchase. Customers often look for P&C insurers that offer better service and/or better price, in particular, an insurer who is reputable in processing claims efficiently and fairly. This explains why a Datamonitor report (2004a) asserts that 80 per cent of the operational costs for P&C carriers are given to claims processing and management. For that purpose, ICT has been deployed to:

- automate first notification of loss (FNOL) or first report of injury (FROI);
- create an initial customer/claimant touch-point while reducing manual processes; and
- streamline the workflow throughout the process.

These are the objectives of the development of proprietary policy and claims administration systems, whose performance is of strategic importance to the insurers. Although these legacy systems can automate claims processing, they are inflexible, user-unfriendly and cannot be integrated with other business processes. A more critical issue is that very few companies have redesigned their claims processing to utilise the capacity of their computerised systems fully.

What customers need today is not just rapid processing, but more communications and more transparency. They want to know the status of claims processing from FNOL to the claims closure. As simple automation of claims processes may not be able to satisfy customers, companies need to study how their customers are treated and what causes the bottlenecks. Methods, such as monitoring, modelling and simulation, and what-if analysis can be used to look for improvements in their workflow.

The Internet is also a convenient channel for communication with customers (policyholders) and partners (such as claims adjusters, investigators and brokers). It can be an enabler for the development of a more comprehensive solution to policy underwriting and claims. For this reason, new P&C insurance systems should implement a message standard (e.g. ACORD XML, see the relevant section) to allow efficient and accurate information exchanges between various parties. With a Web-based jewellery insurance application, such as JEMs for Claims, which uses the ACORD standard 'JCRS-ACORD' created by its vendor JCRS, a customer can understand how the value of their diamond ring has been assessed by the insurer's adjuster, at the time when they purchase the ring and an insurance policy to cover it (JCRS, 2002).

For P&C insurance products that involve complex terms and claims regulations, customers might find more confidence in listening to the explanation from an agent. Unless their prices are really competitive, relatively few P&C products are purchased online. An exception is motor insurance, which is the most common P&C product that is getting more and more customers online.

Motor insurance

The motor insurance market is unique in its being almost fully saturated, i.e., all potential customers have already bought a motor insurance policy. Every insurer in this market needs to fight on two fronts – to retain current customers and to attract new ones. Dumm and Hoyt (2003) quote from the survey result of 2001 national auto insurance study (by JD Power and Associates) that 40 per cent of automobile insurance customers would not switch to another insurer regardless of cost savings. They cherish the services instead.

Gomez, Inc., however, did a survey in 2002 (PeopleSoft, 2003) and found 28.9 per cent of respondents had sought motor insurance online. These people would have no doubt about switching to another insurer if the price was right and the service acceptable. To attract customers, a motor insurance website should have something more than competitive pricing; its website should have detailed product information, FAQs, tools for quotations and application submission. Other services that could be provided online (e.g. claims status cheque and complaints) should also be aimed at enhancing trust in the company.

Compared with other P&C products, motor insurance is a rather simple product that contains standardised terms. Customers may expect fewer pre-purchase services, but once they have claims experience, it can surely affect how they perceive the insurer. Bond and Stone (2004) observe that:

- Non-claimants are more likely to know who their insurers are – maybe most claimants would like to switch to another insurer, thus they tend to forget the identities of their insurers.
- 54 per cent of customers use a 'shopping around' strategy to search for and select an insurer at renewal time, and one in three of them would want 'the cheapest price whatever'.
- Only 23 per cent of customers ask a broker to find an insurer, although the figure may be higher in reality as some customers might have mistaken some large brokers as insurers.
- Older customers (aged over 45) tend to renew their previous insurance with their current insurer – they don't like to answer many questions repeatedly to approach a new insurer.

The authors argue that non-claimants and older customers are more loyal to their insurers. Once a customer becomes a claimant, they might switch to a new insurer and try to look for the highest service level at an affordable price. For example, a customer would expect a replacement car during the claims process once they knew the service was available.

In many countries, the automotive aftermarket has expanded to include PBE companies (the industry that deals with paint, body and equipment for vehicles) and insurance companies to provide a wide range of services to car owners. For example, a driver might get instant assistance from a Web-based or mobile communication system which, in case of emergency, could link up collision repair shops, parts and equipment vendors, tow companies, car rental agencies, third-party administrators (TPAs) and/or insurance companies. These services are managed by an interorganisational system that can integrate the workflow of all parties involved. Figure 5.2 illustrates an automotive claims management system that liaises with various parties via the Internet.

Figure 5.2 Various parties connected by a claims management system

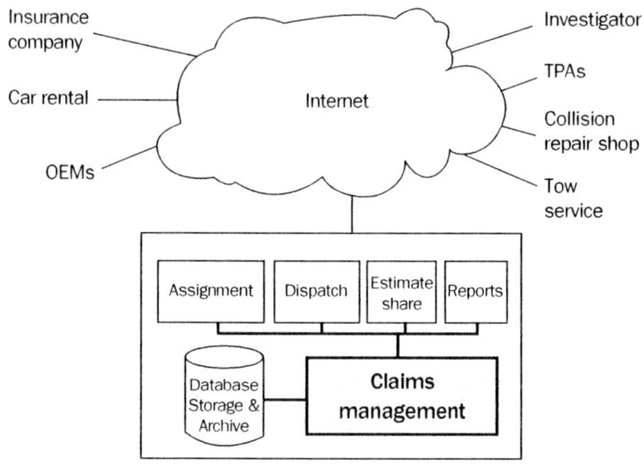

OEM: original equipment manufacturers; TPA: third-party administrator

Life insurance

Life insurance products can be divided into group and individual life policies, the latter of which includes term and whole. Although most of these products are relatively straightforward (there are some exceptions, such as tax-efficient life insurance policies), a large portion of them are sold to customers through captive[4] or independent agents. Just as customers may still be required to see a doctor (say, for a blood test), they prefer face-to-face contact with an agent and they find an insurance website a convenient place only for price comparison or referral services.

The sluggishness of online business does not, however, mean a web presence is not important. Indeed, it has been suggested that those firms whose online services do not support life insurance sales are actually damaging their reputation (Lilischkis, 2002). They could still benefit from applying ICT and Internet technology. However, they cannot count on their Web-based tools for instant quotation and premium calculation to achieve distinctive advantage. To attract customers to their websites, insurers tend to tailor their products to suit customers' individual needs. The life insurance market is already filled with life insurance products bundled with other financial services, such as stocks, investment products, or guaranteed return offerings. There should be more than just information about ordinary life insurance; customers may want to know information, such as risk levels, asset allocation and growth and value investment styles of respective funding options. Gribble and McGing (2000) indicate that life insurer sites are heavily oriented to and better developed for, the funds management side of the business.

Reinsurance

Reinsurance is the process in which a carrier shares the risk on a policy with other insurers (the reinsurers). The process involves an exchange of paperwork between both parties, such an exchange taking place at the outset of searching for an interested reinsurer. Electronic filing and Internet transmission definitely help the information exchange process, but like other insurance businesses, very few reinsurance transactions are carried out on the Internet; however, most practitioners see moving to e-reinsurance to be a very likely eventuality (Best-Devereux, 2003).

The e-reinsurance market seemed to experience a revival period a year after the terrorist attack on the World Trade Center in New York. Major Web-based reinsurers, such as eReinsure, Inreon and ri3k have reported a significant increase in submissions and a surge in reinsurance prices (Best-Devereux, 2003). Reinsurance firms would like to invest in ICT to enhance their strategic advantages.

Some firms focus on the technology of document management systems. For example, the AgoraINS (Insurance Network Solutions) is a system specially designed for the reinsurance process in the Toronto-based Manulife Co. It can turn documents into TIF files, and when they are sent to selected reinsurers, the system keeps track of all file exchanges, their encryption and decryption, and the participation level agreed by the reinsurers (Hyle, 2002). Others may consider other applications, such as credit exposure management. The General Electric Employers Reinsurance Corp (ERC) implemented a ceded agreement system to keep track of terms and conditions from all current reinsurance contracts. The system can calculate the kinds of limits to which the reinsurer would be exposed if, for example, its client, an insurer, was bankrupted due to a hurricane in Florida (Hyle, 2004).

This section briefly described the marketspace created by the customers, insurers, reinsurers and intermediaries taking advantage of the Internet. The insurance industry has so far not produced much profit from the e-insurance movement, but practitioners are learning to accept the technology, and are prepared to use ICT extensively for product development, transaction management and customer services, even if it generally involves large investment and business process re-engineering.

Application of ICT is an important step for e-insurance. The next section covers some important developments in the ICT industry paving the way to e-insurance.

ICT in the insurance industry

Insurance companies are considered to be conservative in applying new ICT, but they have invested generously to extend their activities on the Internet (Lilischkis, 2002). Their e-insurance business has not been very successful so far. Swiss Re (Sigma, 2000) suggests the following factors might be responsible for this limited success:

- product complexity;
- difficulty of standardising claims settlement;
- infrequent contact between the client and the company;
- insecure perception toward the Internet;
- regulatory hurdles.

These may be difficult problems but a solution may be found if an insurance firm finds time and resources. For example, there must be some niche products that would be welcomed by customers on the Web.

Swiss Re analysed the insurance market and evaluated the transaction volume and product complexity of various insurance products. Figure 5.3 illustrates the positions of these products with respect to their transaction

Figure 5.3 **Suitability of Internet distribution**

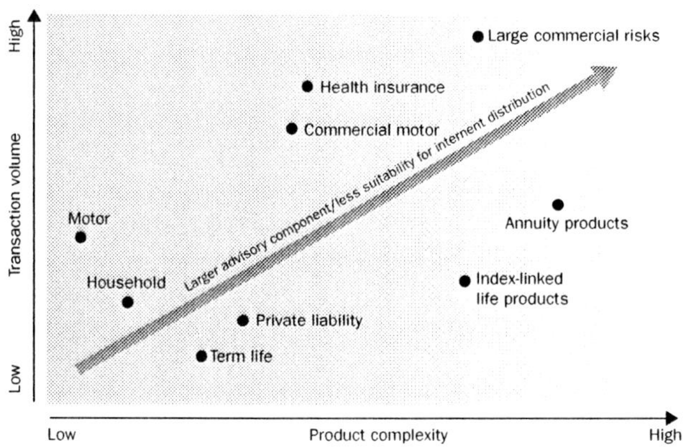

Source: Sigma (2000)

volume and product complexity. Swiss Re suggests that products at the lower left corner are most suitable for Internet distribution.

In an effort to make the e-insurance business a successful reality, the industry has developed several standards and models to guide inexperienced firms toward ICT deployment. The most significant achievement is the ACORD standards, which are described below with a few other ICT models.

ACORD standards

The Association for Cooperative Operations Research and Development (ACORD) is an international insurance association that facilitates and develops the use of standards for the insurance industry. By promoting messaging standards for communications between partners in the insurance industry, the ACORD stakeholders expect to achieve straight-through processing (STP). Table 5.1 summarises a few ACORD standards.

ACORD began to standardise hundreds of forms in the 1970s to help independent agents place business with insurance companies more

Table 5.1 Summary of ACORD standards

AL3	An electronic data interchange standard for communication between P&C insurers and their agents. This standard is based on fixed length messages, where every data element has its own prescribed position in the message.
ACORD XML (for P&C insurance)	A standard created in XML that defines transactional messages for the domains of personal lines, commercial lines, surety, claims and accounting.
ACORD life data model	This defines entities and their relations for describing life insurance and annuities as well as health insurance. This model is the basis for the ACORD XML for life insurance standard.
ACORD XML for life insurance	This comes as two sets of XML specifications. The entities from the ACORD life data model are represented in one XML data type definition (DTD). These entities are then used as content for the transactions that are defined in the XML for life insurance transactions specification, which comes as a separate XML DTD.

Source: IAA Positioning Statement (2001)

efficiently. It developed its AL3 standard for electronic data interchange communications in the 1980s. Subsequently, XML versions of ACORD forms – there are hundreds of them – were introduced to the industry. These standards have been accepted by 1,100 insurance carriers and groups (87 per cent of life carriers and 94 per cent of P&C carriers, according to McKendrick, 2004). Software vendors responded by using web services extensively as building blocks for their distributed systems so that information (in the form of XML) flows efficiently, regardless of platform. It has become a cost-effective means for internal integration for extracting data from legacy systems, to tie up with field agents and to communicate with business partners.

Three standards are now maintained by ACORD, designed respectively for the life and annuity, P&C and the reinsurance sectors. The segment of an ACORD XML message illustrated in Figure 5.4 is a template for the description of a policy. Readers who are familiar with HTML syntax should easily understand that messages are inserted between specialised tags, such as <policy_number> and </policy_number>.

Figure 5.4 **Sample ACORD XML message**

```
<quote_details>
   <quote_generated></quote_generated>
   <alteration></alteration>
   <policy_number></policy_number>
   <tablecode></tablecode>
   <category></category>
   <subcategory></subcategory>
   <inputs id='i0'>
      <label></label>
      <html_label></html_label>
      <existing_value></existing_value>
      <entered_value></entered_value>
      <html_value></html_value>
   </inputs>
   <existing_details id='0'>
      <label></label>
      <html_label></html_label>
      <existing_value></existing_value>
      <entered_value></entered_value>
      <html_value></html_value>
      <html_novalue></html_novalue>
      <display></display>
   </existing_details>
   <new_outputs id='n0'>
      <label></label>
      <html_label></html_label>
      <new_value></new_value>
      <html_value></html_value>
      <html_novalue></html_novalue>
   </new_outputs>
   <quotes_expiry></quotes_expiry>
</quotes_details>;
```

Source: Rai (2001)

In particular, the Life and Annuity Standards are built on the basis of the life insurance data model (OLifE) that was originally developed for data exchange between agents' desktop computing environments and is naturally regarded as a framework for information exchange between applications in a company. OLifE is no longer supported by ACORD since the release of Life and Annuity Standards version 2.6.

The Life and Annuity Standards consist of four levels of guidance. The following describes these levels, starting from the lowest level:

1. *XTbML*: A tabular data model that handles information that is tabular in nature, such as lists and multi-dimensional tables (such as mortality rates and cash value tables).
2. *XMLife*: The object model and data dictionary specific to life insurance business, probably written in JavaBeans.
3. *TXLife*: A framework for defining messages used in business processes in the life insurance industry.
4. *Implementation guides*: These define the standardised workflow and messages.

Interested parties may download specifications and templates from the ACORD website *www.acord.org*.

ACORD XML specifications define vocabulary and line-of-business-specific DTDs and schemas for information exchanges in those businesses, but they have the flexibility to work with the Service Provider eXtensions (SPX) standard, which allows an individual carrier to define and maintain its own unique insurance policy and claims application data requirement. The integration between XML and SPX is done by an application known as XML Manager, which contains a set of business rule templates to help validate data exchange between other applications, such as underwriting and accounting.

The ACORD standards have, however, been accused of having a steep learning curve. The versions keep on changing and the insurance industry lacks sufficient expertise. In May 2001, ACORD announced that its new project, eMerge, would integrate all of its XML standards for insurance into a single global insurance business message specification.

ACORD standards have been accepted by most insurance solutions providers. For example, IBM helps ACORD members adopt ACORD standards in their IBM solution model called 'Insurance Application Architecture'.

IBM's insurance application architecture

IBM studied the requirements of 40 insurance companies worldwide and proposed its own version of a business blueprint called Insurance Application Architecture (IAA) in 1992. Since then, it has been accepted as a reference model for the development of insurance applications and enterprise management solutions.

Using standardisation and communication as the key drivers, the IAA aims to streamline and integrate the ICT applications better in an insurance firm. There are five purposes underlying IAA (IBM, 2004b):

- *Business process analysis*: The architecture provides more than 100 standard processes that can be selected as 'to-be' processes in modelling or re-engineering. These processes focus on the scenarios of acquiring a customer, administering an insurance agreement, managing a claim and developing a product.
- *Application portfolio rationalisation and component-based development*: The functionality of the current system is studied and rationalised by using the service concept (SOA, see Chapter 2). Services identified are coupled into components when the 'to-be' functionality is defined (recall services and components in Chapter 2). The result is a business component blueprint (BCB) which describes business components at both the business level (i.e. business model) and the design level (i.e. interface design model).
- *Integration*: To integrate applications in the model, IAA defines XML messaging standards to interface the components. It also provides data mapping of the ACORD life and P&C XML standards. It is also possible to use the WebSphere Business Integration Interchange Server for integration purpose.
- *Product flexibility*: IAA includes a product modelling guide and product specification diagrams to help develop new insurance products.
- *Data rationalisation and data warehousing*: By normalising customer-related data in a data warehouse (an information insurance warehouse, IIW) and moving business and product rules away from policy administration processes (externalisation of business rules), IAA defines a business model that is customer-centric and facilitates re-use of product components. Based on the IIW, a client information integration solution (CIIS) is constructed to provide operational data store and data services to all other applications.

Figure 5.5 The big picture of insurance application architecture models

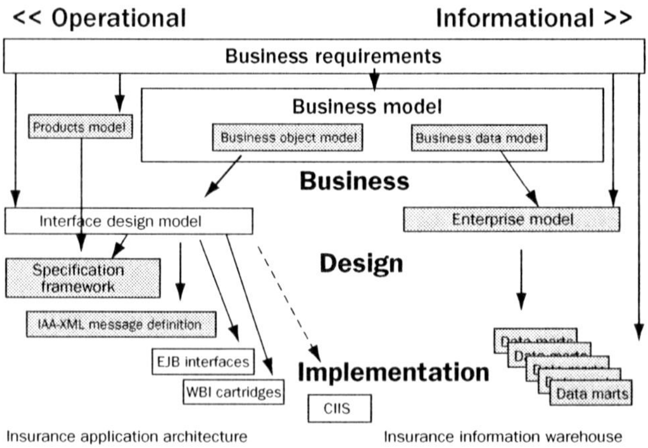

CIIS: client information integration solution; EJB: enterprise JavaBean; IAA: insurance application architecture; WBI: WebSphere business integration

Source: IBM (2004b)

The IAA is a suite of models for the industry. These are: requirement model, business model, product model, design model (of components, interfaces and messages), a generic design framework (for product definition and agreement administration), design models (for the creation of data warehouses) and generation capabilities for XML (DTDs and XML schemas) and EJB component interfaces. Open standards, such as XML and EJB are used to integrate these components. The architecture is shown in Figure 5.5.

Microsoft insurance value chain

Microsoft views the insurance market being made up of an insurance value chain. The software giant allies itself with quite a number of software and hardware vendors to form the so-called Microsoft Insurance Value Chain. Products from the members in the alliance are developed in compliance with open standards, such as ACORD XML and .NET technology. Insurance companies installing these products should have less of a problem in integrating their business processes and offering end-to-end solutions from product sales to claims settlement.

To enhance integration through ACORD XML, Microsoft released the Microsoft Office Solution Accelerator for Insurance Forms in 2004. The package is a collection of software components and templates and can be used to develop a solution to allow products from the members in its value chain – whether they are concerned with rating, agency, or administration – to prepare XML web services-enabled forms from the Microsoft Office environment.

For example, DSPA Software is one of the members in Microsoft's value chain. It created a field administration support and tracking (FASAT) system for the management of distribution and sales compensation for the life insurance industry. Applications in the FASAT solution are divided into four divisions (DSPA, year unknown):

- *Policy administration systems*: Batch or real-time bi-directional feeds supported by ACORD forms.
- *Distribution channels*: E-commission statements and payments, event notification, licence renewals, production summaries, pending new business and commission feed.
- *Corporate systems*: General ledger, corporate disbursements, payroll, tax and document management.
- *Head office*: Producer contracting, compensation rules, compensation management, compliance, online adjustments, *ad hoc* payments, debt management and *ad hoc* queries.

It has been installed in major insurance companies, such as AmerUs Group, Manulife Financial, RBC Insurance and Sun Life Financial (Microsoft, 2004).

Large software vendors, such as IBM and Microsoft wish to provide a comprehensive solution to the insurance industry. Smaller vendors have to ally or compete with them by perfecting their own software products, which are usually targeted to solve problems in specific areas. In the following section, solutions to these specific areas are examined as individual applications of the enterprise e-insurance systems.

E-insurance applications

The Internet may not be able to generate sufficient revenues to draw insurers to the e-insurance business, but it can still demonstrate to the industry how newly designed software applications take advantage of Internet technology. These applications are deployed for the core business processes of the industry. Mostly compliant to ACORD standards, they can communicate with each other freely to construct a straight-through process.

There is a wide spectrum of applications related to e-insurance. For example, as a Web presence may enhance the image and brand name of a corporation, many insurers do not hesitate to build their websites. Even now, because many of these websites are just portals to information about the firms and products, they require a content management system to maintain the flexibility and scalability of the websites so that new products and services may be implemented online easily.

Including the content management system, these applications are designed by using component-oriented methodology and deploy web services extensively. Not only do web services shorten development time and enhance reusability, they also provide an easy connection to legacy systems. As many insurance companies choose to invest in ICT one application at a time, the web service-oriented design guarantees easy integration between applications. Besides, web services remain current with industry transaction standards; they are compatible with the ACORD, .NET and J2EE standards.

Many of these applications reside on a multi-tier server like those mentioned in Chapter 2. Functionally speaking, applications installed on an insurance company's server would include those for security and interfacing, workflow and decision support and applications specialised in the insurance business. An example of high-level component architectures is shown in Figure 5.6. Notice that three core business

Figure 5.6 High-level insurance component architecture

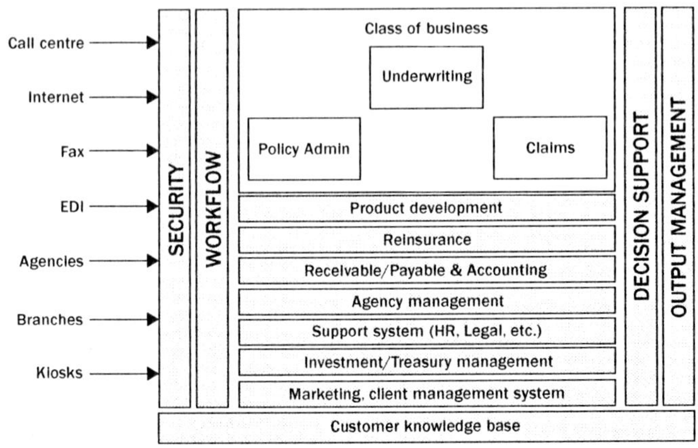

EDI: electronic data interchange

Source: Somasundaram and Eappen (2002)

processes lie at the highest position in the hierarchy. They are supported functionally by the business processes below.

Recall that those three core business processes also appear in the insurance value chain as depicted in Figure 5.1. To illustrate how software vendors respond to the special requirements of the insurance sector, this section examines those in the value chain that are particularly designed to support the major value-added business processes in the industry. They are:

- channel management;
- actuarial services;
- underwriting, including risk management;
- policy administration;
- claims processing.

Channel management

Channel management applications of the insurance industry are used to keep track of the sales volume by sales channels, which include captive and independent agents, direct-sale call centres and the Internet. New breeds of insurance products can even be sold through banks, brokerage houses, auto dealers or funeral homes. For example, CSC's 3r Evolution is claimed to be a customer contact management system that integrates multi-channel access to the customers via contact centres, branches, remote agents, mobile devices and self-service using the Internet or interactive television. It allows its storage of customer data to be shared by all channels so that every channel, when queried, is able to identify a customer with all their transaction history.

Moreover, a channel management system is incorporated into compensation calculation. Keeping records in a database, a channel or distribution management system can calculate agent and broker compensations, bonuses and overrides, evaluate sales campaigns and appraise the performance of an individual agent or a channel. An example is the aforementioned FASAT system, installed by Toronto-based Prudential Financial, which is able to calculate compensation at 'almost "compensation-on-demand" basis', said Doug Powers, Manulife's Assistant Vice President of Distribution Systems (O'Donnell, 2003).

Channel or distribution management may mean more to other vendors. For example, Oracle e-Business Solutions for Insurance regards

Figure 5.7 Oracle's e-distribution architecture

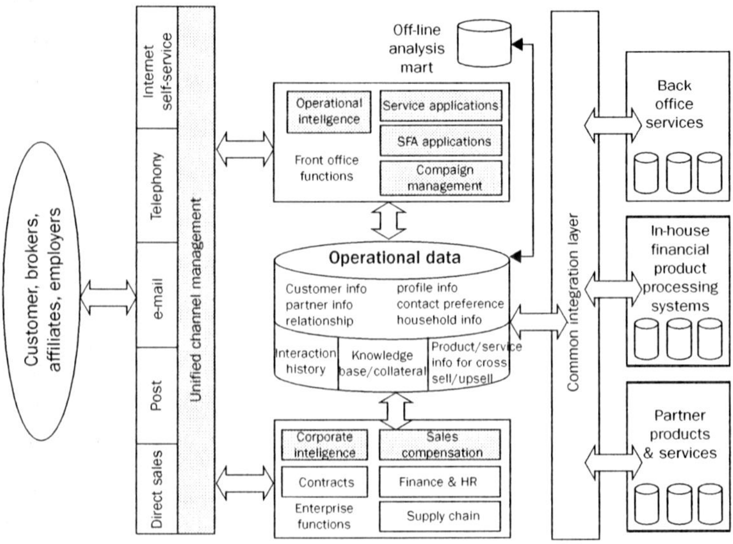

SFA: sales force automation

Source: Oracle (2002b)

sales, marketing and business intelligence as features in its e-distribution solution. With its advantage in database management, Oracle builds an information hub to connect all the stakeholders (customers, employers, suppliers, brokers and affiliates). A unified channel management application is an interface between the hub and the stakeholders (see Figure 5.7)

To improve sales and marketing, channel management tools are also incorporated with a business intelligence or customer relationship management (CRM) system to help insurers identify the best channels (places) and the best ways to reach their customers. Channel management is the beginning of the sales effort. It could also include functions, such as sales force deployment, agent development and channel analysis. While dealing with the Internet, channel management may oversee site navigation and referrer analysis that contribute to the improvement of the e-channel. Information collected in this process can be integrated with applications for other business processes, such as online underwriting systems, business rules engines, or even legacy systems, to achieve vertical integration.

Actuarial services

To establish an insurance product, the insurance company needs to estimate how much it is expected to pay in case of claims. This is the actuarial computation that looks up probability tables to find the likelihood that a potential future event will occur, determines whether the premium charged for such insurance can cover the claims and management expenses, and determines the amount of reserves that should be set aside. In the case of life insurance, actuaries could often deliver long-term health and annuity policies for the insured, wherein returns from investment tools are also considered.

The competitiveness of an insurer depends on how it manages the risks of its customers by pooling large groups of individuals who seek protection against similar risks. In the process of managing and pricing risks of the company, the actuary plays a central role. The art of the actuary is the application of statistics. The insurance market is now offering individualised products, each of which requires careful actuarial analysis before underwriting.

The actuarial process begins by building a mathematical model from available data, such as claims history, demographic data of the insured and mortality rates. The model needs to be verified and updated from time to time and various actuarial tools can be applied. In cases where quantitative methods cannot produce satisfactory results, knowledge of the coverage and experience in matters related to the frequency and severity of claims are necessary to give an educated guess of the profitability of an insurance product.

Tools that accompany an actuarial application include the following functionalities (Popelyukhin, 2001):

- *Adaptive reporting*: Unlike traditional static reporting, which has predefined content and layout, adaptive or dynamic reporting provides an interactive environment (e.g. a spreadsheet) that allows users to shape the report to the level of detail desired. Using this technique, an actuary needs to choose which measurements are of actuarial significance, so that tools (e.g. for filtering, outlining, sorting, formatting and OLAP) can be applied to highlight important issues.
- *Visualisation*: This is a collection of techniques that can be used to explore the meaning of data by transforming and viewing data as images (e.g. charts) and/or animation.

- *Alarm systems*: Algorithms to trigger an actuarial alarm when some predetermined (combination of) circumstances occur.

However, most software applications available in the market (including the renowned TAS Tillinghast's Actuarial Software, and SS&C's (Nasdaq: SSNC) PTS and AnalyticsExpress) have the first two functionalities while alarm systems are found mostly in proprietary applications.

Moving an insurance business to the Internet creates some potentially difficult problems for the actuarial department. It has not been a major problem yet because most products presently sold on the Web are simple and do not require instant actuarial work. If customers demand dynamic products on the Web in the future, an actuary can no longer rely on past calculation but will have to estimate risk on a case-by-case basis. In that case, sensitivity testing and statistical analysis are used extensively and the estimation requires periodic checking and adjustments.

Underwriting

Efficiency in underwriting is usually how customers and agents perceive an insurance carrier. It is important to customers who submit applications because the longer they have to wait for the process, the more likely they are to switch to another carrier. It is also crucial to share underwriting tasks with agents, who can be more productive and profitable if they are able to screen policy applications (Craig, 2004).

The underwriting process is a consideration of risk and profitability of an application. Upon the entry of an application, the underwriting process needs to validate the data submitted, to assess risk (probably by looking up the actuarial tables), to predict potential customers' propensity to make a claim (in P&C cases) and to make a final decision (to approve, decline, or conditionally approve – which is usually granted on the basis of receipt of favourable lab results or other information). The process may involve interviewing an applicant several times and sometimes making referrals to other information sources, such as the Medical Information Bureau (MIB). A Web-based underwriting application could obviously alleviate the problem of data exchange between the various parties involved.

An automated underwriting system (AUS) is usually a rule-based (or knowledge-based) system. It could be incorporated into a business intelligence system with a data warehouse to enable rapid decision making. For example, when the Michigan-based insurance underwriter

Auto Club Group implemented its AUS, the underwriter created more than 3,000 business rules to drive decision processes for home and motor underwriting. (Koscielny, 2005). The process can be done so quickly (in near real-time, in general cases) that vendors call their automated underwriting applications 'jet issue'.

Rules-based underwriting system

Rule-based underwriting emerged when insurers and agents felt the need to reduce travel expense and time. The revolution began as tele-interviewing (in fact, it is tele-underwriting), which gets information directly from the applicant through the telephone by trained personnel. Currently, large insurers in the UK and the USA deploy rules-based systems at their point of sale to help agents collect information from the applicants in general. More complex cases are still referred to the back office for senior underwriters to determine (SelectX, 2004).

Rules-based underwriting systems were first developed for 'jet issuing' simpler products, such as life insurance policies that have lower face amounts and require no medicals. With the success of these systems, insurers are now studying ways to enhance the rules base so that the systems can be applied to term products of higher face amounts as well as whole life products (Gordon and Setteducati, 2004). For example, if the system is interfaced with authorities, such as the MIB, medical records of the applicants can be made accessible to the insurer so that referrals can be automated.

Lying at the centre of a rule-based AUS is a rule inference engine (Figure 5.8), which is a software application that checks the relevant

Figure 5.8 A rule-based underwriting system

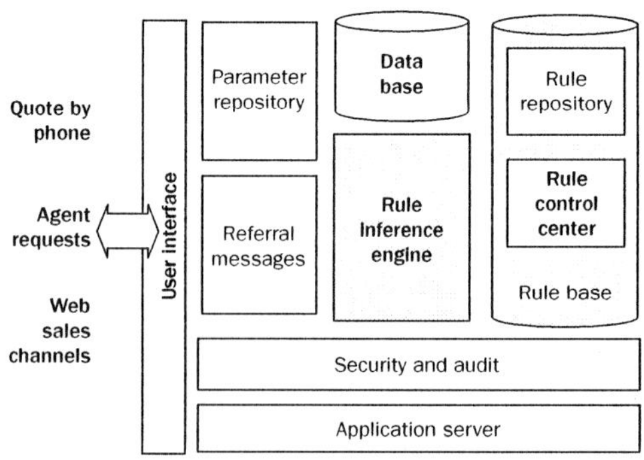

logical rules selected from a rule repository. These underwriting rules are normally implemented as binary propositions[5] that help in reviewing an insurance application. The case of Hibernian below reflects the difficulty a company may encounter when those rules are determined.

Case: Hibernian (Al-Attar, 2002)

Hibernian Group is a life insurer in Ireland. To enhance its strategic advantages, the company implemented a rule-based underwriting system to automate the process of life proposals at the point of application. The system was able to capture underwriting knowledge and handle 51 per cent of the underwriting applications whereas the remaining cases were left for manual processing.

Hibernian was not satisfied with the percentage of automated underwriting but capturing further advanced underwriting rules was very difficult. The company turned to data mining, which found out – of the cases being processed manually – that a significant number of them were underwritten with no or a very small additional premium. The additional premium was far less than the cost of the manual underwriting.

The company decided to apply rule induction analysis to cases being processed manually, using the amount of additional underwriting premium as an outcome. The analysis generated a general pattern of the following format:

> If AGE > 30 & AGE < 41 and HEIGHT – WEIGHT = NORMAL
> then PREMIUM LOADING = 1%

The rule was checked for risk by the actuaries at Hibernian before being added to the rule base. It has since successfully increased the rate of automated underwriting to 78 per cent.

Risk management

According to the Casualty Actuarial Society, risks of an insurance company can be categorised as follows (D'Arcy, 2001):

- *Operational risk*: This includes the largest types of risks. Roughly speaking, it is the office work risk that is related to negligence or misconduct on the part of employees and managers and system risk that is associated with computer stoppages or malfunctioning. Further division could distinguish the underwriting risk, which is the risk stemming from the fluctuation of economic conditions and/or loss incurred from the project made at the time the premium amount was decided. However, underwriting risk may be affected by risks in the other categories, such as catastrophic disaster risk and reinsurance risk. This category also includes *compliance risk*, which is related to laws and regulations and reputation risk that damages the company's image because of some operational failures. Auditing is believed to be a means to control operational risk.

- *Financial risk*:[6] This can further be divided into *investment* risk and *asset management* risk. The former is associated with external economic factors, such as *market* risk (e.g. equity, interest rates and foreign exchange rates), *credit* risk and *asset/liability management* risk. It also includes *liquidity* risk that arises in a cash flow shortage due to a sudden unexpected drain on capital, or on market turmoil. Liquidity risk impacts directly on reserves for claims. Asset management risk refers to risk of loss arising from fluctuations in the value of assets the company is holding and failure to properly take into account the characteristics of liabilities in its asset management (Fuji, 2004). If these risks are subject to market changes, they could be hedged. In this book, Chapter 10 is dedicated to financial risk management.
- *Strategic risk*: This arises from changes in the market, such as the strategy of competitors, mergers and acquisition, customers' demography and their demands and regulatory or political impediments (such as Basel II).
- *Hazard risk*: This refers to events happening to property (e.g. theft, fire), liability (lawsuits), the environment (pollution), natural disasters (e.g. earthquakes, tsunamis) and political environment (e.g. war, terrorism). Recently, catastrophic disaster risk is a hot topic.

The general principle of risk management is to identify the risks first, to assess and optimise them as a perception of opportunities and to communicate the risks to operational management so that proper measures can be used to avoid, minimise, or transfer risks. Figure 5.9 illustrates the general steps in risk management that lead to the implementation of an enterprise risk management (ERM) solution, which is made up of the financial and organisational solutions.

Risk management is largely a management issue and ICT has contributed only to a few areas, such as financial risk and hazard risk. This could be explained by the fact that analysis and quantification of

Figure 5.9 Enterprise-wide risk management workflow

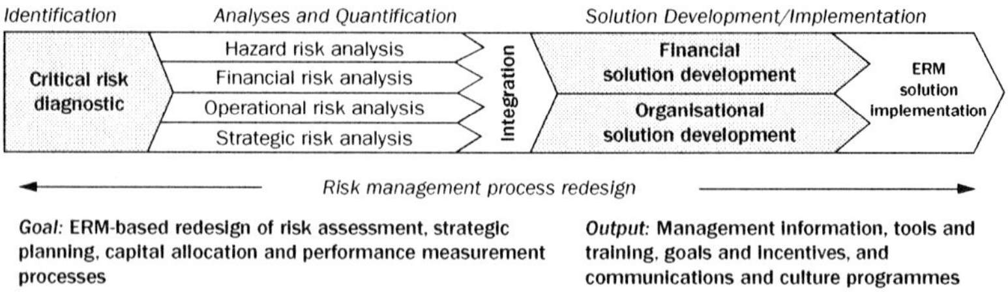

Source: Darlington et al. (2001)

risk are not always possible, as many risks are conceptual in nature and there could never be sufficient data to apply statistical analysis. Even though operational and financial risks are relatively easily quantifiable, their analysis is biased by the tools and metrics by which they are measured. For example, a metric traditionally used is called 'probable maximum loss', which is a measure of the largest loss that is expected to occur. If the probable maximum loss is found to exceed a predefined value, the insurer needs to consider transferring the risk. However, researchers propose a new measure known as 'value-at-risk' (VaR), which represents the loss that a firm expects to occur once over a selected time period. As VaR is believed to be able to provide a more timely view of the risk exposure of the insurer, its management needs to understand both measures.

This explains the composition of the 'ERM solution' in Figure 5.9. Even if ICT is applied to ERM, it would only be effective to help manage the quantifiable risk in the financial and operational categories. The organisational solution is implemented as workflows, procedures and regulations, which means human judgment and decision making is essential in ERM. Thus, risk management is sometimes known as the 'art of risk management'. Further discussion on VaR and ERM is found in Chapter 10.

Operational risk management

Operational risk can be reduced by strict management rules and regulation and auditing procedures. Traditionally, insurers determine the price of insurance products by using conservative static assumptions regarding loss distributions and interest rates. But these classic methods have not been able to price and manage actuarial risks since the 1980s, when interest rates became volatile. To avoid underwriting risk, modern insurers might use specially designed software packages (e.g. SS&C's PTS and Tillinghast's TAS) to estimate the values of insurance policies. Common techniques for pricing include stochastic valuation and simulation.

To avoid the so-called Nick Leeson Syndrome,[7] senior management needs to check constantly over activities in the company. For example, underwriting information can be made available to senior management at all times and a software system can be deployed to give warnings at threshold values.

With new laws and regulations (such as the US Sarbanes-Oxley Act and European Data Privacy Directive) becoming effective one after another, the insurance industry is aware of its compliance risk, which could incur costly penalties if insuring companies fail to comply. To reduce compliance risk, some insurers might also include the following initiatives in their risk management strategy:

- *Compliance with legislation*: such as Sarbanes-Oxley, Basel II, Health Insurance Portability and Accountability Act (HIPAA) and regulations issued by CMS (Centers for Medicare & Medicaid Services).
- *Anti-fraud and anti-money laundering initiatives*: to set business rules and fraud detection filters to check suspicious activities around insurance underwriting and claims.
- *Content management*: including data consolidation, versioning, categorisation, archival and disaster recovery management.
- *Workflow management*: controlling the right person and/or procedures to complete the steps necessary to process information, document internal controls and provide audit trails.

The last two initiatives are crucial to compliance risk because unchecked content and workflow management is believed to be the root cause of non-compliance. Further discussion on regulatory compliance and compliance risk can be found in Chapter 9.

Reinsurance management

There are two kinds of reinsurance: facultative and treaty. The former is arranged on a case-by-case basis while the latter is a longer-term contract that is effected to cover the whole or a certain section of the ceding company's business without the reinsurer receiving details of each individual risk reinsured.

When negotiating with a reinsurer, the cedent may opt for proportional or non-proportional sharing of business with the reinsurer. However, the reinsurer would like to bind a contract such that it can have enough liquidity and the cedent can survive in case of major events occurring. The process of negotiating reinsurance thus requires complex and specialised information/knowledge of the risk and all parties involved. Those involved in a treaty reinsurance contract should also consider the dynamic environment in which the knowledge about risk and the financial condition of each party are continuously changing. A Web-based reinsurance management platform is an ideal place where insurers, reinsurers, brokers and the like can exchange information and manage the reinsurance negotiation process.

In a nutshell, ICT is applied to reinsurance management in processes, such as:

- *Document management*: Document scanning, storage and retrieval of complete underwriting files (probably using XML).
- *Case management*: Review and submit underwriting case file to reinsurers and management of case distribution.
- *Communication management*: To reinsurers, applying ACORD message standards.

Famous vendors of reinsurance management systems include eReinsure and ri3k.

Case: ri3k

The London-based ri3k Ltd. is famous in the treaty reinsurance market. Its product, ri3k, is a hub platform that provides three key services (Ironside, 2003):

- a framework for the administration for all classes of treaty and facultative contracts through one electronic channel;
- automation of premium and claims payment;
- connection between applications and data using ACORD XML.

The hub allows information exchange between cedents, brokers and reinsurers in XML. It helps reinsurance contract negotiation, underwriting, settlement and accounting.

In order to integrate with each party's back-office legacy systems, the hub is constructed using the Simple Object Access Protocol (SOAP)

Figure 5.10 ri3k workflow management system

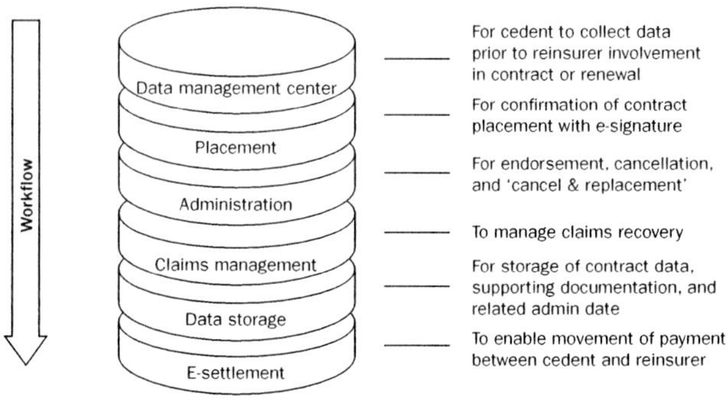

Source: ri3k (year unknown)

standard. In 2004, version 2.2 of ri3k incorporated a workflow management system with its contract management system to streamline processes, as illustrated in Figure 5.10. It also builds in a dataflow system to route data between users' systems in ACORD format.

Catastrophe risk securitisation

Several financial products are related to catastrophe risk, among which catastrophe bonds (CAT bonds), CAT swaps and CATEPut are discussed below.

CAT bonds are risk transfer instruments that offer insurers the ability to hedge risk of a catastrophic scale through the capital market. Since their first appearance after Hurricane Andrew (which caused $15.5 billion of loss by devastating coastal Florida) in 1992, CAT bonds have become more popular in areas that are subject to natural disasters (e.g. earthquakes, hurricanes) and attract the insurance industry as an alternative source of funding for P&C reinsurance. Although the CAT bond market remains small (less than $1 billion each year), it is expected to grow as more and more new perils or new structures are recognised.

Figure 5.11 depicts a common structure that brings catastrophe reinsurers and investors in the capital market together. As a special

Figure 5.11 Catastrophe bond model

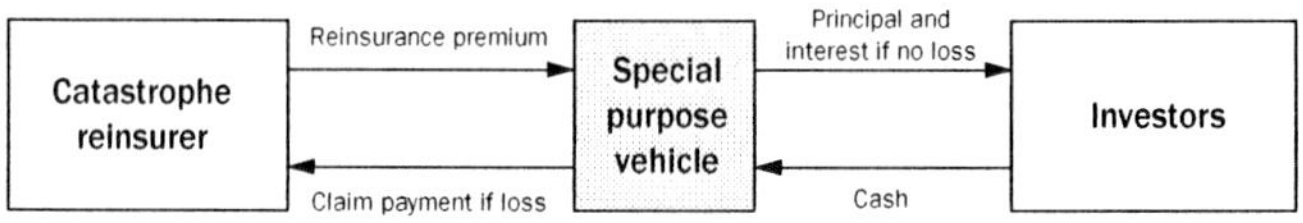

Figure 5.12 A catastrophe model

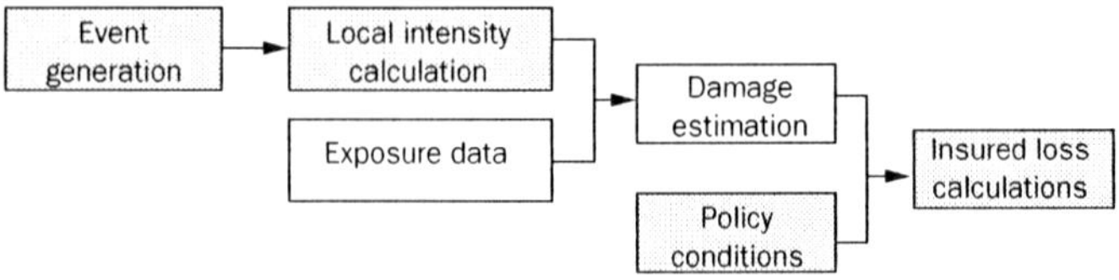

Source: American Academy of Actuaries (2001)

purpose vehicle, the CAT bond is designed to cover a considerable amount of loss if the event occurs. All known factors related to the catastrophe are used to build a catastrophe model (Figure 5.12) to give an educated guess on loss cost at each location, distribution of occurrence and aggregate loss. The size of the CAT bond is determined by a catastrophe index (e.g. Guy Carpenter Catastrophe Index, GCCI)[8] if it can be provided by a rating agency. The compensation amount is calculated by referring to the aggregate loss index or some physical attributes of the event (e.g. distance from the epicentre of an earthquake or the path of a typhoon).

A catastrophe swap, however, is a bilateral agreement, creating reciprocal reinsurance between two insuring companies. For example, an insurance company in Miami can arrange a CAT swap with its counterparty in Kagoshima, trading hurricane risk on the American coast with typhoon risk in Japan. Several markets have been established for this kind of trading.

The Catastrophe Risk Exchange International, Inc. established in 1994 provides Web-based trading and back-office services for the trading of CAT swaps as well as treaty and facultative reinsurance, but the most significant service is its CATEX Trading System which became operational in 1996. Eighty-two of the world's largest reinsurance companies had become CATEX subscribers by 1999 (Cooley et al., 2000). They can get access to real-time indexes and post risks for swapping or requests for reinsurance coverage on the platform. CATEX has found a market niche in the e-commerce era but the industry could not generate enough CAT swap transactions to sustain CATEX, which later evolved to trade other risk products, such as aviation, politics, weather and credit risks.

The catastrophe equity put (CATEPut or CEPut) is an option contract that allows the insurer to sell a predefined number of shares to its counterparty for a fixed price if and after the catastrophe occurs (often the magnitude of the incident is also taken into account). The arrangement mitigates the insurer's burden of lack of equity when it suffers from a catastrophic loss. By selling its shares, the insurer can stand a better chance of maintaining its ratings and continuing its business so that it can recover from the loss.

Policy administration

Often integrated with an underwriting application and/or claims processing application, the policy administration process can offer a comprehensive administrative solution to an insurance company. It could be the core of the entire business of an insurer. If separated from underwriting and claims processing, policy administration is the collection of activities including issuance of new policies, renewals, commission processing, agency licensing, billing and collection, records management and accounting. For a company offering insurance services on the Web, its policy administration system (PAS) may allow web access to policy and policyholder information, while underwriting and policy renewal can both be completed online.

Case: Allstate (Microsoft, 2003b)

Allstate is the largest publicly held personal lines insurer in the USA. Its wide range of insurance products are sold through a group of third parties (sales representatives), who may be exclusive and non-exclusive agents – the latter include banks and securities firms, which are collectively called 'producers'.

As the producers can choose to sell products from other institutions, Allstate feels the need to service them better in order to increase its market share. The management launched a producer connectivity initiative to build a Web-based solution that integrates five policy management systems (Figure 5.13). The solution is extensible in the sense that it can eventually be integrated with systems of the large producers, such as banks and brokerage houses.

The solution is built using Microsoft Visual Studio .NET development system. The integration layer runs J2EE servlets on an IBM WebSphere server, which is exposed for access through the policy management systems by a XML-based interface.

The Web-based interface enables producers to access the policy management systems and allows them to drill down into the database residing in Allstate's host systems. Many transactions against the host systems can be done in real-time. The solution has attracted about 500,000 hits per day and has greatly reduced expenditure on both the call centre and mailing.

Figure 5.13 Allstate's producer connectivity platform

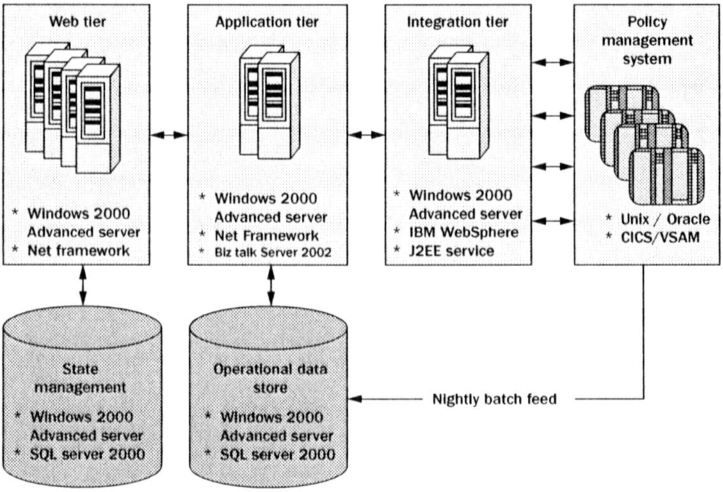

Source: Microsoft (2003b)

Claims management

Claims management is one of the core operations in the insurance business. Traditionally there is a long time-lag between filing and settlement, and it happens while the claimants are suffering some loss. It is also a key performance indicator of the company and any effort to shorten the time-lag should add to its strategic advantage.

However, using technology in claims management is not simple. It is difficult to standardise claims settlements as they often require rigorous information gathering, investigations and a lot of decision making. A typical process is depicted in Figure 5.14. Its complexity requires careful re-engineering – by using business process re-engineering[9] or workflow analysis – before trying to speed it up with automation.

The strategy consultancy Celent proposes a claims processing model as shown in Figure 5.15. Lying in the core layer of the model is the transaction processing system that handles the entire lifecycle of each claim, together with interfaces with other internal and external applications (Light, 2004).

The core solution is supported by applications in the inner ring, which includes content management component, business process (workflow) management component and business rules engine. Tools for claims processing in the outer ring of the model include the following:

Figure 5.14 Conventional claims processing

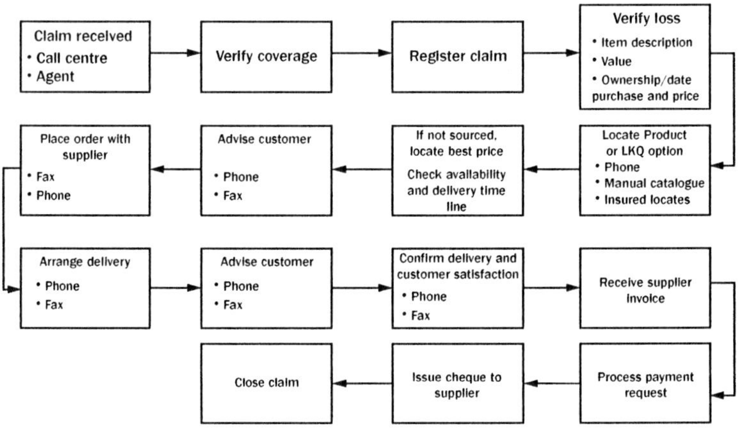

Source: EIU (2001)

- *Estimator tools*: To allow adjusters to identify the property damage or bodily injury costs of a claim.
- *Litigation management tools*: To provide litigation planning and financial management functionality, such as bill review, modelling alternative fee arrangements, budget and case phrase planning.
- *Analytics/fraud detection tools*: To analyse claims activities and to detect fraudulent claims.

Oracle's claims processing system – Claims for General Insurance – is designed for both B2C and B2B markets. The system is prepared to interface with individual claimants as well as corporate clients. Taking claims handling as a key area of interaction with the claimants, Oracle

Figure 5.15 Celent's three-ring model of claims technology

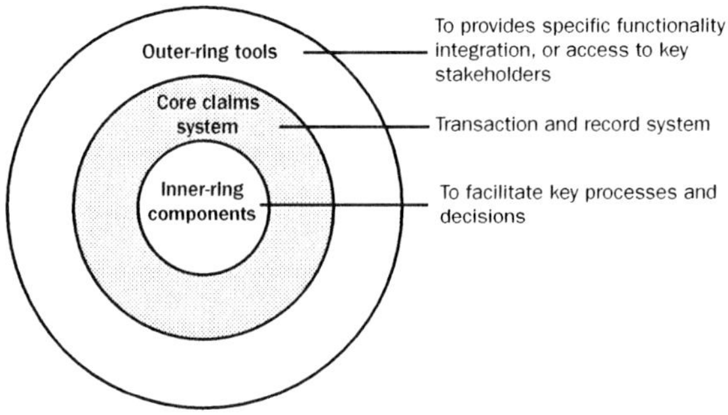

decided that communication is crucial in claims management and established a message hub inside its solution. Its aims are to provide (Oracle, 2002a):

- improved visibility of the claims process;
- faster and more convenient communication; and
- focus on problem resolution, not just cash.

Claims for General Insurance is built with standard Oracle e-Business Suite components. There are three major modules in the system: claims contact centre, claims supply chain management and claims intelligence (Figure 5.16). These are responsible for the interfacing, processing and back-office analytical information of claims.

Notice that the claims supply chain management module provides an environment in which all claims settlement activities are handled. While claims processing is just one of its functions, the module actually caters for the management of the corporate contract lifecycle, from contract negotiation, internal compliance, to supplier service delivery.

The claims processing system is also integrated with health plans that are installed, say, in hospitals or clinics to provide straight-through

Figure 5.16 Oracle claims for general insurance

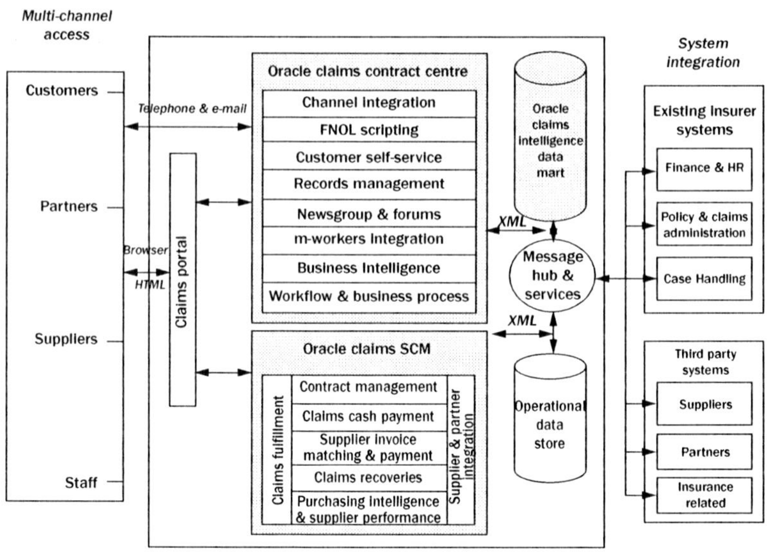

Source: Amalgamation of several diagrams from Oracle (2002a)

processing for patients. Hard copy receipts can be scanned to produce images that can be entered into the claims processing system, which then proceeds to analyse and adjudicate the claims.

Summary

This chapter has taken a top-down approach to explain the present e-insurance marketspace. Although relatively few insurance transactions are completed online today, the industry believes that expanding insurance business to the Internet is a sensible move to strengthen an insurer's competitiveness, whether its business is property and casualty insurance, life insurance, or reinsurance.

To nurture the e-insurance business, large software vendors have joined hands with international standards organisations to promote message standards and their specialised solutions or architecture. The second section of the chapter described ACORD XML standards, which form the basis of rapid message exchange, system integration, interoperability and insurance value/supply chain. It is also adopted in vendors' solutions, including IBM's Insurance Application Architecture and Microsoft's Insurance Value Chain.

The ICT applications deployed in the insurance business were detailed in the last section. Prior to the description on those core functions of underwriting, policy administration and claims processing in the conventional insurance business, the importance of channel management was discussed. The section also examined risk management as one of the tasks in underwriting, although the subject will be brought up once again in Chapter 9, which is dedicated to risk management. The impact of the Sarbanes-Oxley Act was also examined, as compliance risk is serious in the insurance sector.

Questions for discussion

1. The insurance value chain shown in Figure 5.1 is different from Porter's value chain for a general business (Figure 5.17). How would you compare the two and position those activities absent from Figure 5.1 in an insurance company?
2. What would be the impact of e-insurance business on actuarial work?

Figure 5.17 One common illustration of Porter's value chain

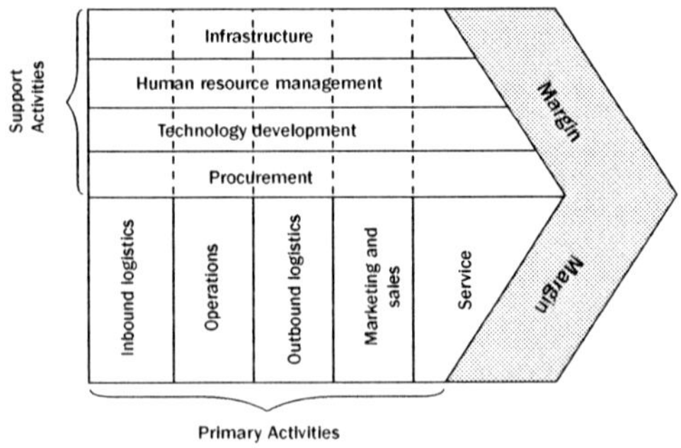

Notes

1. The term 'marketspace' was popularised by Rayport and Sviokla in their 1994 article 'Managing in the marketspace' in *Harvard Business Review*. It refers to the virtual context in which buyers and sellers discover one another and transact business (Clarke, 1997).
2. Life insurance products can further divide into life insurance, health insurance and annuity products.
3. Catastrophe bonds (or CAT bonds) are instruments to protect the insurer from losses from a catastrophe that occurs very rarely (say, less than 3 per cent of the time). Its net effect on the investor is the rate of return times face value, after deducting a part of the face value should a disaster happen.
4. A captive agent is one who works on an exclusive contract with one company.
5. A binary proposition is one which can only be true or false, if the arguments are known.
6. However, in some researchers' definition, financial risks include actuarial and systematic risks besides credit and liquidity risks (Babbel and Santomero, 1996).
7. It refers to the case in which junior underwriters put together loss-making books of business that senior management was not aware of until it was too late.
8. GCCI reports real paid claims. It measures the losses paid by 39 insurance companies for weather damages. The index is updated every three months.
9. Business process re-engineering is a methodology in which an organisation fundamentally and radically redesigns its business processes to achieve dramatic improvement.

6

E-stock trading

Online stockbrokers

'Disintermediation' does not eliminate the intermediaries from stock markets. In the last few decades, those in the intermediation business have been confronted with one crisis after another. We have seen the role of traditional brokers and dealers who connect retail and institutional buyers and sellers in the USA gradually being taken over by alternative trading systems (ATSs) and electronic communications networks (ECNs). But the force of disintermediation does not wipe out the entire population of brokers. Those that remain understand they are serving a new marketplace and a group of new customers, who are getting used to the Internet and all the advantages of e-business. The brokers and dealers in the new century have changed their strategies in ICT applications. Software systems for online brokerage and direct-access trading have become necessities rather than luxuries as the intermediaries know they should enhance and extend their services to niches where ICT can make a big difference.

Since Charles Schwab moved into its Web business in 1997, a profusion of online brokers have emerged to compete on this new frontier, each trying to attract customers by lowering the commission rates and offering enhanced services, such as free online financial information. By now, practically all large brokers have a foot in the e-stock trading business. A Sigma report[1] (2000) even suggests it was the stockbrokers who led the financial services sector to use the Internet.

Having studied the e-brokerage market in the 1990s, Singh (2001: Chapter 20) observes that:

- Companies, having invested in reliable technology and service, are able to stay ahead of those who rely simply on low commissions. In particular, they benefit from technology that enables traders to execute an order at the best possible price.

- Online brokers compete in terms of the information that they provide – with better research and analysis, and detailed, up-to-the-minute quotes.
- They also compete in terms of the range of services offered, such as trading in mutual funds and bonds, cheque writing, access to IPOs and account insurance.

Their competition did not stop even when the bull market ended towards 2000 and when trading (both by online and traditional means) decreased dramatically. According to a survey by Rockbridge Associates (2004), only 10 per cent of adults who surf on the Web trade securities online, compared with 8 per cent in 2000. Similar findings are confirmed in other parts of the world.[2] Even though the figures of e-stock trading are not particularly exciting, customers have already become used to low commissions and easy access to information. Once a revenue generator, the e-stock trading environment has now become the customers' minimal expected level of service. Maintaining the service level is a burden in operational expenses, and online trading is no longer as promising as it seemed a few years before.

Stock exchanges of some major markets look at digitisation from a longer perspective. Besides demutualisation, preparing for the next wave of online trading hype is another possible reason to justify their huge investment in ICT. For example, The London Stock Exchange (LSE) has been launching one ICT project after another since its demutualisation, including the following:

- *Stock Exchange Electronic Trading System (SETS)*: Launched in 1997, three years before LSE demutualisation, SETS is an electronic order book for FTSE 100 securities trading.
- *RSP Gateway*: Became operational in 2002, allowing private client brokers to do business with retail service providers on the extranet.
- *London Market Information Link (LMIL)*: Provides real-time market data feeds, and is being upgraded into a newer system called 'Infolect' in 2005.

Similar endeavours to reduce manual operations and to eliminate the physical trading floor are repeated in many exchanges globally.

These are common scenes in stock markets all over the world – extensive applications of ICT and digitisation in stockbrokerage, trading, clearing and settlement. These are the subjects of the discussion below. In the next three sections, the descriptions focus on e-brokerage, innovations in stock exchanges, and ICT developments for clearing and settlement. The chapter ends with a further section that briefly mentions straight-through processing (STP), a goal that proved too ambitious for the industry.

E-brokerage

The era of e-brokerage began when Charles Schwab (NYSE: SCH) and Merrill Lynch (NYSE: MER) offered their Web-based brokerage services in the late 1990s. They allowed customers to place orders directly into their trading systems via the Internet. They demonstrated how their customers enjoyed more full-services at a lower cost. (Previously, a full-service broker charged an order at $100–300 for up to 1,000 shares; but now the same service charges $5–30 if delivered online.)

The establishment of online brokerage coincided with the emergence of day traders in the 1990s. These investors, who purchase and sell the same securities on the same day, require quick transactions and low transaction costs. The rapid increase of trade volume (double-digit growth in 1998) drew more discount brokers into the e-brokerage market. E-brokerage firms are competing with all kinds of strategies, which include the following:

- *Low commission rate*: To attract day traders and other investors alike.
- *Cost reduction*: For example, by offering a flat (and low) fee for each transaction and reducing management cost.
- *Wider range of business*: Offering quotes, trades and even IPOs online.
- *Banking facilities*: For example, by treating customer accounts like regular checking accounts.
- *Personalisation of information*: Chtaneva (2001) observes two common approaches for personalisation. With the 'pull' approach, the customer sets their preferences and the e-broker sends information compiled to suit these preferences. In the 'push' approach, the e-broker application is capable of estimating the customer's preference through earlier contact history so that it may send information so formatted.

Bakhru and Brown (2005) assert that the firms achieving a critical mass of accounts first stand a better chance of surviving. As their total income is determined by trading volumes and the size of clients' investment assets, e-brokers need to have sufficient customer accounts to strike a balance before they can make profit from economies of scale. Reaching critical mass is difficult especially when the number of online traders declined after 2000. This explains why only a small number of online brokers survive in the market – 12 online brokers (including Comdirect and Consors in Germany) account for more than 70 per cent of all European market online accounts (Schuler, 2002) while in the USA, five companies (Charles Schwab, Fidelity, Ameritrade, E*Trade and TD Waterhouse) hold 85 per cent of the market share and are engaging in acquisition battles in 2005.

E-brokerage models

There are few online brokers like E*Trade that operate in a purely online trading mode. As their business strategies differ, there is no reason to assume all e-brokers follow the same business model. Having studied 179 e-brokerage firms, Looney and Chatterjee (2002) identified four business models: three are brick-to-click types and one is click-only. Complexity of the website functionality increases as the models are described below:

- *Inquiry model*: firms in this category treat their websites as an additional channel for their clients to make inquiries for information, while typical brokerage services are still delivered through human contact (either face-to-face or telephone). Their websites are relatively simple in design and inexpensive to develop. Examples are AG Edwards (*www.agedwards.com*), DA Davidson (*www.davidsoncompanies.com*) and Dain Rauscher (*www.rbcdain.com*).
- *Layered model*: At one time, many full-service brokers including Goldman Sachs and Merrill Lynch offered several options to customers, such as traditional full-service, online trading and flexible full-service by Morgan Stanley, where only the last option allowed customers to have a full-service relationship as well as the flexibility to trade online at the same time. The layered model is becoming obsolete as it is gradually being replaced by other methods. For example, the Choice account offered online by Morgan Stanley is actually a full-service of wealth management which charges members on the basis of the assets in their account.
- *Discount model*: Discount brokerage firms develop their websites as an additional channel for trading, and continue to operate their business in their physical offices and/or by telephone. Charles Schwab

and TD Waterhouse are discount e-brokers that have succeeded to draw in large numbers of clients by lower commissions, after-hours trading and offline customer services.

- *(Pure) e-broker model*: Getting no professional advice, investors who trade on a pure e-broker website prefer rapid execution and low commissions. The e-brokers compete on price and their clients expect no telephone support or hard-copy statements. Extreme cases are FreeTrade.com and BrokerageAmerica (both acquired by Ameritrade; the service is now provided via Ameritrade Izone, see case below). They take the no-fee approach and depend on banner advertisements and kickbacks on order placements from market makers for revenue.

Looney and Chatterjee's modelling focuses on the brokerage functionality offered on the websites. However, due to the competition of full-service brokers, enriching websites with more services has become the consensus within the e-brokerage sector, and the demarcation into these four models blurs in recent years. Looney et al. (2004) propose another model, which focuses on two dimensions: pricing and platform deployment.

Figure 6.1 illustrates the four business models of e-brokerage business. The researchers divide all pricing strategies into two categories: standard and stratified. While a standard pricing strategy refers to a uniform pricing scheme applied to all customers, stratified pricing refers to a more complicated scheme that differentiates each customer – probably a lower commission rate is offered to one who trades more often than

Figure 6.1 Price–platform matrix

Platform	Price: Standard	Price: Stratified
Vertical	**Quadrant I** **Basic model** *Characteristics* – Uniform pricing scheme – Vertical platform support	**Quadrant II** **Incentive model** *Characteristics* – Multiple pricing schemes – Vertical platform support
Polymorphic	**Quadrant III** **Preference model** *Characteristics* – Uniform pricing scheme – Multiplatform support	**Quadrant IV** **Elastic model** *Characteristics* – Multiple pricing schemes – Multiplatform support

Source: Looney et al. (2004)

others. Brokers adopting a stratified pricing strategy use ICT to identify individual customers through their transaction history.

On the other dimension, Looney et al. distinguish a vertical platform from a polymorphic one; they refer to whether the trading platform offers a single or multiple configurations of devices, carriers, or networks to satisfy a customer. Implementing a polymorphic platform, a broker wishes to reach out to more customers who would like to follow the technology trend. Maintaining a polymorphic platform is rather expensive for an e-broker. It might be too futuristic to find one in the elastic model, which uses a polymorphic platform to attract customers in different strata.

Case: Ameritrade

Founded in 1971, the forefather of Ameritrade (Nasdaq: AMTD) began as a retail securities brokerage firm offering equity trades to individuals for negotiated commissions. It was the first brokerage firm to implement automated touch-tone telephone trading in 1988, and also the first to develop an Internet trading platform in 1994.

Since 1997, Ameritrade has used a variable pricing approach to promote its online trading services – their customers trade over the Internet for $8, via touch-tone phone for $12, or with a broker's assistance for $18. The strategy was later ascertained as a reason for effectively building and supporting Ameritrade's brand identity (Cornell Equity Research, 1997). Unlike other firms that offer low commissions, Ameritrade does not make a market in any securities and all orders are routed to the market for execution. All trade confirmations and statements are returned by e-mail. The company provides order execution at a low price, but it offers no advice – thus, there is no need to maintain research staff.

In 2005 Ameritrade launched Izone, to which an investor pays $5 – through a bank wire or brokerage transfer – to open an account for stock trading. Keeping at least $5,000 in the account, the investor can trade. Izone charges $5 per trade unless the investor requires assistance from a broker, who would charge several times more.

Technology for e-brokerage

Most Web-based trading systems are constructed in a three-tiered architecture. The upper tier is the front-end application that receives customer orders and delivers trading and/or market information in a secure way. The middleware in the second tier processes the requests (such as orders, quotes, or requests for information) from customers by routing them to relevant software applications. Due to severe competition in the e-brokerage market, the system is normally expected to have a very short turnaround time (for example, Anthes (2004) reported that in 2003, Ameritrade made a promise to complete trades within five seconds and E*Trade retaliated by lowering its pledge to two seconds). A database management system that keeps the records of all transactions and customers resides on the lower tier. The system may also maintain a linkage with the stock market and/or news agencies to obtain real-time quotations and other market information.

Applications that are characterised as the brokerage information systems often lie in the middle tier of the architecture. Their main functions are to assist e-brokerage firms in account administration, order management, liabilities administration, cash handling, compliance monitoring and operational risk management. Two of the most distinctive systems are examined below.

Order management

The most strategically important brokerage system is the order management system (OMS), which is the centre of the automation for organising and managing trades. But functionalities included in an OMS are not limited to transaction processing; applications complementary to transaction processes are also found for:

- *Extended liquidity functions*: To allow trading of multiple investment instruments, such as stocks, indexes and hedge funds.
- *Multi-currency*: To allow cross-border trading.
- *Increased connectivity*: To connect to various markets and/or trading systems.
- *Consultancy services*: Ranging from simple charting tools to visualise price movement, computational tools to study market trends and even to portfolio modelling tools to devise investment strategies. Some of these tools may give buy or sell signals according to pre-set algorithms and rules.
- *Trade tracking*: Real-time data streaming and news bulletins; multiple screens to view profit and loss.
- *Compliance monitoring*: Rule-based applications to screen out dubious activities.

To make the facilities available on the Web, these systems are Java-compliant and deploy extensive messaging and web services application programming interfaces (APIs) so that they can be integrated with back-office systems. For OMSs that are connected to exchanges and other brokers/dealers, messages can be written in FIX or ISO15022 standards. The case of DEx demonstrates the capabilities of such systems.

Case: BNY Brokerage's Direct Execution Services (DEx)

An innovative brokerage application, DEx, is offered by BNY Securities Group, a subsidiary of the Bank of New York (NYSE: BK). After its acquisition of Sonic Financial Technologies, BNY incorporated three products from Sonic – SonicPort, SonicSmart and SonicCentral – into the DEx suite.

The application executes self-directed trading as well as broker-assisted trading; i.e. investors can take direct control of their trading strategies and execution management if they don't want any assistance from their brokers. Through a market access gateway (provided by SonicCentral), the DEx system is connected to ECNs, Nasdaq, market makers and many exchanges (these are known as 'liquidity points'). It also provides marketplace aggregation tools and smart routing functionality (by SonicSmart, an intelligent routing engine), enabling streaming quote data to all major liquidity points for listed and over-the-counter (OTC) equities. These are housed in a trading strategy server, as illustrated in Figure 6.2.

Figure 6.2 **DEx platform**

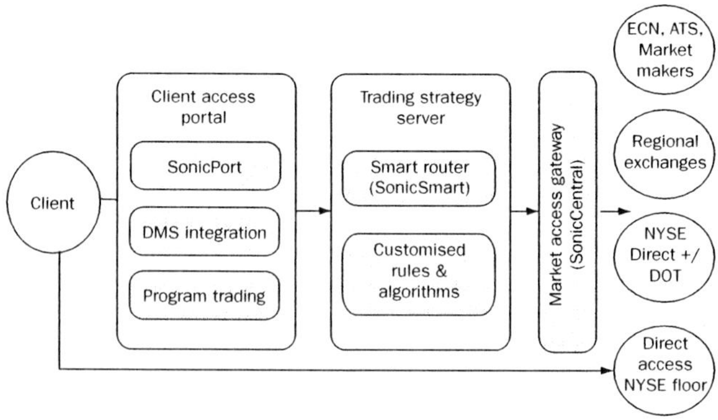

ATS: alternative trading system; DOT: designated order turnaround;
ECN: electronic communications network; OMS: order management system
Adapted from: BNY Brokerage at *http://www.bnybrokerage.com/exmgmt_DEx.asp*

Trading is controlled by the SonicPort application, which lies in the client access portal of the DEx platform. SonicPort is a front-end trading management tool responsible for the streaming of quote data with direct market access and advanced routing strategies to the liquidity point. It can be used as a standalone application or integrated to the client's proprietary OMSs by the FIX API connection.

The workflows of OMS as well as many other information systems in e-brokerage firms are regulated by the authorities. The technology for automating compliance is therefore essential to the streamlined operations in the trading lifecycle.

Compliance automation

As the financial market has been suffering one blow after another in recent years, government and various authorities are formulating regulations to protect investors as well as the financial sector. Operations in a brokerage firm – including those controlled by information systems – must not deviate from these regulations. Management should consider the deployment of computerised compliance tools essential for activity monitoring because they are the only means by which large amounts of data can be handled and decisions made in a fraction of a second. Everybody knows that compliance automation can assure quality operations and the integrity of the firm. But even when the exact capacity of these tools is unknown to the firm, the mere implementation of these tools can already demonstrate the firm's willingness and effort to improve compliance.

Often wrapped in auditing applications or in other systems, compliance automation tools can be used to monitor trading activities and check them against pre-set business rules. These rules are determined by the risk management policies of the firm and can be modified by the profile of individual clients. As the trade activity of each client is monitored in the OMS, a compliance tool can alert when a client acts outside the permitted limits of the personalised business rules. In special cases (such as a market crash), the tool is able to display all inappropriate trading activities in sequence of priority pre-stated in the risk management policy.

Roughly speaking, compliance monitoring is divided into pre-trade, post-execution and portfolio-level. The traditional meaning of compliance checking is post-execution or a back-end process that is activated at the end of a reporting period. The modern concept of compliance requires activities to be constantly checked against rules that are pre-set for the entire firm, an individual account, or a type of activities within an account. Pre-trade checking is essential to prevent breaches from occurring in the first place. In addition, compliance tools provide behaviour analysis and *ad hoc* reporting that enable an early warning to be issued in other levels of compliance monitoring.

Studying various behaviour detection technologies deployed in the financial services industry, a 2003 report from Mantas, Inc., a world-class solution provider, identifies five levels of complexity of the technology, whereby each level encompasses the techniques of the preceding level(s):

- *Level 0 (Sampling with manual investigation)*: With simple tools for sorting and scanning data, detection of suspicious behaviours relies on manual examination. It can only be applied to samples of data, not the entire volume of data.
- *Level 1 (Single events and entities)*: All data are automatically checked individually, without considering their relationships (e.g. trend). It can only spot a suspicious transaction or account because of the peculiar nature of the event or entity.
- *Level 2 (Rudimentary summaries)*: A high-level summary of the behaviour of an account can be drawn. Techniques, such as rule-matching[3] can be used to reveal abuses.
- *Level 3 (Sophisticated summaries)*: Details in account transactions are studied and summarised to detect possible behavioural nuances. Such analysis can reveal patterns that are elusive in higher-level study. For example, an instance in which multiple monetary instruments in the same account are just below reporting thresholds is suspicious but is less obvious at Level 2.
- *Level 4 (Behaviour detection technology)*: More complex algorithms (e.g. link analysis,[4] sequence matching[5]) are used to detect potentially suspicious relationships and/or patterns between events and entities. The study aims to identify networks of related accounts (syndicates of fraud or money laundering), rapid movement of funds and sudden escalation in activities.

Mantas' Behaviour Detection Platform was implemented by the National Association of Securities Dealers (NASD)[6] in the mid-1990s and it is now available to the financial services sector to implement their compliance technologies, including fraud detection or anti-money laundering (AML) applications. Mantas' own compliance technologies (including AML, broker compliance, trading compliance and mutual fund compliance solutions) can be installed on the platform. The platform is also offered to other vendors (such as i-flex and HP) so that their applications can be combined with Mantas' behaviour detection technology.

Web-based stock markets

The emergence of Web-based marketplaces shows us the future of many conventional markets that are still operating in the bricks-and-mortar model. In response to the growing number of investment instruments, market makers, brokers, dealers and investors, bricks-and-mortar markets must follow an evolutionary path that is not limited by their physical space, memberships and trade volumes. Advances in ICT have been powering such evolution, which is seen in Europe, North America and other parts of the world.

At the turn of the century, many teams entered into a race to develop a pan-European equities exchange. In 1997, the German and Swiss consortium Eurex launched the first version of its online trading platform Xetra. It soon became the world largest electronic exchange for options and futures in early 1999, with a trade volume exceeding that of Chicago Board of Trade (CBOT). The race for pan-European exchange has not finished, but by now the winner seems to be Euronext, a joint venture of exchanges in Amsterdam, Brussels and Paris.

On the other side of Atlantic, the New York Stock Exchange (NYSE)[7] has been slow in embracing any automated system, although other electronic stock markets, such as Nasdaq[8] were established quite a few years ago. The auction-based exchange is legendary in its specialists and market participants who believe human involvement is an advantage. Its slow pace of automation is expected to change, especially after the NYSE merged with Archipelago Holdings, Inc. in April 2005 because the latter is an all-electronic exchange.

Setting up larger (and more efficient) stock exchanges is a major driving force of digitisation in the European and North American markets. Their stories of expansion are scattered with cases of ICT applications, which make the backbones of all the web-based marketplaces.

European bourses

Keeping pace with the unification of Europe, exchanges (or bourses) of the European countries must cooperate and consolidate into an international exchange to facilitate cross-border trading. The aforementioned Euronext NV is an attempt to unite all the European exchanges. Since its emergence in 2000, it has successfully merged the exchanges of Amsterdam, Brussels, Paris, London International Financial Futures and Options Exchange (LIFFE) and Bolsa de Valores de Lisboa e Porto (BVLP of Portugal). Its chain of actions to acquire European exchanges – though not always a success – shows no sign of stopping. It serves to remind the financial sector of its ambition to become the only exchange on the continent. In 2005, it offered to acquire the London Stock Exchange and, at the same time, it is busy harmonising the trading and clearing systems of markets in respective countries.

Backed by Deutsche Börse AG and the Swiss Exchange, the Eurex Exchange is still running for trading and clearing of international derivatives products. Eurex is ambitious to move into the US derivatives market. It is also a strong competitor of Euronext when the latter develops its derivatives market. The technology that supports Euronext operations is exemplified by two systems (NSC and LIFFE CONNECT) which are described below.

Euronext NSC system

Euronext runs on an NSC (Nouveau Systèm de Cotation) system, the same system used in the Paris Bourse, Boston Options Exchange, Chicago Mercantile Exchange, Toronto Stock Exchange and a dozen other exchanges. As shown in Figure 6.3, the central system of Euronext is a hub that links to the NSC, Clearing 21 (a clearing system, see the section on clearing), and servers for common delivery and settlement services (including the handling of fill and kill (FAK) orders). Member brokers from all over Europe can connect to the hub through the Internet, using:

- *Euronext Trading Workstations (ETW)*: Created by Euronext, they can handle basic trading functions.
- *Clearnet Clearing Workstations (CCW)*: Originated from Clearnet, the clearinghouse of Euronext, these workstations handle basic clearing functions under the management of Clearing 21. The CCW

Figure 6.3 Euronext ICT support

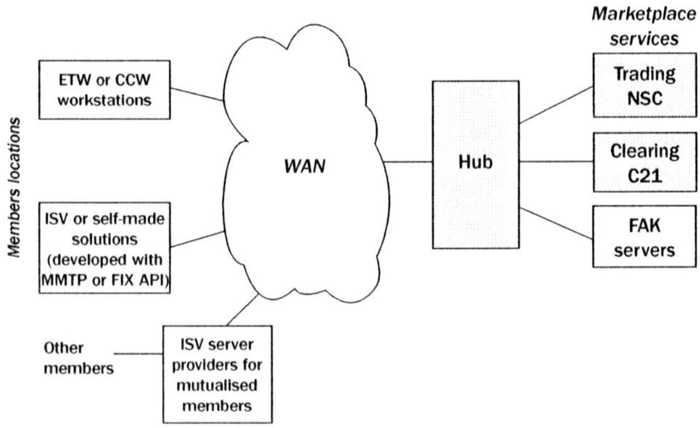

CCW: Clearnet clearing workstations, ETW: Euronext trading workstations; FAK: fill and kill (order); ISV: independent software vendor; MMTP: market message transfer protocol; NSC: Nouveau Systèm de Cotation (a Euronext system); WAN: wide area network.

solution is added to an ETW solution to convert the latter into a trading and clearing workstation.

- *Software solutions*: Self-developed or developed by independent software vendors (ISVs), these solutions communicate with the Euronext system by using FIX and MMTP[9] protocols.
- *Other contact points*: Certified ISVs might develop interfacing applications, including Certified Access Point Interface (CAPI) and Mutualized Access Point Interface (MAPI) solutions, which are designed for the exclusive use of one member and the mutual use of several members respectively.

The NSC is a trading system for cash and derivatives products, but Euronext's NSC is for securities trading purposes. It is a so-called order-driven platform; i.e., orders entering into the market are routed to a public, central, electronic order book using a time-price algorithm[10] to match buy and sell orders in a continuous process. For less liquid securities, orders are aggregated in the order book and auctioned several times per day. The trading becomes an auction. But in individual exchanges (say, Amsterdam) the NSC platform allows some quote-driven trading to stir up liquidity. It incorporates a Euronext Liquidity Provider System (ELPS) in which some traders are required to quote prices when liquidity sinks to a certain level (BIS, 2003a).

Euronext's LIFFE CONNECT

Following the purchase of LIFFE, Euronext formed a derivatives exchange Euronext.liffe, which developed the LIFFE CONNECT electronic trading platform. In just a few years, LIFFE CONNECT has become the trading and clearing system in many major exchanges in the world, including CBOT, Tokyo International Financial Futures Exchange and Nasdaq Liffe Markets. One by one, exchanges under Euronext are migrating their derivatives trading platforms to LIFFE CONNECT. The system has become the strategic tool for Euronext.liffe to compete with its rival derivatives market, Eurex (*www.eurexchange.com*).

The objective of developing LIFFE CONNECT is to integrate multiple markets into a single platform. For Euronext.liffe, this single platform is maintained in London with a backup in Paris. Customers around the globe can access to the system through front-end applications written by ISVs[11] and in-house developers, with appropriate LIFFE APIs.

The platform is the residence of several software modules, including (LIFFE, 2004) the following (see Figure 6.4):

- *Trading host*: The matching engine with a fully anonymous central order book. The system is connected via gateways to members, who may enter orders to the host.

Figure 6.4 LIFFE CONNECT architecture

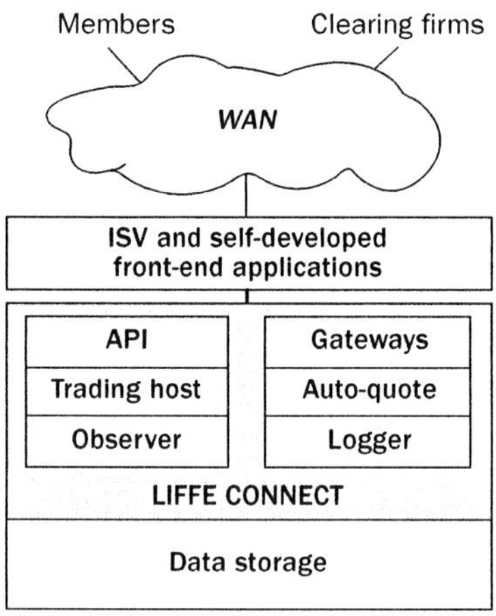

API: application programming interface;
ISV: independent service vendor;
WAN: wide area network

- *Monitor and control platform*: The Observer and Logger applications designed for market management and data audit respectively.
- *Autoquote*: An application to calculate indicative pricing and options settlement.

The trading host is the core of LIFFE's system. Matching of orders is controlled by either of two algorithms: (1) for bond, equity index and Euroyen futures, orders are matched with strict reference to price and time priority; (2) for short-term interest rate products (except Euroyen), matching is done by a price and pro-rata algorithm, but priority is given to the first order at the best price subject to a minimum order volume and limited to a maximum volume cap.

The trading host notifies corresponding traders when an order is executed. The details of the transaction are then sent to the trade registration system which routes the matched trades to the clearing processing system.

The LIFFE CONNECT is implemented on a BEA WebLogic Platform 8.1, making use of the J2EE resources available in BEA WebLogic environment. The database tier is built by Microsoft SQL Server 2000, which is scaled to the levels predicted for at least five years of usage. The server is 32-bit for the moment and could be switched to 64-bit when needs arise.

Case: LIFFE CONNECT in e-CBOT

In 2000, Chicago Board of Trade split into two companies: CBOT and e-CBOT. Developing into an e-trading exchange, e-CBOT first partnered with Eurex in the design and implementation of the Alliance/CBOT/Eurex (A/C/E) system. Hoever, the marriage between e-CBOT and Eurex did not work out. In November 2003, the A/C/E system was replaced by the LIFFE CONNECT solution, which is now implemented on three Sun Microsystem's Fire F15K servers and Sun's gateways. The new system is said to have a number of improvements over Euronext.liffe's version and has more flexible matching algorithms than the A/C/E system.

e-CBOT also gets assistance from the Chicago Mercantile Exchange (CME) to develop a CME/CBOT common clearing link. Besides providing clearing and related services to all CBOT products, the link establishes a standardised online interface and common business practices between the two exchanges. It also supports the web-based electronic delivery system (EDS), which replaces the physical delivery system and offers real-time online reports on the quantities each member firm receives in the delivery process.

The CBOT has been quick in implementing Euronext's LIFFE CONNECT, but the securities markets in the country are not equally keen in adopting the latest ICT development. The difference in attitudes is seen in the following descriptions of the electronic communications networks (ECN) markets Nasdaq and NYSE.

Alternative trading systems and electronic communications networks

Alternative trading systems (ATSs) are trading facilities for securities that are normally traded on regular exchanges or markets. ATSs attract traders by offering special functions and/or services that major exchanges or markets lack. Many times smaller than regular exchanges, most ATSs execute transactions in compliance with private-law contracts but not with stock exchange law. Offering a diversity of services, ATSs are typically classified as follows (Mühlberger, 2005):

- *Bulletin boards*: Traders publish their bids and negotiate with others on the system, which does not provide trade execution.
- *Cross networks*: Stock prices are imported from other trading systems, such as exchanges. Although some cross systems (including the European E-Crossnet and POSIT) still remain in business, they are struggling for survival.
- *Quote-driven, market maker systems*: Market makers exist who, after concluding a transaction with an investor, quote binding bid and ask prices for selected securities. However, after Jiway, Knight Trading and Nasdaq were driven out of business in Europe, the fitness of these systems for the European market has become questionable.
- *Order-driven systems*: In a call auction, orders are batched together and executed at a single price. In continuous trading, orders that are compatible are executed immediately. In either case, buy and sell orders meet directly in an order book. These systems are the largest ATSs and are adopted in all ECNs in the USA.
- *Hit-and-take execution*: Quotes are collected and displayed to market participants, who respond and negotiate until the trade is made. Matching is not automatic, but the spread is small if not totally absent.

ATS is the prototype of ECNs.[12] The US pioneer Instinet began in 1969 as a securities broker specialising in after-hours trading. It subsequently offered a Web-based system, INET, for order routing and matching services for securities trading. Later registered with the Securities and Exchange Commission (SEC) as an ECN, Instinet has drawn a large market share (12.5 per cent in 2001) by providing better prices and lower commissions to retail and institutional investors. It was the largest ECN until 1999, when its leading position was taken over by another ECN, Island. It recaptured the leadership by acquiring Island in 2002. In 2005, it was acquired by Nasdaq.

An ECN can register with the SEC in the USA as either a broker-dealer or an exchange. As a broker, an ECN (such as Brut) is an electronic securities matching system that connects major brokerages and individual traders so that buyers and sellers can trade directly between themselves without a broker. If registered as an exchange, the ECN (e.g. Archipelago Exchange) is regulated by the National Association of Securities Dealers (NASD), the parent organisation of Nasdaq. By doing so, an ECN becomes a self-regulatory organisation and is allowed to connect electronically and trade stocks that are listed on Nasdaq and other US exchanges. For the last few years, ECNs have succeeded in taking over 40 per cent of the transactions from Nasdaq and become direct rivals to the NYSE because ECNs can connect to NYSE and other exchanges over the InterMarket Trading System (ITS, further discussion below). ECNs have become a common place to trade Nasdaq stocks for day traders.

ECNs compete with traditional markets as well as among themselves. The market force drives ECNs to differentiate their cost structures, client portfolio and trading activities. Many ECNs offer after-hours trading and anonymous transactions because these are not possible in conventional exchanges. Some ECNs offer trading in multiple markets, allowing the investor to structure their portfolios that involve more than one market (e.g. choosing stocks of a business sector rather than a country).

ATSs are also found in Europe though they are less successful. Degryse and Achter (2002) argue that this may well be caused by the more automated marketplaces in Europe and the major attention drawn towards Euronext. Their counterparts in the USA, ECNs, are comparatively better off as Nasdaq is a popular trading platform. But when Nasdaq launched SuperMontage (to be discussed later) in 2002, the new trading system triggered a direct competition with ECNs. The market of ECNs is now entering into a period of consolidation. In 2002,

Sungard bought Brut and Instinet acquired Island. Three years later, Nasdaq purchased Instinet, soon after Archipelago Exchange was acquired by NYSE.

Nasdaq

The National Association of Securities Dealers Automated Quotation System (Nasdaq) was originally designed for the over-the-counter (OTC) markets for stocks. It was managed by its parent company NASD and was sold to its members in 2001 in a deal that allowed NASD to keep all the voting rights. Throughout the years, Nasdaq has established listing standards, marketplace rules and regulations that are usually not applied to OTC securities. Nasdaq is the largest electronic stock market in the world.

Nasdaq is a securities information processor (SIP). Trade and quote information from all exchanges and markets that trade Nasdaq-listed securities is collected and consolidated in the Nasdaq system and is disseminated to other exchanges.

As a market, the Nasdaq is a network that connects buyers and sellers, mostly through the SuperMontage trading platform. This is just one of the ICT systems responsible for streamlining transactions in the market. In particular, Nasdaq is famous for its implementation of the following systems:

- *SuperMontage (also known as Nasdaq MarketCenter)*: The order book and trade execution system that started operation in mid-2002. Based on a Unisys 7802 mainframe, it is a real-time system that displays the top five bids and offers. It also integrates quotation and order management capabilities for traders, who are even allowed to enter attributed quote and order data at multiple price levels.
- *Automated confirmation transaction (ACT)*: A system to report the clearing of trades in the market. It speeds up comparison and clearing of pre-negotiated trades.
- *InterMarket Trading System (ITS)*: Introduced in 1978 by the NYSE, the ITS is the trading network that electronically links Nasdaq, the NYSE and seven other exchanges in the USA. As all current bids and offers across those exchanges are displayed on the ITS, specialists can choose the best market for any trade. As the operational speed of the ITS has been under heavy criticism in the last decade, enhanced

features are expected to be added to the system; these include auto-routing to better priced away markets and automatic execution ('auto-ex', see section on the NYSE) of incoming commitments.

- *Securities information processor (SIP)*: The term SIP originally referred to the role of Nasdaq displaying market data related to its securities, which included those listed in Nasdaq and Nasdaq securities placed through other market systems, such as unlisted trading privileges (UTP). The new SIP (also known as 'internal SIP') in Nasdaq specially caters for UTP. It aggregates and consolidates data from the UTP OTC stock markets and then disseminates it to the data distribution vendors.
- *OTCBB*: A bulletin board quotation system that displays real-time, last-sale prices and volume information for unlisted, non-Nasdaq OTC securities, which are generally small companies. It was phased out in 2004.
- *Mutual funds quotation system (MFQS)*: An information processor for mutual fund pricing.

SuperMontage has become a serious threat to the survival of ECNs, as it works very similarly to the ECN, in its faster execution, anonymity prior to transaction and order-routing features. In addition, the system improves transparency of the market and supports the release of new TotalView and PowerView data products as enhanced features of Level II information.

Figure 6.5 illustrates several levels of data the Nasdaq system provides to subscribers. Level I data consist of the current best bid and ask price, together with information of the current trading. Information on the activities (bids and offers) of individual market makers is shown only in Level II data, which is available to traders of NASD members and institutional investors. Level II quotes are essential to traders who like to capture the opportunities of volatility and momentum in the markets and who have the ability to enter orders directly into the market. Thus, day traders might trade on the direct access trading (DAT) systems, which allow an investor to trade directly with another client or a Nasdaq market maker without intermediation. Level II quotes are essential to these systems as they reveal the trend of stock movements to viewers.

The highest level of data, Level III, is available to registered market makers only. This is in fact the electronic marketplace where the market makers may enter their own bids and offers for securities that they have registered.

Figure 6.5 Different levels of Nasdaq data services

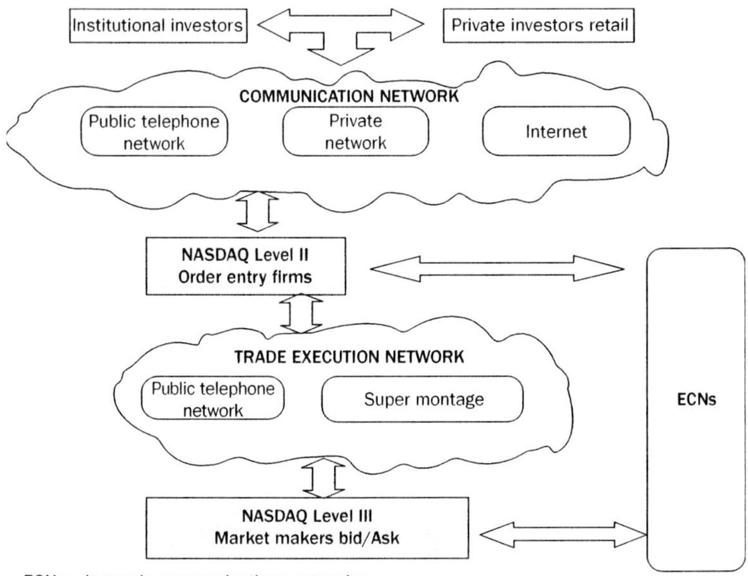

ECNs: electronic communications networks
Adapted from: Benhamou and Serval (1999)

Case: Nasdaq Prime system (Microsoft, 2003b)

The core of Nasdaq SuperMontage is the Nasdaq Prime system, which is implemented on a Microsoft Windows 2000 Advanced Server and SQL Server 2000 Enterprise Edition. The system is able to handle 5,000 to 8,000 quote messages per second, during which it performs the major operations of SuperMontage, including the evaluation of bid and ask prices, transmitting the top five levels, checking the status of quotes, and withdrawal of prices for completed and cancelled transactions.

The system has three tiers (Figure 6.6). The first tier receives quotation information from SuperMontage's HP NonStop Computing mainframe platform from six streams, each through Microsoft Message Queuing (MSMQ) middleware. Each stream is processed by a separate processor in one of the two four-processor Dell 6650 servers.

The second tier is made up of the Windows Server and SQL Server. They follow business logic to review information within the message received, such as state of quoting participants, and prepare transmission of quotation data to subscribers. The third tier retrieves data from the SQL Server database and multicasts it to the subscribers. The work is distributed among three dual-processor Dell 2250 servers, each having a

Figure 6.6 Nasdaq Prime system

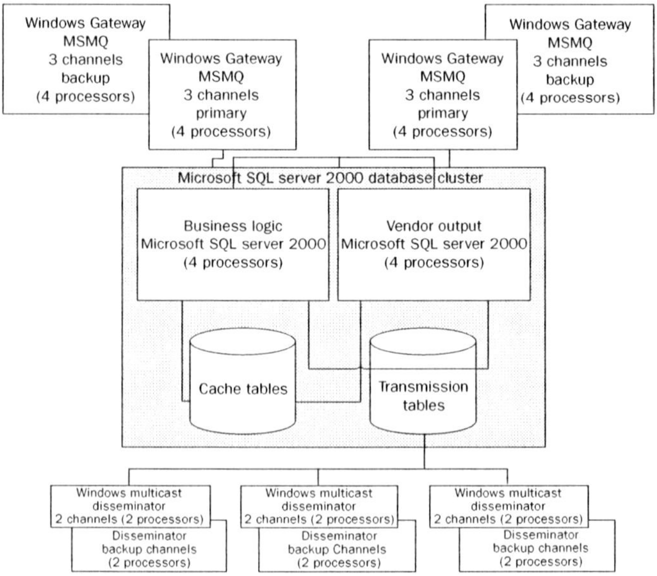

Source: Microsoft (2003c)

backup for failover. To guarantee its absolute reliability, SuperMontage prepares a disaster recovery site even though it has never been used.

New York Stock Exchange

As the second largest stock market and one of the oldest exchanges in the world, the NYSE is controlled by its 353 member firms, which consist of broker-dealer and specialist firms. A specialist stands outside one of the 17 posts in the exchange premises and floor brokers are mobile and visit any post to trade securities of their choice. The NYSE is traditionally an auction market, as the specialists manage actual auctions among the brokers who gather around their posts. There are clerical officials on the floor approving and reporting all transactions.

The NYSE began its e-market project as early as in 1976, when the designated order turnaround (DOT) system was implemented as an order routing system to receive incoming orders from member firms through a message-forwarding device known as a 'common message switch' (CMS). The DOT routes the orders directly to specialist posts, where the orders appear on the specialist's display book. The system also sends post-trade reports to the originators of the orders. In 1984, the DOT was upgraded to SuperDOT to improve turnaround time. However, the system is not an order execution system because the specialists, to whom an order routes, need to execute the orders manually.

Since the automatic execution system Direct+[13] began operations in 2000, SuperDOT sends all limit orders designated for automation execution (called 'auto-ex' limit orders) to Direct+. Without routing to a specialist, these orders are automatically executed at the posted quote (against the specialist). Although many people criticise the sluggish operational speed of Direct+ (orders can only be entered to the Direct+ system every 30 seconds), the system executes nearly 150 million shares on an ordinary day. Pending approval from the SEC, NYSE is going to expand the capacity of Direct+ by allowing the trading of larger share sizes and faster consecutive order execution.

In the early 1990s, the NYSE developed a broker booth support system (BBSS) and an e-broker system. The BBSS is an OMS that enables brokerage firms to route orders selectively and electronically to either the trading post or the booths on the trading floor. The e-broker is a wireless, hand-held terminal used to connect floor brokers to their booth and off-floor locations. Using the e-broker, a floor broker can automate order-flow and communicate order status and 'market look' information[14] to their back-offices (by using SMTP e-mail protocol). The terminal can activate functions in the BBSS, which include receiving and entering orders (e.g. to Direct+), rerouting orders and issuing reports. A newer version of the BBSS is now available on a browser and it is called BOSS (booth overview supervisory service).

Figure 6.7 illustrates how the e-broker and BBSS work with a broker's proprietary system, which connects to the NYSE system via a common access point (CAP) network, using FIX, FCS and SMTP protocols. CAP is an extranet through which the NYSE provides its information products to subscribers and receives orders from its members. Since 2002, NYSE's new datafeed product, OpenBook, has been multicast on the CAP extranet. This is a data service showing subscribers (e.g. off-floor investors) the limit order volume information for all NYSE-traded securities on a real-time basis.

Transaction processing in the exchange is left to the trade capture and reporting service, which transmits messages of trade data (from the SuperDOT or proprietary brokerage systems) to the clearing corporation. Before the transmission, the matching of these transactions must be confirmed in the online comparison system (OCS), which then

Figure 6.7 Broker booth support system as a bridge between e-brokers and specialist posts

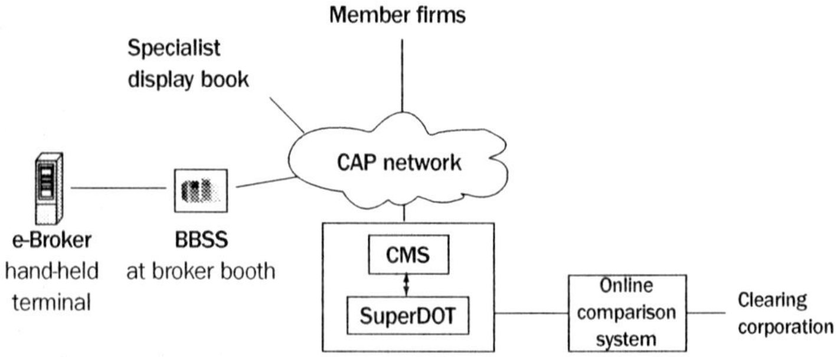

BBSS: broker booth support system; CAP: common access point; CMS: common message switch; SuperDOT: super designated order turnaround (a system at NYSE)

sends equities trades to the National Securities Clearing Corporation (NSCC). Trade details are reported on an intra-day or end-of-day basis.

The NYSE operates a hybrid market, where manual auctions take place between human specialists and floor brokers as well as electronic executions of trading via the CAP. However, the exchange is getting more and more involved in e-stock trading since it bought Archipelago Exchange (ArcaEx) in April 2005. The ECN has been running a fully electronic exchange and is believed to have some effect on the NYSE's progress toward e-stock trading.

NYSE's new order management system: TradeWorks

The BBSS of NYSE is now being replaced by TradeWorks, a new OMS which is specially designed to cope with the 1.6 billion shares traded in the exchange every day. The solution includes 3,000 handheld devices to allow floor brokers to interact with specialists and Direct+. These devices allow users to receive, manage, and execute buy-and-sell orders and send reports to back-office or other OMSs.

The architecture of TradeWorks shows three tiers (displayed vertically in Figure 6.8). The first tier is made up of Linux workstations, on which traders and clerks in the market can forward their requests (by e-broker terminals) through a workload manager.

The middle tier is built on the IBM WebSphere Application Servers and DB2 database management software that runs on a mainframe. To maintain data integrity and accuracy within the database, the system adopts a technique known as 'two-phase commit', which is

Figure 6.8 A high-level view of the TradeWorks architecture

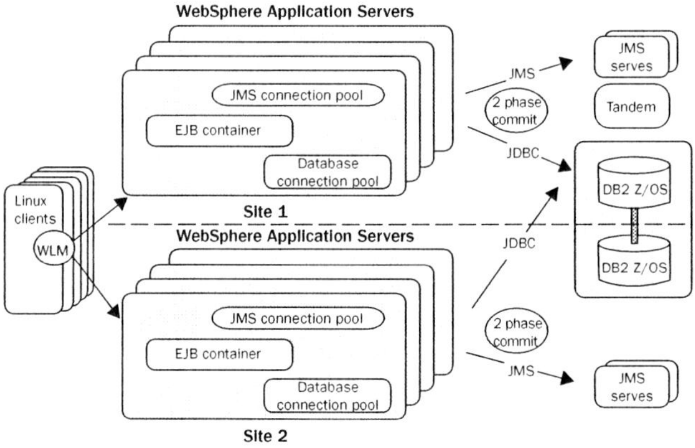

EJB: enterprise JavaBeans; JDBC: Java database connectivity; JMS: Java message service; WLM: workload manager

Source: Coleman and Bowman (2004)

particularly effective in the TradeWorks operating environment, where multiple interacting resources must be synchronised during the process of a transaction.

The paramount concern of the system is the high volume of transactions that the system handles every day. The system is thus provided with applications to handle failovers and load balancing. The tested infrastructure is believed to have 'extreme availability'.

Clearing and settlement in the Internet era

All securities transactions go through three processes: execution, clearing and settlement. While traders and brokers can use ICT to get quotations and place orders at high speed, the other two processes are also enhanced by extensive application of ICT.

In traditional markets, such as the NYSE, traders negotiate with someone inside the exchanges, such as the specialists in the NYSE or the counterparties in some markets where trading is done face-to-face between sellers and buyers. In markets where transactions are automated or anonymous, risk can be reduced if there is an entity that can act as the counterparty in each trade and novate – i.e. shortly after the trade, replace the original contractual obligations to deliver and pay with equivalent obligations. The solution is to establish a central counterparty[15] (CCP), an entity that is able to:

- *Reduce credit risk in the transaction*: It eliminates the risk associated with the participants of different credit ratings.
- *Increase market liquidity*: It speeds up the matching of bids and offers in marketplaces
- *Enable post-trade anonymity*: Anonymity is retained throughout the lifecycle of a trade, keeping trading strategies unknown to others.
- *Netting*: The presence of a CCP reduces the number of settlements the market has to make per day. It reduces settlement costs and operational risk. Members can also enjoy greater efficiency of capital and cost savings from fewer settlements.

It is a common practice for clearinghouses to act as CCPs. In addition to NSCC in the USA and Clearnet in Europe, the Canadian Depository for Securities Ltd. and Hong Kong Securities Clearing Co. Ltd. are all clearinghouses playing their parts as a CCP.

Because of the strong tie between the processes of clearing and settlement, CCPs or other institutions may offer both clearing and settlement services. In the discussion below, however, the two services are separated under their own topics. The integration of these services – either horizontally or vertically – is discerned at the end of this section.

Clearing in the Depository Trust and Clearing Corporation

In the USA, the Depository Trust and Clearing Corporation (DTCC) was set up for the clearing of all stocks traded on the NYSE, Nasdaq and the ECNs. The DTCC provides post-trade clearance, settlement, custody, and information services for equities and other products through its subsidiary NSCC, which also acts as a CCP and provides guarantee of trade completion, netting and risk management services.

To ensure business continuity, DTCC developed a securely managed and reliable technology search (SMART/Search) network, which:

- Provides reliable connectivity between DTCC and its customers by connecting more than one customer's operating location to all of DTCC's multiple processing.

- Allows tight security measures (offered by the Department of Homeland Security) in event of an outage by installing a DTCC router on a customer's premises.
- Offers better communication quality through accessibility over a DS3 bandwidth connection. (A DS3 or T3 carrier has a bitrate of 45 megabits per second, the highest available at present.)

As the facilities manager of NSCC, Securities Industry Automation Corporation (SIAC) sets up a connection between the SMART/Search network and SIAC's Secure Financial Transaction Infrastructure (SFTI, pronounced 'safety'). In response to the September 11 attack, SIAC designed the SFTI as a data communications infrastructure to be more resilient to man-made and natural disasters. The SFTI is implemented by Nortel Networks (NYSE: NT). It provides multiple access centres and redundant connections, power supplies, network equipment and links. The communication pathway is composed of independent, self-healing fibre-optic rings such that a failure at any contact point should not affect connection between other points and the network is able to recover quickly after any crisis.

The joining of SMART/Search and SFTI is a milestone achievement in the US financial sector as, starting from the end of 2004, the SMART/SFTI has become the message hub that provides access to almost all clearing and settlement entities, which are, namely, DTCC/NSCC, Fixed Income Clearing Corporation (FICC) and Emerging Markets Clearing Corporation (EMCC).

The evolution of the DTCC system showcases the consolidation of clearing corporations. The advantages, such as lowering clearing costs, are known to the rest of the world. The DTCC has established a branch, European Central Counterparty Limited (EuroCCP), to provide clearing and settlement services for Nasdaq Europe since December 2001. It competes head-on with many clearinghouses in Europe, including:

- *Crest*: the British central securities depository;
- *Euroclear*: which was set up about the same time; and
- *Clearstream*: the settlement house and depository acquired by Deutsche Börse.

EuroCCP lost its battle when Nasdaq Europe ended its business. Currently there are still a few organisations competing to be the pan-European clearinghouse. The history of LCH.Clearnet shows a glimpse of the European version of financial market consolidation.

Clearnet and Euronext

Clearnet was originally a French institution. Since 2001, Clearnet has been responsible as a CCP to the traders in Euronext and acted for the netting and clearing of all trades on Euronext's cash and derivatives markets. In December 2003, Clearnet merged with London Clearing House (LCH) and the new company, LCH.Clearnet SA became wholly-owned by Euronext. Besides being the CCP for cash and derivatives trading in Euronext, LCH.Clearnet also provides clearing services to other markets, including debt securities and repo transactions.

All clearing services in LCH.Clearnet are managed by the Clearing 21 system, a clearing system developed by CME and New York Mercantile Exchange (NYMEX). As Euronext selected Euroclear to be its settlement organisation, Clearing 21 is integrated into the Euroclear system,[16] the world's largest provider of settlement and related services for cross-border securities transactions.

Figure 6.9 stretches a high-level architecture of the Euronext system. Access to Euronext Paris is provided through LIFFE CONNECT and SWITCH[17], which are connected to a single central order book in Euronext. Clearing 21 then acts as a CCP and provides real-time netting and financial guarantees. The transaction is then routed to Euroclear for settlement.

The figure also illustrates the product model of Clearing 21 installed at LCH.Clearnet in Paris. Receiving trade information from Euronext Paris, the Clearing 21 system handles three types of markets, respectively for:

- *MONEP*:[18] for equity options, index options and index futures; applications include membership administration, market operations and surveillance, technical clearing procedures and control of margin requirements.
- *MATIF*:[19] as a CCP for the trading of futures options, commodities futures and interest-rate futures.
- *Cash product*: for transactions from the NSC system. It takes into account information (e.g. corporate events) drawn from the Fininfo data stream (a financial information source).

The clearing process for derivative products in MONEP and MATIF begins when the clearing fees are calculated by the Fees program. Before the message is sent to Euroclear, a delivery versus payment (DVP) process ensures that securities are delivered if, and only if, the price of

Figure 6.9 Overall architecture of Euronext/LCH.Clearnet in Paris

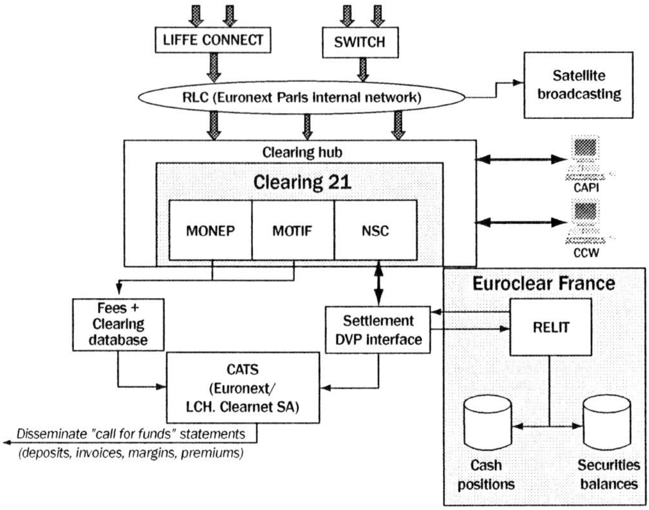

CAPI: Certified Access Point Interface; CATS: Centralised automated trading system; CCW: Clearnet Clearing Workstations; MONEP: Marché des Options Négociables de Paris (Paris traded options); MATIF: Marché à Terme International de France (French Financial Future Market); NSC: Nouveau Systèm de Cotation (a Euronext system); DVP: delivery-versus-payment; RELIT: RLC:Réseau Interne ParisBourse (Euronext Paris internal network)

Adapted from: Clearnet (2004)

the securities is paid, and vice versa. The RELIT system (an alias of 'Relit Grand Vitesse' or RGV) is an application to process a settlement on the basis of the securities balance that has been adjusted with corporate events, if there are any. After each settlement process, Euroclear produces a report of settled and unsettled securities transactions and disseminates it to each participant.

Activities in clearing and settlement are often provided by a single organisation. As shown in the case of LCH.Clearnext in Paris, the work of Clearing 21 is integrated with those in Euroclear France. To differentiate clearing from settlement, the famous Clearing 21 and DTTC's IMS are discussed in the next two sections.

Clearing 21

Clearing 21 is designed with an open architecture, complying with industrial standards. In December 2001, Clearnet and Euronext reached an agreement with SWIFT, that, while the Clearing 21 service is provided

Figure 6.10 Clearing 21 modular architecture

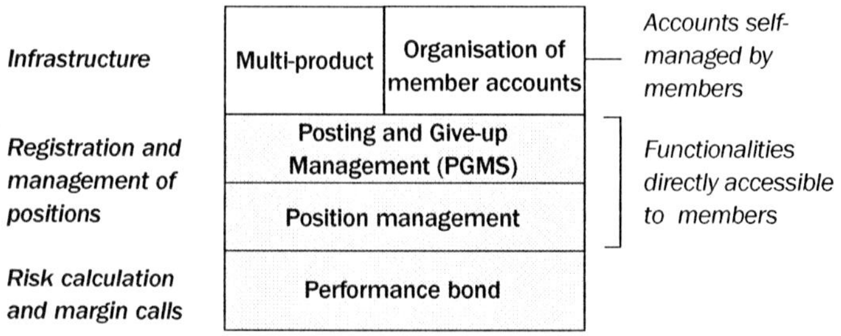

PGMS: posting and give-up management system

Modified from: Clearnet (2002)

to Euronext's NSC trading system, SWIFT would contribute to the message definition under the ISO15022 standard. The open architecture of Clearing 21 is the reason for its compatibility with many trading systems used in the financial sector. The Clearing 21 system consists of five modules, organised into three levels as in Figure 6.10.

The main activities of the Clearing 21 system are concentrated at the lower two levels:

1. Registration and management of positions for the MONEP and MATIP markets:
   - *Posting and give-up management system (PGMS)* – when Clearing 21 receives and acknowledges a trade from a member's trading system, it requires the member to post the trade to one of its accounts or give it up to another member. The PGMS provides real-time management of postings, give-ups, take-ups, transfers and corrections.
   - *Position management* – real-time management of exercise, assignment, abandonment and offsetting.

2. Risk calculation (called 'performance bond' in Clearing 21) and margin calls:
   - *Valuation of products* – risk management is standardised by LCH.Clearnet's risk division. Valuation methods, such as SPAN,[20] Cox Ross Rubinstein formula[21] and the Black 76 model[22] are available. SPAN is used to calculate initial margin requirements.
   - *Margin calls* are disseminated through a centralised automated trading system.

Other than LCH.Clearnet, Clearing 21 is also implemented in the CME and NYMEX as their clearing management systems.

Settlement

Settlement is the conclusion of a stock trading transaction. Exemplified by the DVP system in Clearing 21, the meaning of settlement is exchanging securities and payment. Even though the process may not involve the physical presence of securities certificates, some electronic records must be made to track the transfer of ownership of the securities in a central securities depository (CSD). There is a national CSD in each country plus some international CSDs (or ICSD), like Euroclear and Clearstream in Europe. In the USA, the depository is provided mainly by DTCC.

A depository is an organisation that holds the (physical or dematerialised)[23] securities that are traded in the securities market. At time of settlement, the depository effects the centralised transfer of such securities against payment by making appropriate entries on its books and records. In cases when the investor does not have an account in the CSD, they may authorise a custodian to oversee the delivery and receipt of securities (possibly through another custodian, depository, or sub-custodian). Custodians look after the securities for the investors and offer value-added services, such as receipt of dividends, interest payments and corporate actions.

In the case of a cross-border trade, the transaction involves a far greater number of intermediaries and thus is exposed to higher risk. For example, a buyer may ask a local custodian to claim ownership in a foreign CSD or an ICSD. Or, if the investor is an institutional investor, its custodian collaborates with a foreign CSD to overcome the difference in trading systems and jurisdictions. Today, many ICSDs have expanded their business to custodian banking. Their institutional clients may be offered such services as securities safekeeping, clearing and settlement, securities and cash lending, which were once the specialities of custodians.

Settlement in the Depository Trust and Clearing Corporation

In the USA, the services of securities depository, custody and asset servicing are provided by DTCC and its subsidiaries, in particular, Depository Trust Company (DTC) and NSCC. The settlement process in DTCC is a team effort by several ICT systems. Three systems described below (CNS, TradeSuite and IMS) can briefly demonstrate DTCC's effort in upgrading their depository and settlement services to the ultimate goal: straight-through processing.

Continuous net settlement

The continuous net settlement (CNS) system was first launched in 1974 by NSCC. After several rounds of rewriting and redesign, the current CNS provides real-time settlement management such that trades (practically all broker-to-broker equities and bonds trades in the USA) can be settled within three days after the actual trade is done.

Trades eligible for CNS are settled on a net basis, i.e. they are matched to available securities in order to net receive or net deliver positions. The new CNS that came into being in 2004 is able to net trades intra-day and generate reports for all participants.

Information (such as intra-day trade messages and positions reports) can be released to participants through their Web-based participant browser service (PBS).

TradeSuite

DTC's TradeSuite is the trade messaging and settlement solution for equity and fixed income securities. Developed by Omgeo LLC (a joint venture between DTCC and Thomson Financial), TradeSuite consists of four applications:

- *TradeMessage*: Exchanges of post-trade messages (such as block trade notices of execution, and confirmations and affirmations[24]) between brokers, custodians and institutions. Messages are sent in SWIFT, TCP/IP, or ISO15022 protocols.
- *TradeMatch*: Centralises matching investment managers' allocations with brokers' trade confirmations. The application also sends trade affirmation messages.
- *TradeSID*: Processes settlement with allocations, trade confirmations and settlement data from DTC's standing instructions database (SID). Settlement instructions are then routed to custodian banks and broker's clearing agents.
- *TradeHub*: As a single access point for counterparties, investment managers and custodian banks, it is a message centre for settlement notification, reconciliation information and other trade details.

Omgeo plans to replace these applications using its own STP system, Central Trade Manger (CTM, discussed below in the section on STP). However, the progress of replacement is sluggish. Omgeo is still offering members of NSCC who register as 'prime brokers' an interface between TradeSuite and CNS so that with a TradeSuite account they can forward transactions that are affirmed in TradeSuite directly to CNS for netting and settlement.

Inventory management system

The core settlement process is managed by DTCC's inventory management system (IMS). Affirmed deliveries received from TradeSuite are processed by the IMS, and at the same time trading information is given to brokers, custodians and other participants so that they can have better control over the settlement. Implemented on an IBM WebSphere server with a DB2 database and MQSeries messaging middleware, the IMS incorporates the following applications:

- *Authorisation capabilities*: Replacing the old authorisation and exception features in TradeSuite, these allow participants to authorise transactions for automated settlement from multiple matching utilities.
- *Transaction prioritisation system*: Allows participants greater control over the timing and order of their deliveries using predefined profiles, based on transaction type and asset class.
- *Transaction warehousing*: Stores delivery instructions so that they can be directed to the processing system as night delivery orders (NDOs) that are due to settle on the appropriate settlement day.
- *'Dropped' deliveries*: Controls permitting the retention of failed deliveries for re-submission on the following settlement day (eliminating participants' need to re-input failed delivery instructions).

Completed in 2004, the IMS offers custodians and brokerage firms greater control over their trade settlements within DTCC. The system supports a wide range of settlement services, which include:

- giving special clients a higher (different) priority in the queue;
- inquiry on trades within 21 days;
- viewing summary of each transaction, e.g. a client can examine their NDO to see what has been processed, authorised, or rejected.

Horizontal and vertical integration

Consolidation of clearing and settlement operations chooses between two models: horizontal and vertical integration. The aforementioned LCH.Clearnet takes the horizontal model by consolidating processes at the same level – namely the levels of trading, clearing and settlement – across different markets and jurisdictions, so as to provide for economies of scale in various processes, such as those in commercial or user-governed utilities. Other benefits include reduced competition and redundant infrastructure and improved efficiency.

In contrast, Eurex Clearing, the competitor of Euronext and LCH.Clearing, follows a vertical model by integrating processes at the three levels (Figure 6.11). This model is regarded as a full integration across key processes of the investment cycle. This model is believed to facilitate internal decision-making processes, harmonisation of rules, and fast and safe transaction processes.

Chanel-Reynaud and Chabert (2005) describe a more flexible model that is demonstrated by the Virt'x framework of the Swiss stock exchange (SWX) – see Figure 6.12. Famous as a pan-European 'blue-chip' securities exchange, Virt'x is a joint venture of SWX and Tradepoint, a British ECN. Instead of competing with existing stock exchanges in Europe, Virt'x cooperates with Crest, SIS (Swiss clearinghouse), and Euroclear to set up an integrated transaction

Figure 6.11 Horizontal integration of Euronext

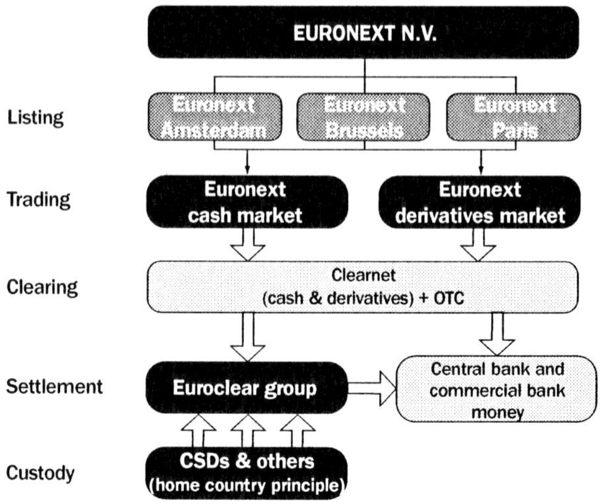

CSD: central securities depository; OTC: over-the-counter

Source: Euronext (2001)

Figure 6.12 Virt'x model of clearing and settlement

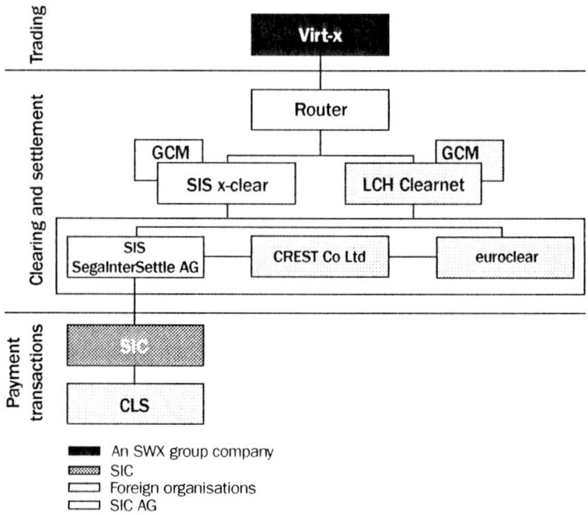

CLS: continuous linked settlement; GCM: general clearing member; LCH: London clearinghouse; SIC: Swiss Interbank Clearing (an interbank payment system); SIS: SegaInterSettle (a settlement network); SIS x-clear: a subsidiary of SIS Swiss Financial Services Group AG offering CCP services for Virt-x participants

Source: SWX (2005)

processing network. Thus, Virt'x is an exchange as well as a provider of clearing and settlement services. Customers trading on Virt'x can freely choose their preferred service provider at each step of the transaction process.

The consolidation that is going on in the European market seems inevitable. It is the effort of the financial services sector to enhance their competitiveness, in response to globalisation and deregulation, which are two challenges that have come to life in the age of the Internet. In North America, Europe and across the world, the financial services sector has once again become eager to achieve straight-though processing (STP). Although STP has never materialised for a number of reasons, it is believed to be the ultimate goal of the financial market.

Straight-through processing

In view of the growing competition in the market, the financial services industry has to revise its strategies and re-engineer its operations to meet new challenges. Streamlining the transaction cycle – trading, clearing and settlement – has become a consensus in the industry; the only uncertainty is how efficient the cycle may become. The US Securities Industry Association (SIA) set up a committee to promote the idea of STP. It defines STP as:

> the integration of systems and processes to automate the trade process from trade execution to confirmation and settlement without manual intervention or data re-entry. (*Gartner*, 2003)

The STP initiative is a rectification of the current problems – an inefficient trade processing cycle characterised by manual procedures, incompatible data and a diversity of standards. Integrating all trade processes into an STP system can reduce error rates, settlement risk and operational costs. In 1998, the establishment of the Global Straight-Through Processing Association (GSTPA) – a consortium of over 60 leaders in the financial sector – marked the official opening of the project to implement STP throughout the global market. According to SIA and GSTPA, the short-term goal toward STP is to shorten the trading process to T+1 day (one day after trading).

The quest for STP is contagious in Europe and Asia/Pacific, especially in areas where strong governing institutions exist. STP is believed to be a possible development for domestic trades through ICT deployment, local laws, regulations and market practices. However, promoting STP on a global basis is more difficult. This may be one of the reasons why GSTPA dropped out of the race to lead the STP initiative a few years ago.

Towards straight-through processing

STP is made possible if trading, clearing and settlement organisations are willing to cooperate. However, the problem is far more than connecting different organisations; internal trade processes need to be integrated as well. Pareek (year unknown) depicts the iterative consideration of STP objectives inside an organisation (Figure 6.13). Notice that the STP implementation process requires constant revisions as the market environment keeps changing.

Although STP is not entirely about ICT, using ICT to build an infrastructure for automated institutional trade matching, central management of information flow, and centralised enrichment of trades with standing settlement instructions (SSIs) is a major investment for the STP initiative. SIA developed an STP model and indicated that the core

Figure 6.13 **Formulation of internal straight-through processing objectives**

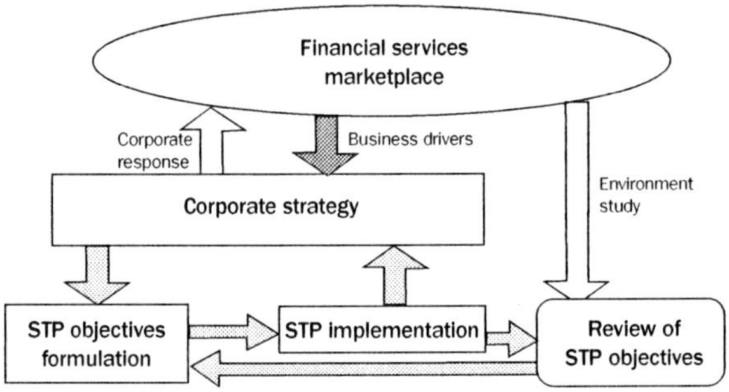

STP: straight-through processing
Source: Pareek (year unknown)

of the model is a virtual matching utility (VMU), which centralises trade processing functions within a utility module (Figure 6.14). With the SSI enrichment capability, the VMU should be able to check if there is any settlement instruction applicable to a trading situation so that the transaction can be so modified and appropriate parties can be notified. The SSI is essential to the automation of the transaction.

All players in the STP initiative accepted the VMU idea. For example, GSTPA's cross-border trading model has a central VMU hub. GSTPA named it 'Transaction Flow Manager' (TFM), which directs messages to relevant participants in the trading cycle. However, the construction of the TFM model seemed to have exhausted the consortium's €90 million funding. GSTPA ceased operations in 2002 when it found its rival Omgeo was offering its own version of VMU, the Central Trade Manger (CTM).

Figure 6.14 **The flow of messages in a future straight-through processing system**

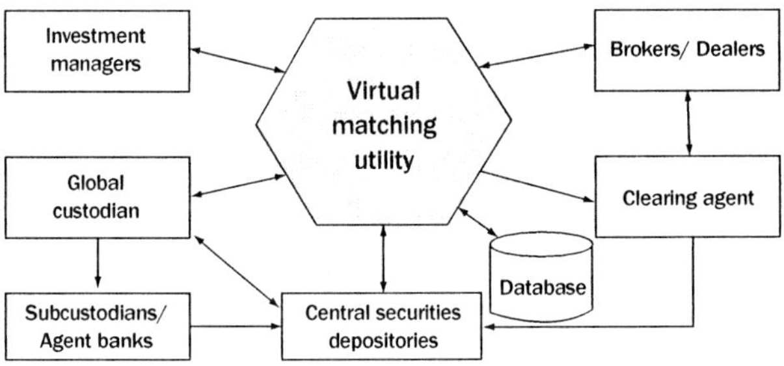

Omega CTM

Backed by DTCC, Omgeo's CTM system is a cross-border and non-US domestic STP solution. A broker/dealer can connect to the CTM directly through an interface or through the gateway of a solution provider.

The CTM matches trade data at two levels. In Omgeo's terminology, they are known as trade level (TL) or trade details (TD) information (see Figure 6.15). These are information on block (execution) and allocation respectively. The first step in processing begins as follows:

- *Trade validation*: The information is checked, for example, to see if all required data fields are present.
- *Security ID cross-referencing*: Both investment manager and broker/dealer are required to supply a security ID and a security type code.
- *BIA enrichment*: The broker/dealer's internal account number (BIA) is retrieved and cross-referenced with the investment manager's account.

Matching is performed with both TL and TD messages, which apply to match block and allocation respectively. Before matching, TD and TL information is enriched by relevant instructions from a central Omgeo ALERT database for SSI, if investment managers do not provide them

Figure 6.15 **Central trade manager tradeflow**

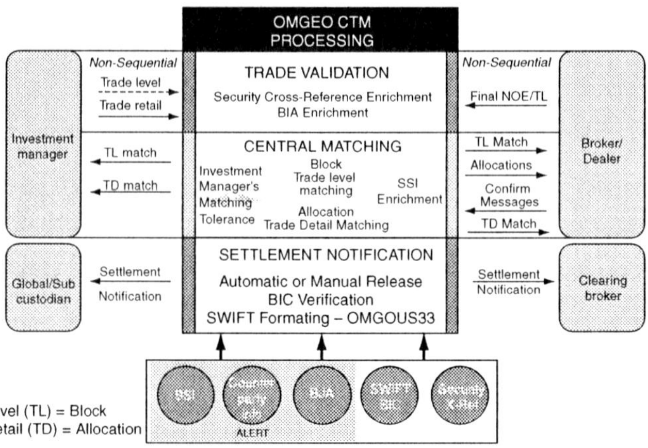

Trade Level (TL) = Block
Trade Detail (TD) = Allocation

CTM: central trade manger; BIA: broker/dealer's internal account (number); BIC: bank identifier code; NOE: notices of execution; OMGOUS33: the bank identifier code (BIC) of OMGEO; SSI: standing settlement instructions; TD: trade detail; TL: trade level; X-Ref: cross reference.

Source: Omgeo (2004)

manually. The process of central matching includes checking with matching and tolerance profiles, which are matching criteria and tolerances (e.g. exact match, a variation by percentage and the like) set by investment managers.

STP is provided by the automated settlement notification process, which occurs when trade details match but prior to trade validation. The latter is a process in which all settlement parties are validated against a directory of bank identifier code, which is called OMGOUS33 and has been available on the SWIFT FIN Network since 2001. In the USA, settlement notification is sent directly to DTCC.

CTM represents the endeavour of the securities industry to achieve STP. But streamlining interorganisational processes alone cannot solve all the problems; brokerage firms may also need to re-engineer their internal operations. An example of an STP solution offered by a vendor is shown below.

Canadian STP (TATA, 2004)

The Canadian Depository for Securities Limited (CDS) is the central hub of the country's securities depository, clearing and settlement system. Its two legacy systems – respectively called debt clearing service (DCS) and securities settlement services/book-based system (SSS/BBS) – do not have the flexibility and functionality to support CDS to achieve STP. In 2000, CDS decided to launch a giant project to reengineer the clearing and settlement system. Tata Consultancy Services won the contract and worked for three years to build a new system called CDSX.

The new system allows matching and confirmation. It automates a number of manual procedures, integrates the legacy systems, and offers new functionality. Users can settle their OTC equity trades – or debt and money market transactions – by several methods, including continuous net settlement (CNS), batch net settlement (BNS), and real-time trade-for-trade (TFT) settlement. The new system also incorporates ISO15022 messaging standards to facilitate real-time messaging between participants, including clearinghouses and depositories. It shortens securities settlement time to T+1 or even T+0 on a bilateral or industry-wide basis.

Summary

Unlike other sectors, the securities industry has experienced a period of interorganisational collaboration in the so-called STP initiative to enhance their operational efficiency by increased connectivity, automation, standardisation, newly devised rules and regulations. The endeavour seems to have come to a halt in the past couple of years, but the advantages it once promised are still valid and will soon rekindle new efforts to shape the industry.

The beginning of this chapter described the application of ICT in brokerage firms for streamlining their business processes and to offer better services to their clients. The emergence of online brokers and their solutions proved to the world that the Internet has not disintermediated the securities market, but instead has triggered a series of changes in investors' behaviour, broker/dealer services, operations in exchanges, clearinghouses and other authorities in the industry.

These changes were mentioned in the second and third sections, augmented by a few cases that outlined special features of ICT solutions in stock markets, clearing and settlement institutions. The chapter ended with a review of STP endeavours in the industry and an STP solution by a vendor, as an unfinished story of the quest for a better future of the increasingly globalised securities industry.

Questions for discussion

1. When compared with other markets like Nasdaq, the NYSE has been slow in digitisation. Its Direct+ system only processes 10 per cent of the exchange's volume, leaving the rest to the traditional floor-based trading. What are the advantages of the traditional method?
2. Several factors were once believed to be the driving force behind STP. These include explosive growth of securities transactions, shortening of the settlement cycle, increased competition and technological advancements (this is not an exhaustive list). With recent slackening of the STP initiative, are these factors no longer driving forces?

Notes

1. Sigma is the research arm of Swiss Re.
2. According to Société Générale (2004) 9.6 per cent of French people visit their bank's website for stock market transactions, available at: *http://www.efma.com/pdf/Report191.pdf*, p.8.
3. The technique of rule-matching can find all accounts that satisfy a rule, for example, those with more than ten wire transfers and more than $1,000,000 deposited.

4. Link analysis is a technique to find hidden links between accounts. The link could be a common address and/or shared cell phone number.
5. Sequence matching is a technique to detect particular orders of events that hint at some hidden relationships.
6. A financial regulator whose jurisdiction covers virtually all securities broker-dealers in USA.
7. Established in 1789, the NYSE is the largest stock market in the world. 2,760 companies are listed on it with a total market value of $20 trillion at the end of 2004 (Anderson, 2005).
8. Nasdaq is the world's largest electronic stock market. Since it was born in 1971, it has listed 3,271 companies, with a total market value of $3.7 trillion, as at the end of 2004 (Anderson, 2005).
9. MMTP is a protocol for clearing messages.
10. The matching of sellers and buyers is determined by two factors: time and price. For example, a buy order with the highest limit will be executed first and if there is more than one such order, the earliest one arriving at the order book trades first.
11. There were 19 certified ISVs for LIFFE CONNECT in 2004.
12. Although the two terms, ECN and ATS, are often used interchangeably, ECN is a latecomer.
13. Direct+ is an automatic execution service for limit orders of up to 1,099 shares. It lets users opt for an immediate execution at the best bid or offer, without a fee and with anonymity and speed.
14. 'Market look' information is information of trading interest that brokers can convey to their back office; e.g. number of buyers and sellers in a stock and the quantity bid or offered.
15. A CCP is the buyer to all sellers and the seller to all buyers.
16. Euroclear Bank is the parent company of Euroclear France. It has already taken over several settlement houses and depositories, which include the Dutch depository (Negicef), the Belgian depository (CIK) and the settlement-delivery company of LSE (Crest).
17. SWITCH is a trading system for derivatives offered by Euronext Amsterdam; it is planned to migrate SWITCH to LIFFE CONNECT.
18. Marché des Options Négociables de Paris (Paris traded options).
19. Marché à Terme International de France (French Financial Future Market).
20. Standard portfolio analysis of risk, a standard risk-based portfolio simulation method.
21. It is used in pricing equity options and index options.
22. Another model for the evaluation of futures and options on futures.
23. Dematerialised securities are those that exist only through account records on the books of the issuer or appropriate intermediary.
24. In cases when a customer places an order on behalf of other parties, they should notify the broker how to allocate the transaction among the corresponding parties. It happens after the receipt of notices of execution. The broker returns a 'confirmation' of the customer's instruction. After the customer verifies the allocation, they send the broker an 'affirmation'.

7

E-fundraising and other services

Introduction

The impact of the Internet is seen in all walks of life. Not only are large service institutions like banks, insurers, and stockbrokerage firms being influenced, other institutions and individuals who might come into contact with the financial sector have also found new applications of Internet technology making things very different from the past. There are unlimited ways to use the Internet and the related technologies, ranging from some back-office automation technologies to a business model innovation. This chapter is dedicated to several less conspicuous (but nonetheless important) areas of the financial services sector where people are experimenting with new Internet applications.

Also known by e-philanthropy, e-giving, e-advocacy and other names, the activities of raising funds on the Web is called 'e-fundraising' (or online fundraising) in this chapter. According to Bartlett et al. (2000), the impact of the Internet on the charity industry can be assessed at four levels for innovation – marketing, channel, product/service and business model (Figure 7.1).

One focus of this chapter is to examine Level 4. Although there are a few Web-based products/services specially designed for e-fundraising (e.g. online gifts, such as screensavers and e-cards), they are less substantial than business model innovation and related ICT applications. Level 2 has been a topic in Chapter 4 and Level 1 is obviously beyond the scope of this book.

Fundraising is usually considered as the kind of activities pertinent to charity or nonprofit organisations. Other institutions or individuals seeking financial support from the market may resort to methods like venture capital (VC), private equity and initial public offering (IPO). The latter two areas are included in this chapter, where ICT is not just automating back-office workflows. In the second and third sections

Figure 7.1 Framework to assess the impact of the Internet on the charity industry

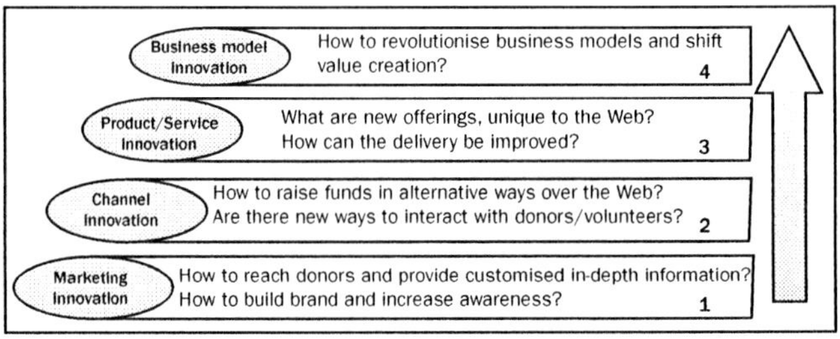

Source: Bartlett et al. (2000)

below, online VC and e-IPO are discussed not because they have produced a very significant impact on the financial services sector, but for the potential that they could ignite a revolution if the economic atmosphere permits.

E-fundraising

The potential of raising money on the Internet is demonstrated by the donation appeal for the September 11 relief. One hundred and fifty million dollars was raised via the Web in the first six months (Miller, 2002), making up to 10 per cent of the total individual relief donations. The story set a record high until the aftermath of the 2004 Boxing Day tsunami (see Table 7.1). But even before the disaster happened, online donations in general had already exceeded $2 billion in the year of 2004 (Stein & Kenyon, 2004).

However, these success stories do not mean online fundraising is a proven means for every charitable organisation to get financial aid.

Table 7.1 Online donations to US charities in the first ten days after the tsunami struck South Asia on 26 December, 2004

Charity	Donations
American Red Cross	$57 million out of $106 million
UNICEF	$20 million
Doctors Without Borders (US branch)	$16 million
Oxfam	$12 million out of $15 million

Data source: Wallace-Wells (2005)

Charities can only be certain about one thing – that their websites provide an efficient channel for information dissemination. Whether a forceful and far-reaching fundraising appeal online can materialise into real support depends on many factors, such as the nature of the incident, size of audience, their trust and the economic environment. With that many uncertainties, no one would completely replace conventional fundraising methods with an online campaign. These success stories can only demonstrate that e-fundraising is not an option but a further requirement.

In addition to getting direct funds online, online activities can also reward an organisation in raising the public's awareness and building relationships with current and potential donors. This idea has become so popular lately that the author and activist James Gregory Lord (1999) argues that the fundraising profession should begin looking at themselves as relationship managers rather than development directors (Kelly, 2001). In the same respect, King (2001) suggests that the objectives of Web-based fundraising can be summarised in *three Rs*: raising money, recognition and reaching out. Not only do these Rs set some goals for donor relationship management, they also imply the inseparability of these objectives in most e-fundraising activities.

Even when e-fundraising is perceived as just another channel of getting funds, organisations need to consider making recognition and reaching out as two other functions of their websites. Features on their websites could be aggregated to three levels, each catered for by one of the Rs.

- *Membership services*: Features for information dissemination, including e-mail and e-newsletter services. These improve member relationships and help them recognise the aim and commitment of the organisation.
- *Fundraising processes*: Features for the management of a fundraising campaign, including dissemination of action alerts, donation appeals, the 'Donate Now!' button and mechanisms to process online donations (e.g. credit card payment processor).
- *Member recruitment*: Features that are open to the general public to make them aware of the existence, goals and achievements of the organisation, including web pages of history, annual reports, reciprocal links with other organisations, as well as a discussion forum to support a community that pays attention to the organisation's activities.

Compared with traditional methods, building a website to attract Web surfers is simple and inexpensive. With traditional means, such as sales, grants, letters, phone calls and face-to-face appeals play the leading role in a fundraising campaign, the website can still play a subordinate role with its three levels of features.

When the organisation is prepared to take e-fundraising more seriously, the strategy of its online operations may become the strategy of the entire campaign. Such a campaign always requires careful planning, probably involving the following steps (Kelly, 1998) that are known by an acronym ROPES:

1. *Research* in three areas: (a) the readiness of the organisation; (b) the opportunity for raising gifts, and (c) the interests of the donor community. The aim of the research is to see whether these three areas conflict with one another.
2. *Objectives* are set to support the organisation's goals of fundraising. Measurable objectives are recommended and these can be divided into two areas: the result and the impact.
3. *Programming* to plan and implement activities to attain defined objectives. Activities are broken down into two areas: (a) cultivation and (b) solicitation of donors. Cultivation is important in building trust in the donor communities.
4. *Evaluation* can be carried out to assess the preparatory steps, the process, and the programme itself. The results are monitored and, if necessary, adjustments are made to improve effectiveness in the current exercise and/or the next.
5. *Stewardship* to ensure reciprocity, such as appreciation and recognition and responsibility, such as the proper use of funds. The campaign also needs to report regularly to donors and to nurture relationships. Smith (1993) asserts that the recipients of charitable funds are effectively the stewards of those funds and are expected to use them in accordance with the goals of those who provide them.

Three kinds of activities mentioned in the ROPES planning are cultivation, solicitation and stewardship – three words often found in the literature. Their meanings more or less coincide with the three Rs – reaching out, raising money and recognition – respectively. Besides specifying the activities in a fundraising campaign, the ROPES planning exemplifies a top-down process that begins by studying the aim of the campaign and building a business model for the exercise. Without the model, it is hard to coordinate activities for cultivation, solicitation and stewardship.

Business models

E-fundraising is often compared with e-marketing, both of which contain online activities to engage stakeholders, build relationships and cultivate customers (donors in the case of fundraising). Like e-marketing, while e-fundraising campaigns do not find ICT a critical success factor, technology can help the individual process. They should consider how the fundraising or marketing activities are coordinated to achieve the overall goal of the campaign. In other words, choosing an effective business model is the most critical success factor for an e-fundraising campaign.

The model is developed at the first two stages of ROPES, together with the processes that deal with steering committee selection, budgeting, long- and short-term objectives, staffing and all legal matters. The model must align with the objectives and resources available to the campaign. It also controls what activities should be chosen for the campaign and how they should be integrated.

If other factors remain the same, success cases of e-fundraising efforts bear a few unique characteristics, which include the following:

- *Brand name*: National and international organisations are in a better position to win recognition and credibility. Organisations whose physical establishments are less significant can build a brighter brand name online by e-marking methods, such as allying with other institutions (e.g. sponsors and search engines). Epner (2004) also suggests that the charity organisation's domain name should end with .org and have its .com counterpart reserved to be sure that no one surfing on the Web will miss it.
- *Content*: An attractive website that has informative content must be frequently updated. Websites of nonprofit organisations should avoid an oversupply of information and keep their layout clean and tidy, with all important messages clearly written and posted in some easily accessible pages. The pages should still have multimedia content, as this is generally more explanatory and more entertaining; however, it can often slow down the loading of a page and may have negative effect on people who have become used to the 'eight-second rule'.[1]
- *Prospective community*: Regardless of the model chosen, organisations with a large member community have an advantage over the others. Membership organisations hold verified lists of prospects with whom the organisations presumably keep in close contact all the time. The members trust their organisations and may easily be mobilised when they are alerted by an e-mail or a letter of a

fundraising appeal. For non-membership organisations, prospective communities are made up of their visitors, affiliates, guests, enquirers, volunteers, supporters and other acquaintances. They may need a little more effort to cultivate, perhaps by e-mail communications.

- *Fundraising pitches*: With the list of prospects ready, the online fundraising solicitation is implemented as planned. Following whatever model, the donation appeals appear on the splash page of their websites. The wordings are passionate, sincere, but not overwhelming. The page lets viewers read and immediately see that the cause can justify the action. An entry on the fund-receiving web page (such as a 'Donate Now!' button) is easy to find and the form filling procedure gives a pleasant experience.

Although organisations with prestige brand names are certainly capable of receiving funds and grants on and off the Web, smaller organisations can also benefit from the Internet. With a majestic website, any small organisation may look as large as other organisations. Stein and Kenyon (2004) assert that smaller charitable organisations have the advantage of tying a much more intimate relationship with their donor communities. Sometimes, the choice of a fundraising model is more important than the brand names. The authors quote a case in which a five-person organisation – Ruckus Society (*www.ruckus.org/index2.html*) – raised $170,000 online by exchanging donations with War Profiteer Playing Cards.

In the last decade, a few Web-based business models for fundraising have emerged. They range from having just a simple 'Donate Now!' button on a website to teaming several organisations together on a charity portal. The following models are popular among nonprofit organisations:

- *Web advertising*: Charities can sell their website space for advertisements in the form of banners or hyperlinks. Organisations might have more bargaining power if their websites have a high volume of traffic; for example, having a large member community.
- *Online auction*: If the size of member (or audience) population is large enough and there is attractive merchandise of interest to many people, an auction site is a fundraising opportunity. This method may also attract donors who care about tax deductions. Auction sites, such as WebCharity.com offer a tax deduction scheme for purchases over a certain amount, whereas other kinds of purchases, such as through a charity mall, are not tax deductible.

- *Charity (or donation) portals*: Sites like charitableway.com and helping.org offer directories of nonprofits that accept donations. These portals may also refer all donations to a centralised site and later redistribute the monies to relevant charities. Particularly suitable for small charities, these portals operate on the belief that they may attract heavier traffic and offer less total cost of ownership (TCO) in Internet security and credit card transaction processing. However, many such portals have been shut down because of poor management. An e-commerce strategist, Larry Cohen (year unknown) accuses them of three problems: (1) they often take control and revenue away[2] from charities that join them; (2) they require a percentage of donations or access to information on the donors; and (3) they work against the preference of younger donors to contribute directly to the nonprofit of their choice.
- *Charity malls*: Specialised cyber-malls, such as charitymalls.com and iGive.com aggregate e-retailers (or e-tailors) who agree to donate a commission to the malls from where customers are referred. This commission will be shared among the member charities. Paying no effort in building websites and administering donation payments, charities may find this model very appealing, although some of Larry Cohen's concerns remain valid.
- *Commercial co-ventures*: Taking advantage of the affiliate plans of many e-commerce institutions, charities may place a banner or hyperlink in their websites that leads viewers to those commercial websites where purchases can be made. Commercial institutions would then funnel their commissions to any sites sending consumers to them. Such a relationship offers donors an online store as well as a place for 'buying to give'. However, it might affect the status for unrelated business income tax (UBIT, discussed again in the section of legal issues) of the charity organisation.
- *Online storefront:* Selling merchandise is also a means to fund a nonprofit. Management of such online storefronts would be no different from a common B2C storefront. The merchandise to be sold could be manufactured for the campaign or be donations from their members. As many charities do not have the capacity to create and manage the online storefront, they rely on a service provider. Adopting the model, either the charity or service provider of the storefront might be required to register as professional solicitors in most US states.

Charities can choose more than one model for their fundraising campaign. Some might outsource the construction and management work of their e-fundraising projects, others might look for the right kind of ICT applications to help them manage their fundraising activities. In a typical case, software solutions for general business management, budgeting and accounting, human resources management, project management, auditing and decision making may provide sufficient support for most operations. A few vendors have also developed special ICT systems for the management of fundraising campaigns.

E-fundraising technology

Although fundraising is more about social relationships than technology, those activities on the Web can be better managed with the use of ICT. Nonprofits can use software tools for general management, such as project planning and credit card transaction processing; there are also specialised ICT solutions that provide more integrated control over selected fundraising models. Besides solicitation, these solutions also build in a database of donors and prospects and some software tools for cultivation and stewardship.

When compared with the management information systems of other businesses, e-fundraising solutions are characterised by their versatility in content management, donor relationship management and transaction management. Some might be designed for a special business model (such as a portal or auction) and some excel in campaign management or marketing. These features are discussed as follows:

- *Content management*: To edit and publish website contents so as to improve the online experience of members and donors. To cultivate constituents, these websites need to assure and encourage visitors to concern themselves with the vision and objectives of the organisations. As these websites are channels for interaction between the organisations and constituents, there are contents linked to a constituent database to facilitate webpage personalisation and online feedback. Information in the constituent database is also required when delivering messages, including expressions of donor appreciation, (tax) receipts and acknowledgments.
- *Donor relationship management*: There is a saying, 'donations are a by-product of a successful relationship'. The success of a fundraising campaign does not entirely depend on the efforts put into the campaign, but on the long-term relationship with donors. Donor

relationship management is always compared with the customer relationship management (CRM) systems in other business sectors, as both are used to recruit and retain prospects by providing them with optimal value.

Among nonprofits, the concept of 'constituent relationship' covers an even larger area than 'donor relationship'. Constituents of a charitable organisation could be donors, subscribers, members, friends, volunteers, vendors, media, or anyone interested in the goals of the organisation. They could all be prospective donors, if intrigued by the right timing and appeals. There are ICT solutions (also abbreviated as CRM) that are used to cultivate loyalty among constituents by using some of the following techniques:

- *Viral effect*: Constituents are becoming regarded as a virus as their passion can spread from person to person. CRM solutions, such as Convio's Teamraiser provide tools to encourage constituents to forward messages to their friends, whenever they receive the message from the charities. Viral marketing tools are effective in expanding the constituent population.
- *Segmentation*: A fundraising campaign may be more appealing to one group of constituents than others. Information of constituents' profiles should thus be segmented to find target lists to which e-mail, newsletters, action alerts or fundraising appeals may have the strongest effect. As constituents differ in their previous actions, interests, needs, values and demography, the segmentation process uses software tools in CRM solutions to find the correlation between the possibility of donation and the complex and multidimensional profile of a constituent.
- *Easy response tools*: Used to construct response forms for constituents to return their comments on special issues. These forms may have pre-fill items or combo boxes that turn form-filling into a few easy clicks.
- *Single view*: The CRM system opens a window that allows a single view of a constituent in spite of the bulk volume of data in the constituent database. The single view lets everyone in the organisation have a consistent perception of a constituent, so that cultivation and fundraising efforts can be coordinated better.
- *Miscellaneous tools for easy access to constituent and activity information*: These include directories, search engines, event calendars and communication tools.

(Note that the abbreviation CRM refers to customer relationship in the rest of the chapter.)

- *Credit/debit card processor*: Charitable organisations usually outsource their credit/debit card processing operations to service providers. It is thus important to select the provider whose services and security levels (including fraud handling) satisfy the organisation. In addition, charities should also be careful about indemnity and protection against legal actions while binding a contract with the provider.
- *Online auction solution*: Service providers, such as Epiq (Nasdaq: EPIQ) and cMarket release online auction solutions for the management of auctions. These solutions include tools to develop auction websites, online categories, constituent lists and e-mail promotion. These can manage the auction process, which includes pricing, bidding, closeout and payment processing, and pertinent accounting routines.
- *Marketing software*: Most fundraising solutions include e-mail marketing tools that can be used in tasks like e-mail authoring, e-mail list building and prospect segmentation. For organisations that run an e-auction or online sales as a major fundraising event, direct notification by e-mail is necessary to promote and gather sufficient participants for the event.
- *Campaign management*: Within the scope of fundraising, a campaign management application encompasses tools for the planning, tracking, managing and streamlining of a campaign. It is basically a database-driven system that contains up-to-the-minute information of the campaign status (e.g. funds received and the distance from the target) and allows users to track user-defined data fields (e.g. revenue, cost). By linking its operations to marketing and donation processing, a campaign management solution can streamline the campaign by simplifying data capture, organising all fundraising scripts and event reports, and automating constituent communications.

The functionality of a fundraising management system varies with the business model of its user. In the following case, the organisation's effort to become the hub among a large number of other organisations gives it the reason to deploy a totally different management system.

Case: Aidmatrix.com

At *www.aidmatrix.com* you will find a nonprofit, Web-based service that supplies advice, technical help and online tools for other nonprofits.

Launched by the i2 Foundation in 2000, Dallas-based Aidmatrix applies supply chain management (SCM) methods to build up a network of international, regional and local agencies to channel food, clothing, building, medical and educational supplies to people in need. The SCM solution itself is a donation from i2 Technologies, Inc. (Nasdaq: ITWO), a world-class expert in SCM.

In 2003, the organisation started to provide a service known as 'virtual food drive' with the technology consultant Accenture. The backbone of the application is implemented on a Sun ONE Portal Server and Sun ONE Directory Server, which facilitates collection of donations and fundraising for humanitarian aid. Charitable organisations can register as one of its food drives and the 'virtual food drive' plan can help the charity to set up specialised web pages to accept monetary donations. Items in need are detailed on the web pages so donors can decide to give money to buy exactly the right items or just to give money. Aidmatrix's platform also calculates the number of families fed per month by this donation and gives a better picture of the impact of each donation.

The idea supports the construction of 'virtual aid drives' and 'Aidmatrix Asian Tsunami Virtual Drive' after the disaster struck at the end of 2004. In times of less turmoil, Aidmatrix offers its expertise in SCM and Web-based operations to deliver humanitarian aid around the world in a scheme called 'Global Relief Network'. Apart from its partnership with US charitable organisations, Aidmatrix is also involved with the European Federation of Food Banks in its fight against hunger and waste.

Legal issues

The Internet is borderless, but raising money and many other online activities that are common practices in a charitable organisation are subject to regional regulations. To wrap up the discussion on e-fundraising, we examine a few legal issues below.

Mercer (1998) asserts that any local government may have the right to regulate any fundraising website if someone residing in their jurisdiction makes a donation through the website. Some US state governments might even require the owner of such a website to register in their office in person. It is desirable that charitable bodies seek legal advice to comply with these 'solicitation laws' at state level or in a lesser jurisdiction. In the USA, a charitable body may use a 'unified registration statement'[3] to fulfil the requirements of all states requiring registration once and for all. However, the Internet service provider (ISP) supporting the campaign may also be subject to other regulations for registration requirements.

Nonprofits are usually classified as tax-exempt organisations. In the USA, however, income that they generate in a way that is unrelated to the mission of the organisation is subject to tax, under the UBIT[4] law. Although income derived from fundraising activities is not considered to be UBIT, the Internal Revenue Service Department has been sceptical in some instances – for example, the issuance of affinity credit cards and the sale of items for 'suggested minimum contribution' (Hurwit & Associates, 2004).

Mercer is also aware of the problem of 'credit card laundering' which may happen to organisations that wish to accept credit card donations but have no merchant account. This kind of service is commonly offered by service providers – i.e. they process credit card transactions without requiring the organisation to obtain its own merchant account from a bank or some third-party provider. However, this is illegal in some states (including Florida) and is considered to be a misconduct case by credit card companies.

Personal data that organisations can capture from their website could again be a problem, especially in places where a law similar to the UK Data Protection Act is in place. Such regulations may require that the usage of the data is stated in a conspicuous place on a charitable website to demonstrate the transparency and justifiable causes of the data handling procedures. Because charities may capture personal data and activity history of their constituents, these data could be used for communications for cultivation and solicitation purposes. At one end, using the bulk of data for sending e-newsletters would turn normal communication into spamming. At the other extreme, using a carefully selected group of constituent data would also constitute an abuse of personal data; for example, hospitals targeting their fundraising appeals to former patients of a special segment without their prior written consent violate the HIPAA Privacy Rule.

There are numerous traps into which a charitable organisation may fall. Besides the aforementioned laws and negligence over security matters, nonprofits should also be certain that the contents of their websites comply with intellectual property laws and do not conflict with laws on trade secrets or defamation.

Venture capital

The Web is also a venue for individuals and institutions to seek capital for financing start-ups and the development and/or expansion of an established organisation. The owners of venture capital will invest in a business that they consider profitable in return for assuming a portion of ownership of that business and/or to place some persons in the management board. To these venture companies,[5] a change in ownership and/or management board may not be desirable. However, venture companies understand that getting venture capital is different from borrowing money from a bank. For various reasons, venture companies may not be able to satisfy the usually harsh condition of lending and it is not surprising to find the capitalists (also called 'angels') eager to maximise return on investment may expect a return higher than that from other investments.

The volume of venture capital committed reached its peak in 2000. It was at the height of the e-commerce bubble when ICT start-ups usually got the largest share of investment (they *were* called 'e-ventures') and the marketplace, on and off the Web, was filled with individual and corporate investors looking for investment opportunities. Besides traditional financial services, such as investment banks, online venture capital firms also appeared helping investors and venture companies find each other. Since 2000, only a few of these online capital firms have remained in business, including AlwaysOn-Network.com and Garage Technology Ventures.

To both e-ventures and online venture capital firms, their business is largely influenced by the relationship with their investors. They tend to use ICT solutions to tie closely with the decision-making process of the investors. For example, Figure 7.2 shows the functionalities of a venture capital management system of an online venture capital firm, which provides a trading platform for registered investor and venture companies. One of the objectives of the system is to let investors and venture companies understand each other better by facilitating meetings and information exchange.

The structure shown in Figure 7.2 represents an investor relationship management (IRM) system, which is a specialised CRM system serving at least two groups of clients. These groups differ in their agendas and wish to have specialised information at their disposal:

- *Investors* wish to learn the context of the ventures – the development history, environment, due diligence and valuation methods.
- *Venture companies* need to understand the financial implication of their ventures, including their business models, development, capitalisation plans and even post-investment controls.

The discussion on IRM is thus divided into two subsections below.

Figure 7.2 Functions of the five modules that build up an online venture capital management platform

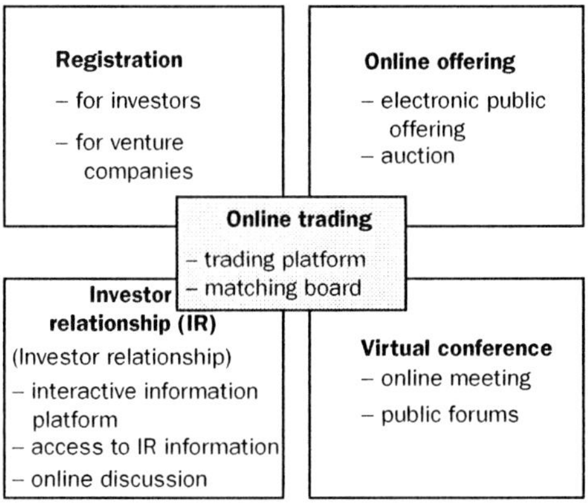

Source: cin/technology (year unknown)

Investor relationship management from an investor's perspective

As with any CRM system, an IRM system should help retain and recruit investors. Online venture capital firms supply information and other services to bind investors to venture projects. During the pre-investment phase, investors are provided with information of investment opportunities. They can also find assistance for their selection of ventures and there are ICT tools for financial due diligence, deal negotiations and the trading process. In the post-investment period, the investors keep track of their investment profiles by using those wealth management tools provided by the IRM solution.

Due diligence is a complex exercise that may take days or weeks. It is a rigorous investigation and assessment of an investment opportunity to see if it fits with the investor's criteria[6] of investment. The exercise is carried out in a series of meetings, interviews, analysis, documentation and processes of approval. The investigation is aimed at drilling down into each problem discovered in the exercise to determine whether the venture is competitive in terms of its internal management, customer preference, technology trend (including intellectual property), value chain and liability and risk.

Often implemented as a major component of an IRM solution, FundRunner, for example, a Web-based document management system, is helpful to the due diligence exercise. Using techniques in workflow management and document imaging, the document management system manages document templates, versioning, archiving, indexing and searching. Those processes are controlled by pre-set business rules and are compliant with laws, such as the Sarbanes-Oxley Act and anti-money laundering legislation. The platform must also be able to provide a secure environment as most of these documents are highly confidential. Figure 7.3 shows the architecture of an IRM system.

Another objective of due diligence is to negotiate price and deal terms. The investor should continue its meetings with the venture company to find out the optimal deal structure, which is often selected to maximise the investor's return and protection as well as to fulfil the company's requirements. The deal will detail the financial instrument[7] in the deal, percentage of ownership, controls, staged commitments and exit mechanism (such as IPO or bankruptcy).

The meetings and negotiations would likely go on for a couple of months before the deal can be closed. This occurs at the time when due diligence is completed and both parties have found trust in each other. They come to an agreement on the deal structure and lay down each item in the deal in contracts. Details, such as all legal terms, anti-dilution protection (common methods include full-ratchet, weighted average and pay-to-play), management fee, and the company disclosure schedule must have been discussed and consensus reached before the investment closes.

After the deal has been made, the investor should have its investment profile constantly monitored to see if any agreed terms are infringed. The capability to retrieve real-time information and generate reports dynamically is thus essential. Web-based IRM systems can integrate all relevant track records, analytics, and documents in a personalised web page to which only the investor can get access.

Figure 7.3 **Investor relationship management platform**

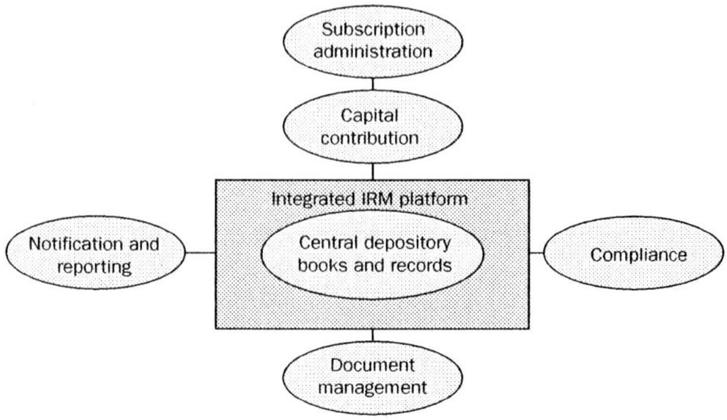

Investor relationship management from a venture company's perspective

When registered to a venture capitalist firm, a venture company expects to find information on the IRM system of possible investors and other ventures that are competing in the same market. To prepare for any enquiry, the company needs to organise its management team for due diligence and get all necessary documents ready and uploadable on the IRM database. When negotiating a deal with an investor, the venture company can let the capitalist firm offer its expertise in determining the term sheets and setting business milestones and other metrics. The IRM could also administer meeting records, document consolidation, repository and distribution.

After investment, the investor becomes a major stakeholder and may take over some or all control of the venture company as defined in the deal structure. Theoretically speaking, a venture company may acquire business skills besides finance from the investors. It is not surprising to see a re-structuring of the management board after investment, with one or more board members or even the CEO replaced. Thus, the IRM system from then on could exhibit different forms – from being a bridge between the company and an hands-off investor to a simple intra-company reporting system – depending on how investors get into the daily operations of the venture companies.

Assuming that a company values its relationship with its investors, it might have an IRM system to manage communications between the company and its investors. As investors are the stakeholders, work in IRM might be taken as one of the functions of the stakeholder relationship management (SRM) system, which disseminates information to all stakeholders as well. In any case, the company is obliged to send reports to its investors in accordance with the types, frequencies and qualities of information delivered as specified in the investment deals. For this purpose, a Web-based IRM or SRM system could automate the generation and distribution of those reports, perhaps in the form of web pages or e-mail messages. It could also be integrated with some performance monitoring tools, such as balanced scorecard, to let investors know the strengths and weaknesses of the business.

For investors who are not interested at the daily operations of the company, IRM should provide strategic level decisions of the company. Figure 7.4 illustrates this investor relationship model in two loops, where the IRM loop at the top is linked with the internal management loop below. The loops imply that IRM as well as planning and performance

Figure 7.4 **Integrating investor relationship management with strategic planning**

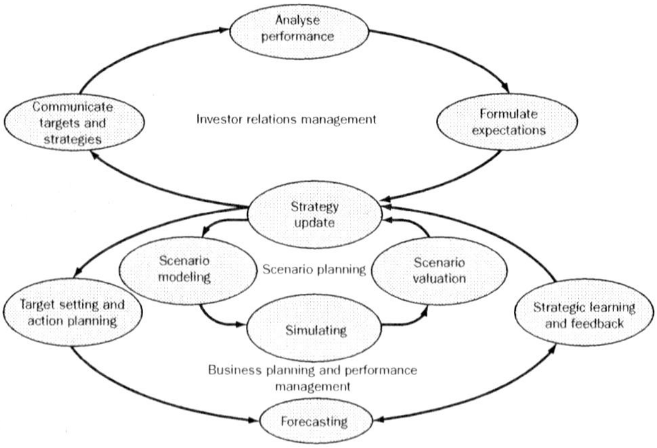

Source: Wung (2004)

management in a company are constantly modified by feedback controls. Note in the internal management loop that both the strategic modelling (scenario planning) and operational business management are aligned whenever the strategy is updated. The business strategy determines what parameters and targets should be communicated to investors.

Venture capitals are scarce in the market when compared with their heyday in 2000. However, individuals and venture companies alike may still find other financial alternatives in the market, which gathers a large number of institutional investors, private equity funds, hedge funds and individuals who are always seeking investment opportunities. As far as the financial services sector is concerned, their application of ICT extends no further than the IRM functionalities discussed above.

E-IPO

IPO is perhaps the most remarkable transformation of any private company. This is a process of going through a prolonged period of underwriting, accounting and legal procedures, and at the end the private company can raise a substantial amount of money by selling its shares to the public. The procedure is generally known to be complicated, expensive, paper-intensive and potentially error-prone.

The history of Web-based IPO started with the Spring Street Brewing Co. in 1996 (see the case described in the next section). Its success has triggered a series of attempts in the USA as well as in other parts of the world – most in countries developing at a fast pace. A typical example is the Securities and Futures Commission (SFC) of Hong Kong, which tested its e-IPO model with the offering of the local subway corporation MTRC in September 2000. Compared with an IRM system or the Spring Street's system, the e-IPO model of Hong Kong is structurally simple. It is only an alternative channel of logistics (other than mailing) with every other process remaining unchanged.

Note that the e-IPO system in Hong Kong differs very much from Spring Street Brewing. The former was created by the city's securities authority but the latter was developed by an issuing company and was originally used for its own IPO. Even though the models operated in different communities, both posted IPO information on the Internet. As the Internet is an inexpensive way to reach millions of people, intermediary firms, such as investment banks and underwriters, might also provide e-services for IPO clients by creating websites to release company information, including the prospectus, filings, management overviews, progress of the IPO, latest and forecast prices, and bullish/bearish rankings. Storing and editing this information can become a value-added service to clients and business news subscribers. For a fee, they might release tracking resources and detailed IPO data (including an aftermath report) to them.

Nonetheless, e-IPO in Hong Kong is a collaborative effort between brokers, banks and regulatory bodies. Considered as a value-added service, many banks (including HSBC, Bank of America and Standard Chartered) join as IPO service providers and each sets up its website to collect subscription applications from its clients and uses its internal banking platform to manage applicants' payments. The SFC maintains a securities and derivatives network to collect applications electronically from those banks which, at the same time, submit consolidated applications and subscription monies to the receiving banks. The subsequent notification and refund processes would be paper-based.

In a case more general than Hong Kong's model, e-IPO should include a wider range of activities. The financial market has seen several attempts to harness the Internet in mitigating the problems of IPO. Each of these e-IPO models was designed to replace parts of the manual or paper-based processes and many have met resistance and controversies in the financial sector. Until now, e-IPO is still experimented with by one institution after another. There are many processes that make up the IPO workflow (as depicted in Figure 7.5) and in theory each process can be digitised and has the potential to be included in an e-IPO model. There is plenty of room for the financial sector to create new e-IPO models.

Figure 7.5 Workflow of a typical IPO

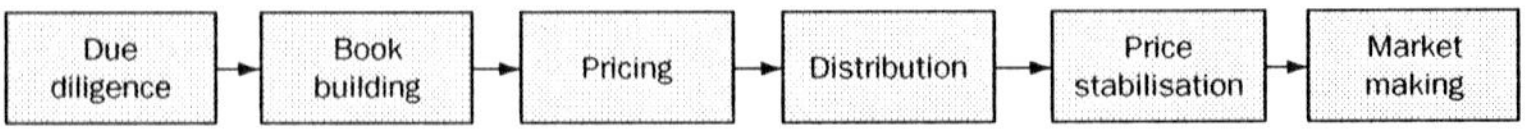

The entire procedure of an IPO traditionally takes one or two years of preparation, during which the underwriter plays the most important role. The underwriter conducts due diligence about the issuer. It also participates in the filings and registration, and most importantly, administers book building and determines share price of the stocks. Several e-IPO incidents in the USA – including the Spring Street Brewing case – took a disintermediatory approach and circumvented the underwriters. Their approach has set an example to followers, showing them how issuing companies can take better control over their IPO.

The following two cases demonstrate how issuing companies use the Internet for pricing their shares without the intervention of any underwriter. Incidentally, both cases used a modified version of the Dutch auction method in pricing their stocks.

Case: Hambrecht's OpenIPO

WR Hambrecht & Co. is an investment bank founded in 1998. It distinguishes itself by offering several Web-based auction services to investors and issuing companies; two of those services are:

- *OpenBook*: A Web-based platform used for online auction of corporate bond issues. In 2000, Dow Chemical raised about $300 million in a two-hour auction window which aggregated 57 participants in the bidding. During the auction, every order when entered was made known with its size and price (but not from whom) to every participant on the platform. They could also see how the demand curve changed in real-time.
- *OpenIPO*: A platform used in hosting Web-based IPO auctions. The OpenIPO platform was a replica of OpenBook until the SEC expressed concerns over the transparency of the operations on the platform, as it can show demand in real-time, and it was feared that sudden demand surges could shock investors. The OpenIPO is thus designed to operate with sealed bids such that investors could not see specific bids for a particular stock by any group of bidders (O'Connor, 2001). Anyone can open an account on OpenIPO with $2,000 and bid for a stock.

One of Hambrecht & Co's clients is RedEnvelope.com, a San Francisco-based e-tailer of valuable gifts. Its IPO was in September 2003, after two consecutive years of having deficits. Using the OpenIPO platform, RedEnvelope succeeded in selling 2.2 million shares, each priced at $14. When bids entered OpenIPO, they were sorted by price and the number of shares. The auction platform tallied the bids, and people who bid highest won the shares. However, the platform also calculated the lowest bid price that would allow for the company to raise the targeted funds. The bid price was made known to RedEnvelope which then finalised the real offering price after taking other things into consideration. The company (Nasdaq: REDE) shares have traded on the Nasdaq ever since.

The auction model adopted in OpenIPO is a modified form of Dutch auction. It is in fact based on the theory of the Nobel laureate William Vickrey.[8]

Case: Google IPO

When Google Inc. went IPO in 2004, it caused a sensation. Instead of asking its underwriters Morgan Stanley and Credit Suisse First Boston to price the IPO, the top search engine company conducted a Dutch auction on the Web, trying to raise $2.718 billion. It planned to sell 25 million shares at $108–135.

One of its co-founders, Larry Page, posted a seven-page letter entitled 'An Owner's Manual for Google's Shareholders' on google.com. The manual was supposed to be read by the public investors as it detailed the reasons behind the arrangement of the IPO. However, rival search engines had also studied its content to find weaknesses in Google's operations.

More than information delivery, the company was confident enough to apply its experience in running AdWords to its own IPO. Being an auction-based advertising system, AdWords technology was once again used in the new IPO platform, which was built with some advice from Morgan Stanley and Credit Suisse First Boston. It supported a website that would capture bids into a database. Information on the bids would be vetted and used to build order bookings. There was an application written to review and choose the winning bids by some mathematical methods.

Google chose 13 August, a Friday, to open its auction. The incident aroused much debate as no companies larger than Google had gone through an IPO auction before. The market was sceptical about the auction, which had been attacked by some investment banks. Although the GoogleIPO website received a large volume of bids, they were mostly institutional buyers who bid at a lower price. Five days later, Google realised it had to lower its original target. The new target was set to 19.6 million shares to be sold at $85 (i.e. 37 per cent below the original top price.) Since then, shares of the search engine have traded on the Nasdaq under the ticker symbol GOOG. The share price soared to over $420 at the end of 2005.

Direct public offering

The Internet has also revolutionised the financial market to allow a simpler way than IPO that helps small to medium-sized enterprises (SMEs) and startups to collect capital from the public. Direct public offering (DPO) in its traditional form is a small business (e.g. a local bank) selling its stocks directly to its customers (now called 'affinity group') without soliciting assistance from the underwriters. The Internet is a perfect venue for DPO as it can easily be turned into a bulletin board for the affinity group. For example, as Google's investors are mostly Web surfers who have confidence in Google's technology, its IPO is also referred to as a DPO and during the exercise, the GoogleIPO website was a venue for investors to obtain company news.

Although securities administrators still require DPOs to be registered, the offering procedure is simpler and far less costly. The aforementioned IPO of Spring Street Brewery Co. is commonly quoted as the first case of online DPO. It began in 1995 when the company created a website for people interested to find DPO information, such as financial reports and subscription agreement. The website was open for ten months, selling shares on a 'first come, first served' basis to more than 3,500 investors (some overseas). The DPO raised about $1.6 million without any underwriter. To provide a secondary market, the company built a bulletin board system known as Wit-Trade, which consisted of a buyers' bulletin board and a sellers' bulletin board on which investors could trade their shares via e-mail. Payment was managed by Spring Street manually.

Even though they were not listed on any stock exchange – which is a characteristic of many DPO issuers – the stocks of Spring Street traded in the Wit-Trade mechanism pretty well. But the SEC worried that the system was not giving adequate protection to small investors. Soon after Wit-Trade began operations, it was shut down for two weeks. At the end of the period the SEC agreed that Wit-Trade could open again on condition that a few operations would be modified. Having realised that the Wit-Trade mechanism could turn into a digital stock market, the brewery established Wit Capital (Nasdaq: WITC), an online investment bank and e-brokerage firm combined. It bought Soundview Technology in 1999, a technology stock research operation spun-off from Gartner Securities Corp, to become Wit Soundview and then E*Trade's underwriter E*Offering. It remained one of the pioneers of online IPO and DPO service providers until it was acquired by Charles Schwab in early 2004. It is currently called Schwab Soundview Capital Markets.

The success of Wit-Trade demonstrates how the technological and legal hurdles of online DPO can be cleared. Compared with e-IPO, online DPO is not widely accepted by public investors as well as companies. It is believed that 'information asymmetry', which refers to the problem where the issuer knows the quality of the securities being offered but the investor does not, is a major reason.

Summary

This chapter wrapped up a few niche areas in the financial services industry where institutions and companies are able to get financial support from others. The first section detailed e-fundraising models and related technologies. The second section examined how venture capitalists and startups benefit from ICT solutions. Lastly, some real-world cases were used to illustrate the feasibility of e-IPO and e-DPO.

When compared with developments in other e-financial services areas, those business models and ICT solutions discussed in this chapter are still experimental to see if they are acceptable to the public, the financial services sector and regulatory bodies. Nonprofits and charities are aware of the potential capability to raise money on the Web; but they understand their success relies very much on how they cherish the relationship with their constituents. Thus the Internet is used to foster relationships, which include constituent relationships to fundraising organisations and investor relationships to venture capital firms.

Seemingly more premature is e-IPO. Subsequent incidents of e-IPO in the USA, have caused speculation. One such incident, Google, which was described as a typical case of pricing without underwriting, explained why the idea is not welcome to many investment banks and underwriting firms. But there must be more to come.

Questions for discussion

1. If your nonprofit organisation outsourced the processing of online donations to a service provider, what would you expect that the service should include?
2. Why do you think an investor wants to invest in a new company in the first place? What would thus be the possible strategies of the investor when they take control of the company?
3. In spite of its size and unprofitable track record, RedEnvelope (see Hambrecht's case) succeeded in raising $31 million in its IPO. Why do you think this could happen?

Notes

1. A Web surfer is said to have patience to wait for no more than eight seconds for a page to load from the Web.
2. For example, the portal would not redistribute monies received until the donations aggregate over some thresholds set up by the portal. Many small charities find it difficult to reach the threshold and can never get paid.
3. Details available at: *http://www.multistatefiling.org/index.html* (last accessed: 2 December 2005).
4. Unrelated business income tax (UBIT) is income derived from (1) a trade or business, (2) which is regularly carried on, and (3) which is not substantially related to the performance of tax-exempt functions.
5. 'Venture companies' is the term used to exemplify all investees, which include entrepreneurs and portfolio companies.
6. Many investors have their preference of ventures which can be distinguished by their industry sector, stage of development, geography and size.
7. Such as loan, shares, warrants and options.
8. For further information, see: *http://torque.oncloud8.com/archives/cat_google_ipo.html*.

8

Security management

Introduction

The unsuccessful hype of B2C e-business in 2000 was explained by several reasons, in which online security was everyone's concern. A 2004 global security survey by world-renowned financial advisor Deloitte Touche Tohmatsu (DTT) even found that 83 per cent of the surveyed financial firms admitted that they were attacked in 2003 (compared with 39 per cent in 2002) and 40 per cent suffered some financial losses (DTT, 2004a). DTT findings were confirmed in similar surveys[1] in the UK. These findings indicate that the financial services sector must take some measures to defend itself against possible attacks when it enters the treacherous waters of the Internet marketspace.

When the findings of the 2004 survey (DTT, 2005b) are compared with those of the previous year, they show some signs of improvement. The percentage of the surveyed firms having been compromised drops to 30 per cent. This apparent success may be attributable to the investment on security, which is about 4–6 per cent of the total IT budget, as mentioned in the survey. With increasing awareness of management boards, security budgets also show a gentle upward trend. In addition, the 2005 survey reveals more interesting findings, including the following:

- small organisations (fewer than 5,000 employees by DTT's standard) are less likely targeted by outsiders;
- thirty-five per cent of the attacks occurred from the inside (compared with the 14 per cent in the previous year).

The first result can be explained by the fact that the fame and fortune of larger organisations make them more attractive to hackers. In spite of their heavy investment in security technology, there may be operational practices in which hackers find weaknesses.

The second finding suggests that security is not merely a technological issue. McCue (2004) highlights three sources of vulnerability – collusion between employees and criminals, disgruntled employees and portable storage devices. Most organisations now believe that a risk management strategy is very important. They would agree with the concept of a 'culture of security', which was defined by the Organisation for Economic Cooperation and Development as:

> a focus on security in the development of information systems and networks and the adoption of new ways of thinking and behaving when using and interacting within information systems and networks. (OECD, 2003)

A culture of security is strengthened by rules and regulations, and the financial services industry finds no shortage of them. As the Internet can reach almost every corner of the world, institutions that serve foreign customers or partners should treat compliance as an international business. This implies that the financial services sector is engaging in a battle with two frontiers – security and compliance. On both sides, every institution needs to spend a large sum of money on technology. HAL Knowledge Solutions (2005) Cost of Complexity Survey discovered that despite the fact that financial sector IT departments *do* understand and commit to an IT governance strategy, over a third of financial sector organisations are still struggling to meet the regulatory standards. Even worse, no one is certain if the spending can reduce the risk of security breach, data abuse, or employee misconduct. The industry can only speculate about the cost of not spending the money, only to have an insecure or noncompliant system running.

For the financial services industry, security and regulatory compliance go side by side as strategic concerns. Compliance is a major feature of most security-management solutions. Because of the complexity of legal issues, the discussion on compliance is mainly left to Chapter 9. But this does not prevent the titles of some laws and regulations being brought up in this chapter, thereby illustrating their tight relationship with the security strategy of the financial services industry. Chapters 8 and 9 should be viewed together as one long description of those security management solutions providing comprehensive protection that includes most security aspects of the e-financial services as well as legal compliance.

The aim of this chapter is to describe the security management framework adopted by e-financial services and the problems of security and risk management that arise from the use of ICT. The term 'risk management' is restricted to operational risk management in this chapter whereas matters arising from financial risk management are left to Chapter 10. In addition, the term 'security management' is not to be confused with 'risk management' as the former refers to the offering of a secure operational environment to the financial services institution while the latter focuses on managing risk to an acceptable level. Risk management is thus considered as one of the major components of security management.

Security management

In theory, the security management strategy should be viewed as a means to strengthen consumer confidence and market discipline; this, in turn, would improve the Web into a safer place for the financial services industry. But in reality, fighting crimes on the Internet seems to be an endless war, as new viruses, malware and attacks emerge every day. The World Bank researchers Glaessner, et al. (2002) reduce the objectives to implementing security measures to three general axioms:

- attacks and losses are inevitable;
- security buys time; and
- the network is only as secure as its weakest link.

These axioms draw the bottom line of any security management strategy.

The last of these axioms explains why a holistic security management strategy is needed. The weakest link could occur in workstations, applications under development, physical areas, human resource areas, or working procedures. Without security management at a high level, an organisation may not have an overview of all its vulnerabilities and may have its security expenses spent unwisely over areas that are not facing the greatest risk.

Thus, the validity and effectiveness of a security management strategy requires an iterative reviewing process that may be divided into several stages, as in Figure 8.1. The review process is necessary to appraise current security management practices and to cater for new risks that have emerged since the last review. Notice that the process is a collaboration of internal and external efforts – the latter is provided by local governments and regulatory bodies. Thus, regulatory compliance

Figure 8.1 An information security risk management framework

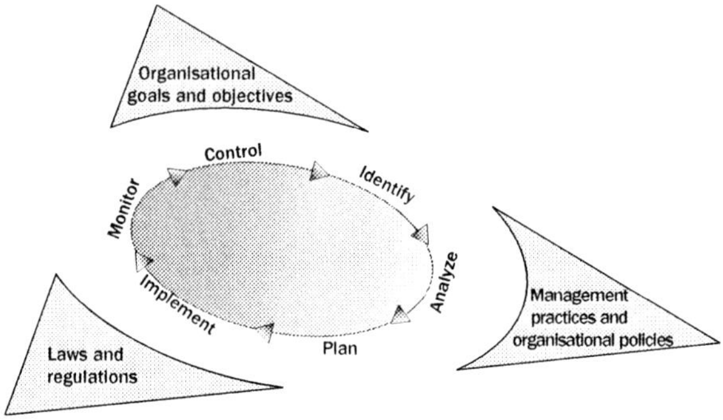

Source: CERT (2003)

that is to be discussed in the next chapter is an indispensable component in a security management policy.

A chief security officer (CSO) or chief risk officer (CRO) is often found overseeing all security matters in an organisation. To be competent in security management, this person or any team responsible should be knowledgeable in the following areas (Hong, et al., 2003) and their relationship is illustrated in Figure 8.2:

- *security policy*: its establishment, implementation and maintenance;
- *risk management*: risk assessment, control, review and modification;
- *internal controls*: control systems establishment and implementation;
- *information auditing*: audit trail and audit tools; and
- *contingency management (business continuity planning)*: in the sense that security management should be dynamic and contingent upon environmental variables, such as threats, vulnerabilities and impact on an organisation.

Figure 8.2 Major tasks in security management

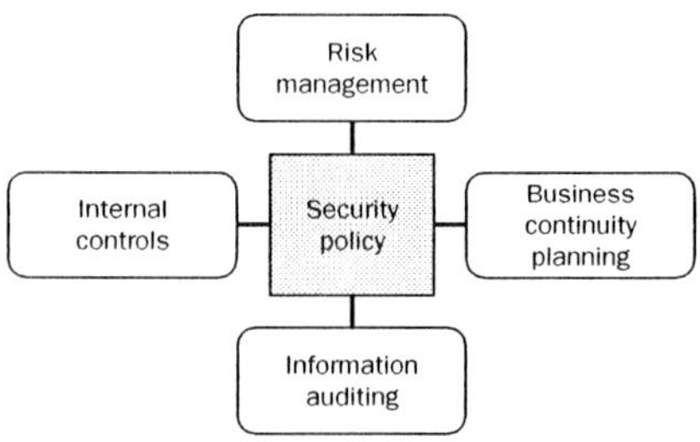

This chapter is laid out in a sequence of these five areas, each being examined in one section. In the security management theory of Hong et al., a security policy is central to the other four components and should be established first.

Security management policy

A security management policy lays down a framework of all matters concerning security in the organisation. While doing so, the CSO must leverage trade-offs between protection and investment as well as the socio-technical problems in the four other components. The job is difficult. Bradley and Josang (2003) identify the following five hurdles for an effective security management policy:

- *Policy divide* between the establishment and implementation of the policy. This is generally the consequence of miscommunications between technical and managerial staff.
- *Reproducibility* of a security solution relies on the expertise of a few persons and/or some working conditions; i.e. the organisation is unable to defend itself if those persons leave. This problem may be mitigated if some standard configuration languages are in place.
- *Consistency* is difficult to maintain between configurations of devices (e.g. firewalls from different vendors).
- *Coverage* is never enough because of the huge effort required for initial configuration and maintenance.
- *Proprietary and inflexible systems* currently in use may not be configured to comply with new security requirements.

The security policy is a guideline for the implementation of security measures. It contains the high-level technical information for the technical staff to configure and operate each security defence, and also contains management information for the CSO and other managers to measure and assess the effectiveness of various security measures. Security management is not entirely a top-down process because the security policy requires reviews and revisions from time to time when lessons are learned from implementation and auditing.

A security policy defines the security perimeter, security appetite and risk tolerance of an organisation. For example, financial services institutions that offer easy 24/7 contact to their customers might stretch their security perimeters to include all internal processing but allow transaction messages to pass the defence line. The policy should be high-level and implementation-independent, detailing only conceptual information, such as security functions at the perimeter (to prevent unauthorised access) and within the perimeter (for intrusion detection). At this level, security technology is not of major concern. Some policies may also specify a hierarchy of standards, guidelines and procedures to assist policy implementation.

The security perimeter is also related to the risk appetite and risk tolerance of an organisation. Written in the security policy, the statement of the risk appetite of an organisation broadly identifies the levels of risks that could be acceptable to the organisation, and the statements of risk tolerance spell out, perhaps quantitatively, the variations from objectives. Moreover, the perimeter can only be established after the process of risk assessment. To help a business organisation draw its security policy, many security models have been set up. Some of them are discussed below.

Industrial security models

Security models are (less mandatory) guidelines drawn by professional bodies and international standards organisations. They are meant to help the business sector, in particular the financial services sector, to prepare for IT security. Among the famous ones, the following will be referred to in our discussion:

- *ISO17799 Code of practice for information security management*: Equivalent to the British Standard BS7799, this is a baseline reference for IT security effectiveness for the preservation of information confidentiality, integrity and availability. The guideline details security measures at the operational level.
- *IT infrastructure library (ITIL)*: Proposed in the 1980s as a UK government initiative for standardising IT processes, it has now evolved into a collection of best practices, including security management and continuity management via service level agreements (SLA) with service providers.
- *COSO*: The guidelines issued by the Committee of Sponsoring Organisations of the Treadway Commission. It emphasises internal controls standards that oversee financial matters.
- *Control objectives for information and related technology (COBIT)*: Issued by the IT Governance Institute, this is a reference framework for security practitioners.

- *Operationally critical threat, asset and vulnerability evaluation (OCTAVE)*: Released by the Software Engineering Institute of Carnegie Mellon University in 2001, the pilots of the model were monitored by the US Government and Department of Defense. It is a risk-based strategic assessment and planning technique.

ISO17799

Generally accepted as an information security standard, the first version of ISO17799 was issued in 2000, based on the BS7799 standard. (A newer version, ISO17799:2005, was released in June 2005.) It provides a comprehensive guideline covering a host of security issues, including templates for security policies and resources for risk assessment, such as checklists and questionnaires for the discovery of errors and/or misstatements. The objectives of those controls are divided into 11 sections (as shown in Table 8.1).

Without specifying the technology of security controls, ISO17799 can be seen as a code of practice. The standard includes the specifications in the original BS7799 Part 1 and Part 2 that detail recommendations for

Table 8.1 **Ten security controls of ISO17799:2005**

Sections	Objectives
Security policy	To provide management direction and support for information security
Organisational security	To manage information security within the company To maintain the security of information and processing facilities with respect to external parties
Asset management	To achieve and maintain appropriate protection of organisational assets To ensure that information receives an appropriate level of protection
Human resources security	To ensure that employees, contractors and third parties are suitable for the jobs they are considered for, understand their responsibilities, and to reduce the risk of abuse (theft, misuse, etc.) To ensure that the above are aware of information system threats and their responsibilities, and are able to support the organisation's security policies To ensure that the above exit the organisation in an orderly and controlled manner

Table 8.1 Ten security controls of ISO17799:2005 (*cont'd*)

Sections	Objectives
Physical and environmental	To prevent unauthorised physical access, interference and damage to business the organisation's information and premises To prevent loss, theft and damage of To prevent interruption to the organisation's activities
Communications and operations management	To ensure the secure operation of information processing facilities To maintain the appropriate level of information security and service delivery, aligned with third-party agreements To minimise the risk of system failures To protect the integrity of information and software To maintain the availability and integrity of information and processing facilities To ensure the protection of information in networks and of the supporting infrastructure To prevent unauthorised disclosure, modification, removal or destruction of assets To prevent unauthorised disruption of business activities To maintain the security of information and/or software exchange internally and externally To ensure the security of e-commerce services To detect unauthorised information processing activities
Access control	To control access to information To ensure authorised user access To prevent unauthorised access to information systems To prevent unauthorised user access and compromise of information and processing facilities To prevent unauthorised access to networked services To ensure information security with respect to mobile computing and tele-networking facilities
Information system acquisition, development and maintenance	To ensure security is an integral part of information systems To prevent loss, errors or unauthorised modification/use of information with applications To protect the confidentiality, integrity or authenticity of information via cryptography To ensure the security of system files To maintain the security of application system information and software To reduce/manage risks resulting from exploitation of published vulnerabilities

Table 8.1 **Ten security controls of ISO17799:2005 (*cont'd*)**

Sections	Objectives
Information security incident management	To ensure that security information is communicated in a manner allowing corrective action to be taken in a timely fashion To ensure a consistent and effective approach is applied to the management of information system issues
Business continuity management	To counteract interruptions to business activities and protect critical processes from the effects of major failures/disasters To ensure timely resumption of the above
Compliance	To avoid breaches of any law, regulatory or contractual obligation and of any security requirement To ensure system comply with internal security policies/ standards To maximise the effectiveness of and to minimise associated interference from and to the system audit process

Source: ISO17799 Information and Resource Portal, available at *http://17799.denialinfo.com/whatisiso17799.htm* (Last accessed: 3 December 2005)

information security management and the specifications of a model known as the information security management system (ISMS) respectively. The ISMS model specifies a number of requirements, which can be divided into four phases as shown in Table 8.2.

Supported by software toolkits and certification, ISO17799 and BS7799 offer business organisations an internationally recognised benchmark to develop their IT security framework. In addition to security controls, ISO17799 provides guidelines for the aftermath of an incident, such as the analysis of the cause, remedies, audit trails, reporting and communication with those affected. Information on those incidents should be collected for the purposes of problem analysis, forensic evidence and compensation negotiation.

ITIL

ITIL defines the objectives of implementing IT services to fulfil two fundamental requirements for IT governance – an accountability

Table 8.2 **Information security management system requirements divided into four phases**

Plan phase	Do phase	Check phase	Act phase
▪ Define the ISMS scope ▪ Define an ISMS policy ▪ Identify the risks ▪ Assess the risks ▪ Select control objectives and controls for the treatment of risks Prepare a statement of applicability	▪ Formulate a risk treatment plan ▪ Implement the risk treatment plan ▪ Implement controls selected to meet the control objectives	▪ Execute monitoring procedures ▪ Undertake regular reviews of the effectiveness of the ISMS ▪ Review the level of residual risk and acceptable risk ▪ Conduct internal ISMS audits at planned intervals	▪ Implement the identified improvements in the ISMS ▪ Take appropriate corrective and preventive actions ▪ Communicate the results and actions and agree with all interested parties ▪ Ensure that the improvements achieve their intended purpose

Source: Humphreys (2003)

framework typically made up of well-defined roles and responsibilities in the IT management process (CGI, 2005). The library consists of seven sets of standards: service support, service delivery, planning to implement service management, ICT infrastructure management, application management, security management and the business perspective. The financial services industry is interested in three of these disciplines: service delivery, service support and security management. Shown in Figure 8.3, these disciplines are interrelated and are inseparable from security management.

Note on the left side of Figure 8.3, the disciplines of service support fall into two groups – a cycle consisting of the management of change, configuration, and release and another group supporting the service desk. Lying in the centre of service support is a configuration management database (CMDB), which stores the information of

Figure 8.3 **IT infrastructure library service management and security management disciplines**

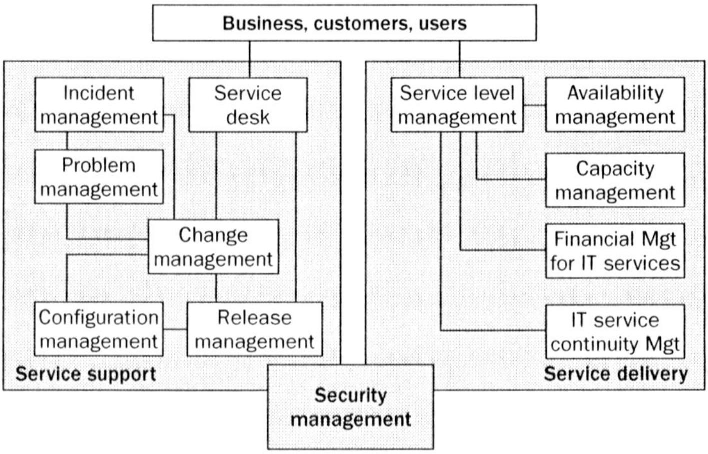

Source: Micromuse (2004)

identification, control, maintenance, and verification of service and asset configurations within the IT infrastructure of the organisation.

To administer services that are delivered by providers, there is a service level management discipline overseeing asset availability, capacity, performance, finance and business continuity. Security management is no exception; it is also managed from the perspective of a service provider. The management needs to identify the level of security required by the organisation. In particular, security management is associated with the management of SLAs in relation to external providers as well as the management of the service desk (together with the management of incidents, problems and change).

In spite of its UK origin, ITIL has gained quite a few important clients worldwide, including Procter and Gamble, IBM and Boeing.

COSO

The report 'Internal Control – Integrated Framework' (COSO, 1992) is one of the guidelines of quantitative risk analysis and assessment frequently referred to by information risk specialists. The report is unique in focusing on the concept of 'internal control', a process that assures (a) effectiveness and efficiency of operations; (b) reliability of financial reporting; and (c) compliance with applicable laws and regulations.

The control framework consists of five components, all of which contribute to the effective operations of internal control. These five components are:

- *Control environment*: The environment that is made up of management philosophy, operating style, organisational structure, ethical values, code of conduct and involvement of the board of directors.
- *Risk assessment*: Identification and analysis of risks from external and internal sources (see later sections on risk identification and analysis).
- *Control activities*: Policies and procedures (such as system reviews, physical controls, segregation of duties, proper authorisation procedures, account reconciliations and information processing controls) to safeguard assets and ensure reliability and timely generation of financial statements.
- *Information and communication*: Employees are able to receive information on their roles and responsibilities in the internal control system. The system should also ensure effective communication with external parties, such as customers, suppliers, regulators and shareholders.
- *Monitoring*: Reviewing and evaluating qualities of the control system and take actions as necessary.

COSO is chosen by companies to comply with the Sarbanes-Oxley Act or Public Company Accounting Oversight Board (PCAOB) Standard 2. In 2004, COSO collaborated with PricewaterhouseCoopers LLP and proposed an enterprise risk management (ERM) framework that expands the internal control concept in the control framework to address risk management across the entire enterprise. The ERM framework is discussed in Chapter 10.

COBIT

COBIT is an open standard published by the IT Governance Institute (*www.ITGI.org*) with joint effort from the industry, especially DTT and the Information Systems Audit and Control Association (ISACA). The standard consists of six components, which include executive summary, management guidelines, framework, control objectives, implementation toolset and audit guidelines.

ITGI views 'IT governance' as the leadership, organisational structures and processes to ensure that an organisation's IT sustains and extends the corporate strategy. The responsibility for IT governance is divided into five areas:

- *Business-IT strategic alignment*: IT strategy should align with business strategy.
- *Value delivery*: Expense on IT is cost-effective.
- *Risk management*: Effective to safeguard assets and recover from disasters.
- *IT resource management*: With the help of relevant know-how, infrastructure and partners.
- *Performance measurement*: All the above activities are measurable and transparent.

IGTI believes its COBIT is a framework for IT governance.

In the COBIT framework, enterprise governance is interrelated with IT governance as most business processes take information from IT processes. COBIT identifies 34 control objectives, one for each IT process. Each IT process can be subdivided into 318 detailed objectives and audit guidelines. The IT control objectives are grouped within four domains, as shown in Table 8.3.

The COBIT framework associates the business objectives with IT efforts, which can be organised in a hierarchy of three levels: domains,

Table 8.3 Control objectives in COBIT

Planning and organisation	
PO 1	Define a strategic IT plan
PO 2	Define the information architecture
PO 3	Determine technological direction
PO 4	Define the IT organisation and relationships
PO 5	Manage the IT investment
PO 6	Communicate management aims and direction
PO 7	Manage human resources

Table 8.3 **Control objectives in COBIT (*cont'd*)**

Planning and organisation	
PO 8	Ensure compliance with external requirements
PO 9	Assess risks
PO 10	Manage projects
PO 11	Manage quality
Acquisition and implementation	
AI 1	Identify automated solutions
AI 2	Acquire and maintain application software
AI 3	Acquire and maintain technology infrastructure
AI 4	Develop and maintain procedures
AI 5	Install and accredit systems
AI 6	Manage changes
Delivery and support	
DS 1	Define and manage service levels
DS 2	Manage third-party services
DS 3	Manage performance and capacity
DS 4	Ensure continuous service
DS 5	Ensure systems security
DS 6	Identify and allocate costs
DS 7	Educate and train users
DS 8	Assist and advise customers
DS 9	Manage the configuration
DS 10	Manage problems and incidents
DS 11	Manage data
DS 12	Manage facilities
DS 13	Manage operations
Monitoring	
M 1	Monitor the processes
M 2	Assess internal control adequacy
M 3	Obtain independent assurance
M 4	Provide for independent audit

Figure 8.4 The COBIT cube

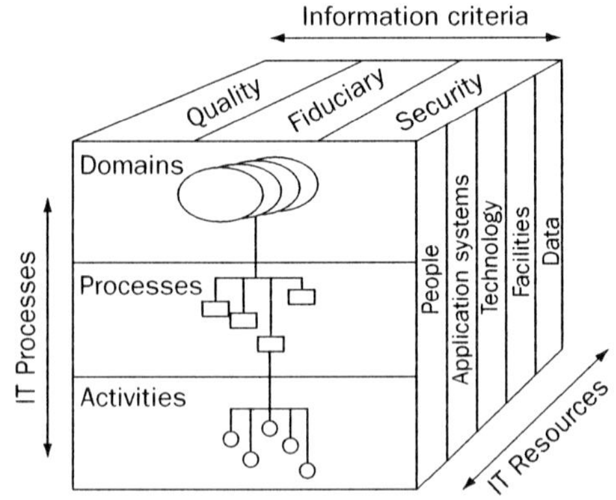

Source: COBIT (2000a)

processes and tasks/activities. Each level serves a different purpose as each domain has a responsibility, each process has a control objective, and each task/activity has a discrete/cyclic lifespan. These IT processes spend various resources but should all be able to produce information that supports the business objectives. The information produced is assessed by three principles:

- *Quality*: quality, cost, delivery.
- *Fiduciary*: effectiveness and efficiency of operations, reliability of information, compliance with laws and regulations.
- *Security*: confidentiality, integrity and availability.

The framework can thus be illustrated as a three-dimensional cube (Figure 8.4).

Control objectives that focus on information security appear in every domain. For example, PO2 (define the information architecture, referring to Table 8.3) encompasses the control objectives 'data classification scheme' and 'security levels'; common security controls, such as transaction authorisation, non-repudiation, and firewall architecture are recommended in DS5 (ensure systems security). The CSO or the responsible team can identify and assess possible threats in each domain.

In 2004, COBIT formulated a security baseline as 39 essential steps to guide the planning of information security. The first two steps were as follows (Pabrai, 2005):

1. Based on a business impact analysis for critical business processes, identify data that must not be misused or lost, services that need to be available and transactions that must be trusted.
2. Define specific responsibilities for the management of security and ensure that they are assigned, communicated and properly understood. Be aware of the dangers of delegating too many security roles and responsibilities to one person. Provide the resources required to exercise responsibilities effectively.

One year later, COBIT released six survival kits, each written respectively for home users, managers and executives alike.

ITGI also proposes tools for getting management's awareness, which include the 'IT governance[2] self-assessment' (Woodbury, 2004) and 'management's IT concern diagnostic'. Both of these are tabular forms that let management fill in their understanding of various control objectives. For example:

- *IT governance self-assessment*: Against each control objective, management is asked how the risk is evaluated, who is responsible for the process, whether it has been audited, and who is accountable.
- *Management's IT concern diagnostic*: Risk factors in six areas of concern (Table 8.4) are examined.

COBIT has become a standard model for IS controls. As it is frequently referred to in other standard practices, such as ISACA, many vendors

Table 8.4 **Risk factors considered in management's IT concerns diagnostic**

Management
1. IT initiatives in line with business strategy
2. IT policies and corporate governance
3. Utilising IT for competitive advantage
4. Consolidating the IT infrastructure
5. Reducing cost of IT ownership
6. Acquiring and developing skills
Internet/intranet
7. Unauthorised access to corporate network
8. Unauthorised access to confidential messages

Table 8.4 Risk factors considered in management's IT concerns diagnostic (*cont'd*)

9. Loss of integrity – corporate transactions
10. Leakage of confidential data
11. Interruption to service availability
12. Virus infection
Enterprise packaged solutions
13. Failure to meet user requirements
14. Failure to integrate
15. Not compatible with technical infrastructure
16. Vendor support problems
17. Expensive/complex implementation
Client-server architecture
18. Failure to coordinate requirements
19. Access control problems
20. Not compatible with technical infrastructure
21. End user management problems
22. Control of software versions
23. High cost of ownership
Workgroups and groupware
24. Quality control
25. Access control
26. Informal procedures
27. Data integrity
28. Configuration control
Network management
29. Availability
30. Security
31. Configuration control
32. Incident management
33. Costs
34. Support and maintenance

Source: ITGI (2000)

like to offer financial services applications that are certified COBIT compliant (e.g. Finacle Core Banking solution).

Case: Charles Schwab (ISACA, 2005)

Charles Schwab adopted the COBIT model in its IT implementations when the company acquired US Trust and increased regulatory exposure. The senior management then learned the value of COBIT from the internal audit team and was convinced that COBIT was a tool to ensure consistency in risk management and to facilitate communications between IT audits and IT managers.

The audit team identified 14 key elements and the level of risk associated with each of them was studied. Findings were presented in a general outline for audit planning documents. Some focal points are shown in Table 8.5.

Subsequently, the COBIT model was implemented in the following steps:

- *Mapping to other standards*: These included the Federal Financial Institutions Examination Council examination guidelines, COBIT's high-level control objectives, and COBIT's detailed control objectives.
- *COBIT control assessment*: Risk assessment exercise and evaluation of existing processes and control mechanisms.
- *Client relationship management*: Proactive activities to evaluate effectiveness of controls and to ensure collaboration.
- *Auditing*: Results of the risk assessment were analysed, documented and validated, using COBIT audit guidelines.

Charles Schwab is prepared to maintain a long-term relationship with COBIT and to expand its COBIT-based audit approach.

Table 8.5 **Examples of focal points**

Audit focal points for information security	Audit focal points for infrastructure
Access control	Structure and strategy
System security configuration	Methodologies and procedures
Monitoring and incident response	Measurement and reporting
Security management and administration	Tools and technology

Source: ISACA (2000)

OCTAVE

Created by the computer emergency response team (CERT)[3] of Carnegie Mellon University, OCTAVE is a popular model of security management that lays down a pathway for enterprises to identify their vulnerabilities and to develop practice-based protection strategy and risk mitigation plans. The methodology is based on a series of workshops that can be separated into three phases:

- *Phase 1*: Organisational evaluation – to build an asset-based threat profile of the organisation;
- *Phase 2*: Technological evaluation – to identify vulnerabilities in the infrastructure of the organisation; and
- *Phase 3*: Strategy and plan development – to create a protection strategy and risk mitigation plan.

Note also the main purpose of these workshops is evaluation. OCTAVE also defines a few criteria for the evaluation. Each workshop should have its fundamental concepts or objectives to drive the evaluation. It should also have distinctive qualities or characteristics in the methods and metrics used. As a result, each workshop produces a predefined list of results of the evaluation. Figure 8.5 shows the flow of the three phases as well as the targets and outputs of each of the phases.

Phase 1 is dedicated to identify assets, assess the current security practices and to establish the security requirements to protect each

Figure 8.5 OCTAVE phases

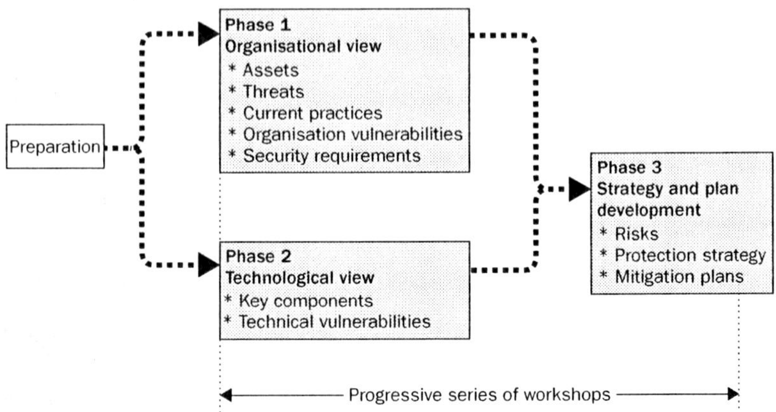

Source: Alberts et al. (2003)

identified asset. OCTAVE categorises security practices into two main areas: strategic practices and operational practices. Security practices at the higher management level are concerned with security policies, regulations, contingency planning and training. Operational practices are divided into three aspects – physical, IT and staff – as shown in Table 8.6. Practices in these aspects can be selected into the mitigation plan and action plan.

At the end of Phase 2, the CSO or security analysis team selects the key components of the right security strategy for the organisation. At this stage, the experience of IT staff and resources available to support a selected strategy must be considered. Areas with significant technological vulnerability must be addressed in the final security management strategy, which is produced as a long-term policy document for the organisation in Phase 3. At the same time, the team should also prepare a mitigation plan that details operational practices to deal with risks to critical assets. For an organisation that is currently under threat, Phase 3 is also a time to formulate an action list that can be effective immediately.

CERT also proposed an OCTAVE-S that is specially devised for small organisations (fewer than 100 employees, according to CERT). Besides having a slightly simpler staging structure (having the same three phases), the OCTAVE-S methodology introduces the use of probability to evaluate the likelihood that a threat will occur. CERT provides a worksheet for organisations adopting the OCTAVE-S approach. A security analysis

Table 8.6 Operational practices areas

Physical security	IT security	Staff security
Physical security plans and procedures Physical access control Monitoring and auditing physical security	System and network management System administration tools Monitoring and auditing IT security Authentication and authorisation Vulnerability management Encryption Security architecture and design	Incident management General staff practices

Source: CERT (2003)

team needs only to answer the structured questions on this worksheet to evaluate asset risks.

Risk management

The financial services industry may adopt comprehensive models, such as COSO and COBIT to direct their security management initiative. But as far as IT security is concerned, risk management could be viewed as a cyclical process consisting of just a few steps. For example, the National Institute of Standards and Technology (NIST) defines risk management as the combination of three processes (Stoneburner et al., 2002):

- *Risk assessment*: To determine the extent of the potential threat and the risk associated with an IT system throughout its lifecycle.
- *Risk mitigation (risk control)*: To prioritise, evaluate and implement appropriate damage-reducing controls recommended from the risk assessment process.
- *Evaluation and assessment*: To evaluate the effectiveness of ongoing risk-reducing measures and to look into the necessity of replacing or updating them.

Since the beginning of ICT applications, various standards, guidelines, techniques and tools have been developed for risk management. Some of these are discussed below, in a sequence that roughly follows the three processes mentioned by NIST.

Risk assessment

This is the process to systematically identify and analyse threats, hazards and perils that might impact an organisation. The ISO list of controls (Table 8.1) provides several directions where risk elements can be identified.

In practice, risk management tends to focus on risk elements that allow quantitative measures. The identified risk elements are subject to analysis to determine their likelihood of occurrence and their impact. However, at the time of risk assessment, there may not be sufficient data to compute the level of each risk element. Suggestions, such as those found in the 2004 edition of the National Fire Protection Association's Standard on Disaster/Emergence Management and Business Continuity

Programs (code name NFPA 1600) illustrate the abundance of techniques, which include the following (NFPA, 2004):

- *What-if analysis*: Its effectiveness relies on knowledgeable individuals who are subject experts.
- *Checklist*: This compares as-is or to-be situations with accepted standards.
- *What-if/checklist*: Checklists are used to encourage the creativity of the what-if process.
- *Hazard and operability study*: A systematic method to identify hazards and operability[4] problems.
- *Failure mode and effects analysis*: A bottom-up approach in which each risk element is examined individually and collectively to determine the effect when one or more elements fail. It relies on the determination of the risk priority number (RPN) of a risk element by the formula:

  RPN = severity × frequency of occurrence × likelihood of detection
- *Fault-tree analysis*: A top-down approach in which an identified risk is backtracked to its potential causes so that the interrelationship of all possible causes of a risk element is studied.

Note that the computation of RPN coincides with the arithmetic formula that treats risk as a multiplicative product of three parameters:

Risk = asset value × threat × vulnerability

The process of risk control is to find and deploy appropriate countermeasures to decrease the one or more of these parameters so that the risk can be contained at an acceptable baseline level.

At a later stage, risk assessment is performed within system monitoring and auditing processes. Risk elements can be converted to key performance indicators (KPIs) which are monitored constantly to see if the measurements deviate from a predefined baseline (see Table 8.7). KPI measurements are compiled in documentation for evaluation and auditing purposes.

The convenience of quantitative metrics does not restrict management to find qualitative ones for the assessment of system security. However, qualitative metrics also need to be formalised in ordinal ranking and maintained at a central repository so that they can be converted to numbers and figures that can be treated quantitatively.

A few tools for risk assessment are described below.

Table 8.7 **Common quantifiable key performance indicators for security management**

Key performance indicator	Explanation
Security incident detection indicator	Ratio of successful detection of security attack. An ideal indicator is 1:1.
Security defence incident indicator	Ratio of successful defence controls when a security attack is detected. Ideal ratio is 1:1.
Security breach indicator	Number and types of security breaches identified.
Security breach recovery	Elements of recovery from a security breach; those elements include recovery time, completeness of data recovered, volume of data loss and number of users affected by the incident

Source: Microsoft (2005)

BITS' Kalculator

Since 2004, the Banking Industry Technology Secretariat (BITS) has promoted its product – Key Risk Measurement Tool for Information Security Operational Risks (Kalculator) – as a tool for financial institutions to identify key information security risks. The tool is designed as a spreadsheet template for a CSO to identify high-risk factors related to information security as well as their vulnerability or likelihood. In addition to ISO17799 domains for information security (Table 8.1), the tool refers to those Level 1 categories of loss events proposed in Basel II (BITS, 2004a):

- internal fraud;
- external fraud;
- employee practices and workplace safety;
- clients, products and business practices;
- damage to physical assets;
- business disruption and system failures;
- execution, delivery and process management.

The spreadsheet template can also be used to prioritise risk factors, so as to decide the degree of defence to each identified threat, but it is not able to produce risk management reports. The Kalculator is simple to use and has the following advantages (Zeichner Risk Analytics, LLC, 2004):

- It standardises information security risks as part of operational risk, as defined in the Basel II Accord.
- It produces risk assessment results that can serve as a critical benchmark for outsourcing purposes.
- It helps enhance awareness of senior management relating to information security risks.

The template has wide applicability and is suitable for enterprises of all sizes.[5]

CRAMM

The UK Government recommends a Central Computer and Telecommunications Agency (CCTA)[6] risk analysis and management method known as CRAMM. It is referred to in the ISACA model as a means to identify and contain risk to an acceptable level with justifiable expenses. Developed in late 1980s by the CCTA, the CRAMM methodology has been revised several times and the latest version – 5.1 – was released in 2003. The CRAMM toolkit encourages and assists in security audit, system modelling and contingency planning.

The general principle of CRAMM is to compute risk impact by considering asset value, threats and vulnerability. CRAMM considers software, hardware and data as assets. The values of software and hardware are estimated by their replacement costs, while data assets are evaluated by asking users' assessment in four different scenarios – denial of access to data, destruction of data, disclosure of data and modification of data.

Using questionnaires that are compliant with BS7799 (the UK version of ISO17799), a CSO can evaluate the threat and vulnerability of each asset, giving a 'triple' set denoting the values of asset, threat and vulnerability. The CRAMM methodology consists of a library of over 3,000 countermeasures from where one could be chosen to meet the security requirement of each 'triple'. These countermeasures are divided into about 70 groups, which include hardware and software, communications, procedural, physical, administrative, environmental, voice communications and wireless networking. When a countermeasure is selected, the CRAMM toolkit is able to generate documents, such as reports and policy. It also provides tools for backtracking, what-if analysis and prioritisation.

The toolkit is also compliant with GLBA and HIPAA, the two laws that have aroused a lot of controversy in the USA. These laws will be discussed in Chapter 9.

BITS' Expectation Matrix

In 2004, BITS proposed the IT Service Provider Expectation Matrix for the financial services industry to identify risks and comply with regulatory requirements at the time of outsourcing IT-related services. Divided according to the security control areas of ISO17799 (Table 8.1), the Expectation Matrix is made up of ten spreadsheets. Each spreadsheet describes a high-level expectation toward a control area and presents a list of sample questions for the manager to validate the expectation. A few questions are shown in Panel 8.1.

There are questions in the matrix to evaluate the expectations for information security, physical security, personnel security and business continuity management. Answers to those questions provide a consistent view that financial services institutions, service providers and auditors can use to close the gaps in the assessment and audit processes.

BITS' Expectation Matrix was derived from the Framework for Managing Technology Risk for IT Service Provider Relationships (called Framework) that was proposed in 2001. The Framework was divided into eight sections, the first of which gives a general view of the workflow (Figure 8.6) of the risk management strategies for outsourcing. The Framework is not a regulatory document, but is proposed as a voluntary guideline complementary to industrial regulations.

The 2003 revision of the Framework is presented in nine sections (Table 8.8) and is considered as a guiding document of the criteria against which IT service provider relationships can be effectively evaluated and managed.

Risk assessment is the process to analyse and quantify risks so that they can be prioritised and risk control methods can be arranged to avoid or mitigate risks. The CSO needs to document the results of risk assessment and work out a risk management plan in which risk control methods are specified.

Panel 8.1 A small part of the spreadsheet concerning 'organisational security' (BITS, 2004b)

2.0 Organisational Security: One or more security rules, procedures, practices, or guidelines imposed by an organisation upon its operations. The set of laws, rules and practices that regulate how an organisation manages, protects and distributes sensitive information.

Documents that May Be Requested: Information security organisation chart (including where information security resides in the organisation), roles and responsibilities, job descriptions, overview of access administration processes and procedures, third-party security reviews/assessments and SAS 70 or SAS 70-equivalent reports, due diligence performed on third parties, performance reporting for third parties, legal clauses and templates.

2.1 Information Security Infrastructure High-Level Expectation: A management framework should be established to initiate and control the implementation of information security within the Service Provider's organisation.

Questions/Control Activities

2.1 Who is/are the person(s) responsible for information security?

2.2 Are there written job descriptions for all information technology/ security job functions?

2.3 Please document the following roles and responsibilities, indicating if the responsibilities are outsourced

- 2.3.1 Security user administration
- 2.3.2 Application security
- 2.3.3 Security management

Risk control

While risks are identified and assessed, they are coped with by mitigation methods, which are roughly categorised as follows:

- *Risk reduction (temper, prevention)*: To reduce the possibility of the risk by methods such as improving internal controls, or to lessen the severity of the damage done if the risk turns into reality.

Figure 8.6 BITS framework flow diagram

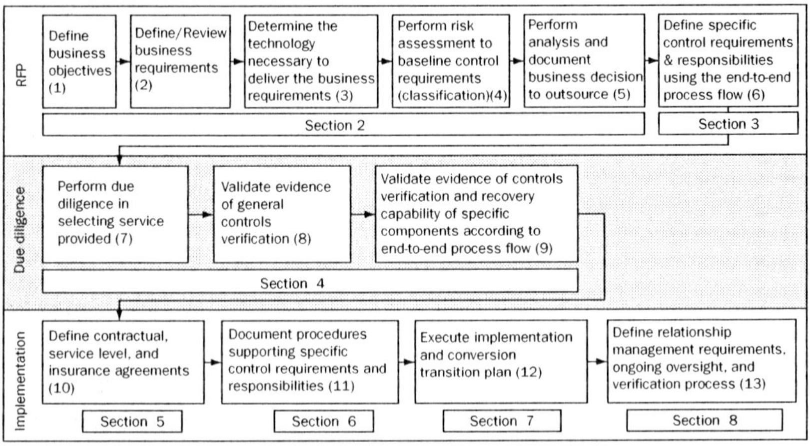

RFP: request for proposal

Source: BITS (2003)

Table 8.8 BITS framework

Framework application and flow chart	Provides framework overview of the steps a financial institution should take in evaluating a decision to outsource IT services Clarifies that the framework is not an audit checklist but rather a guide for selecting and managing IT service provider relationships Supplements the financial services company's risk assessment, risk management and due diligence processes Use of the framework will be driven by the specific outsourcing activity under consideration
Business decision to outsource	Provides guidance on which factors to consider in defining objectives and making the business decision to outsource Defines the application, systems or services to be provided and the associated level of risk Details a cost analysis for comparing internal *vs.* external sourcing
Request for proposal considerations	Provides guidance on and defines factors to consider in developing the request for proposal (RFP) Helps to identify a set of qualified vendors with the skills required to meet the business objectives Defines the specifics of what is required to ensure the integrity of information and transactions

Table 8.8 **BITS framework (*cont'd*)**

Due diligence considerations	Verifies how the service provider will deliver the requirements specified in the RFP Provides assurance that the service provider has a well-developed plan and adequate resources to deliver acceptable service Identifies service provider's reputation, experience, financial condition and reliance on other third-party service providers Ensures that the extent of due diligence is commensurate with the risk of the outsourced service
Contractual, service-level and insurance considerations	Contractual considerations will be driven by the specific outsourcing activity Contractual considerations in the framework are intended to supplement those developed by legal counsel at each institution Service arrangements should be reflective of contractual considerations associated with regulatory requirements (e.g. Interagency Guidelines, section 501b of GLBA, etc.)
Procedures supporting specific controls	The receiver company retains responsibility for ensuring sound risk management practices To ensure successful operations and a sound risk management programme, it is essential to document technology control procedures and responsibilities of both receiver and provider companies The receiver company must consider the level of risk associated with the outsourced service in order that the cost of the control process not exceed a reasonable risk/return formula
Implementation and conversion plan	Highlights the need for a detailed conversion/implementation plan Details transition planning issues and implementation activities Outlines implementation risk management activities Identifies the need for a post-implementation review
Ongoing relationship management	Highlights the importance of ongoing management of an outsourced service Describes business and technological changes Emphasises the need for technology risk management process
Cross-border outsourcing	Identifies industry requirements for establishing and managing cross-border relationships

Source: BITS (2003)

- *Risk avoidance*: To avoid the risk completely, say, by changing the security environment. Methods to avoid risk, if they exist, are much more expensive in cost or effort than those for risk reduction.
- *Risk transfer*: To transfer risk or share risk with others by using insurance, outsourcing, or joint venture.
- *Risk retention*: To accept the risk and live with it. The organisation should therefore strengthen its capacity in contingency management so as to ensure business continuity. Technologies, such as mirror sites are essential for this tactic.

For each risk element identified, one or more of the above categories is chosen according to the amount of risk exposure determined by the organisation's risk appetite. There are still a vast number of methods and technologies in each category and management needs to justify its choice with the budget and the assessed residual risk.

The management may like to consider a change of policy or procedure if it suits the risk control method selected. The formulation of new policies or procedures is a social issue that may become a task for change management. Risk control needs the cooperation of IS personnel, end-users and vendors; thus management skills are critical to the success of risk control. From a technological point of view, implementation of various security technologies is believed to be crucial to many security standards, such as ISO17799 and World Bank's Twelve Core Layers (Glaessner et al., 2002). Many security controls are common, as reviewed by Tables 8.1 and 8.9.

Many financial services institutions outsource their implementation projects to solution providers, for the sake of lower total cost of ownership. The monitoring and management of outsourced technology is largely dependent on the quality of service written in the service level agreements (SLAs). Managing security technologies that are developed in-house or by external parties is part of the duties of a CSO.

Risk control, which is a process to monitor vulnerable areas and enforce security rules and procedures defined in the risk management plan, often deploys more than one kind of technology. As this book cannot include an exhaustive list of these technologies, only a few technologies that are common in well-established security standards are described in the following sections. These are perceived as the foundation of current research and development of security technologies that protect the information flows of electronic financial services.

Table 8.9 World Bank's 12 layers of e-security

Information security officer	To oversee all measures are carried out in accordance with the best practices.
Risk management	A broad based framework based upon CERT's OCTAVE paradigm for managing assets and relevant risks to those assets.
Access controls/ authentication	To set up and administer an identification and authentication system, using passwords, tokens, biometrics and public key infrastructure
Firewalls	To configure and enforce a boundary between two or more networks.
Active content filtering	To filter all material that is not appropriate for the workplace at the browser level.
Intrusion detection system	To detect break-in attempts. Monitoring methods vary depending on types of attacks expected, origins of attacks, types of assets and levels of concern.
Virus scanner	To detect attacks from worms, Trojans and other viruses.
Encryption	To protect information while it is in transit or exposed to theft of the storage device by encryption.
Vulnerability testing	To discover knowledge of vulnerabilities on the computer system or networks.
Proper systems administration	To integrate with the best practice of administration.
Policy management software	To control bank policy and procedural guidelines vis-à-vis employee computer usage.
Business continuity/ incident response plan (IRP)	To define how a corporation will identify, respond to, correct and recover from a security incident. The IRP should be tested periodically.

Source: Glaessner et al. (2002: 52–3)

Identity management

One of the oldest techniques for computer security is that of user identity and password. This has become an access control system that grants access right(s) (the privilege to read or write) to each user in accordance with the user's role in the organisation. This technology is collectively known as 'identity management' or 'identity and access management' (IAM).

Besides password authentication, biometrics (using fingerprint, iris, voice, or facial features for recognition purpose), smartcards and other authentication techniques are also common in today's identity management solutions. Biometric data for identity management are conveyed through industrial standards, such as the eXtensible Common Biometric Format (XCBF) and the ANSI X9.84 banking industry biometrics initiative.

IAM is now integrated into many corporate information systems, including ERP, CRM, SCM and e-business suites. The key technology is known as 'single sign-on' (SSO), which has the capacity to allow users who have been authenticated in one domain to be recognised in other domains without additional authentication processes. This technology enables centralisation of user rights and password administration. The workflow of an SSO server is depicted in Figure 8.7.

SSO is central to IAM. Besides user authorisation and authentication, SSO is also associated with access management, with the following enabling technologies:

- *SAML (Security Assertion Markup Language)*: Developed by the Organisation for the Advancement of Structured Information Standards (OASIS), SAML is an XML-based framework that provides a security environment for messages across a corporate system. Assertions or facts about a user are often found in different databases in the system. Those assertions can be extracted by using SAML to

Figure 8.7 Single sign-on process and its components

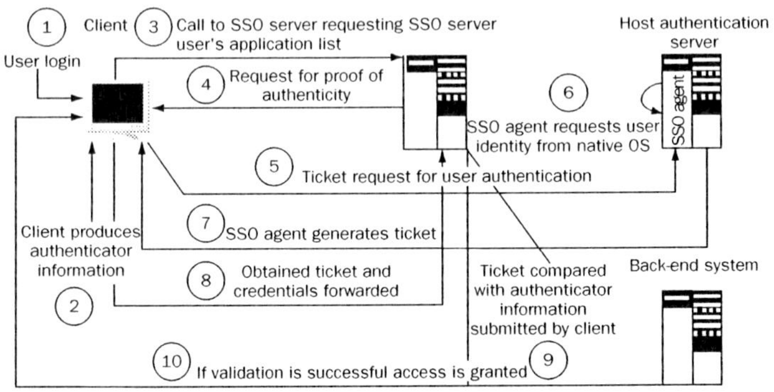

Source: Datamonitor (2004b)

become the user's profile that can be shared in different domains of the system. SAML 2.0 was released in 2005. It has become a *de facto* standard for the exchange of identify and authorisation data.

- *User provisioning*: This is the automated process of delivering goods or services to a user based on the user's identity throughout the identity lifecycle. Those services could mean access rights to storage and application systems, as determined by the workflow delegated to the user's role. Provisioning also includes the password, e-mail account, facilities and even cell phone assigned to a person at time of hire or position change. In this context, provisioning is managed by the human resource function.
- *Directory services*: A directory is the specialised repository of data structured to support rapid searching functions for users. Traditionally, the OSI standard X.500 provides a guideline for structuring the hierarchy of directory entries. But X.500 is so complex that only large enterprises can afford it. The University of Michigan at Ann Arbor created LDAP (Lightweight Directory Access Protocol) as a simpler version of X.500, keeping the hierarchical directory structure in one or more LDAP servers (Figure 8.8). When a user requests data (e.g. an e-mail program, such as MS Outlook or Eudora, looks up contact information) from an LDAP server, the latter may refer the request to another LDAP server if it cannot satisfy the request. The newest version, LDAPv3, is now the *de facto* standard for directory information over a distributed system on the Internet.

Figure 8.8 **Architecture of a directory system**

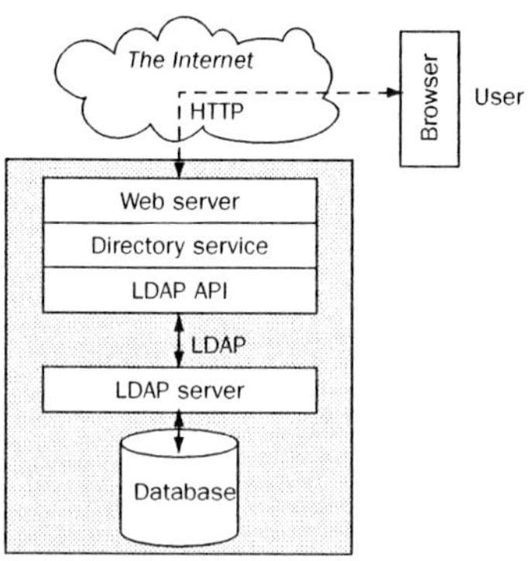

API: application programming interface;
LDAP: Lightweight Directory Access Protocol

- *Federated identity*: For organisations that partner with other companies to conduct transactions (such as banks teaming up with insurance and/or securities firms), SSO might be applied to more than one corporate system. There could be a highly distributed federation of networks or systems on which, if identity can be managed by an SSO server, a user may get access to databases and applications safely and easily.
- *Liberty service*: Some financial services institutions, including American Express and Wells Fargo & Co., adopt the liberty service concept to set up 'circles of trust' covering their electronic contact points, such as websites and intranets. Their authorised consumers are offered SSO when entering these circles of trust (Sullivan, 2003). The Liberty Alliance[7] has maintained an open architecture and sets of liberty specifications for connecting federated networks as circles of trust, which can also be linked when needed for the sake of maximising scalability, interoperability and collaboration.
- *Web services management*: Web services can be used in federated networks to integrate business partners at the application and messaging layer. For security reasons, the user identity is checked to enable binding of web services. OASIS Web Services Security (WS-Security) adopts SAML for this purpose and the latter is believed to be able to accelerate the secure deployment of service oriented architecture (SOA). Liberty Alliance also proposes the Identity Web Services Framework (ID-WSF) that defines protocols and methods for a Web service provider to interact with a user.

Today's IAM solutions often take the 'identity lifecycle management' approach that provides a comprehensive service from the creation to termination of an identity account. For example, Datamonitor (2004b) indicates four core areas of an IAM framework, which cover:

- *Identity lifecycle management*: provisioning, self service password management, password synchronisation and self registration.
- *Access control*: access and privacy management, authentication, SSO and identity federation.
- *Identity repositories*: directories and directory services.
- *Auditing*.

Most IAM solutions today still rely on a password, which is usually protected by encryption. Some of the basic technologies that support IAM and other risk control mechanisms are discussed below.

Encryption

While authorisation and authentication is provided by IDS, confidentiality and integrity of messages transmitted over the Internet is usually supported by the encryption technologies. In simple terms, the principle of an encryption system is to use an algorithm to convert sensitive data into unreadable and scrambled data (i.e. ciphertext) with a specified bit-string known as a 'key'. Anyone who wants to revert the ciphertext into the original data must use the special key with the algorithm in the reverse direction. In theory, the key is the most vulnerable part of the entire mechanism because anyone who knows the key is able to decrypt the ciphertext into original data.

Created in the last decade, the public key infrastructure (PKI) is believed to be able to offer a secure environment for business transactions on the Web. The system uses a public key for encryption and a private key decryption; thus the system is said to be 'asymmetric'. Having been given a key pair, a user can release the public key to anyone who might want to send them an encrypted message. The person should keep the other key – the 'private key' – secret. It is used to decipher any messages encrypted by the public key.

To Web surfers, the secure sockets layer (SSL) is the most familiar PKI protocol as it is incorporated in most Web browsers today. Using cryptography algorithms, such as RSA,[8] AES,[9] and ECC,[10] the SSL provides a secure passage for confidential information on the Internet. Created by Netscape Communications, SSL was originally designed to protect the transmission of credit card data over the Internet. In addition to communication privacy, it also offers other protections, including:

- *Data integrity*: The protocol uses the public key to generate a digital signature for each message transmitted. The encrypted message is transmitted together with the signature. When received and decrypted, the message is used to compute the digital signature which can then be compared with the previous one to see if the message has been tampered with.
- *Authentication*: To subscribe to an SSL system, both the users and the servers obtain digital certificates from a third-party certificate authority (CA). The digital certificate (X.509 certificate[11]) contains the identity as well as the public and private key pair of the certificate owner.

To prevent eavesdroppers from guessing the key, financial institutions implement SSL systems that use keys of 128 to 2048 bits. This may require browsers that provide only 40-bit encryption to upgrade their keys before they can do business on the Web. Several security mechanisms have been developed on the basis of SSL, including the following:

- The secure electronic transaction (SET) system developed by MasterCard and Visa in 1996 was a modification of SSL. It was used to identify and authenticate cardholders. The system was later replaced by 3-D secure and secure payment application (SPA) by Visa and MasterCard respectively, but both these new methods are still SSL-based.
- A simpler version of SSL called Wireless Transport Layer Security (WTLS) is designed for applications that use wireless application protocol (WAP). As most wireless devices have limited memory and processing capabilities, WTLS deploys simpler (thus weaker) encryption methods.

Firewalls

A firewall product is a software or hardware installation to restrict network traffic between internal networks and the Internet. It is set up at the perimeter of the corporate network and examines all messages going in or out of the perimeter, filtering off those that violate the security policy of the organisation. It often excludes a demilitarised zone (DMZ) where a few servers are made accessible to the public. There are three types of firewalls, among which the stateful packet inspection firewall is the third generation:

1. *Packet filter*: The mechanism checks the IP address of the source and destination on each data packet[12] in the traffic and accepts only those allowed by the access control rules. It is considered as the first defence.
2. *Application proxy (or gateway)*: Checking of packets is delayed in the application level, where the firewall software resides. It is efficient but not too flexible as it may have difficulty handling newly developed protocols.
3. *Stateful firewall*: This records all connections between internal and external addresses in a 'state table'. No traffic is allowed if there is no connection recorded. It is effective in recognising denial of service (DoS) and DDoS (distributed DoS) attacks.

Firewalls are installed to protect corporate networks against hackers as well as active content (e.g. ActiveX, cookies and viruses) that sneak in with e-mails, file downloads and HTML pages. They can also be used to set up virtual private networks (VPNs) as intranets or extranets.

The financial industry is familiar with VPNs that secure communications on the Internet as if they were transmitted along a dedicated line. The basic technology of VPN is to build a logical connection on the Internet in which data packets are encrypted with some protocol. The passage of such data packets is called a tunnel. Two common types of VPNs exist: SSL and IPSec (Internet Protocol Security) VPNs.

- An SSL VPN restricts any navigation command unless it comes from a secure connection known as 'HTTPS' (HTTP secure). For example, a browser may set up an SSL VPN with a remote Web server by exchanging public keys. The SSL encryption forms a tunnel connecting the browser and a corporate network. This type of VPN allows any authorised user to connect to a corporate network with any device (PDA, laptop or cell phone) with a browser from various locations (home, hotel or client's office).
- An IPSec VPN sets up a firewall on either side of the tunnel that connects two hosts. Assuming the firewalls are able to secure the host at the end points, the IPSec VPN encrypts all information passing through the tunnel. It supports all applications that use the IP for communication and is considered the best choice for connections that are to be set up for a long time, because the VPN needs to be configured each time the connection is established.

The SSL and IPSec technologies are not mutually exclusive. It is not surprising to find vendors offering VPN solutions that have functionalities of both types.

Technology for intrusion detection

From the functional perspective, the workflow of an intrusion detection system (IDS) has three stages: traffic monitoring, data analysis and incident response. The system provides a risk prevention function within the firewall-protected zone; i.e. it checks on abnormal activities in data storage and business systems, whether they originate from the inside or hackers who have passed through the firewall. A security service provider would offer its IDS through its security operations centres. Network traffic is monitored on a 24/7 basis and any event that is recognised as an intrusion attempt will alert the security engineers at the centre.

There are host-based IDS (HIDS) that monitor activities in the host computer and network-based IDS (NIDS) which check against attacks, misuse and anomalies on the network. Most tools (commonly called 'sensors') used are pattern recognition tools that search for suspicious activities through data sources – including metadata and log data (in the case of HIDS) or packet-transmitted data, such as sizes and destinations (in a NIDS). These operations require fast storage devices best equipped with load balancing functionality.

Further analysis unveils two groups of intrusion detection techniques:

- *Anomaly detection* based on deviations from established normal operations. Common techniques include threshold detection, rule-based measures, agent-based tools, statistical measures and heuristic methods.
- *Misuse detection* based on known patterns (e.g. specific strings of data transmitting on the network) for malicious activities. Such patterns are known as 'signatures'.

An organisation may choose to respond either actively or passively against intrusions. Bace and Mell (2001) summarise those responses as in Table 8.10.

Recently, a new intrusion detection technology called 'honeypots' has been the subject of discussion among security experts. This is a decoy-based method that sets up an emulation of the real system without much protection. As the decoy uses a file naming system similar to the real system, hackers are deceived into attacking the decoy. Their activities cause no damage to the organisation as the decoy is non-productive; but they can be recorded and studied to reveal the hackers' targets and tactics.

Case: HSBC's anti-fraud plan (Thomas, 2005; Marlin, 2005)

HSBC suffered from a loss as large as $788 million in credit card fraud in 2004, after a loss of $882 million in the previous year. In 2005, HSBC started to upgrade its anti-fraud technology. Incorporating SAS's Fraud Management for Banking solution, with HSBC's anti-fraud system, the

Table 8.10 **Responses to intrusion detected**

Active responses	Passive responses
Collect additional information Change the environment Take action against the intruder	Alarms and notifications – to users SNMP traps and plug-ins – to network management system

Source: Bace and Mell (2001: 21–3)

international bank wanted to build a system to monitor and analyse customer spending patterns in real-time.

The new system is called 'Advanced Card-Fraud-Detection System'. It is a behavioural analysis system that includes sophisticated analytic intelligence, real-time decision making at the point-of-sale, and it is integrated with the chip-and-PIN technology that is often used in the credit card industry. The system examines every piece of data in a card transaction, such as a change of address or telephone number. It is believed to be more effective in fighting against card fraud.

The first stage is to implement the system in the USA. By 2007, the same system will be available in the UK as well as Hong Kong before it is extended to other regional markets.

Anti-phishing

Financial institutions operating on the Internet are constantly at the risk of phishing. There are fraudsters who try many means to trick Web surfers into disclosing their personal data, including bank or credit card account numbers and passwords, so that they can impersonate the victims and transfer their savings from the Internet accounts. A common phishing case is to forge a bank website that appears so authentic that customers can easily be attracted to log on to it by entering their user ID and passwords. Phishing can be a low-tech crime, such as sending an e-mail disguised as a legitimate bank notice to all the staff in an organisation, asking them to update their account information for security reasons.

Joining financial institutions, e-commerce providers, Internet service providers and software vendors, the Anti-Phishing Working Group (APWG) offers four solutions to fight against phishing:

- *Strong website authentication*: All users of an e-banking site need to authenticate themselves strongly by using a physical token, such as a smartcard.
- *Mail server authentication*: All e-mail messages passing through a gateway server must have their source code verified.
- *Digitally signed e-mail with desktop verification*: Institutions that believe they are under a phishing attack need to sign all their outbound e-mails digitally.
- *Digitally signed e-mail with gateway verification*: Instead of asking the recipient to verify its e-mail, this solution relies on the gateway server for the verification.

Newer technologies have been used to prevent phishing; most belong to the first solution in APWG's list. For example, a 'two-factor authentication' scheme requires users to have two passwords – one determined by the user and the other supplied by the financial institution – in order to log into the institution's website. The one supplied by the institution is usually a single-use password that becomes invalid once it is used to log into a website. In Hong Kong, HSBC's customers are given their single-use passwords through their cell phone once they enter their own passwords. In places where cell phones are not as popular, the single-use passwords may be delivered by special remote devices (such as a RSA Security's SecurID) provided by the financial institution. Alternatively, it can be printed as a list on documents, such as monthly statements of personal accounts that are mailed to the users. These passwords can be hidden under silver paint that the user can scratch off to read a password at any particular time (Brandt, 2004).

Furthermore, customers should be educated to understand how fraudulent websites or e-mails can be differentiated. Organisations that operate websites or communicate with their customers online are also responsible for taking sufficient precautions to deter phishing activities. These measures include adopting the four solutions suggested by APWG, carefully designed websites that cannot be mimicked too easily, and the deployment of anti-phishing or anti-spamming utilities. These software utilities screen off incoming e-mail scams that ask recipients to enter information.

The US government has also enacted a number of anti-phishing laws, including the Anti-Phishing Act 2004 (S.2636), Spy Block Act 2004 (S.2145), and the Safeguard Against Privacy Invasions Act 2004 (HR 2929). Both phishing and spamming are considered criminal offences.

To summarise risk control briefly, the aforementioned risk control technologies have been applied to tackle problems of vulnerabilities in data storage (transmission), network access and e-mail. But risks in other areas – for example, fraudulent use of applications – require organisational measures rather than technical solutions. Once a risk event is detected, the CSO needs to execute pre-specified risk control measures and procedures. The event must also be documented and studied so that the organisation can learn and revise its security management plan. Most importantly, the organisation is living through the aftermath of the event. It should resume its business as soon as possible. Business continuity is thus an essential part of the organisational security management plan.

Business continuity

Business continuity management is closely related to security management and the two should be considered at the same time, for example, at the time of risk identification and assessment. Originally, security management included a procedure for disaster recovery but this is now expanded to business continuity management, which not only stresses quick recovery from disaster (zero-interruption) but provides proper channels of communications to let staff, customers, vendors, and all related parties get the latest information on the disaster and the recovery process.

The attention towards business continuity reached its climax immediately after the terrorist attack on September 11, 2001. The financial industry experienced large-scale disruption of payment and settlement services and learned their weaknesses and inadequate management effort in protecting business continuity. However, provision of a business continuity plan is not as easy as it might seem. An organisation needs to identify its vital operations and their supporting resources, and leverage the optimal business continuity strategy that is affordable to the organisation. Several years have passed since 2001, and the financial services industry is still reviewing whether their operations are sufficiently robust to withstand another crisis.

In the USA, both the NASD and NYSE released their regulations for business continuity and contingency planning in 2004 – NASD's Rules 3510 and 3520 and NYSE's Rule 446. These rules aim to establish business continuity and contingency plans in their member organisations so that they could still meet their obligations to their customers during times of emergency or significant business disruption. In particular, the rules emphasise that a business continuity plan should be disclosed to customers and requires special attention in setting up alternative communications to related parties. The rules converge to ten minimum requirements:

1. Books and records backup and recovery (hard copy and electronic).
2. Identification of all mission-critical systems and backup for such systems.
3. Financial and operational risk assessments.
4. Alternative communications between customers and the firm.
5. Alternative communications between the firm and its employees.
6. Alternative physical location of employees.
7. Critical business constituent, bank and counter-party activity.
8. Regulatory reporting.
9. Communications with regulators.
10. How the member or member organisation will assure customers prompt access to their funds and securities in the event the member or member organisation determines it is unable to continue its business.

By the term 'mission-critical system', NYSE means any system to ensure prompt and accurate processing of securities transactions, including order taking, entry, execution, comparison, allocation, clearance and settlement of securities transactions, the maintenance of customer accounts, access to customer accounts and the delivery of funds and securities (NYSE, Rule 446). Technically speaking, these mission-critical systems need to have backup to ensure business continuity.

The European Central Bank issued an issues paper entitled 'Payment Systems Business Continuity' (ECB, 2005a). Unlike the NYSE rules that target stockbrokerage firms, the European paper addresses business continuity requirements to payment systems under the headings of three key elements:

- *Business continuity plan*: With business continuity objectives well-defined and critical functions identified. The business continuity plan is to implement measures to allow fast recovery and resumption of these critical functions at the time of malfunction.

- *Secondary site*: This can replace operations at the primary site, under a variety of plausible scenarios, including major disasters affecting a wide geographical area. The secondary site is supported by a well-structured crisis management team and formally defined operational procedures.
- *Testing and disclosure*: The business continuity plan and secondary site should be reviewed periodically to allow improvement of the business continuity plan. The reviewed plan should also be disclosed to the general staff from time to time.

Although these guidelines emerged after the September 11 disaster, they are applicable not only to the recovery from a disaster, which includes natural disaster, war-time attack, or even a power downtime, but these business continuity requirements can also guide a business to maintain normal service in crises of a less violent nature, such as hardware or software failure, human error, or a virus attack. These requirements are rather generic elements in a business continuity plan and they become topics of discussion in this chapter.

Business continuity planning

The Bank of Japan (2003) outlined a business continuity planning chart that can be used as a roadmap to business continuity management. It consists of the following four sections:[13]

- *Formulating a framework for robust project management*: To establish a basic policy, designate a firm-wide control section, and implement project management procedures.
- *Identifying assumptions and conditions for business continuity planning*: To recognise disaster scenarios, prioritise critical operations and decide target times for operational resumption.
- *Introducing action plans*: To study specific measures for the business continuity plan, set up a data backup mechanism, provide adequate managerial resources, such as staff, IT equipment and telecommunication lines, set up decision-making procedures (command and reporting lines) and emergency contact lists and prepare practical manuals.
- *Testing and reviewing*: To conduct testing/training programmes at least annually. (Organisations like MasterCard claim to test their ability to respond to a disaster all year round.)

The first step in the business continuity planning is to determine the scope of operational activities that the firm believes are vital to its normal business. However, the scope is related to the kind of disaster that is threatening the firm. Therefore, it is essential to consider various disaster scenarios and to speculate about different levels of destruction and interruption to normal business activities. For a financial services institution, these activities may include trading, sales, settlement, clearance, custody and funding. The 'business impact analysis' is a long process of studying the effect of disasters. As in the process of risk assessment, each business activity identified should be assessed and prioritised.

The business continuity plan should identify options to obtain substitute resources to support recovery from any disaster and recommend the most efficient and cost-effective option to management. In many cases, the business continuity plan is executed with the aid of a supplier, who may offer consultation in the course of business impact analysis. In practice, a business continuity plan includes the statement of minimum acceptable recovery capabilities (MARC), which is the consensus of all parties involved and the documentation of the agreed level of business activities that are to be maintained before full recovery is possible. The establishment of a secondary site is essential to provide the MARC.

Secondary site

A secondary site is a physical or virtual location where hardware and software are available and are capable of taking the job of information processing up to the service level determined by the MARC. The secondary site is generally not considered as a replacement of the primary site as the former is operational only in times of crisis; thus, maintaining a hot site[14] is seldom cost-effective. There are a few approaches for the building of a secondary site. For example,

- *Active/backup model*: This is the traditional way of maintaining an active (primary) site and a secondary site for backup. The model relies on the ability to relocate operations swiftly to the secondary site at a time of crisis.
- *Active/active ('split operational' model)*: This is implemented by establishing several hot or warm sites that share the mission critical activities and inherently backup for one another. Using the Internet, operation of remote sites may not involve physical transfer of staff.

While planning a secondary site, the following should be considered:

- *Data centre recovery alternatives*: Where duplicates of critical data are kept.
- *Back-up recovery facilities*: For the recovery of lost transactions or backlog of activities.
- *Geographic diversity*: Safety and convenience should be leveraged as demanded by recovery time objectives and business unit requirements.
- *Back-up and storage strategies*: Back-up priorities, file types, frequency of back-up, and technology are essential in the strategies.
- *Data file backup*: The ability to generate a current master file that keeps transactions accurately up to the point of operational disruption.

Thus, backup technology lies at the centre of a secondary site. Technologically, business continuity is assured by establishing facilities to provide backup of critical data and software systems so that normal operations are not affected at time of disruption. Solution vendors offer storage technology for backup, restoration and failover. For example, the so-called 'Disaster-Tolerant Data Center Solution' offered by HP and Cisco makes use of a storage area network to provide real-time, hot backup between data centres (HP, 2004b). The vendors claim that their solution has no data loss and has zero recovery time. In the business continuity plan recommended by the vendors, data are replicated to several data centres on a regular basis. The infrastructure allows a backup data centre to take over the processing capacity within a few seconds should the primary data centre be down in a risk event.

Besides data storage technology, server backup is also crucial to provide business continuity. A secondary site may be implemented as a cluster of servers. Operating either using the failover or load balancing approach, a server cluster is able to maximise continuous availability of critical software applications.

Case: Sybase triple layer resilience solution

Sybase Inc. (NYSE: SY) claims that its business continuity solution provides multiple levels of availability in various disaster and emergency circumstances. The architecture depends on the following three key products, which are all recommended to the financial services sector (Sybase, 2002):

- *Adaptive Server Enterprise-High Availability (ASE HA)*: This is a software and data host that supports the establishment of hot or warm sites. Using failover technology, the ASE HA does not disrupt information processing when the operation on the primary site is moved to the secondary site.
- *Replication server*: This automates server failover across a LAN or WAN so that large amounts of data can be replicated to and from heterogeneous hardware and data sources. The server operates in a warm standby mode. It works with the OpenSwitch to switch the direction of replication and automatic switchover at time of disaster.
- *OpenSwitch*: This is a gateway application that provides continuous availability to remote clients by offering transparent client connection failover, transparent client connecting routing, load balancing and central management. The OpenSwitch can seamlessly route clients from the primary system to a secondary site in the event of a disaster.

Datamonitor (2002) describes a three-layered resilience business continuity solution by using Sybase products. Figure 8.9 shows the solution in three layers of presentation, applications and storage in the centre. Two ASE HA databases established as the primary and secondary sites lie in the middle layer. Both sites run applications so that should the primary site fail, the secondary site can take up the processing by failover. The direction of data replication is controlled by the replication server which, at any time when the primary site is down, routes transactional data from secondary site to the primary site. As the primary site is not working then, transactions queue up at the secondary site until the primary site resumes processing. The re-routing of data guarantees no data loss. In the storage layer, the OpenSwitch provides continuous monitoring over server availability. It can transfer client connections automatically without any loss or disruptions in the connections. With the Replication Server and OpenSwitch, the solution enables continuous availability.

Sybase promotes its product as a 'high availability' solution instead of a 'fault tolerance' one. Commonly seen in the building blocks of a business continuity plan, the two approaches refer to means to maximise application and system availability by resource backups. However, in addition to the minimal downtime that high availability implies, the term 'fault tolerance' should also refer to mirroring those resources required by the application. Thus, fault tolerance is essential to financial services systems. For example, banking applications cannot afford any loss of

Figure 8.9 **Technical infrastructure of Sybase triple layer resilience solution**

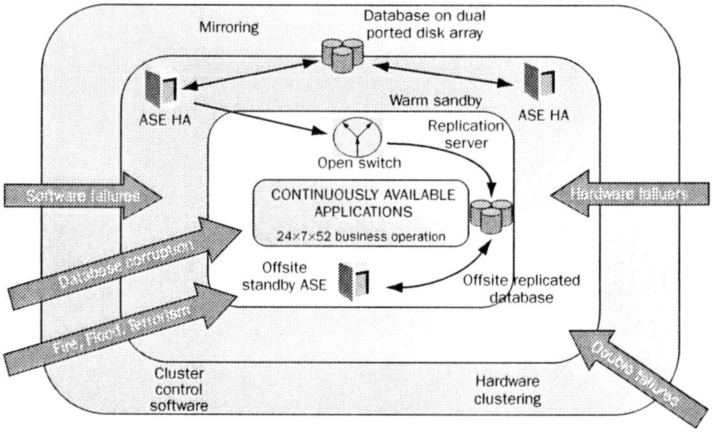

ASE HA: adaptive server enterprise-high availability

Source: Datamonitor (2002)

data. The Sybase business continuity solution makes use of its replication server and OpenSwitch to mimic the performance of fault tolerant systems.

Disclosure

The business continuity plan needs periodic appraisal and review. The performance of the business continuity mechanisms and procedures during both the testing and actual disaster recovery period can be reported to both the management and business functions concerned. These reports should be reviewed by internal audit or a consultant so that the effectiveness of the business continuity plan can be assessed and assured.

To comply with NASD Rule 3510, a broker-dealer must also disclose to its customers the implementation of its business continuity plan. NASD specifically requires a broker-dealer to:

- provide specific scenarios of varying severity: for example, a firm-only business disruption, a disruption to a single building and a regional disruption;
- state whether business will be continued during each scenario: if so, provide a planned recovery time; and
- provide general information on its intended response.

The broker-dealer needs to provide information on its business continuity plan to its customers at the time when they open accounts – and on the corporate website. Such disclosure statements are easily found on the Internet; they include a brief description of the business continuity plan, the existence and operation of the secondary site and contact telephone numbers for emergency. NASD Rule 3520 also requires a broker-dealer to provide the names of two persons whom NASD can contact in the event of a major business disruption.

Responsibilities of the CSO include the construction of a secure ICT environment for the business operations of a (financial services) company. Elements like security policy, risk assessment and control, and business continuity planning that were discussed earlier are daily work for the CSO. To appraise the effectiveness of the security plan as well as the performance of the CSO, the security plan is reviewed periodically by internal or external auditors, whose jobs are detailed in the next section.

Auditing

Auditing is a systematic process to appraise policies, practices, and procedures of strategic information systems in an organisation, to identify suspicious activities, potential weaknesses and possible non-compliance. It differs from intrusion detection, which has a reactive purpose, as it includes tools to predict threats so that they can be dealt with proactively.

Auditing is major component of many security management models, such as ISO17799 and COBIT. Auditors may follow the guidelines or standard questionnaires to check the effectiveness and performance of every security measure, including the security management policy and procedures. Automated processes to monitor those quantitative KPIs (like those in Table 8.8) may provide data to reveal potentially high vulnerabilities in the IT environment. However, manual auditing is indispensable as it can give a clear picture of how closely the security procedures are followed in practice. The auditing process is painstakingly time-consuming and most organisations do not have the resources to put every aspect of the systems under scrutiny. Besides KPI, auditors may prioritise their targeted subjects according to other criteria, such as activities that are related to financial benefits or losses, security loopholes, and areas that were audited in the last exercise.

Not only are internal and external auditors the key people in an audit, they may also contribute to IT governance by ensuring the long-term effectiveness of the technology deployed. They help select performance metrics, and search through huge volumes of transaction data to spot errors, fraud, or weaknesses.

An audit begins with a plan that defines the scope of the audit (operations, finance, applications, or other elements). The process is guided and evaluated by the audit management. Modern security management applications gather an event log across the corporate system in a centralised repository. But auditors still need to involve themselves in direct observation, inquiry and interviewing. The quality of auditing depends on the auditors' professional judgment. ISACA (*www.isaca.org*) includes in its model curriculum the following auditing concepts which can be taken as the basic skills of an auditor:

- *Materiality*: The information (on an incident, say, an error) collected is 'material' if its misstatement has a strong impact on business decisions. However, the materiality of a piece of information is determined by the auditor's professional judgment, and audit risk could increase if the materiality level is wrongly assessed. For IS auditors, materiality can be assessed by (1) the aggregate level of error acceptable to management and (2) the potential for the cumulative effect of small errors or weaknesses to become material (ISACA, 1999).
- *Evidence*: The conclusion of the audit must be based on solid 'audit evidence' which comprises source documents and records. The quality of evidence is evaluated by its sufficiency (quantity of evidence) and appropriateness (relevance and reliability).
- *Independence*: The auditor should not be biased and must maintain objectivity and integrity throughout the audit. As the auditor must have some knowledge of the subject matter of the business, competence renders 100 per cent independence as being unrealistic.
- *Audit risk*: The risk of carrying out the audit work is considered to be the multiplicative product of three kinds of risks: inherent risk, control risk and detection risk. They are respectively referred to as the perceived level of risk in that an error occurs in the system when internal control is absent, it is not detected by the internal control and it is not detected by the auditor.
- *IS and general audit responsibilities for fraud detection in relation to laws, regulations, professional ethics*: Towards the end of 2002, the Auditing Standards Board issued the Statement on Auditing

Standard 99, 'SAS99: Consideration of Fraud in a Financial Statement Audit', which states that the auditors have the responsibility to plan and perform the audit to obtain reasonable assurance about whether the financial statements are free from material misstatement, whether caused by error or fraud. That is, the auditor needs to (1) gather information needed to identify risk of material misstatement due to fraud; (2) assess these risks after taking into account an evaluation of the organisation's systems and controls; and (3) respond to the results.

- *Assurance*: All weaknesses should be reported by the auditor, who should also provide qualified opinion on material weaknesses.

An audit may identify several platforms or systems for investigation and each may initiate a series of auditing processes. ISACA defines five requirements for each investigation if it is done according to COBIT guidelines (Table 8.11).

For each IT process, COBIT (2000) recommends that a general audit is carried out in four steps:

1. Obtain an understanding of risks related to business requirements and relevant control measures.
2. Repeat the evaluation of each control measure identified in Step 1 by the following process (Steps 3–4).
3. Assess compliance by testing if a control is functioning, consistently and continuously, as it is expected.
4. Substantiate by analytical techniques the risk incurred if a control objective is not met.

To illustrate the complex task of auditing in practice, we shall focus on auditing in e-banking.

Auditing in e-banking

As proposed by the Basel Committee, one of the risk management principles for e-banking is:

> Principle 9: Banking should ensure that clear audit trails exist for all e-banking transactions.

For this purpose, the bank should maintain sufficient logs for all transactions to establish an audit trail and to assist dispute resolution.

Table 8.11 **Audit process requirements**

Define audit scope	Business process concerned Platforms, systems and their interconnectivity, supporting the process Roles, responsibilities and organisational structure
Identify information requirements relevant for the business process	Relevance to the business process
Identify inherent IT risks and overall level of control	Recent changes and incidents in business and technology environment Results of audits, self-assessments and certification Monitoring controls applied by management
Select processes and platforms to audit	Processes Resources
Set audit strategy	Control risk Steps and tasks Decision points

Source: COBIT (2000: 22)

The auditors should assess whether the e-banking systems are capable of capturing forensic evidence (BIS, 2003b, Appendix IV: 27).

In general, auditors should examine and evaluate the financial and information systems, management procedures and internal controls of an e-bank. The bank should ensure that all necessary records are accurate and all controls are adequate to provide a secure environment for daily operations. Blanco (2002) suggests that a clear audit trail is provided by a carefully planned workflow while auditors should pay special attention to the following aspects:

- the opening/closing and modification of customer accounts;
- transactions with financial consequences;
- any authorisation granted to a customer to exceed a limit; and
- any granting, modification, or revocation of system(s) access rights or privileges.

Auditors could also follow the ISACA guidelines that define a wider coverage of potential weaknesses in an e-banking system (ISACA, 2003):

- *Organisational aspects*: Due diligence, risk analysis, business model, management skills, segregation of duties and management reports.
- *Policy aspects*: Policies dealing with customers, suppliers, security, audit trail, corporate website, privacy, change control and compliance.
- *IS infrastructure aspects*: Scalability, security, paths between website and internal network, dataflow security, potential areas of vulnerability, automated and manual controls and transaction records.
- *Telecommunication infrastructure aspects*: Appropriateness for e-banking operations, appropriateness of network protocols, physical controls, IDS, penetration testing, VPN and encryption techniques.
- *Authentication aspects*: Control features for customer identity, authentication, data integrity, and transaction confidentiality, non-repudiation and fault tolerance.
- *Third-party service provider aspects*: Due diligence, contracts, internal or external audit reports, their security procedures, business continuity and contingency plans, software escrow agreement and security architecture evaluation.

In cases when the transaction system remains the responsibility of a third-party service provider, the bank needs to ensure that the service provider is maintaining relevant audit trails that meet the bank's standards.

Auditing is an essential mechanism to provide an independent and objective evaluation of the effectiveness and efficiency of all decision-making processes of an organisation. While many operations in an e-financial services institution are completed in a virtual space – on the Web or over the phone – auditing is particularly important for management. An audit could ensure that all transactions in cyberspace proceed under the controls designated for security as well as compliance purposes.

Summary

This chapter provided an overview of security management in the financial services sector. It outlined the components generally found in the security management effort – security policy, risk management, internal controls, auditing and business continuity planning. The chapter gave a brief discussion on each of these components.

A number of security models are available and should be considered when a security management policy is being formulated. This chapter introduced ISO17799, COBIT and OCTAVE, among others. These models emphasise that security management is a dynamic process that should be ready for changes in the business environment, which in turn is affected by technological advances and changes in the legal infrastructure.

Not only does security management require periodic updating and improvement, operational procedures and security technologies that are deployed should always be reviewed and monitored to assess their effectiveness to deliver the protection as planned. It should not be surprising to find some of the technologies mentioned in this chapter will become obsolete in a few years' time, but the setup of the security team or risk analysis team and the procedures these people follow will remain more or less the same.

Although new threats to the e-financial services sector keep emerging, the general public sees a more secure business environment that is constructed collaboratively by the security management efforts given by the sector and the legal infrastructure laid down by governments and regulatory bodies. The next chapter gives an account on the regulatory compliance issue that, to a large extent, is an essential part of a comprehensive security management plan.

Questions for discussion

1. It is now well-known that 'information security is as much a human issue as it is a technology issue (Ernst & Young, 2004: 12). Discuss the implication of this statement.
2. Security technology is neither a short-term nor a small investment. In addition to the benefits it can bring, what factors should also be considered by a CSO (or CIO, if investment needs the approval of a higher level) before such an investment is made?

Notes

1. The National Hi-Tech Crime Unit and the Department of Trade and Industry in the UK report respectively that 83 per cent and 94 per cent of surveyed firms reported being attacked (FSA, 2004).

2. According to COBIT, 'IT governance' is a structure of relationships and processes to direct and control the enterprise in order to achieve the enterprise's goals by adding value while balancing risk versus return when it comes to IT and its processes (Skyview, 2004).
3. CERT belongs to the Software Engineering Institute of the university and OCTAVE is thus sometimes referred to as SEI's OCTAVE.
4. Operability is defined as any operation inside the design envelope that would cause a shutdown that could possibly lead to a violation of environmental, health, or safety regulations or negatively impact profitability (AcuTech, 2002).
5. People who are interested can download the template free of charge from the BITS' website: *http://www.bitsinfo.org/downloads/Publications%20Page/BITS%20Kalculator/bitskalculatorspreadsht.xls*.
6. The CCTA is a UK Government taskforce investigating risk analysis and management methods in central government.
7. A global industry consortium formed in 2001 as a premier open standards organisation for federated network identity management.
8. The technology is named after its creators Ron Rivest, Adi Shamir and Leonard Adleman.
9. Advanced Encryption Standard, a US federal standard since 2002.
10. Elliptic Curve Cryptography, an encryption algorithm based on the mathematical features of an elliptic function. ECC works in a constrained environment (such as a mobile phone, PDA, or a smartcard that has very small memory).
11. A variation of the X.500 authentication standard.
12. Data transmitted on the Internet is wrapped in a packet with a header that provides routing information.
13. See also MasterCard Factsheet at: *www.mastercardintl.com/docs/business_continuity.pdf*.
14. A hot site is the place where a company sets up pre-configured hardware, software, data centre, and a network that mirrors the operations in the original site. These can take over the original site in the event of a disaster. The site may belong to the company or be provided by the vendor.

9

Regulatory compliance

Introduction

The financial services industry has seen governments and regulatory bodies mandating more and more laws and regulations in the last decade. The objectives of these regulations are obvious – they help financial service institutions establish working procedures to establish a more secure environment and attain better transparency. However, issuers of these regulations seem to have ignored the questions of whether the market is over-regulated and whether compliance is too expensive.

For public financial institutions in the USA, compliance is to observe the so-called 'three primary regulations' – Health Insurance Portability and Accountability Act 1996 (HIPAA), Gramm-Leach-Bliley Act 1999 (GLBA) and Sarbanes-Oxley Act 2002 (SOX). These laws have become so important that almost every major ICT system deployed by the financial service sector in the USA has incorporated some compliance mechanism.

The European Commission takes a different view to controlling the financial markets in its vast territory. In 2001, the so-called 'Committee of Wise Men' led by Lamfalussy published a final report, which recommended a four-level pathway to reform securities legislation in the EC (see Appendix for a description of the Financial Services Action Plan in Europe). In the UK, the Financial Services Authority (FSA) has also established a regulatory framework for e-commerce through the Financial Services and Markets Act 2000 (FSMA). The Act requires financial services institutions to observe the FSA's 'good regulations', which include economy and efficiency in the use of resources, responsibilities of senior management, and facilitation of innovation and competition.

Besides regulations for the financial services industry in general, there are regulatory standard-setting bodies offering rules and directives for special sectors. As the banking sector needs to observe Basel II,[1] the securities and insurance sectors are regulated by the International Organisation of Securities Commissions (IOSCO) and the International Association of Insurance Supervisors (IAIS) directives respectively. Furthermore, the accounting practice in financial firms is also bound by standards set by local and international accounting professional bodies.

A financial services institution may respond to these regulations in a passive way; but a better strategy is to regard compliance efforts as a necessary strategic investment. As required by the three primary regulations, better corporate governance can be seen as a means to reduce legal liabilities, harm to the firm's reputation, and the possibility of productivity loss. Compliance is not just a requirement for publicly listed companies; these regulations have come to be regarded as 'best practices' for private companies. But any way you look at it, compliance is expensive – a survey (EIU, 2005) reveals that 53 per cent of respondents confirm that IT expenditure on compliance increases over 10 per cent a year and the total spending will exceed $80 billion between 2005 and 2009 (Hagerty, 2005).

The high cost of complying with regulations proves the complexity and diversity of the regulation landscape that the financial services industry is facing. In this chapter, we study three types of regulations that find ICT an effective tool for compliance. These regulations focus respectively on corporate governance, personal privacy and anti-money laundering. Although some regulations are interrelated or overlapped, each type of regulations is discussed in a separate section. These sections are followed by a discussion on ICT compliance solutions. Basel II is left for the next chapter as its main theme is to oversee financial risk.

Compliance and corporate governance

'Good corporate governance' is now perceived as a panacea for all problems in the business sector, especially after the outbreak of scandals in the financial sector in the last few years – the cases of Enron[2] (2000) and AOL Time Warner[3] (2002) are just the tip of the iceberg. However, a yellow brick road to good corporate governance is not easy to find. To help the business sector and to rebuild confidence of the market, many governments and professional bodies have not hesitated to offer their own version of assistance. Certainly, these laws and regulations can strengthen a company's capability in controlling its operations, but whether they are easy to comply with or whether the already congested landscape of laws and regulations is too crowded is another matter.

The business sector receives compliance with mixed feelings. Since the enactment of SOX in 2002, the financial section – especially companies listed in US markets — must review the quality and reliability of their internal controls and the disclosure of their financial statements. No doubt the capital markets are regaining investors' trust, but at a cost that many business executives believe unjustifiable (Quigley, 2005). However, in a survey on ethics and compliance, DTT (2003) teamed up with the *Corporate Board Member* magazine and found that 83 per cent of the US companies surveyed have developed formal codes of ethics or conduct; and 98 per cent of survey participants agreed that an ethics and compliance programme is essential for corporate governance.

In the EU, the issue of corporate governance has also been discussed recently, only to discover that many member states hold different views on the issue. It was not without effort that about 40 corporate governance codes have been adopted at national and international level from 1994 to 2003 (Bolkestein, 2003). Table 9.1 summarises a few of these codes that originated in the UK.

Table 9.1 shows the variety of corporate governance codes and their targets. Although they differ slightly from each other, these targets can be summarised as follows:

- *Management board*: Structure, election, directors' remuneration, operations and performance.
- *Stakeholder relationship*: Responsibilities of stakeholders and dialogue with institutional investors.
- *Accountability and audit*: Financial reporting.
- *SOX section 404*: Internal control effectiveness.
- *Disclosure*.

ICT is obviously able to help corporate governance in the last three targets, especially the requirements of SOX and reporting. The rest of this section is devoted to these two topics.

Sarbanes-Oxley Act 2002

The Enron scandal demonstrated the possibility of collusion between senior management, research analysts, trading and underwriting divisions in banks, legal firms and accounting firms. Its bankruptcy, and

Table 9.1 **Corporate governance codes offered in the UK**

Code title	Sponsorship	Targets
Cadbury (1992)	Financial Reporting Council (FRC), London Stock Exchange (LSE), and some accounting professionals	Composition of the board; role of directors in implementing internal control; establishment of audit committee; code of best practice for UK plcs
Greenbury (1995)	Confederation for British Industry (CBI)	Disclosure of directors' remuneration
Hampel (1995)	LSE	Investor protection in listed companies
Combined Code (1998)	Financial Services Authority (FSA)	Structure and operations of the board; directors' remuneration; accountability and audit; relations with institutional shareholders; responsibilities of institutional shareholders
Turnbull (1999)	Institute of Chartered Accountants in England and Wales	Guidance on internal control and compliance with the Combined Code; compliance with SOX section 404
Smith (2003)	FRC	Roles of the audit committee, in compliance with the Combined Code
Higgs (2003)	Department of Trade and Industry (DTI); HM Treasury	Roles of non-executive directors
Combined Code (2003)	FRC	Consolidation of Combined Code 1998 with Smith and Higgs' codes

several others, led to the enactment of the Public Company Accounting Reform and Investor Protection Act 2002 (better known as the Sarbanes-Oxley Act or SOX), which aims to protect investors by combating corporate crime and improving corporate governance. SOX ignited a mandatory public company accounting reform.

The law covers many areas in the corporate accounting process, but most importantly it holds the senior management responsible for preventing financial fraud and for the implementation of procedures and control functions related to financial management. A few sections that are particularly relevant to financial services institutions are briefly mentioned in Table 9.2.

Under SOX sections 101 and 103, the Public Company Accounting Oversight Board (PCAOB) was established for the purpose of supervising and regulating auditors of public companies. The PCAOB recommends the COSO framework (see Chapter 8) as a *de facto* standard for compliance management; thus, all layers in the COSO framework must be considered when internal controls are being assessed. Other models, such as COBIT and ISO17799 are also applicable.

The essence of the highly publicised section 404 of the law is to require chief executives to attest to the effectiveness of 'internal controls' that encompass all ICT systems. SEC-registered companies are even required

Table 9.2 **Summaries of six sections of the Sarbanes-Oxley Act 2002**

Section	Brief description
Section 103 (Auditing, Quality Control)	All audit-related records (including electronic ones) must be maintained for seven years
Section 302 (Financial reports)	The senior management (CEO and CFO) is required to certify the appropriateness and fairness of the financial statements and disclosures contained in periodic reports
Section 404 (Internal controls)	Each annual report should contain an 'internal control report' which states the management's responsibility in providing adequate internal controls and assesses the internal control effectiveness
Section 406 (Code of ethics)	The firm is required to disclose a code of ethics for its CEO, CFO, principal accounting officer and the like
Section 409 (Real-time reporting)	Public companies must disclose changes in their financial condition or operations in real-time (meaning four working days) to protect investors from delayed reporting of material events
Section 802 (Five-year audit records)	Public companies must retain records, including electronic records that impact the company's assets or performance, for a period of five years
Section 906 (Corporate responsibility for financial reports)	CEOs and CFOs are required to ensure all financial reporting (including annual and periodic reports) fairly presents, in all material respects, the financial condition and results of operations of the issuer and that they conform and comply with the Act

to report the assessment of their internal controls on their financial statements. In general, the management of internal controls consists of the following elements:

- *Risk assessment*: To assess the controls over physical security, access to information and systems, business continuity planning and change management.
- *Control identification*: To identify existing controls.
- *Control testing*: To test the effectiveness of existing controls.
- *Gap analysis*: To identify areas that require additional efforts.
- *Education/training*: To educate end-users to ensure smooth transitions to new/improved control structure and procedures.
- *Remediation*: To check if identified gaps have been closed.
- *Process documentation.*

Note that internal control is a means to enforce policies and procedures. Its effectiveness can be assessed by its ability to detect and manage exceptions early. Independent auditors are required to attest the assessment of the management and evaluate the implications of their findings.

As section 409 requires real-time disclosure, public companies are required to assess their real-time information processing capability. Chan and Lepeak (2004) suggest six areas for assessment:

- *Quality of financial modelling capabilities*: In relation to the firm's ability to anticipate and to avoid awkward reporting situations.
- *Availability of internal and external portals*: To route information rapidly to investors and other relevant parties.
- *Breadth and adequacy of financial triggers and alert*: The effectiveness of triggering off disclosure, as required by section 409.
- *Adequacy of document repositories*: For event monitoring and audit disclosure.
- *Adequacy of captured document audit trails*: To establish adequate disclosure.
- *Capacity to be an early adopter of XBRL*: The eXtensible Business Reporting Language (XBRL) is recommended as a tool to integrate and interface transactional systems, reporting, and analytical tools, portals and repositories. XBRL will be examined in more detail later in this chapter.

While section 409 focuses on disclosure, section 802 implies that a complete set of critical documents should be stored in a secure location where auditors may have timely access. Chan and Lepeak argue that compliance practices based on sections 409 and 802 can improve financial process visibility and transparency, which in turn can offer services of better value to customers.

SOX has now become an essential concern in corporate governance, information system development and security management practice. As internal controls are explicitly described as the direct responsibility of senior management, corporate governance practice has to be integrated with security management. However, security in ICT is a common requirement in many laws and regulations. Laws, such as HIPAA and GLBA even highlight the necessity of IT governance (see Chapter 8), as is discussed in the next section.

Corporate governance and security management

SOX and many other laws and regulations require financial institutions to protect their operations and data storage areas with proper internal controls. This explains the key role played by compliance technology in many security-management solutions. For example, HIPAA and GLBA provide some guidelines for data security while SOX requires IT governance practice to ensure the consistency, reliability and security of the company's information assets. To comply with the requirements of SOX as well as other regulations, organisations often adopt standard models of security management and IT governance, as exemplified by COBIT and COSO in Chapter 8.

For federal agencies in the USA, their ICT projects are managed under the jurisdiction of the Federal Information Security Management Act 2002 (FISMA). Proposed by the National Institute of Standards and Technology (NIST), FISMA outlines a comprehensive framework for security controls over all information resources in the federal government. In particular, the Act specifies that the agency's information security responsibility rests at senior management level and requires detailed reporting and measurements on Internet security for all agencies. To report an agency's FISMA compliance status, senior management should verify compliance for every IT system within the agency by comprehensive validation testing and remediation planning. Although FISMA targets government IT projects and is not mandatory for the private sector, it can still be seen as a reference for proper security management (BSA, 2003).

Figure 9.1 Four pillars of the Sarbanes-Oxley Act 302/404/906

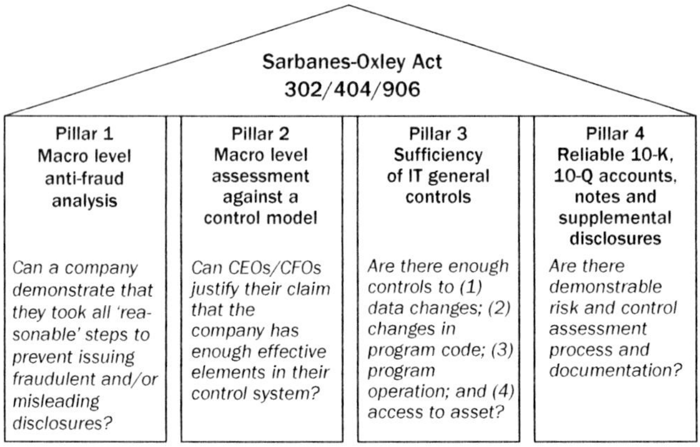

Source: Leech (2004)

To comply with SOX, companies must demonstrate that the proper and adequate measures to maintain good records management are in place. Coincidentally, these measures are called 'the four pillars' of SOX by several authors, one of whom explains the pillars as in Figure 9.1 (Leech, 2004).

Note that SOX compliance covers a vast area, in which internal controls and security management are just parts of the issue. ICT vendors include compliance as one of the features of their solutions. SOX compliance is expensive. A Financial Executives International survey shows public companies have already spent $4.3 million to comply with section 404 (Irsfeld, 2005).

Case: Peakflow X (Abor Networks, 2005a–c)

Arbor Networks' Peakflow X is a communication network dedicated for internal use by corporations, such as a financial firm. Its user tracking features enable security officers to monitor anomalous activities among employees and outsiders, such as contractors. Its intrusion prevention system can be used to implement security measures to combat insider misuse, phishing, botnet armies and zero-day attacks.

In addition, Peakflow X is famous as being a SOX compliant platform that adopts the COBIT model of internal controls. That is, features of Peakflow X can be mapped directly to those COBIT control objectives in Table 8.3. For example, DS5 (ensure system security) can be supported by specific Peakflow X features that meet lower levels of specification (Table 9.3).

Table 9.3 Peakflow X's support for COBIT DS5.x

COBIT DS5.x Requirements	Peakflow X support (Type of feature)
DS5.1 Manage security measures	Direct (A, M)
DS5.2 Identification, authentication and access	Direct (A, M)
DS5.3 Security of online access to data	Direct (A, M, E)
DS5.4 User account management	Indirect (M)
DS5.5 Management review of user accounts	Indirect (M)
DS5.7 Security surveillance	Direct (M)
DS5.8 Data classification	Direct (M)
DS5.9 Central identity and access rights management	Indirect (M)
DS5.10 Violation and security activity reports	Direct (M)
DS5.11 Incident handling	Indirect (M)
DS5.16 Trusted path	Indirect (M)
DS5.19 Malicious software prevention, detection and correction	Direct (E)
DS5.20 Firewall architectures and connections with public networks	Direct (E)
DS5.21 Protection of electronic value	Direct (A, M, E)

A: Assess; M, Monitor: E, Enforce
Source: Arbor (2005)

The network provides either direct or indirect supports for each of the COBIT requirements. There are three types of features – assessment, monitoring and enforcement – that depend on a relational model and two special engines, as depicted in Figure 9.2

The foundation of the Peakflow X capability is made up of two engines: total session reconstruction (TSR) and stateful flow reassembly (SFR). The TSR engine is responsible for reconstructing all traffic in a session to reveal the route of anomalous traffic while the SFR engine fully reassembles all flow information collected from switches, routers and firewalls on the internal network so that the network can evaluate and detect changes to all transactions.

To provide a safe communication environment on the internal network, Peakflow X takes a 'relational model' that puts all traffic under surveillance, i.e. it keeps an eye on who talks to who and how. The model learns the behaviour of all users and applications on the network.

Figure 9.2 **Peakflow X capability**

ASSESS	MONITOR	ENFORCE	
REPORTING	DETECTION	QUARANTINE	HARDENING
Log violations Simplify compliance HIPAA, SOX/COBIT Identify assets Spot vulnerabilities Monitor AUP	N - Dimensional Single packet Includes Learning & zero - learning engines Active threat feed	Safe Quarantine Worm Vaccine Instantly generate switch & firewall rules	Hardening and segmentation Virtual perimeters Visibility and application footprint
RELATIONAL MODELLING WHO TALKS TO WHO, HOW?			
TOTAL SESSION RECONSTRUCTION (TSR)		STATEFUL FLOW REASSEMBLY (SFR)	

Source: Arbor (2005b). NB. Safe Quarantine and Worm Vaccine are Arbor's software products

This model supports the control features at a higher level. A few of them are as follows:

- *Active threat feed* (ATF) is a list of current security threats provided and updated by Arbor Networks' security response team.
- By continuously checking the identities of entities that communicate on the network against a list of legitimate traffic, *safe quarantine* software can instantly block any malicious communication discovered.
- *Worm vaccine* activates a defence before threats or attackers launch a real attack on the network.
- Firewall rules can be generated on the network to define *virtual perimeters* of segments of resources to satisfy special security or compliance requirements.
- Critical resources on the network, such as data centres and branch offices can be hardened (with a higher level of security protection) by changing network virtual perimeters. *Hardening* and *segmentation*

capabilities allow Peakflow X to isolate and harden the resources in response to a virus attack to avoid cross-infection.

With its relational model, Peakflow X can be customised to comply with HIPAA, GLBA and other regulations.

Regulatory reporting

To enhance transparency of operations in a publicly listed company, regulatory bodies like the SEC require the company to disclose information, such as the structure of its management board, adequacy of internal controls, financial status and activities that are important to the company. This might even include disclosure as a responsibility of the senior management, as SOX does.

The current best practice of the management boards and independent auditors is to provide regulatory reporting on both tangible and intangible areas. The former could be financial statements in annual reports. The latter includes corporate governance and compliance, such as SOX demanding that management evaluates the elements specified in the regulations against a defined standard and reports the assessment publicly.

The SEC issued the final rules to implement the internal controls reporting requirements of SOX in 2003. The rules define the form and content of management's annual report on internal controls as follows (Grant Thornton, 2003):

- a statement of management's responsibility for establishing and maintaining adequate internal control over financial reporting;
- a statement identifying the framework used by management to evaluate the effectiveness of this internal control;
- management's assessment of the effectiveness of this internal control as of the end of the company's most recent fiscal year; and
- a statement that an auditor has issued an attestation report on management's assessment.

In addition, auditors are required to follow the standards issued by the PCAOB. The external auditors should audit the internal control assessment of the management in addition to assessing the internal control that is related to the audit of financial statements (PCAOB, Standard No. 2). According to the SEC, financial statements should be prepared in accordance with the Generally Approved Accounting Practices (GAAP) standards. To enhance accuracy, timeliness and reliability of the financial statements, SEC recommends the following internal control policies and procedures (Grant Thornton, 2003):

- records of transactions and dispositions of the assets of a company (the registrant) should be maintained in reasonable detail, accurately and fairly;
- transactions should be recorded to allow preparation of financial statements in accordance with GAAP, and receipts and expenditures of the company are made only in accordance with the authorisation of senior management; and
- unauthorised acquisition, use or disposition of the company's assets that could have a material effect on the financial statements should be prevented or timely detected.

On the other side of the Atlantic, listed companies in the EU (including Australia[4]) should adopt the International Financial Reporting Standards (IFRS). Starting from 1 January, 2005, these companies must prepare their consolidated accounts on the basis of the standard that has incorporated the previously mandatory 'International Accounting Standards' (IAS). It is up to each member state's decision whether to extend IFRS to private companies. The entire set of IFRS consists of five standards and several relevant IASs as shown in Table 9.4.

In addition to the accounting industry, the financial services sector is also affected by the IFRS. For example, in accordance with IFRS4, life insurers must disclose more information on the types of insurance risks as well as the sensitivities of their business to fluctuations in interest rates, equity prices and mortality (Swiss Re, 2004). Companies must also be prepared to modify their balance sheet and income statement so as to comply with IAS32 and IAS39 (Standard & Poor's, 2004). Because IFRS is still evolving and has been mandatory for only a short while, the effects of its adoption are still not clear.

Foreign companies wishing to comply with the SEC regulation are required to reconcile to the GAAP standards. However, as a continuous effort to harmonise global accounting standards, there has been discussion between SEC and EU companies to lift such a requirement by 2009 (DTT, 2005b).

Disclosure

Section 404 of SOX requires management to certify the adequacy and effectiveness of internal control in the company's annual reports while

Table 9.4 **Standards included in international financial reporting standards/international accounting standards**

Standards	Description
IFRS1	First Time Adoption of IFRS Explains how an entity should make the transition to IFRSs from another basis of accounting
IFRS2	Share-based Payment Prescribes the financial reporting by an entity when it undertakes a share-based payment transaction
IFRS3	Business Combinations Prescribes the financial reporting by an entity when it undertakes a business combination, i.e. bringing together of separate entities into one reporting entity
IFRS4	Insurance Contracts Prescribes the financial reporting for insurance contracts by their issuers
IFRS5	Non-current Assets Held for Sale and Discontinued Operations Prescribes the accounting for assets held for sale and the presentation and disclosure of discontinued operations
IAS1	Presentation of Financial Statements
IAS2	Inventories
IAS7	Cash Flow Statements
IAS8	Accounting Policies, Changes in Accounting Estimates and Errors
IAS10	Events After the Balance Sheet Date
IAS11	Construction Contracts
IAS12	Income Taxes
IAS14	Segment Reporting
IAS16	Property, Plant and Equipment
IAS17	Leases
IAS18	Revenue
IAS19	Employee Benefits
IAS20	Accounting for Government Grants and Disclosure of Government Assistance
IAS21	The Effects of Changes in Foreign Exchange Rates
IAS23	Borrowing Costs
IAS24	Related Party Disclosures

Table 9.4 **Standards included in international financial reporting standards/international accounting standards (*cont'd*)**

Standards	Description
IAS26	Accounting and Reporting by Retirement Benefit Plans
IAS27	Consolidated and Separate Financial Statements
IAS28	Investments in Associates
IAS29	Financial Reporting in Hyperinflationary Economies
IAS30	Disclosures in the Financial Statements of Banks and Similar Financial Institutions
IAS31	Interests in Joint Ventures
IAS32	Financial Instruments: Disclosure and Presentation
IAS33	Earnings per Share
IAS34	Interim Financial Reporting
IAS36	Impairment of Assets
IAS37	Provision, Contingent Liabilities and Contingent Assets
IAS38	Intangible Assets
IAS39	Financial Instruments: Recognition and Measurement
IAS40	Investment Property
IAS41	Agriculture

Refer to IAS summary website: *http://www.iasb.org/standards/summaries.asp* (last accessed 3 December 2005)

section 409 requires business companies to release real-time reports to the public at the time of some material events. Thus, disclosure is not simply the issuance of reports but a workflow consisting of investigation, reporting and certification. For example, before management can disclose the 'material weaknesses' in the company's internal controls, in accordance with section 404, management needs to study and certify the findings on the weaknesses.

The requirement of real-time reporting (section 409) suggests that companies should automate, perhaps in a rule-based workflow, at the time of material events (typical ones are shown in Table 9.5), which will result in a substantial impact on the financial conditions or operations of the companies. An automated workflow can ensure a consistent format and completion of audit trail, besides being rapid in production. Furthermore, the information system compliant to this requirement should have the complete, timely and accurate information in a readily accessible database.

Table 9.5 Triggering events recognised in the securities and exchange commission form 8-X

Sections	Items
1. Registrant's Business and Operations	1.01 Entry into a material definitive agreement 1.02 Termination of a material definitive agreement 1.03 Bankruptcy or receivership
2. Financial Information	2.01 Completion of acquisition or disposition of assets 2.02 Results of operations and financial condition 2.03 Creation of a direct financial obligation or an obligation under an off-balance sheet arrangement of a registrant 2.04 Triggering events that accelerate or increase a direct financial obligation or an obligation under an off-balance sheet arrangement 2.05 Costs associated with exit or disposal activities 2.06 Material impairments
3. Securities and Trading Markets	3.01 Notice of delisting or failure to satisfy a continued listing rule or standard; transfer of listing 3.02 Unregistered sales of equity securities 3.03 Material modifications to rights of security holders
4. Matters Related to Accountants and Financial Statements	4.01 Changes in registrant's certifying accountant 4.02 Non-reliance on previously issued financial statements or a related audit report or completed interim review
5. Corporate Governance and Management	5.01 Changes in control of registrant 5.02 Departure of directors or principal officers; election of directors; appointment of principal officers 5.03 Amendments to articles of incorporation or bylaws; change in fiscal year 5.04 Temporary suspension of trading under registrant's employee benefit plans 5.05 Amendments to the registrant's code of ethics, or waiver of a provision of the code of ethics

Table 9.5 Triggering events recognised in the securities and exchange commission form 8-X (*cont'd*)

Sections	Items
6. (Reserved for future use)	–
7. Regulation Fair Disclosure	–
8. Other Events	–
9. Financial Statements and Exhibits	–

Source: SEC (2005) *http://www.sec.gov/answers/form8k.htm*

Among the disclosure requirements stated in IFRS, IAS30 is an industry-specific standard that requires the attention of banks and similar institutions that are involved in deposit-taking, lending and securities activities. IAS30 requires financial institutions to disclose information on their income, expenses, assets and liabilities. Moreover, they should also observe the requirements in IAS32, as companies in other sectors do, to disclose factors that affect the amount, timing and certainty of their future cash flows. If their assets involve financial instruments, such as derivatives and bonds, their records must also satisfy IAS39 such that any changes in their value can be disclosed through income statements.

Note that the main goal of both SOX and IFRS is to enhance corporate governance by promoting internal controls and transparency in corporate transactions. Even though it is difficult to equate disclosure with transparency, it is generally accepted that transparency depends on the disclosure policies. For example, Nier (2004) suggests to the banking industry a quantitative measure of transparency by constructing a composite 'disclosure index', which is basically an average of the indexes of 17 measurements.[5] The index can be used to compare the risk profile a bank discloses in its annual accounts. Regulatory bodies would also request more disclosure from time to time. SEC issued Rule 11Ac1-5 in 2004 to require all US-based securities market centres to disclose statistical information regarding their order execution practices (Saraoglu and Ascioglu, 2004).

Disclosure is sometimes required by regulations on other areas, such as regulations concerning personal data. For example, an organisation that collects personal data must be prepared for the disclosure of data to a data subject, whose right is bestowed by the HIPAA in the USA and the Data Protection Act in the UK. In addition to personal data, there are other areas in privacy regulations to which the financial services sector should pay attention, as described in the next section.

Privacy

In view of the vast amount of personal data gathered by various business sectors from their customers and their practice of sharing information, governments in many countries legalised – in the last century – their data protection guidance to protect privacy. This protection is even more crucial when ICT has developed fast and cheap means to collect and transfer large volumes of data via the Internet.

Legal protection of privacy has a long history in the USA. For example, the Privacy Act 1974 was primarily enacted to limit the potential of misuse of Federal records on US citizens. At the time when business transactions are being migrated onto the Web, several new laws have been established to prevent misuse of customer data. Two of them – the GLBA and HIPAA – command the attention of every business.

The UK Data Protection Act 1984 is another piece of pioneering legislation. The law has been revised several times to cope with the development of the EU, but its eight principles (Table 9.6) remain more or less the same (Tyacke, 2005):

1. It shall be processed fairly and lawfully and, in particular, shall not be processed unless specification conditions are met.
2. It shall be obtained only for one or more specified and lawful purposes and shall not be further processed in any manner incompatible with that purpose or those purposes.
3. It shall be adequate, relevant and not excessive in relation to the purpose or purposes for which they are processed.
4. It shall be accurate and, where relevant, kept up to date.
5. It shall not be kept for longer than is necessary for that purpose or those purposes.
6. It shall be processed in accordance with the rights of data subjects under the Act.
7. Appropriate technical and organisational measures shall be taken against unauthorised or unlawful processing of personal data and against accidental loss or destruction of, or damage to, personal data.
8. It shall not be transferred to a country or territory outside the European Economic Area unless that country or territory ensures an adequate level of protection for the rights and freedoms of data subjects in relation to the processing of personal data.

Table 9.6 **Health Insurance Portability and Accountability Act 1996 security standards**

Administrative	Physical	Technical
Security management process Assigned security responsibility Workforce security Information access management Security awarencess and traning Security awareness and training Security incident procedures Contingency plan Evaluation Business association contracts and other arrangement	Facility access controls Workstation use Workstation security Device and media controls	Access control Audit controls Integrity Person or entity authentication Transmission security

Source: Fadlalla and Wickramasinghe (2004)

According to the 1998 law, a financial institution needs to appoint a data controller to be responsible for the protection of personal data. This person should register a notification with the Data Protection Commissioner and submit the purposes for the data to be collected and processed.

Such regulations on privacy or personal data became controversial when organisations started to use modern ICT to collect personal data for the sake of tracking and monitoring user activities on the Internet. In 2001, Microsoft and some related services – including e-Wallet – were criticised for collecting and disclosing detailed personal information without the data subjects' consent and sufficient guarantees of privacy.

Gramm-Leach-Bliley Act

The Financial Modernisation Act 1999 is better known as the 'Gramm-Leach-Bliley Act' or GLBA. All financial institutions are affected, including those doing 'non-traditional' business, such as financial advice and credit counselling, as well as lending, brokering, transferring money and preparing tax returns. (Incidentally, colleges and universities would be regarded as 'financial institutions' if these institutions are engaged in student loan-making activities.)

GLBA removes the previous restrictions on the merger of banks, stockbrokerage firms and insurance companies. To prevent the abuse of the vast amount of personal data as a result of a merger, GLBA states specifically that privacy must be protected. There are three principles in the privacy requirements:

- *Financial privacy rule*: All financial institutions that receive customers' personal financial information must protect the confidentiality of the information. These institutions should notify customers of their information collection and sharing practices.
- *Safeguards rule*: All financial institutions need to design, implement and maintain safeguards to protect customer information.
- *Pretexting provisions*: Personal financial information obtained under false pretences (i.e. pretexting, such as fraudulent statements and impersonation).

The safeguards rule is the provision to protect consumers' personal financial information held by financial institutions, whereas 'customer information' refers to their personal information as well as information on financial transactions. The objectives of the safeguards rule are threefold:

- to ensure the security and confidentiality of customer records and information;
- to protect against any anticipated threats or hazards to the security or integrity of such records; and
- to protect against unauthorised access to or use of such records or information which could result in substantial harm or inconvenience to any customer.

Electronic financial services must provide enough protection for their websites, including threats from Internet connectivity and hosting arrangements.

The rule is particularly interesting for compliance solution vendors, as they can help financial institutions develop an 'information security programme' for the protection of customer information and to assess their compliance level on a continuous basis. Such a programme would require management involvement and the deployment of administrative, technical and physical safeguards:

- *Administrative level*: Employee management and training safeguards.

- *Technical level*: Technical measures, such as encryption and backup technologies to safeguard ICT systems and stored records.
- *Physical level*: Password administration to physical assets, including workstations and data storage areas.

The programme would also include employee training to implement security and privacy procedures. Safeguards are also required by HIPAA, which was enacted a few years earlier.

Health Insurance Portability and Accountability Act 1996

The Health Insurance Portability and Accountability Act 1996 (HIPAA) is generally regarded to be a piece of legislation that safeguards protected health information (PHI, including electronic PHI or e-PHI) from being shared without the patient's consent. This is one of the focuses of the 'administrative simplification' provision of Title II of the Act (there are five titles in total). The provision addresses how e-PHI is transmitted and stored. By the term PHI, HIPAA refers to health information that can reveal the individual identity of a person.

The insurance industry is particularly concerned with HIPAA, as insurance firms can get access to, store, maintain, or transmit patient-identifiable information. They should understand the requirements and implications of the law. Three rules are included under the 'administrative simplification' provision:

- *Transaction and code sets*: To improve the transmission of quality healthcare data by adopting transaction standards for professional and institutional claims, enrolment, eligibility, payment and coordination of benefits.
- *Privacy standards*: To regulate the use, availability and disclosure of PHI by healthcare plans, medical providers and clearinghouses.
- *Security standards*: To guarantee confidentiality and integrity of PHI by implementing various safeguards in three categories – administrative, physical and technical – as illustrated in Table 9.6.

The privacy standards specify who has the right to access PHI. In particular, the patients (data subjects) are entitled to the right to access their medical records and to request an accounting of any disclosure of their medical records. The standards also establish criminal and civil sanctions against use or disclosure of PHI for a reason beyond the intended purpose. An insurance carrier should therefore obtain an authorisation before it can ask any physician performing pre-insurance physicals to release their findings.

To help management comply with the security rules, the HIPAA recommends a 'security standards matrix' that summarises the 'implementation specifications' of each security standard. The specifications briefly describe how the corresponding standard can be done. The matrix can be used as a checklist to evaluate how an organisation complies with the standards. The specification of a standard is the explanation of what an organisation must do to meet the standard. Table 9.7 shows a few sample rows of the matrix (the three rows chosen represent the three categories of security standards).

Note that in the column of implementation specifications, each specification is marked either as '(R) required' or '(A) addressable'. The former label is given to those required implementations as stated in the HIPAA while the latter label is for those specifications in which more than one option is available. A final rule published in 2003 explains that whether a specification is addressable depends on a variety of factors, such as the entity's risk analysis, risk mitigation strategy, existing security measures and implementation cost.

If compared with the privacy regulation in Europe, the US approach (HIPAA and GLBA) appears decentralised and sectoral (Baer, quoted by Tallman, 2003). The following subsection will explain this.

European Union Data Protection Directive

Although most countries in Europe have their own law to protect privacy, the EU issued the Data Protection Directive 95/46/EC to encourage those member states that had not done so to enact corresponding national laws. The Directive provides a few general guidelines as follows (Coudert Bros LLP, 2004).

- *Registration*: The processor of information should notify the local data protection authority before carrying out any automated processing operation.
- *Legitimate processing and data quality*: Personal data should be collected for specified, explicit and legitimate purposes and be

Table 9.7 A part of a security rule matrix

Standards	Sections	Implementation specifications
Contingency plan	164.308(a)(5) Standard: Establish (and implement as needed) policies and procedures for responding to an emergency or other occurrence that damages systems that contain e-PHI	Data backup plan (R): Establish and implement procedures to create and maintain retrievable exact copies of e-PHI Disaster recovery plan (R): Establish (and implement as needed) procedures to restore any loss of data Emergency mode operation plan (R): Establish (and implement as needed) procedures to enable continuation of critical business processes for protection of the security of e-PHI while operating in emergency mode Testing and revision procedures (A) Applications and data criticality analysis (A)
Device and media controls	164.310(d)(1) Standard: Implement policies and procedures that govern the receipt and removal of hardware and electronic media that contain e-PHI into and out of a facility and the movement of these items within the facility	Disposal (R) Media re-use (R) Accountability (A) Data backup and storage (A)
Transmission security	164.312(e)(1) Standard: Implement technical security measures to guard against unauthorised access to e-PHI that is being transmitted over an electronic communications network	Integrity controls (A) Implement security measures to ensure that electronically transmitted e-PHI is not improperly modified without detection until disposed of Encryption (A): Implement a mechanism to encrypt e-PHI whenever deemed appropriate

Source: ZipLip (2005) and Centers for Medicare & Medicaid Services (2005)

processed fairly and lawfully. Measures to ensure accuracy and security in data processing are essential.

- *Data subject rights*: Notice and access: data subjects must be notified of the identity of data controllers and the purposes of collecting and processing their data. They also have the right to obtain access to their data from the controller, without excessive delay or expense.
- *Security*: The controller must implement appropriate technical and organisational measures to protect personal data against accidental or unlawful destruction or loss, alteration and unauthorised disclosure or access.
- *Transfers to countries outside the EU*: Transfer of personal data to non-EU nations that do not meet the European standard for privacy protection.
- *Remedies*: The judicial systems of member states must impose sanctions to ensure full implementation of the Directive.

To cover the need to protect data in communication channels, the EU issued Directive 97/66/EC – The Data Protection Telecommunications Directive – in 1997. Member states were requested to ensure confidentiality of communications on public telecommunications networks and publicly available telecommunications services. Subscribers of these services should be protected against eavesdropping, interception and surveillance without their consent.

The Directive is the impetus that drives the replacement of Data Protection Act 1984 by the newer Data Protection Act 1998 in the UK. But the EU Directive keeps on evolving. In 2002, a newer version (2002/58/EC) was issued to apply to data recorded on paper and computer files, including video and tape recordings. The Directive allows traffic of data for billing and payment purposes; but these data should only be retained in specific cases and the retention period should be as short as possible. It also prohibits newer forms of communications without the consent of the data subjects. For example, a private individual or a business needs to designate an 'opt-in' system so that they allow marketing spam (unsolicited or uninvited e-mails). Notice that it is different from the 'opt-out' approach in the USA, where the CAN-Spam Act 2003 allows advertising spam unless the recipients explicitly disapprove the spam.

The issue of cross-border data transfers causes some difficulties in financial services multinational institutions that operate in Europe and other countries. The sectoral approach of the USA, which consists of a mix of legislation, regulation and self-regulation, is different from a relatively comprehensive legislation in the EU (*http://www.export.gov/safeharbor/*). There has been some sign of a solution to this problem when the EU and the USA agreed on adopting the seven 'safe harbour' principles (Anonymous, 2000):

1. Notice must be given to individuals informing them of the purposes for which their data has been collected and how it will be used.
2. Choice must be offered to individuals, allowing them to choose (opt out) whether and how their personal information is disclosed to third parties or used for purposes which differ from the ones which were originally notified.
3. Onward transfer of personal data by organisations to third parties must be consistent with the principles of notice and choice.
4. Security of personal data must be maintained using reasonable precautions.
5. Data integrity must be ensured so that personal data are relevant for the purposes for which they are used, not processed in ways which are incompatible with the purposes for which they have been collected and steps taken to ensure that the data remain accurate.
6. Access to personal data must be maintained so that individuals can ensure that data be corrected or deleted where inaccurate.
7. Enforcement should be available through independent recourse mechanisms to deal with complaints, disputes and remedies and provide sufficiently rigorous sanctions to ensure compliance.

Under the agreement, US companies wishing to receive personal data from European companies can do so by certifying the seven privacy principles of the safe harbour. However, financial institutions are excluded from the scope of the agreement.

In most countries, regulations on data protection seldom apply to law enforcement, who should have no difficulty collecting personal data from the controllers in the name of criminal investigation or national security. The UK Data Protection Act does not forbid the law enforcement agencies to get access to personal data without the data subject's consent, provided that it is necessary for the purpose of prevention and detection of an unlawful act and seeking the consent of the data subject to the processing would prejudice those purposes and the processing. However, the US

Patriot Act 2001 enacted after September 11 brings the controversy to a new climax. This issue is discussed in the next section.

Anti-money laundering

The financial services industry has long been aware of the regulations concerning money laundering, which were enforced by regulators and law enforcement agencies as a means to combat dirty money and funds raised by criminal enterprises. Money laundering was once considered as a disruption of the stability of the world markets (Price, 2002). For example, the Bank Secrecy Act 1970 authorises the Secretary of the Treasury to implement rules that require banks to report on activities that have a high degree of usefulness in criminal, tax, or regulatory investigations or proceedings. The Act refers to the suspicious activity reports (SARs), currency transaction reports[6] (CTRs), reports of cross-border movements of currency and monetary instruments and reports on foreign bank accounts.

The Financial Action Task Force on Money Laundering[7] (FATF) has been advising governments and the financial sector on anti-money laundering (AML). In April 1990, the FATF published a report that concluded with 40 recommendations, as a comprehensive action list for fighting money laundering. The recommendations have been revised twice (1996 and 2003) to cater for issues such as electronic payments and terrorist financing. The FATF Recommendations can be categorised into four parts (FATF, 2003):

- *Part A – Legal systems*: The scope of the criminal offence of money laundering; provisional measures and confiscation.
- *Part B – Measures to be taken by financial institutions and non-financial businesses and professions to prevent money laundering and terrorist financing*: Customer due diligence and record-keeping; reporting of suspicious transactions and compliance; other measures to deter money laundering and terrorist financing; measures to be taken with respect to countries that do not or insufficiently comply with the FATF Recommendations; regulation and supervision.
- *Part C – Institutional and other measures necessary in systems for combating money laundering and terrorist financing*: Competent authorities, their powers and resources; transparency of legal persons and arrangements.

- *Part D – International cooperation*: Mutual legal assistance and extradition; other forms of cooperation.

After the September 11 attack, money laundering has become a threat to national security. Title III of the US Patriot Act is in fact the International Money Laundering Abatement and Anti-Terrorist Financing Act 2001, which requires all financial institutions to clear themselves from money-laundering operations through regulatory scrutiny, reporting and record-keeping requirements. The AML compliance has since been regarded as a long-term investment. The AML laws and regulations are explained below.

US Patriot Act 2001

In October 2001, the US Congress passed the Patriot Act to give federal officials the authority to track and intercept communications for criminal investigation and foreign intelligence gathering purposes. Financial institutions are required to clear themselves from money-laundering activities and be careful with their relations with foreign individuals and entities – that is, financial services institutions should identify suspicious activities from all customer interactions and verify the identities of their customers. For example, section 326 of the Act requires banks to implement a customer[8] identification programme to:

1. verify the identity of any person seeking to open an account;
2. maintain records of the information used to verify the person's identity (for five years after the account is closed); and
3. determine whether the person appears on any lists of known or suspected terrorists provided to the banks by any government agency.

Verification of a customer's identity may be accomplished by additional identity information, such as driver licence, passport, certified articles of incorporation, partnership agreement, or trust instrument. For this purpose, financial institutions are required to develop written compliance policies and procedures, and delegate the training and execution of AML operations to compliance officers. At the same time, international law enforcement agencies, such as The Office of Foreign Assets Control (OFAC) and the Financial Crimes Enforcement Network (FinCEN)[9] in the USA and the Bank of England,[10] prepare high-risk databases and watch lists to help financial institutions reveal the true identities of their customers.

Verifying the identity of the customers can easily be amalgamated with a customer relationship management system, but only if financial institutions can afford to probe deeper into information, such as each customer's employment, income, investment objectives and investment history. This is also known as the 'know your customer' policy. Customer information is useful in monitoring customers' activities. However, searching through a huge volume of transaction records and customer profiles is impossible without the help of ICT.

Section 352 of the Act requires financial institutions to improve their ability to detect and prevent money-laundering activities by developing an AML programme, which is a set of written policies and procedures, designating a compliance officer, some ongoing employee training and an audit function to test the AML programme. The AML testing assesses the effectiveness of the AML procedures by addressing the following issues (DTT, 2003a):

- employee training;
- OFAC requirements;
- adoption of AML policies;
- customer identification procedures;
- SAR requirements;
- Bank Secrecy Act;
- cash/cash equivalent requirements;
- correspondent/private banking compliance;
- foreign 'shell' banks

There are automated solutions that help the financial services sector comply with AML regulations. These applications provide continuous monitoring over customer and employee behaviour, to detect and analyse suspicious activities and prepare documents, such as the daily CTR and SAR. Figure 9.3 shows the workflow of Complinet's AML solution, which offers monitoring and checking on two frontiers: watch lists and customer transactions. Using the newest edition of watch list, the solution may identify some of their customers as individuals or their beneficiaries who may be involved in risky business. The figure also shows how a software tool called Complicheck is used to put all transactions under surveillance.

Figure 9.3 **Anti-money laundering solution**

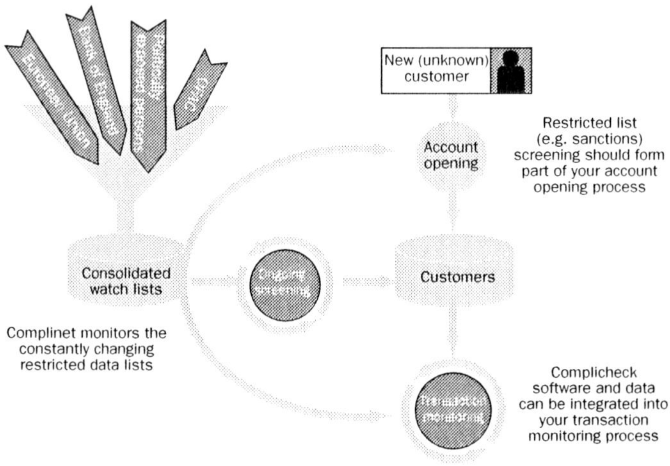

Source: Complinet (year unknown)

Behaviour detection is the main objective of transaction monitoring. AML solutions may have knowledge discovery tools[11] to check transaction patterns of customers and employees. Sophisticated techniques may be able to isolate important transactions and spot relationships among events and individuals. Notice that not only customers are under surveillance. In investment firms, for example, brokers and employees may also be involved in problematic practices. All account holders may be grouped logically into entities for easier detection of group activities. Many AML solutions are effective in detecting the following common scenarios:

- *Abnormal behaviour*: This can be revealed by comparing an entity's current behaviour against historical patterns. For example, an activity that differs substantially from the past 12 months' activities should be flagged.
- *Structuring*: To avoid being recorded on a CTR, money-laundering activities may take the form of structuring; that is, a large amount of cash is broken down into amounts under $10,000 and moved on different days. More complex structuring can involve multiple parties and transactions conducted at multiple locations of one or more institutions, which is known as 'smurfing'.

- *Velocity*: If there is a high number of debits and credits flowing through an identified account over a certain period, it is possibly a velocity case. Cases where the velocities exceed a predefined threshold should be reported in the SAR.
- *Hidden relationships*: The AML expert Mantas (2005) indicates several ways to discover hidden relationships, such as detecting patterns of funds transfers between customers and other entities and recurring originators/beneficiaries in funds transfers.

The US laws exert a far-reaching influence on the financial services sector of both the local and foreign markets. No doubt most off-the-shelf ICT solutions are tuned to comply with US laws which, as described above, focus on three issues: personal privacy, documentation/reporting and AML. However, these issues are not just the concerns of the US Government. European countries, especially the EU, initiate their own efforts to tackle these problems.

EC's Anti-Money Laundering Directive

Since 1991, the European Commission has issued a series (91/308/EEC) of Directives with respect to AML. The latest (third) version was presented to the European Parliament in June 2005. The Directive aims to incorporate the FATF's 40+8 recommendations as an international standard to combat money laundering and terrorist financing.

However, unlike the FATF recommendations, which are not mandatory, the EC Directive imposes several obligations on the financial institutions in the member states, some of which are as follows (Galvão, 2001: 274):

- Their customers should be identified by means of supporting evidence when entering into business relations (e.g. opening an account).
- A copy or the references of the evidence required for customer identification should be retained for a period of at least five years after the end of the customer relationship.
- Special attention should be paid to any transaction that is regarded as likely to be related to money laundering.
- AML authorities should cooperate by informing the authorities, on request or their own initiative, of any fact that might be an indication of money laundering without alerting the customers concerned.

- Adequate procedures of internal control and communication should be established in order to forestall and prevent operations related to money laundering.

Financial institutions are required to file SARs (EC may prefer using the term 'suspicious transaction reports' or STRs instead) to local authorities if there are sufficient reasons to believe transactions are related to criminal activities.

The second version of the Directive (2001/97/EC) widens the definition of criminal activities and extends the obligations to include non-financial businesses and professions, such as auditors, external accountants, tax advisers, real estate agents, notaries and independent legal professionals, and dealers in high-value goods and casinos. Rules on customer identifications are revised to cover new types of transactions on Internet banking, direct banking and other non-face-to-face means. Accountants and lawyers are considered as playing the role of a gatekeeper who may 'open' the gate to financial transactions that can be used for money laundering. They should be regulated by the authorities of respective professions.

In the UK, the effort of combating money laundering is demonstrated in several laws – including the Criminal Justice Act 1988, the Drug Trafficking Act 1994 and the Terrorism Act 2000. In particular, the Financial Services Authority (FSA) is authorised by the Financial Services and Markets Act 2000 to issue regulations to the financial services sector. One of these regulations is enforcing the *Money Laundering Sourcebook* in 2001, and since then a number of banks have been fined because of violating the rules.

Similar to the AML programme (mentioned in the US Patriot Act), the FSA regulations[12] stress the importance of customer identification, staff awareness, training and the responsibilities of the money laundering reporting officer (MLRO). The latter is a person based in the UK and has sufficient seniority and resources to be responsible for (a) receiving internal reports; (b) making reports to the National Criminal Intelligence Service (NCIS); (c) obtaining and using national and international information relating to deficient regimes; and (d) training and making annual reports to management.

Since its first publication, the *Money Laundering Sourcebook* has been criticised for having too many uncertainties. Based on a survey of over 135 compliance experts, Brownlow (2004) observes a few ambiguous cases, which can be illustrated in the following statements. Problems lay where the words are in italics:

- An organisation must exercise its own judgment to establish its AML procedures consisting of *reasonable steps*.
- The AML procedures may take a *blanket approach*.
- An organisation may have committed an offence if there are *reasonable grounds* to have known or suspected money laundering but fails to report to NCIS.

Most regulations apply to businesses of all sizes. This is the blanket approach that makes compliance a heavy burden to small- and medium-sized enterprises, especially as small financial services are less likely to be involved in money-laundering activities. All institutions in the financial services sector have heard about compliance technology, which is discussed next, but whether the technology is cost-effective is another question.

Compliance technology

Software vendors have seized upon regulatory compliance as an opportunity to market their ICT solutions. Their products may offer one or more functions, such as database management, dataflow monitoring, performance measurement, content and record management. But there are also vendors that take an integrated approach. For example, Oracle (2005) proposes a comprehensive compliance architecture that combines data security with compliance processes. The vendor indicates a three-step roadmap to build the compliance architecture.

1. *Enforce corporate and regulatory policies and improve workforce governance*: By automating internal controls, ensuring accuracy, reliability and security of information, and enforcing accountability for compliance across the organisation.
2. *Build a strategic compliance platform*: By identifying common business requirements associated with the compliance initiatives, and building auditable, repeatable processes to enforce and sustain compliance.
3. *Establish a unified information architecture*: By eliminating information silos and turning information into a competitive advantage.

Figure 9.4 shows the integration of several separately developed systems in the Oracle E-Business Suite. The security and identity management

Figure 9.4 Oracle's compliance architecture

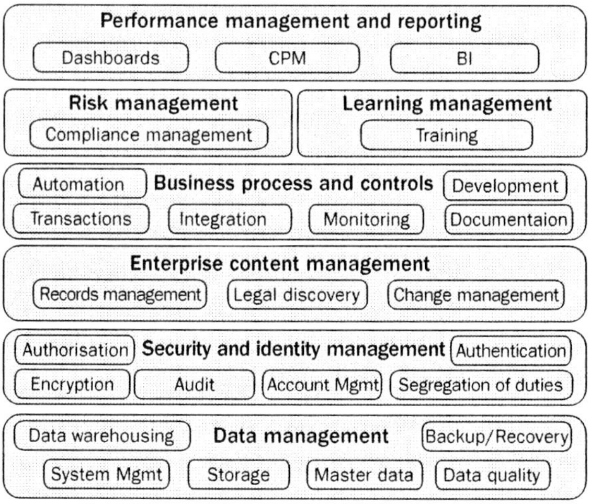

BI: business intelligence; CPM: corporate performance management

Source: Oracle (2005)

layer works with the business process and controls layer to provide the necessary internal controls to the architecture. Not shown in Figure 9.4 is the Oracle Internal Controls Manager, which can track special locations of any workflow. Features of the enterprise content management are supported by Oracle Content Services 10 g (formerly known as Oracle Files), which deals with retaining, auditing, archiving content and supervising electronic communications.

Compliance architecture can be viewed as an integrated collection of applications, as in the Oracle solution. Technology analysts O'Grady (2004) recommend the use of service-oriented architecture (SOA, explained in Chapter 2) to simplify the construction of compliance architecture by using web services. O'Grady calls it a compliance-oriented architecture (COA) in which compliance is separated into various services. A mini-case at the end of this section demonstrates how SOA helps compliance.

Even in such a complex architecture, compliance technology is most effective in two functions: monitoring and reporting (Table 9.8). Besides controlling business processes, the monitoring function requires preparatory work, such as establishing identity and access management policies, and efforts to integrate audit and compliance tools with transaction processing systems. At the same time, the reporting function

Table 9.8 **Two functions of regulatory compliance**

Compliance monitoring	Definition of identity and access management policies to be monitored within IT security management, or integration of audit and policy compliance product log data Incident management and workflow
Compliance reporting	Collection and storage of all log records Long-term data retention Compressed information store Ability to search entire log archive

Source: Williams (2005)

is supported by data management systems that collect and store log records to guarantee their legibility, auditability and authenticity. Both functions contribute to the quality of governance of a corporation.

Monitoring and reporting technologies are discussed in the rest of the chapter.

Compliance monitoring

The monitoring requirement is a part of a financial institution's risk management system. Compliance technology used for monitoring checks whether a rule or regulation is breached or whether a transaction triggers a reporting procedure. For example, Sun Microsystems' Identity Management solution consists of three products – Identity Manager, Access Manager and Directory Server – all of which focus on only one aspect of security management – and it claims to be GLBA compliant (Sun, 2004).

There are other solutions that are more thoughtful. HP, Misys and Intel jointly offer the eagleye solution, which is a flexible and scalable platform to allow the implementation of existing and future rules. The *n*-tier architecture is implemented in a Microsoft.NET server (Figure 9.5), where the internal controls provide both pre-trade and post-trade limit checking. To monitor transactions before they are consolidated, the system is integrated with the order management and trading system to obtain data for pre-trade limit checking.

Rule-based checking is common in compliance monitoring. These rules are often simple and mechanical formulae that can be used to check whether a transaction has exceeded a predefined limit. The eagleye

Figure 9.5 The eagleye architecture

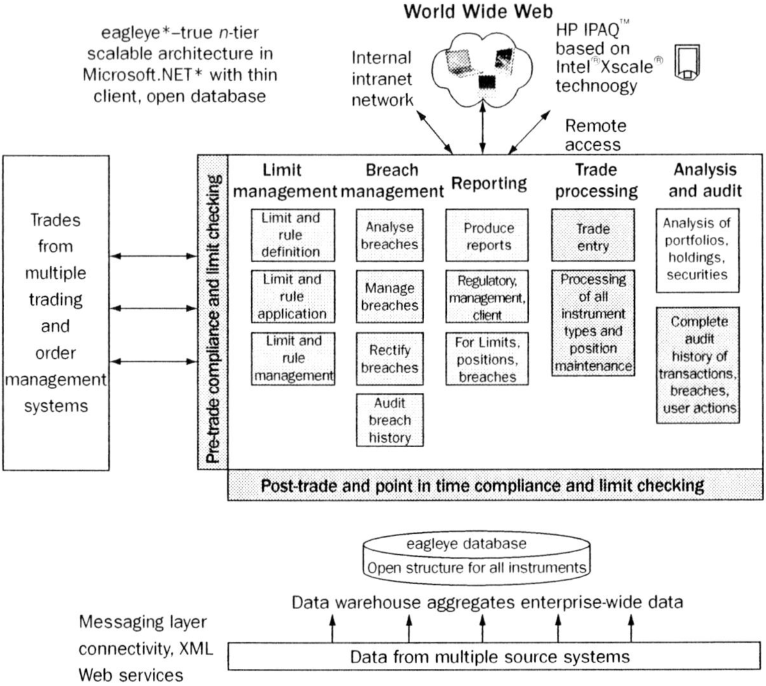

Source: Intel (2003)

system offers a limit checking function which can be customised to cater for different requirements of the rules, such as (Intel, 2003):

- non-iterative rules that check a single limit for each portfolio to which they are applied;
- iterative rules that check multiple limits for each portfolio to which they are applied;
- simple rules involving single measurements (e.g. measuring market value or simple percentage limits); and
- complex rules involving multiple measures and conditions (e.g. compound and conditional limits).

Corporations may adopt a process-based approach to compliance. For example, SunGard (2003) recommends a process-based GLBA compliance solution. It involves a coordinated information security programme that covers several process actions, such as responsibilities of the board of directors, access rights administration, claims management, training, service provider management, programme adjustment and board reporting. Systems that follow the ITIL framework (explained in Chapter 8) may find a process-based approach more appropriate.

For organisations that wish to comply with NASD[13] (Rules 3010 and 3110) and SEC[14] (Rule 17A-4) regulations for tracking and archiving e-mail communications, a monitoring tool could be installed on the Internet server. For example, Veritas' (now merged with Symantec) Vault Compliance Accelerator is a configurable add-on to Veritas' Enterprise Vault, a data repository for Microsoft Exchange Server. Originally, the Enterprise Vault archived and indexed all messages passing through Exchange Server; but the addition of Compliance Accelerator provides structured review functionality to search, sample and check archived e-mail against predefined compliance policies.

Compliance reporting

The technology for compliance reporting is easily converted from data management or record management technologies. A relatively simple framework of compliance reporting is illustrated by FileNet (Figure 9.6). The Business Process Manager controls the workflow of digital documents and enforces policies and standard operating procedures.

Figure 9.6 **FileNet's compliance framework**

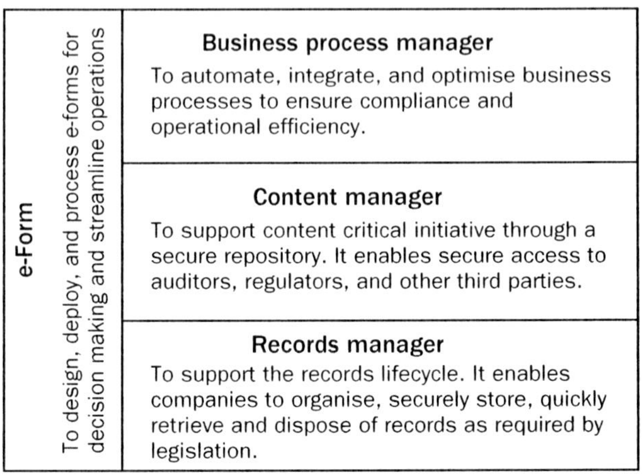

Source: FileNet (2005)

It also handles information processing, audit trail generation and exception approval. To comply with regulations like SOX, the software can identify critical events ('material changes') and respond automatically. At the same time, content management is supported by a record manager, which oversees the entire record lifecycle, and an e-form application that enables easy design, deployment and processing of electronic forms for management decision making.

As compliance reporting solutions are usually rule-based, the same technology can also be applied to security reporting. Specialised regulatory compliance reporting software may have a standard suite of operational and executive report templates that comply with SOX, HIPAA and GLBA requirements. But they can still be used to generate reports of threats against predefined corporate assets or incident trends when the reporting tool is integrated with monitoring tools.

Case: HP OpenView compliance manager

HP promotes its OpenView as a series of 'management solutions for adaptive enterprises'. HP assumes that an adaptive enterprise needs to synchronise business and ICT systems to profit on changes. Its OpenView aggregates best practices to help enterprise customers – including financial institutions – attain quality of service and reduce operational costs. The solution covers four areas of management (HP, 2005a), such as infrastructure management, application management, IT service management (ITSM) and business service management (BSM). The OpenView family also includes plug-ins, toolsets and services.

The latest addition to the family is OpenView Compliance Manager in 2005. It is claimed to be able to help financial institutions in regulatory compliance by automating monitoring of internal controls and offering a dashboard view.

The OpenView Compliance Manager identifies several relevant compliance metrics – called 'key control indicators' (KCIs) and 'key risk indicators' (KRIs) – which are selected from security management frameworks, such as COSO and COBIT. It can collect information from multiple servers, applications and third-party systems. The information is used to compare with preset policies and the results can be shown on the dashboard.

Besides the dashboard, which gives the CIO a view, Compliance Manager is also equipped with a set of reporting functions and instrumentation focused on compliance with regulatory requirements. For example, the application can automate the design, review, approval, testing, and reporting of internal control compliance and IT risk information in a centralised dashboard view.

Being released at almost the same time in 2005, the HP OpenView SOA Manager helps developers manage SOA applications and web services deployed in the system (HP, 2005b). The SOA can greatly lower the development cost of applications and services. Adopting the web service model, each business service is supported by a number of web services, while a 'service delivery controller' (SDC) manages the workflow of the web services that constitute the business service.

The SOA Manager has four major components (HP, 2005b): Web Services Management (WSM), Management Integration Platform (MIP), Business Services Catalog and Business Service Designer (BSC/BSD) and Identity Management. The last component provides the secure control to the web services deployment, and the other three components work together to provide the SDC function, its interaction with resources, and the interaction between different SDCs.

XBRL

eXtensible Business Reporting Language is an extension of the XML standard that is now widely used in the exchange and extraction of financial information across most ICT platforms. Being a variant of XML, XBRL is royalty free and platform-independent. XBRL web services can be deployed to automate the processes of collecting, validating, and transforming business data into information that can be shared and presented as reports to satisfy each stakeholder's need.

Financial service institutions can define their own data structures using XBRL and map business information to the XBRL structures so that the information can be shared between disparate systems within an organisation or between organisations. A source document can be marked up with XBRL tags to become an 'instance document', which can be read by application software or an end-user. Computer programs can be used to check anomalies on the instance documents or to generate reports according to the format specified in a style sheet.

To promote the use of XBRL, descriptions of contents of various financial statements and business reports are promulgated by regulatory bodies across the world, such as the US GAAP and IAS. This is called 'taxonomy' and is often associated with local accounting standards. For example, there are taxonomies representing financial statement-based reports of public and private companies in the financial services industry, such as the IFRS General Purpose (IFRS-GP) taxonomy. Using these taxonomies, an institution can produce business reports at real-time – to meet the requirement of SOX section 409, for example. When electronic documents, such as balance sheets conforming to the same taxonomy are sent to regulatory bodies, they can be validated and reviewed in an automated process.

Many regulatory bodies are accepting XBRL as a mandatory or voluntary reporting format, including the US SEC and the UK FSA. Software vendors are beginning to incorporate XBRL features into their business reporting solutions to comply with internal control requirements, such as SOX – for example, Microsoft Office-based XBRL solution to help in converting source documents to XBRL instance files.

Summary

The financial services industry knows the importance of regulation compliance and the cost of non-compliance. The Collaboration in Financial Services conference held in New York in 2004 made compliance the number one concern of the US banking industry (Dawson, 2005). There have been a few cases where financial services institutions were prosecuted for non-compliance, which could mean great losses in penalties as well as in their reputation. However, management is also warned that compliance may undermine innovation, which is a critical success factor of many banks and financial services firms.

The financial services sector should consider compliance very seriously. This chapter gave a brief account of a few of the laws and regulations that have been highly publicised recently. The main objectives of these regulations fall into three categories: to improve corporate governance, to safeguard privacy and to restrict money-laundering activities. Laws associated with each of these objectives were discussed respectively in three sections.

Discussion on the technologies applied to compliance was left to the last section, where the ICT solutions for two requirements in most regulations – monitoring and reporting – were briefly described. This section recapped two low-level technologies – SOA and XBRL – that were mentioned in Chapter 2.

Regulatory compliance is also regarded as essential to a comprehensive risk management system as well as many transaction processing systems in a financial services institution. Some regulations are formulated to supervise financial risk management in the industry, as will be discussed in Chapter 10. It is the aim of the book to present a fuller picture of risk management in these last three chapters – 8, 9 and 10.

Questions for discussion

1. In reference to SOX, Lee Dittmar, principal with Deloitte Consulting LLP, once said, 'section 404 is principle-based regulation, not rule-based. There could be more than one way to comply' (Jendrey, 2005). What is the implication of such an assertion?
2. The stricter law on AML proposed in EC's Third AML Directive[15] causes further controversies as it gives more uncertainty to (a) data protection, (b) independence of lawyers (are they still acting under their professional secrecy obligations), and (c) responsibility of financial institutions to find out the identity of the beneficiaries of their customers' transactions. To what extent do you think the AML (or patriotism) movement should go (or stop)?

Notes

1. Most of the members of the Basel Committee – including the G10 countries – have plans to transform Basel II regulations into their national laws.
2. In the Enron case, the USA's biggest energy trader was accused of a series of shady dealings, including disguising debt so that their profits could look larger in the company's accounts.
3. AOL Time Warner was accused of erroneously inflating its revenue from advertisements to keep stock prices higher during the time of the merger with Time Warner in 2001.
4. IFRS is adopted by many countries beyond the EU, including Australia, Canada, Japan, and New Zealand. Some Asian countries including China are showing interest to converge to the standard.
5. Nier's disclosure index involves the following 17 measurements: loans by maturity, loans by type, loans by counterparty, problem loans, problem loans by type, securities by type, securities by holding purpose, deposits by maturity, deposit by type of customer, money market funding, long-term funding, reserves, capital, contingent liabilities, off-balance sheet items, non-interest income, and loan loss provisions.
6. The Bank Secrecy Act requires banks to record transactions in excess of $10,000 to a CTR.
7. The FATF was founded in 1989 by the G7 Group (sponsored by the OECD) in response to growing concerns about money laundering.

8. The Patriot Act defines a 'customer' as a person who opens a new account. It does not impose any retroactive provisions although any changes in an existing account may be regarded as a 'new' account.
9. OFAC and FinCEN are two departments of the US Treasury. They enforce trade sanctions based on US foreign policies and deal with money-laundering problems respectively.
10. The Bank of England releases a consolidated list of suspects in which the UN, EU and UK have found relations with Al-Qaida and the Taliban, Burma/Myanmar, Federal Republic of Yugoslavia and Serbia, Iraq, terrorism, and/or Zimbabwe; see *http://www.bridgerinsight.choicepoint.com/descriptions.htm.*
11. Data mining tools, such as segmentation, pattern recognition, predictive modelling, adaptive profiling, and link analysis.
12. According to a description on the FSA's *Money Laundering Sourcebook*, at *http://www.bovillconsulting.co.uk/articles/article008.aspx.*
13. According to these rules, members firms are required to provide active sampling, supervisory review, and reporting to monitor correspondence of each registered representative according to firm-set procedures.
14. According to SEC Rule 17a-4, SEC registrants are required to preserve all original broker-dealer e-mails for three years, including inter-office memoranda and communications.
15. As described in euractiv.com (2005).

10

Financial risk management

Introduction

The financial services industry is changing its perception on risk management. Before deregulation, the Internet and the abundance of new financial products, risk management was aimed at monitoring and limiting potential losses in trading and banking book positions (Porada, year unknown). The industry is now turning towards a short-term orientation – risk management is essential but it should not stand in the way of investment opportunities. Risk has become something that may be retained for a value position and can be bought and sold in its own right as a commodity.

Although many kinds of risks relate to the financial position of an organisation, they are often classified by their origin, and fall into three important types:

- *Credit risk*: The risk that a business partner (customer, borrower) will not pay an agreed amount in full when due. It is managed by periodically monitoring and reviewing the credit limit of the business partner, as well as obtaining collateral and corporate/personal guarantees.
- *Liquidity risk*: The risk derived from events, such as unexpected cash outflows, loss of business, or credit rating fall so that its own liquidity becomes uncertain. As liquidity risk compounds other risks, it is seldom managed as a single type of risk.
- *Market risk*: The risk arising from the effects of unexpected fluctuations in currency exchange rate, interest rate, asset prices and liabilities.

The three types of risk are interrelated, however, and these definitions do not draw a clear distinction between them. For example, an organisation having solvency (liquidity) difficulties would eventually find its creditability affected; which, if it happened across many organisations in an economy, market risk would surely increase.

The success of a risk management system depends on three key factors: corporate culture, risk model and procedures execution. It is the corporate culture – including the code of ethics and corporate attitudes on risk aversion of the financial institution and its associates – that influences the decision-making process to establish a risk model. From an organisational point of view, it is up to the board of directors to decide a risk limit that aligns with the corporate strategy, and to delegate a risk management committee to oversee various aspects, including risk model development and procedure execution.

The model forms the basis of the risk management mechanism, which includes an analytical model, risk management policy, compliance, legal and finance personnel, and the ICT infrastructure that supports all computational and controlling processes. To control financial risks, there are models to estimate market value and sensitivity to interest rates. Some are built to benefit from the dynamics of the financial market by testing hedging strategies and/or management of market risk portfolios. The discussion of the three classic types of financial risk is therefore augmented by a brief note on dynamic risk management.

The execution of risk-controlling procedures is delegated to front-office personnel. Due to the complexity of today's investment instruments, risk management personnel rely on ICT to build risk models, compute risk levels, and exchange information with customers, associates and other business functions. They must also be aware of the laws and regulations that provide a baseline for the management of financial risks. This chapter also includes a discussion on the financial risk management directive included in the Basel Accord.

To wrap up the three chapters on risk management, the last section of this chapter describes enterprise risk management (ERM). This is a system consisting of personnel, policies, and ICT applications that brings operational, liability, asset and financial risk to an integrated model for risk assessment, capital allocation, (re-)insurance and investment decisions.

Financial risk models can range from simple to highly complex with hundreds of correlated and/or evolving parameters. The scope of this book allows only a simple introduction to these models and the underlying theories. As many models are built on statistics, using some statistical terms to illustrate these models is inevitable. Before the three types of financial risk are introduced, we need to examine a few metrics and models that are common in financial risk management.

Risk metrics and modelling

Financial risk management is based on a risk model from which risk is quantified using metrics. Models and the associated metrics are important to risk management as they can be used in risk assessment, design of risk management policies, risk monitoring and appraisal. Many of the metrics have become so popular that the same ones are used to compare risk levels of different systems (portfolios, markets and the like). This section briefly discusses these metrics and comments on risk modelling in general. Special risk models will be described in sections on respective types of risks.

Value-at-risk

Value-at-risk (VaR) is a metric that is widely used in financial and non-financial sectors to represent the level of market risk. It has also become a regulatory and management standard in the financial services industry. VaR is defined as:

- the measure of the worst expected loss under normal market conditions over a specific time interval at a given confidence level; or
- the lowest quantile of the potential losses that can occur within a given portfolio during a specified time period.

To explain the meaning of VaR in an example, let us assume that the revenue of a portfolio is a normal distribution of mean equal to 0 and standard deviation σ. If we are interested to know the worst case of loss that happens at 5 per cent of chance, we can consult a statistics textbook and know that with a normal distribution the level of loss is 1.65 times the standard deviation (i.e. 1.65σ). The right side of Figure 10.1 shows a normal distribution of the portfolio's revenue (in a vertical and reverse position – meaning gain is represented on the lower end of the curve as losses are expected). The shaded region on the top of the curve represents extreme loss that results from unexpected events. If the area of this region corresponds to 5 per cent of the area under the entire curve, this extreme loss is indicated at 1.65σ from the mean of the curve.

Note that the confidence level should reflect the abundance and accuracy of available information, and the time span is chosen to suit the targeted use of the VaR. In the banking sector, daily VaR is calculated and used to monitor trading activities. The Basel Committee

Figure 10.1 Distribution of loss (left); value-at-risk distribution (right)

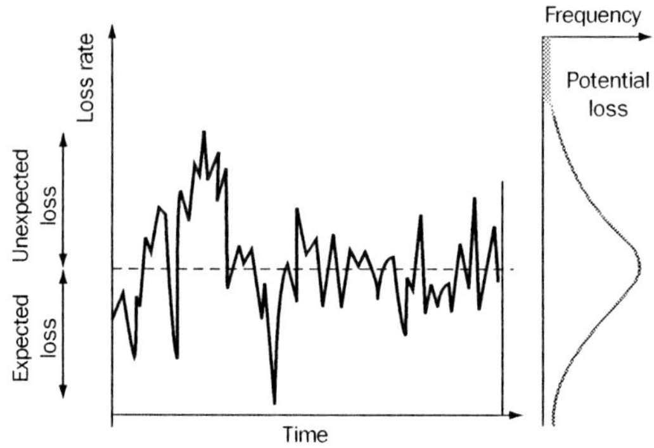

accepts VaR as a guide to determine capital requirements for banks. Financial intermediaries are also encouraged to disclose their VaR (BIS, 1994).

VaR works on a single level as well as multiple levels. The VaR of a portfolio can be viewed as dependent on several factors, such as the change in exchange rates, interest rates, equity and commodity prices. It is not surprising to find a bank taking hundreds or thousands of such factors into account. If the VaR is calculated by analytical methods, it is necessary to assume normal probability distribution for various factors and to approximate pricing functions of the financial instruments in the portfolio. This assumption causes no problem in measuring market risk, because market value distributions are mostly bell-shaped.

A common tool for the calculation of VaR is JP Morgan's RiskMetrics, which is a set of methodologies and datasets that covers a wide range of investment instruments, such as fixed income, foreign exchange, equity and commodities. (Further discussion on RiskMetrics is delayed until the section on market risk.) Both the methodologies and datasets are freely available in the public domain. JP Morgan later formed a subsidiary RiskMetrics to sell and support the RiskMetrics packages.

The original definition of VaR aimed at measuring market risks but the concept has also been applied to credit risk and even operational risk. The financial services sector has developed models that are based on credit VaR to measure the potential loss in investment instruments, such as derivative securities and bond futures, that have large amounts of historical data showing the market trend.

Credit value-at-risk

Like the concept of VaR, the credit VaR is determined as the maximum capital loss if unexpected loss exceeds economic capital; such cases happen at a probability less than a certain level, across a certain time horizon and at a certain confidence level. The credit VaR is also used to estimate the amount by which the losses arising from credit risk might exceed the expected standard risk costs within a year.

Credit VaR models could be divided into two categories (Altman et al., 2003):

- *Default models*: Credit risk is identified with default risk. As only two states with regard to default are considered (default and not default), credit loss occurs only when a default occurs. These models usually adopt a binomial approach.
- *Mark-to-market (MtM) models*: These take all possible changes of the borrower's creditworthiness into consideration. That is, credit loss occurs any time when the creditworthiness changes.

Unlike market value distributions, changes in credit risk tend to be small in size and the distribution is skewed with a fat tail (Figure 10.2). To avoid the normal distribution assumption, these tools may use simulation methods, such as replacing the normal distribution assumption with some distributions generated by historical data. However, this method relies on historical data that may not be valid in predicting future movements of a portfolio.

The Basel Committee on Banking Supervision requires credit VaR be measured with a 99 per cent confidence level over a period of ten days. The financial services industry can find several risk management tools,

Figure 10.2 A typical credit return

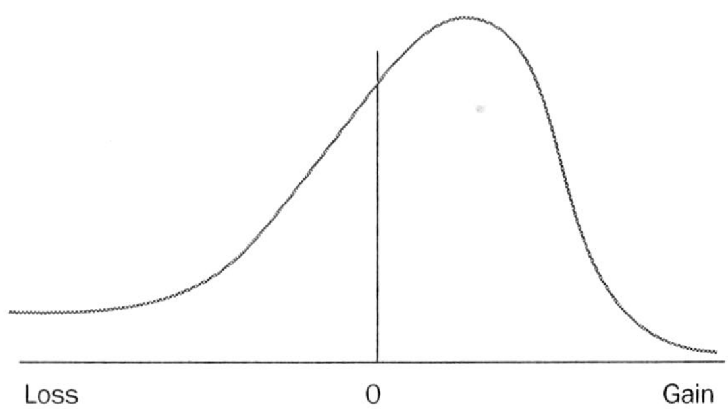

including JP Morgan's CreditMetrics, McKinsey's CreditPortfolioView, Credit Suisse Financial Products' CreditRisk+, and KMV's PortfolioManager, on which to base their evaluation on credit VaR, although they may use different approaches to calculate VaR.

Although it is popular, VaR does not always alert its users to potential disasters. Critics believe that failures could be caused by the historical data used to evaluate VaR. The input data do not include all the market information.

Miscellaneous metrics

There are plenty of other metrics that cannot be classified into the three methods above. A few of these are discussed below.

Greeks

Greek letters are used exclusively to denote certain features (mostly sensitivity) of the price of an option. Mathematically speaking, they are partial derivatives in the first and second orders. Five well-known metrics in Greek are as follows:

- *Delta* measures the sensitivity of the price of an option to a change in the price of the underlying asset, assuming all other variables remain the same. That is, if the price of the underlying asset rises by one dollar, the price of the option will be changed by an amount known as delta. It is an indicator of the risk level of an option and is often called the 'neutral hedge ratio' as it can be used to determine a 'delta hedging' to immunise the movement of the option price. This is done by taking an opposite position in the underlying asset equal in size to the delta value of the option.
- *Gamma* measures the rate of change of delta for each dollar rise in the underlying asset. This metric is used to forecast how delta of an option will change. Anyone delta-hedging an option wishes to see a small gamma because it means the hedge can provide the neutralising effect longer in time. A large gamma, however, indicates a severe change of sensitivity that means a small change in asset price could annihilate the effect of the delta-hedging. Gamma-hedging is done using options. To the bonds market, gamma is known as 'convexity'.
- *Theta* (also called 'day decay') measures the depreciation of the value of an option due one day closer to the expiration date.

- *Vega* (or *Kappa*) measures the sensitivity of the price of an option relative to the volatility of the underlying asset. In general, the option price increases when volatility increases and vice versa.
- *Rho* measures the change in the price of an option with respect to the domestic risk-free interest rate.

Strangely, although alpha and beta are also famous Greek letters used in risk management, they are generally not included with the 'Greeks' metrics.

The mathematical definitions of the Greeks measures are well-defined and their values can be calculated by simple software or even spreadsheets. They have been used in pricing and hedging financial instruments, such as options and bonds. However, the computation of these measures assumes that the returns of the underlying asset have an unrealistic (lognormal) distribution.

Duration and convexity

In the context of bonds, duration and convexity are two common metrics. Duration is the number of years for the price of a bond to be repaid by its internal cash flows. In 1938, Frederick Macaulay developed a formula to calculate duration, which is taken as a weighted average term to maturity. Mathematically, it is expressed as the sum of the present values of all cash flows divided by the bond price:

$$\text{Macaulay duration} = \frac{\sum_{t=1}^{n} \frac{t \cdot C}{(1+i)^t} + \frac{n \cdot M}{(1+i)^n}}{C \cdot \left[\frac{1 - \left[\frac{1}{(1+i)^n} \right]}{i} \right] + \frac{M}{(1+i)^n}}$$

Investors should know that bonds with longer durations have higher price volatility. Macaulay's formula was subsequently modified to measure the sensitivity of bond prices to interest rate changes. It can be shown as a graph (see Figure 10.3) of the value of a bond price versus the interest rate (i.e. yield to maturity), and the modified duration is the slope of the curve. In other words, the modified duration is measured on a linear approximation of the curve at a given interest rate. The 'modified duration' is defined as:

$$\text{modified duration} = \text{duration} \div (1 + (\text{yield to maturity}) \div n)$$

Figure 10.3 **Convexity of the relationship between bond price and yield**

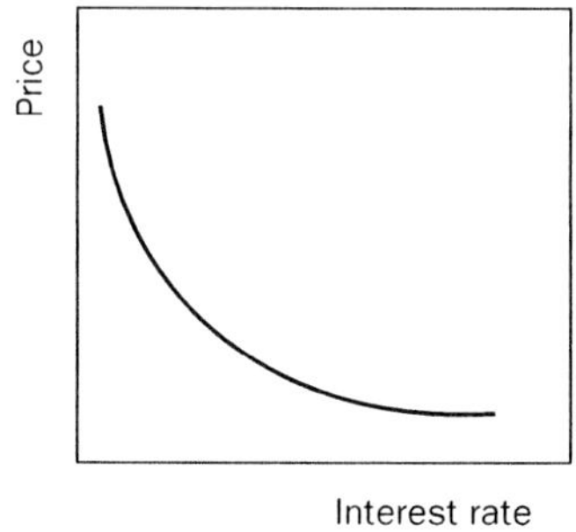

where n is the number of discounting periods in a year (e.g. 2 for semi-annual pay bonds).

The validity of the duration depends on the shape of the curve in Figure 10.3. It is more accurate if only a small part of the curve is considered (i.e. the change in interest rate is small). Otherwise, the convexity of the curve should be considered. The convexity measures the change in curvature of the curvilinear relationship between bond price and yield for a given bond. If the convexities of two bonds are compared, the price of the bond with less convexity falls at a slower rate as interest rates increase. Mathematically speaking, convexity is the second derivative of price with respect to yield.

Duration and convexity are useful in the measurement of bond price volatility and interest rate risk. Knowing the duration of its liabilities, an institute may match it with the duration of its assets to reduce market risk.

Beta

The volatility of a stock or a portfolio can be measured against the market by using beta, a percentage of price change with respect to each percentage of the market change. Beta is defined as the slope of the linear regression of a stock price in correlation with that of the market index. If the two regressions have similar slopes, beta of the stock is near to 1. Stocks with a beta greater than 1 are more volatile than the market, such as those high-tech stocks listed on Nasdaq; they move further positively or negatively in value. Beta is said to be able to measure the co-movement of a stock price with the market, or the sensitivity of the related asset to the market. Mathematically, it is defined as:

$$\beta = \text{(covariance of a stock with market)} \div \text{(variance of market)}$$

In an extreme case, the betas of certain stocks are negative, which means the stocks move in the opposite direction to the standard benchmark. Negative beta is highly unlikely but it exists, for example, in some stocks related to gold.

The concept of beta can be used to measure the fluctuation correlation of a stock and interest rates, another stock, or other investment instruments; but the calculation depends on historical data, which may not reflect the present volatility of the assets. When the benchmark is the market index, beta is often taken as a measure of the systematic risk of the market, which is the risk associated with the 'system' of the market, such as the regulatory framework and its relations with economic and political factors that impact the market as a whole. The idea of separating systematic and non-systematic risks comes from the well-known capital asset pricing model (CAPM). It asserts that the expected rate of return of a security is the sum of a risk-free rate of return and a risk premium that is proportional to the systematic risk of the security. In a mathematical expression, it is written as:

$$\text{Expected rate of return} = \text{(risk-free rate of return)} + \text{(systematic risk)} \times \text{(risk premium)}$$

where the risk premium is given by the difference between average market return and risk-free rate of return. Beta in CAPM is regarded as an indicator of systematic risk. As the risk-free rate of return (i.e. the non-systematic risk) can be eliminated by taking a diversification strategy, the expression above also indicates the expected rate of return depends on only one factor – the undiversifiable systematic risk.

Risk modelling

Most financial risks can be traced to exogenous reasons that are not fully understood or controlled by an institution. There may be historical records with which it is possible to study the correlation between the changes in various factors before and at the time of risk events, and hopefully the relationship can be described analytically with a mathematical model. Artificial intelligence methods, such as neural networks and fuzzy logic have also been used to establish heuristic models that mimic the interrelationship between internal and external factors and the model output. In both cases, the success of a model depends on its capacity to bind various factors together in a way that can explain a potentially risky event.

Factors are often selected because the corresponding data samples are available and they seem to have a persistent and significant contribution to the outputs. However, financial modelling would encompass only a selected collection of factors and neglect the others. The interrelationship of factors as prescribed in the model is based on its creator's assumptions. Although these assumptions are logically plausible, the choice of factors and their interrelationship may only present an over-simplified case, which gives rise to model risk.

To laypeople, risk models are black boxes that produce expected outcomes, such as risk level by assumptions and mechanisms inside the boxes and input data called 'random variables' (in cases where a statistical model is used) or 'parameters'. There are two main types of models:

- *Analytical models*: The mechanism assumes that the correlation between input and output can be described by mathematical functions. Both input and output also assume probability distributions, thus these models are mainly deterministic (i.e. the output is absolutely determined by the value of input) and are subject to statistical variables, such as level of confidence. These models exist if the input–output relationship can be expressed mathematically. In order to simplify calculations in practical problems, many variables that may have influence on the output are ignored.
- *Simulation models*: The mechanism refrains from representing the input–output relationship explicitly in mathematical terms. It assumes that values of factors in the portfolio fluctuate in some user-defined probability distributions. The input–output relationship is found by heuristic 'trial and error' methods, which make simulation models capable of mimicking complex and more realistic investment plans.

The CAPM mentioned in the previous section is a classic model of risk management, but it is rarely used in professional risk modelling. The beta values computed for many company-based investments are not able[1] to reflect the expected return of the related securities.

Risk models are constructed to explain the relationship between input and output. The models can also be subject to further studies, such as scenario analysis and stress testing, which are mentioned below.

Scenario analysis

If historical data are considered insufficient or irrelevant, an investment portfolio can be assessed by building a model to mimic scenarios of loss or gain under plausible circumstances. Many factors can affect the value of a portfolio, for example, interest rates, exchange rates, equity prices and commodity prices. Scenario analysis is used to estimate the change in the portfolio value as the result of the changes in the underlying factors.

Referring to modelling market risk, Aragonés et al. (2001) indicate three types of scenario construction:

- *Using recent history*: Past events can provide real data on which a scenario can be built. For example, the 1994 peso crisis and the 1997 Asian crisis could be simulated to see how the market reacts to similar incidents.
- *Using predefined parameters*: Effects on a fictitious model of changing in one or more parameters in a predefined magnitude (within 1 standard deviation or a certain percentage) can be studied.
- *Using mechanical search*: Computer programs can be used to find the results in the worst possible cases.

The first type of scenario needs the historical records of how the factors change with the portfolio value and assumes that the behaviour of the portfolio does not change with time. Besides market risk, the second and third types can be used in the estimation of credit risk or operational risk. A scenario should allow changes in its parameters; it is common to vary prices, volatilities, correlation, and the time horizon to study how the portfolio value responds to the changes.

The third type of scenario is often used with 'stress testing' to estimate the losses or gains in a scenario/portfolio due to abnormal, hypothetical but plausible, market movements. For this reason, scenario analysis is particularly suitable for the modelling of 'tail events' – those that occur in a way that is far away from the mean. Basel II suggests that banks use stress tests to find out how their portfolios behave in times of economic or industry downturns and various liquidity conditions.

However, analysts recognise that stress testing is not appropriate for day-to-day risk management (Pyle, 1997).

Dynamic financial analysis

The financial services industry may not be satisfied by the fixed or static modelling methodology that assumes many market features are unchanged for a long time. Methods such as scenario analysis that use stochastic or variable parameters have been developed to model the more changeable nature of the market. Dynamic financial analysis (DFA) is the application of stochastic simulation to, say, a financial cash flow model under special assumptions on distributions of major variables that can reflect future uncertainty.

DFA has been applied to various areas. For example, it has been modified to perform dynamic solvency testing (DST). This is the process to project a company's solvency position into the future, to assess its financial strength, and to identify the major risk factors that could affect the company's solvency. The test aims to estimate a distribution of possible surplus to keep the company's position solvent in spite of the risks. In the USA, insurers are statutorily required to use DST in determining the solvency position of the insurers in various scenarios for regulatory valuations.

Again in the insurance sector, insurers are no longer satisfied with traditional asset/liability management (ALM) approaches that tend to regard liabilities as deterministic due to their low variability. ALM is often used to coordinate investment portfolio and liabilities management to achieve financial objectives. With techniques in DFA, the ALM process can analyse assets and liabilities from a dynamic perspective. Risk mitigation strategies, which include adjusting exposure through reinsurance, hedging, securitisation and other investment policies, can then be formulated.

The DFA approach is particularly popular within the insurance industry. Its capability of stochastic simulation offers underwriters and financial managers better understanding of the risks and potential profitability of a company. However, DFA is not free from model risk. No matter how many stochastic parameters are included in the model, it may never be able to capture a full picture of the complexity of real-life economic and financial markets. Model builders should also be aware of the increase in computational effort and model risk if more parameters are considered. In addition, larger models tend to obscure the effect of individual parameters and make scenario analysis difficult.

The quantitative metrics and models introduced in this section show only a part of the spectrum of metrics/models that have been developed and used in the financial services industry. Many other metrics and models might be equally popular, but the previously discussed VaR, Greeks and beta represent the basic knowledge to operate ICT solutions for financial risk management, to which risk managers may apply scenario analysis and dynamic analysis techniques. They form the foundation of the following discussion on financial risk management and regulatory compliance.

Credit risk

Credit risk is concerned with the counterparty of a financial services institution. As counterparties may range from individuals and institutions, to governments, with possible obligations, such as auto loans, derivative trading and debt, a financial institution needs to consider many types of credit risk. This is a problem for large enterprises as well as SMEs and e-financial services.

Credit risk management

Credit risk management could be implemented as an information system that assesses an obligor's (borrower's) credit quality, models individual instruments to mitigate credit risk, consolidates the net credit exposures and monitors and manages portfolio credit risk across the organisation (Algorithmics, 2001). It may include processes to keep the loan repayment under surveillance, to review credit rating and to prepare for loan loss.

BIS (2000) suggests four areas in a comprehensive credit risk programme for the banking industry:

1. *Establishing an appropriate credit risk environment*: The board of directors should have responsibility for approving and reviewing credit risk strategy and relevant policies, with strategy implementation delegated to senior management.
2. *Operating under a sound credit-granting process*: Within the criteria that the banks should understand their borrowers or counterparties thoroughly and establish overall credit limits individually. The process

includes procedures for approving new credits and amendment, renewal and re-financing of existing credits.

3. *Maintaining an appropriate credit administration, measurement and monitoring process*: By developing an internal risk rating system, information systems, and analytical techniques to control the composition and quality of credit portfolios.
4. *Ensuring adequate controls over credit risk*: By establishing an ongoing system to assess credit management processes, controls to manage the credit-granting function properly and a system to manage problem credits.

For many years, the Basel Committee has been regulating the banking industry to prepare for insolvency. Credit risk is the primary concern of the banking industry as well as other financial services sectors. It is recommended that – based on the VaR model – the quantities of probability of default (PD), exposure at default (EAD) and loss-given default (LGD) can be used to calculate the expected loss of an organisation (details are described in the section on the Basel Accord). Models that are specially constructed for credit risk include the following three famous ones: KMV, CreditMetrics and Z-score.

KMV model

KMV is a software implementation of Merton (1974) and Black and Scholes' (1973) theories in credit risk estimation. It supposes that a company's asset level determines PD. The following briefly explains the KMV model.

As the asset value of a company changes over time, the company hopes that the market value of its asset at its maturity date is sufficient to pay off its liabilities. If the asset value is plotted against time, the time series is like the left side of Figure 10.4. By counting the number of days that the price reaches a certain price value, a frequency distribution curve can be drawn like the one on the right of Figure 10.4. Note that the dotted line in the diagram represents the level of liabilities. The KMV model adopts Merton's theory in treating equity as a call option on the company's asset and suggests that if the asset price falls before the liabilities, the company will default. On the frequency distribution, the shaded area below the line of liabilities represents the PD or expected default frequency (EDF). It is obvious that the PD increases if the asset value decreases, the liabilities increases, or the volatility of the asset price increases.

Figure 10.4 **Movement of asset price through time (left) and frequency distribution of asset price (right)**

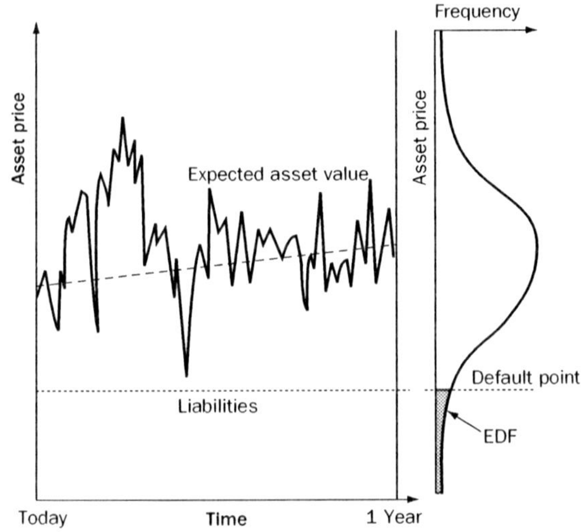

EDF: expected default frequency

The KMV model is able to calculate the 'distance to default' (DD) in terms of the number of standard deviations of the frequency distribution depicted in Figure 10.4. DD measures the distance between the current status (asset value) and the default point. Assuming that the asset value moves in a lognormal process, DD is defined as:

$$DD(h) = \frac{\ln(p) - \ln(d) + (\mu - 1/2\sigma^2)h}{\sigma\, h^{1/2}}$$

where

p = current asset price;

d = default point;

h = horizon;

μ = expected asset price; and

σ = standard deviation of the distribution (volatility of the asset price).

(Note that p, μ and σ are measured at the same time – at the time of calculating DD). The larger the DD, the smaller the company risk of default.

Moody's implements the KMV model in its software application PortfolioManager, which is now a very popular analytical tool for credit

Table 10.1 KMV threshold values to Standard & Poor's and Moody's ratings

Rating	Standard & Poor's	Moody's	KMV
A1	AAA	Aaa	0.02
B1	A–	A3	0.19
C1	BB	Ba2	1.2
D1	B–	B3	5.0
E1	CC	Ca	14.0

risk. It generates a probability distribution from the stock prices of the company whose liability is estimated by information from the company's historical data. The Credit Monitor tool is used to calculate EDF as a function of the company's capital structure, volatility of its asset returns and its current asset value.

Credit risk of a company can be estimated by using DD or EDF. The predictive power of the KMV model has been studied and confirmed. Table 10.1 shows the relationship between KMV values and corporate rating scales of Standard & Poor's and Moody's.

CreditMetrics

JP Morgan released its CreditMetrics in 1997 as a credit risk modelling tool. It is a mark-to-market (MtM) model because it calculates the present value of a portfolio of assets that are sensitive to credit risk. The principle is to look at the credit state (or credit quality) of obligors that are rated and compute the probability of their migrating to another credit state. In the simplest case of a standalone exposure, its credit risk is estimated in three steps as follows (JP Morgan, 1997):

1. *Credit rating migration*: The process constructs a transition matrix[2] (such as that shown in Figure 10.5) consisting of the likelihoods of the obligor's credit state migrating to another state, including default. Knowing the current credit state, the probabilities of the future states are given in just one row of the matrix. Note that the transition matrix collects the probability of changing from one credit state to another within a one-year horizon. The numeric probabilities are produced by rating agencies such as Moody's and Standard & Poor's, which have studied the dynamic changes of states of corporate bonds for many years.

Figure 10.5 **An example of transition matrix, using Standard & Poor's eight-class scheme**

	Aaa	Aa	A	Baa	Ba	B	Caa	D
Aaa	93.38%	5.94%	0.64%	0.00%	0.02%	0.00%	0.00%	0.02%
Aa	1.61%	90.53%	7.46%	0.26%	0.09%	0.01%	0.00%	0.04%
A	0.07%	2.28%	92.35%	4.63%	0.45%	0.12%	0.01%	0.09%
Baa	0.05%	0.26%	5.51%	88.48%	4.76%	0.71%	0.08%	0.15%
Ba	0.02%	0.05%	0.42%	5.16%	86.91%	5.91%	0.24%	1.29%
B	0.00%	0.04%	0.13%	0.54%	6.35%	84.22%	1.91%	6.81%
Caa	0.00%	0.00%	0.00%	0.62%	2.05%	4.08%	69.19%	24.06%

2. *Valuation*: To estimate the change in the present value created by a change in the obligor's credit state. The result is a row of estimated present values of the obligator's asset.
3. *Credit risk evaluation*: With the probabilities and present values, the credit risk is given by the standard deviation of the present values.

CreditMetrics is a model which, when implemented on a software package, gives rise to the CreditManager PC Program. The software can handle most credit instruments, such as bonds, loans, commitments, letters of credit, and market-driven instruments, such as swaps, forwards and credit derivatives.

Altman's Z-score

Banks may use the Z-score model to predict whether a counterparty is likely to go bankrupt within one or two years. The method was developed by Edward Altman in 1968. It takes variables, such as current assets, total assets, net sales, interest, total liability, current liabilities, market value of equity, earnings before taxes and retained earnings. The Z-score is basically a sum of five weighted financial ratios. The weights were supplied by Altman. The prediction of a public company going bankrupt is made by the following expression:

$$Z = 1.2x_1 + 1.4x_2 + 3.3x_3 + 0.64x_4 + 0.999x_5$$

where

x_1 = working capital ÷ total assets

x_2 = retained earnings ÷ total assets

x_3 = earnings before interest and taxes ÷ total assets

x_4 = market value of equity ÷ book value of total liabilities

x_5 = sales ÷ total assets

Figure 10.6 Interpretation of Z-score

Z score			Likelihood to bankruptcy
Public company	Private manufacturer	Private general firm	
3.0 or more	2.9 or above	2.6 or above	Most likely it is safe
Grey area			Probably safe; below safety threshold.
			Likely to go bankrupt within two years; some dramatic action may revive the business
1.8 or below	1.23 or below	1.1 or below	Highly likely to go bankrupt; little chance to recover

To calculate the Z-score for a private company, the five weights are replaced by 0.717, 0.847, 3.107, 0.420 and 0.998 respectively. The resulting Z-score is interpreted as in Figure 10.6.

Z-score has been used for decades and is accepted as a fairly accurate indicator of likelihood of bankruptcy. However, its predictive ability does not extend beyond two years. There are several other methods that use a similar summation function as the Z-score to evaluate credit risk. For example, the logit model (Stickney, 1996) uses seven weighted financial ratios and it calculates the probability of bankruptcy as $1/(1 + e^y)$ where:

$$y = 0.23883 - 0.108x_1 - 1.583x_2 - 10.78x_3 + 3.074x_4 + 0.486x_5 - 4.35x_6 + 0.11x_7$$

and:

x_1 = average inventories ÷ sales

x_2 = average receivables ÷ average inventories

x_3 = (cash + marketable securities) ÷ total assets

x_4 = quick assets ÷ current liabilities

x_5 = (income from continuing operations) ÷ (total assets – current liabilities)

x_6 = (long-term debt) ÷ (total assets – current liabilities)

x_7 = sales ÷ (net working capital + fixed assets)

Case: Risk management in IIB (SAS, year unknown)

The Irish bank IIB is a merchant bank wholly owned by the Brussels-based KBC NV. In 2003, IIB decided to develop a risk management system to meet the requirements of Basel II. Having missed KBC's internal deadline of October 2003, IIB outsourced the implementation of a risk management solution to SAS. Although the outsourcing decision was made in just six months, SAS later proved to be able to provide the statistical and risk management expertise that IIB lacked.

The prototype system installed in the following May won the confidence of management. SAS Risk Management for Banking was able to manage market, credit and operational risk. The solution provides a single environment where analytical tools can be used to calculate credit scoring, VaR, scenario analysis and stress testing for all relevant risk types.

To manage risk in residential home loans, the system keeps homogenous pools of mortgage data and calculates individual customer credit ratings that reflect PD, EAD and LGD. The information is sent to the customers, who are thus segmented according to their risks so that different services can be offered.

The solution also generates a 'movement report' that shows how many records in each pool change in time and why. The management and the regulator are able to monitor the validity of the model by watching these activities in each pool.

The financial industry in the Internet age tends to abandon the 'silo' perspective on credit risk management. Their database of credit risk is integrated with management systems of other types of risks in order to evaluate the risk level at the enterprise level. As credit risk management is so important, some authors recommend that credit risk analysis and decision makers (like fund managers) should be segregated so that the analysis remains objective, although this might not be practical for small organisations.

Liquidity risk

For financial institutions, such as banks and insurers, balance sheet liquidity needs to be closely watched to ensure there is adequate funding or that assets can be liquidated to meet obligations as they come due. In general, all business organisations should be aware of the potential loss arising from urgently selling an asset at a price below its fair market value. Thus, liquidity risk exhibits in the following forms:

- *Market liquidity risk*: This arises when an organisation is not able to conclude a transaction (especially a large one) at a price near to the current market price.

- *Funding liquidity risk*: This arises when an organisation is not able to obtain funds to meet its cash flow obligations.

Thus, liquidity risk is partly determined by the market condition. When referred to a stock market, liquidity risk has a different meaning in the Internet age. With high-speed information passing and efficient program trading, market liquidity is affected by the trading programs, which tend to become homogeneous in design and the trading algorithms employed. As program trading amounts to a very large proportion (more than half in 2005) of the daily volume of shares traded, individual investors might also be attracted to the trend led by trading programs. Program trading is a major reason for the weakening of market liquidity in recent years (Quillian, 2005).

As far as the liquidity of a company is concerned, both external reasons (e.g. market liquidity falls or interbank rate rises) and internal reasons (e.g. credit rating falls) could bring it down. The liquidity risk of a company has a compounding effect on other types of risks. For example, a large company losing some of its liquidity would increase market risk as well as its credit risk. In spite of its importance, liquid risk lacks a standard metric and, as a result, the overall financial risk is always underestimated.

Metrics for liquidity risk

By definition, liquidity risk is related to future net cash flows. A sudden increase of negative net cash flow can be interpreted as a danger to liquidity. If cash flows can be described in a model, scenario analysis and stress testing can also be applied to find potential causes of negative cash flows.

To manage liquidity risk effectively, a financial services institution needs to identify certain indicators so that its liquidity level can be monitored. These indicators are commonly expressed in terms of ratios, such as liquidity ratio and dependency ratio, which are explained below:

- *Liquidity ratio*: Measures a company's exposure to liquidity risk over a specified time frame. The ratio can be defined as the short-term funding divided by deposits and short-term liabilities. That is:

Liquidity ratio = [(net cash) + (short-term and marketable assets)
+ (maturing loans)]
÷ (net deposits and short-term liabilities)

Liquidity ratio is often used by authorities in the banking sector to control the prudential level maintained in a bank, or as a basic requirement for licensees to retain a financial services licence.

- *Dependency ratio*: Measures the extent of volatile liabilities within an institution's funding base. It is defined as:

$$\text{Dependency ratio} = \frac{(\text{volatile liabilities}) - (\text{short-term investments})}{(\text{total earning assets}) - (\text{short-term investments})}$$

  A positive dependency ratio is interpreted as a signal that the organisation is using its long-term assets to fund volatile short-term liabilities.

Although VaR is not intended to study liquidity risk, the term 'liquidity-at-risk' also appears in different contexts, although there is no consensus in its definition. Alan Greenspan (1999) defined liquidity-at-risk as a country's liquidity position under a range of possible outcomes for relevant financial variables including exchange rates, commodity prices and credit spreads, among others. When applied to the liquidity of a company, this concept is interpreted as the maximum cumulative margin calls requiring cash payments during a relevant time horizon.

Market liquidity risk

In a secondary market, liquidity risk is characterised in the following three dimensions (Kyle, 1985):

- *Tightness*: The distance between transaction prices and mid-market prices (i.e. the bid–ask spread). A market is tight if there are many quotes at a price close to the last trading price.
- *Depth*: The largest volume of trades being processed without significantly affecting the prevailing market prices. It is measured by order size and the relevant spread for that order.
- *Resiliency*: The length of time required to recover after a price fluctuation. A market is resilient if it takes a relatively short time to drive the price of an asset back to its fundamentally justified level after a temporary imbalance.

Note that the first two dimensions measure a market at a given point in time. The dynamics of the market are measured by its resiliency. Other metrics have also been used to capture market liquidity from other aspects; for example, the metric 'order imbalance' measures the difference between selling and buying limited orders; another metric 'immediacy' measures the time between an order being placed and the time it is executed.

These metrics are often aggregated to provide a composite metric so that market liquidity can be assessed from multiple angles. For example, Muranaga (1999) devised a metric 'market resiliency', which takes metrics from several dimensions together:

$$\text{Market resiliency } (\gamma) = \frac{\text{ratio of bid–ask price change}}{\text{restoration time of bid–ask spread}}$$

The idea of resilience is sometimes taken to explain prudential regulation. A higher prudent level is regarded as a means to enhance resilience of a financial system or a company. In the UK, the FSA offers a 'resilience test' to all life insurance companies. It tests the companies' liquidity and requires them to demonstrate their funding can withstand a major fall in asset prices (say, by 25 per cent) and a rise in long-term interest rates (say, by 3 per cent).

Management strategies dealing with liquidity risk measure and forecast cash obligations and identify times when cash flows might have problems. Methods to mitigate liquidity risk might include diversification of funding sources and preparation of quick access to liquid assets. A general framework is exemplified below.

KPMG liquidity risk management framework

Solution providers might offer their special approaches in liquidity risk monitoring. Their choices of metrics and indicators are encompassed in their liquid risk management models. KPMG (2000) propose a liquidity risk management framework for banks. The framework is a three-stage process:

1. *Review and gap analysis*: To review the existing liquidity risk framework that is made up of areas of responsibility, liquidity strategies, data sources, quantification and analysis tools, information flows, and management and controlling mechanisms.
2. *Redesign*: A series of four steps:
   - Re-assign management responsibilities and redefine a liquidity strategy.

- Clarify reporting needs according to the firm's risk profile and liquidity strategy.
- Quantify liquidity risk by modelling (including model validation) and data supply to generate the liquidity indicators, which the management compares with defined limits.
- Build a framework for liquidity crisis management.

3. *Result*: To design a new liquidity risk policy according to the firm's risk profile and strategy.

KPMG's risk measurement process is based on a 'liquidity maturity transformation model' that calculates the liquidity gaps between cash inflows and outflows in the form of a maturity ladder (like the one in Figure 10.7). Note that the net funding requirements are represented as the black line among the bars of cash inflows and outflows. Those bars on the right of the 'value date' represent only projected inflows and outflows. KPMG checks regularly on the validity of the maturity ladder and whether the bank's liquidity can meet its payment obligations. The position on the maturity ladder is monitored by KPMG-defined liquidity-at-risk figures. By using stress testing, the model can predict the liquidity situation of a bank during crisis.

Case: The People's Bank of China (Asian Development Bank, 2001)

The early warning system (EWS) model is used by central banks in the USA, France and the Philippines. It is now being implemented by the

Figure 10.7 **A maturity ladder showing cash inflows (upright bars) and outflows**

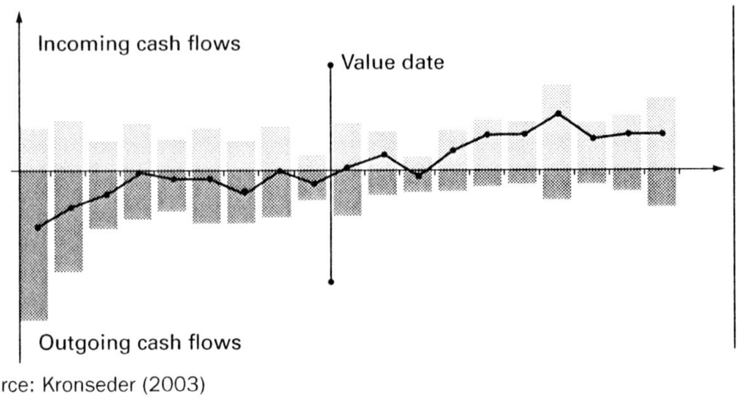

Source: Kronseder (2003)

People's Bank of China to forecast a bank's future financial condition in order to identify high-risk domestic banks.

The model makes use of an indicator known as 'non-performing asset (NPA) coverage ratio' to measure the bank's financial health.

$$\text{NPA} = \frac{\text{capital} + \text{loan-loss reserves} - \text{non-performing assets}}{\text{total assets}}$$

The NPA coverage ratio is a variation of the capital-to-asset ratio that takes into consideration the loan–loss reserves and non-performing assets. The People's Bank of China believes that NPA coverage ratio is very efficient in reflecting the condition of a bank. If a high-risk bank is identified, the bank would conduct more comprehensive analysis of the financial statements of the bank.

To monitor the financial condition of a bank, the EWS must collect information, such as consolidated balance sheets, income statements and macroeconomic data in a database from which the NPA coverage ratio can be calculated. The NPA coverage ratio is accumulated to generate a one-month-ahead forecast. If a bank is found to have its NPA coverage ratio deteriorating, the People's Bank of China would seek an explanation from the bank's supervisors.

Market risk management

Market risk is the risk of a loss in a position or portfolio due to changes in the underlying factors. It is obviously a composite risk determined by one or more market prices, interest rates, financial indices, price volatilities of underlying instruments inputted from option prices, correlations and other market factors, such as liquidity (Morgan Stanley, 2002). Market risk has greatly increased in recent years due to the development of more derivatives and globalisation of markets. It has significant consequences on a financial institution's earnings or economic capital.

The following elements contribute to the market risk:

- *Interest rate risk (IRR)*: This results from the unpredictable fluctuations in the spread between the lending rate and the return on the loan portfolio. It may also arise from repricing of assets, liabilities and contractual maturities. A bank usually uses a cost pass-through formula to limit the interest rate sensitivity of the spread earnings on the bank's loan portfolio. Investment banks may also mitigate their IRR by taking offsetting positions in cash or derivative markets.

- *Exchange rate risk*: This is associated with the current holdings and future cash flows denominated in foreign currencies. An institution can mitigate foreign exchange (FX) risk by buying FX options, currency swaps, futures, forwards and deposits.
- *Equity risk*: This occurs as the price of securities (including bonds, securities and commodity prices) is sensitive to the market dynamics.
- *Commodities risk*: This arises in the holding or a position-taking in commodities, such as agricultural products, minerals (including oil) and precious metals (excluding gold, which is treated as foreign currency).

Financial institutions can monitor their volume limits – the maximum open position that is carried overnight or during the course of a trading session–and ensure that the limits do not expose the institution to excessive risk. The limits, however, vary with differences in currencies as well as estimated potential losses during the trading session. These limits are unable to provide adequate protection to the institutions when new derivatives are introduced to the market.

Models using VaR are recommended by the financial industry. In the simplest case, a VaR model can be built to find out each portfolio component's sensitivity to a small change in interest rate or exchange rate. As early as in 1993, the Basel Committee proposed a standardised model for measuring market risk for the banking industry. It came under severe criticism and was later abandoned. The banking industry prefers their VaR models (also known as 'internal models') for market risk estimation.

In other models, metrics, such as beta and the Greeks are also used to quantify market risk. Aragonés et al. (2001) point out that stress tests should be complementary to VaR methods, as the tests can provide information on extreme events.

The two major types of market risks (interest rate and FX) are discussed separately in the following section.

Interest rate risk management

A financial institution's earnings and portfolio is subject to the influence of interest rates, but how much a portfolio is affected depends on the characteristics of individual instruments, such as:

- *Maturity (for fixed-rate instruments)*: A longer maturity will decrease future income if the interest rate increases.
- *Repricing (for floating-rate instruments)*: Instruments, such as floating-rate loans that reprice frequently are less sensitive to interest rate changes. Maturity/repricing risk occurs from differences between the timing of rate changes and the timing of cash flows.
- *Yield curve*: A yield curve depicts the comparison between long-term rates with respect to short-term rates. A change in interest rates may change the curve by making it flatter (if long-term rate increases are less than short-term rate increases at time of rate change) or steeper.
- *Basis risk*: This arises when a rate change does not result in similar changes in different instruments.
- *Embedded options*: If any exist in assets, liabilities, or off-balance-sheet (OBS) portfolios, these would affect the timing of the cash flows generated by the related instrument.

As components in a portfolio react to interest rates differently, it is possible to reduce the overall sensitivity by including instruments that are less sensitive in the portfolio.

Note that a change in interest rate can result in earnings. For the banking industry, a change in interest rate can affect a bank's net interest income and other interest-sensitive income. The Basel Committee issued a consultative document (BIS, 2001) to promote sound IRR management practices and asserted that a bank's IRR management system should address all material sources of IRR, including repricing, yield curve, basis and option risk exposures. A simplified technique given in the document is a 'maturity/repricing schedule' which allocates interest-sensitive assets, liabilities, and OBS positions into different 'time bands' according to their maturity or the time to the next repricing. The schedule can be used to study the gap between assets and liabilities plus OBS exposures within each time band, revealing the bank's repricing risk exposure – a process known as 'gap analysis'. It can also be used in stress tests.

Foreign exchange risk management

Whenever an institution takes a new FX position (in spot, currency futures, or currency options), the position is exposed to FX risk because the exchange rate may move against it. The risk persists until it is covered by an offsetting transaction.

The exposure to FX risk is measured with the value of an institution's assets, which are usually compiled by methods based on accrual accounting. However, these methods provide data that often fail to show the point-in-time effects of FX rate changes. It is thus recommended to decompose the FX exposure into three elements as follows:

- *Translation (or accounting) exposure*: Loss occurs when accounts that are denominated in foreign currencies are translated into home currency for consolidation purposes.
- *Economic exposure*: The likelihood that the future operational cash flows are affected by an expected change in exchange rate.
- *Transaction exposure*: Risk occurs from a transaction getting more or less than it was contracted prior to the exchange rate changes.

Although there are models to explain the FX mechanism, such as the CAPM variants, FX risk management in practice seldom refers to such models. Institutions prefer to rely on hedging to reduce investment risks arising from potential changes of exchange rates. They should choose among the following derivatives to construct a portfolio that consists of some long-term foreign currency assets and some short-term foreign assets, such that both sides can offset one another.

- *Futures contracts* (e.g. forward options): The purchaser is obliged to buy or sell an asset at a specified price, quantity and future date. They are rarely used to hedge FX risk as the counterparties may not honour the contracts at the date agreed upon (counterparty risk).
- *Futures*: Forward contracts that trade on organised exchanges, which guarantee high liquidity but require higher transaction costs.
- *Options*: The purchaser is given the right, but not obligation, to buy or sell an asset at a specified price, quantity and future date.
- *Swaps* (e.g. interest rate swaps and currency swaps): Counterparties are obliged to exchange one asset for another by a contract, at a specified future date.

Note that not all FX exposures impact adversely on the institution. For example, if a foreign currency weakens, institutions that are holding a liability position in that currency will benefit. In this case, the transaction exposure can turn into profit if no hedging has been made or instruments like call options have been bought. Thus the decision of 'to hedge or not to hedge' must be made before choosing a hedging strategy to minimise FX exposure. Hedging is discussed further in the next section.

Case: RiskMetrics

Developed by JP Morgan in the 1994, RiskMetrics has become a standard tool for market risk assessment. It provides a framework to measure market risk in terms of VaR. For a financial institution, RiskMetrics reveals how much value a portfolio of assets could potentially lose should market conditions move adversely.

Assuming returns for each asset are normally distributed, the calculation of VaR is based on a so-called 'variance-covariance approach'. This method requires only the standard deviations (volatility) of the market returns and the correlation between these returns. It supposes that the value of a portfolio changes linearly or quadratically with changes in market risk factors. The variance of a portfolio $\check{R}$ is first computed as:

$$Var(\check{R}) = \Sigma_i \Sigma_j w_i w_j \sigma_{ij}$$

where:

w_i = weight of asset i in the total portfolio value

σ_{ij} = covariance of asset i's returns with asset j's returns

The market VaR is obtained as 1.65 or 2.33 times the square root of $Var(\check{R})$. The two options give the 5 per cent quantile and 1 per cent quantile of the worst result (i.e. VaR) respectively.

The computation is simplified but the assumption of normal distribution is criticised as being unrealistic. The model is not suitable for a portfolio with options as its underlying asset because the price of options is known to follow a nonlinear fashion. The result of RiskMetrics tends to underestimate VaR.

RiskMetrics Group became a company independent of JP Morgan in 1998. It continues to support the RiskMetrics (and CreditMetrics) technology by issuing technical documents, journals and free datasets (supplied by Reuters) of volatility and correlation information across multiple assets and instruments all over the world. The new company developed RiskManager and CreditManager applications. The latter allows users to calculate credit risk while the former expands the toolset of market VaR calculation to include Monte Carlo simulation, historical simulation and stress testing.

Monte Carlo simulation requires no assumption on the linear relationship between portfolio value and market risk factors. Large numbers of scenarios can be constructed based on derivative positions, interest rate factors, currency exchange rate and other factors whose interrelation can be established by values randomly selected from predefined distributions. However, it is accused of being too slow to produce the result.

If ample historical data are available, the simulation process can draw values from distributions that are based on historical records. Its advantages include that it does not assume any probability distribution of the underlying assets and can be applied to both linear and nonlinear instruments.

The three major types of financial risks – credit, liquidity and market risks – were briefly discussed in the previous three sections. Many of the models described are essentially static as they capture the risk level at one point in time. Although these models are well-known and have strong theoretical bases, modern risk management needs some tools to capture the dynamic nature of the financial market, especially when they are interested in hedging.

Dynamic risk management

A static risk model does not always produce satisfactory results. Some are even described as layers of useless bureaucracy that work only in theory. Fehle and Tsyplakov (2005) raise some questionable assumptions that are common in static models, such as:

- The use of hedge ratio and maturity of risk management instruments cannot be adjusted or reversed over time.
- Risk management instruments do not expire as time progresses. Their life is assumed at least as long as that of the firm. Thus, the timing of initiation and sequence of risk management decisions are unimportant.
- Transaction costs associated with initiation and adjustment of risk management contracts are neglected.

Consultants and solution vendors promote their risk management systems as being capable of 'dynamic risk management' because they allow more flexibility in model construction. The aforementioned DFA, DST and ALM are examples of dynamic risk models.

From the perspective of risk management, a dynamic model can use short-term instruments to hedge long-term holdings, such that the transaction costs of initiating and prematurely terminating risk management contracts are considered (Fehle and Tsyplakov, 2005). Availability of these short-term instruments supports the dynamic risk management model. For example, credit derivatives (e.g. credit default swaps) can be bought or sold to protect against a debtor's default and are regarded as an effective means to diversify credit risks (Banque France, 2002). Dynamic risk management may involve many kinds of instruments for diversification and hedging, such as securities, cash equities, swaps, futures and derivatives.

Securitisation and hedging are major techniques for dynamic management for liquidity and market risks. Netting and collateralisation are effective for mitigating credit risks. These are discussed below.

Liquidity risk mitigation: securitisation

Since the mid-1990s, the method of securitisation has emerged and drawn a lot of attention. It is typically seen as a risk-sharing technique and is a means to promote efficiency of the financial market. For example, the insurance industry believes that securitisation could be applied to catastrophe risks (Table 10.2). The banking sector would like to reduce credit risk and market risk by securitising their loan book, asset finance options, liabilities and so on. The process involves structuring and selling assets to marketable securities, which are funded by the issue of securities secured primarily by these assets. Securitisation enhances cash flow and separates the credit risk of the issuer from the securities transaction.

Table 10.2 **Instruments for insurance securitisation**

Purpose	Tools	Remarks
Risk transfer	Reinsurance	Transfers risks to re-insurers
	Swap (including risk exchanges)	Transfers risks to other insurers or to the capital markets
	Catastrophe bond	Transfer risks to the capital market
	Exchange-traded derivatives	Transfers risks to the capital markets
Contingent funding	Line of credit	Right to borrow
	Contingent surplus note	Option to borrow contingent upon the occurrence of an event

Source: Gorvett (1999)

There are many financial vehicles for securitisation, such as trusts, corporate loans, or a special-purpose vehicle (a subsidiary company set up for a special purpose, such as asset securitisation). The selected vehicle issues securities that are structured so that interest and principal payments are supported by cash flows from the underlying pool of loans. The process is relatively expensive in terms of administration and legal implications.

If an insurer chooses to transfer underwriting risk to the financial market by securitisation, portfolios made up of financial instruments as those in Table 10.2 can be used. Note in the table that those called 'contingent' may not be issued immediately after the risk occurs; they are prepared for future use. Two types of tools – reinsurance and catastrophe securities – were discussed in Chapter 5. Securitisation management has become an essential feature in many underwriting applications. Sharing the same database, a securitisation management module can consolidate and transfer asset summaries, which are frequently required by rating agencies and investors. The module may also be able to track and monitor the status of documents and transactions so that the originators and issuers alike can monitor the performance of the portfolios.

To attract investors, it is common that the selected securitisation vehicle builds mechanisms into its structure to protect against credit risk, using techniques, such as collateralisation, letters of credit and third-party insurance. A more sophisticated securitisation management solution would get access to the database of creditworthiness scores of the assets and assist the process of collateralisation – a concept discussed below. In asset securitisation, it is common that the amount of securities issued is over-collateralised in order to protect investors against the risk of non-payment or late payment.

Market risk mitigation: hedging

Technically speaking, hedging is associated with a transaction that will cause a loss on the same occasion that the hedging generates a gain. This is a common method to reduce holistic risk that includes market risk and even credit risk, although it is also believed that hedging credit risk is more difficult because of information asymmetries.

There are many hedging instruments. The choice of a hedging instrument needs to consider the relationship between the hedging instrument and the assets or liabilities being hedged. The hedge must be highly effective in achieving offsetting changes in the value of the hedged item; this attribute is known as 'effectiveness' of the hedge. The measurement of effectiveness is presented with some mathematics in the following.

Relative risk reduction

The description below summarises a white paper by Coughlan et al. (2003). Suppose that hedged item of value U is hedged by instrument of value H. The portfolio P is therefore made up by:

$$P = U + r \cdot H$$

where r is the hedge ratio; i.e., h units of the hedging instrument are used to hedge one unit of the hedged item. As hedge effectiveness is related to the changes in the fair value (i.e. marked-to-market value), the change in the fair value of the portfolio is found as:

$$\Delta FV_P = \Delta FV_U + h \cdot \Delta FV_H$$

If we assume that the changes in the fair values of U and H are normally distributed with zero means and standard deviations σ_U and σ_H, the change of fair value of P is also normally distributed with a standard deviation as:

$$\sigma_P = \sqrt{(\sigma_U^2 + h^2 \cdot \sigma_H^2 + 2h \cdot \sigma_U \sigma_H \cdot \rho)}$$

where ρ is the correlation between changes in fair value of the hedged item and hedging instrument. The selected hedge is effective if $\sigma_U > \sigma_P$. A quantity known as 'relative risk reduction' (RRR) is a metric of effectiveness:

$$RRR = (\sigma_U - \sigma_P) \div \sigma_U$$

The International Accounting Standard (IAS) 39 and the FAS 133 for US GAAP provide the standards to recognise, measure and report the use of financial derivatives in hedging. IAS 39 was endorsed by the European Commission as regulations concerning accounting for hedging instruments. These standards recognise three types of hedges:

- *Fair value hedge*: Protects against a change in the fair value (marked-to-market) of assets and liabilities. Examples include interest rate swaps that can hedge possible changes in interest rates.

- *Cash flow hedge*: Protects against a change in the value of forecast cash flows generated by existing or future assets or liabilities. Examples include selling an option to hedge the changes in price of the associated securities held.
- *Foreign currency hedge*: Protects against a change of a net investment in a foreign operation generated by a change in FX rates.

Institutions that choose to hedge accounts must satisfy IAS requirements in documenting the detailed hedging relationship and monitoring the effectiveness of the hedge on an ongoing basis. For fair value hedges, variations in the value of the hedged item are kept in the item account while that of the hedging instrument remains unchanged. For cash flow hedges, the accounting for the hedged items is not changed but that of the hedge instrument varies.

Credit risk mitigation

Although the calculation of credit risk often assumes that one counterparty is independent of another, there remains systemic risk, in which any one default case could affect the asset values of others. If credit risk is not mitigated, the investor can risk a potentially devastating 'domino effect'. Even if no systemic risk is involved, methods to reduce credit risk still lower market risk and the credit risk of the counterparties.

The Counterparty Risk Management Policy Group[1] (CRMPG) proposed a contextual framework for counterparty risk management that consists of the following six significant building blocks (CRMPG, 1999):

1. *Information sharing between counterparties*: As knowledge of counterparties is the foundation of risk management of the counterparties.
2. *Evaluation and leverage of market and liquidity risks*: By using an integrated analytical framework.
3. *(Liquidation-based) estimates of potential counterparty credit exposures*: By systematic evaluation of the integrated effect of market, liquidity and credit risks.
4. *Internal credit practices*: Taking into consideration estimates of counterparty credit exposures and potential liquidation cost estimates.

5. *Enhancements in quality of risk information*: For senior management, board of directors and regulatory authorities.
6. *Compliance with document standards*: Including standards for completion and control of documents, particularly focusing on valuation and legal certainty.

Two common strategies of risk mitigation – netting and collateral – are discussed below. Both should be implemented and monitored by the risk management function, which is responsible for the preparation of pledge documentation and legal support of the strategies. The International Swap and Derivatives Association (ISDA) has been lobbying jurisdictions to support the netting and collateral practices, including the use of a master agreement.

Netting

Netting is an agreement between counterparties to offset their obligations. There are several forms of netting, as described below:

- *Settlement netting*: All deals between two counterparties are settled on a net cash basis and in the same currency.
- *Netting by novation*: A new obligation replaces an existing one. This is used to reduce credit risk and liquidity risk and can be repeated many times until the preset settlement date. Usually, the new obligation amalgamates all other obligations on the same date.
- *Close-out netting*: All outstanding liabilities are settled by one single payment immediately after the occurrence of a default or other adverse event that is specified in the contract. It changes neither the credit nor liquidity risk. ISDA launched the Netalytics software tool to help members manage close-out netting.

Netting was first available between two counterparties but more institutions have subsequently participated in the arrangement, known as 'multilateral netting'. Some of the Lamfalussy standards (BIS, 1990) focus on interbank multilateral netting systems, which are expected to:

- have clearly defined procedures for the management of credit risks and liquidity risks;
- be capable of ensuring the timely completion of daily settlements in the event of an inability to settle by the participant with the largest single net-debit position;

- have objective and publicly-disclosed criteria for admission that permit fair and open access.

While bilateral netting could be set up between two parties, multilateral netting requires a central netting agent or a clearinghouse that also acts as a legal counterparty. Modern netting schemes can be implemented as e-settlement systems. The central agent can operate a system administration site to provide system-wide reconciliation, clearing facilities including trade acknowledgment, netting arrangements, guarantees of contractual performance and surveillance of counterparties.

Collateralisation

To mitigate credit risk, a financial service institution may reach an agreement with its counterparties to adopt the collateral approach. The collateral is cash, securities, bank guarantees and equities that both sides agree to post when an event of credit risk occurs on their side of the contract. In case of default of the counterparty, the collateral taker (the institution) may take the collateral as an asset and transform credit risk into market risk.

The insurance sector may be required to maintain a certain level of statutory surplus by holding more assets than liabilities (Garzone, 2005). If they want their receivables to be considered as legitimate assets, the receivables must be supported by collateral. Rating agencies like Standard & Poor's, Moody's and Fitch also consider collateral held by an insurance company as its ability to satisfy anticipated liabilities.

ISDA published the *Collateral Review* in 1999 which confirmed that many institutions had greatly reduced credit loses by their effective collateral arrangements. The review gave 22 recommendations (ISDA, 1999), including the following three, by which an institution is required to:

- Regard collateralisation as a complement to credit analysis, which focuses on traditional metrics (current credit exposure, potential future credit exposure and PD), estimate of the size and nature of the exposure of the counterparty to the market as a whole (including its liquidity and leverage), and the effect of collateral.
- Review the composition of its collateralised portfolios regularly to assess the collateral risks (which include risks on the legal, operational, collateral issuer, concentration, correlation and liquidity

aspects). Collateral risks should be reported to management and actively managed where appropriate.

- Structure the collateral function so as to minimise operational risk. Extensive process automation and the implementation of a rigorous control environment are critical. The institution should consider centralising the collateral function or developing a series of linked 'hub and spoke' operations.

In Europe, central counterparty clearinghouses play an important role in collateral administration. For example, they require their members to regularly re-value (MtM) their collateral, together with the re-assessment of relevant 'haircuts' – a discount to the full value of the collateral as a protection for the institution against price volatility. For example, if $10,000 worth of securities is taken as collateral, only a part of the value is counted as the real effect of the collateral and the rest is haircut. There are other haircuts and their sizes depend on several factors, including collateral maturity, liquidity and price volatility. After haircuts are applied, the value of the collateral is adjusted according to the following formula:

$$\text{adjusted value of collateral} = (\text{collateral value}) \div (1 + H_E + H_C + H_{FX})$$

where:

H_E = haircut appropriate to exposure

H_C = haircut appropriate to collateral

H_{FX} = haircut appropriate for currency mismatch between collateral and exposure

Collateral management solutions, such as Clearstream Banking AG's Xemac, can provide real-time adjustments of collateral exposure values and automate releases and allocations of collateral in accordance with contractual arrangements between counterparties. Many risk management systems also incorporate collateral management as one of their features.

Collateral management is important – especially when the institution wishes to raise its credit ratings. With a clear understanding of its collateral positions with the counterparties, the institution should have a consolidated view over its liquidity. The Basel Committee is changing its view on collateral and has accepted a wider range of collateral in its new Accord. As the Basel Accord is a controversial regulatory model that will affect the banking industry in years to come, the following section re-examines it from a risk management perspective.

ICT in dynamic risk management

To help manage financial risk in such a dynamic market, ICT can be deployed in the following processes:

- *Data consolidation*: To consolidate investment data and to generate and distribute documents that are used in investment decisions as well as reports on monitoring and controlling investment exposures.
- *Analysis and pricing procedures*: Techniques include computerised modelling (such as scenario modelling, weather modelling and simulation), financial engineering (such as securitisation and hedging policies), and sensitivity analysis (including stress testing by specified problem situations, reproduction of historical situations and/or extreme scenarios generated by stochastic models).
- *Portfolio management*: To identify key accumulations, allocate capacity, determine needs for risk transfer and benchmark risk against solvency requirements, possibly in a real-time and multi-currency fashion. For example, many banks monitor their VaR on a real-time basis.

Program (or algorithmic) trading is particularly suitable for hedging. Many hedge funds are operated on quantitative strategies and depend on an interactive hedge design application to leverage risk impact of various investment instruments. Brokerage firms may incorporate their trading strategies to their order management systems to allow customers to design their own hedging algorithms. Collateral management solutions are also available for financial institutions to automate their collateral activities, which are usually centralised in order to reduce operational risks.

Although ICT is advantageous to individual institutions in financial risk management, it might have negative effects on the market as a whole. Many stock market crashes have been attributed to highly efficient program trading and quick transmission of market information. ICT increases volatility and systemic risk because many market participants react in the same way at almost the same time.

The Basel Accord

To ensure continued financial viability, a financial institution is required by Basel II (see Chapter 3) to bring in internal controls and to maintain an appropriate capital percentage that is proportional to the risk profile of the institution. The Basel Committee proposed the Standardised Approach in its first Accord (1988). Basel I required all banks[4] to designate buffer capital in proportion to each of the bank's assets (such as mortgage portfolios, credit card portfolios, defaulted loans and the like). In the new Accord, the Basel Committee describes its innovative regulations on a bank's capital ratio in its first pillar – minimum capital requirements.

Basel II is not for European banks only. It is scheduled to be fully implemented in the USA by 2007. It is also a reference for all financial services institutions seriously considering risk management; for example, the EU Capital Adequacy Directive applies Basel's capital requirement to non-bank financial services firms. They should be aware of two new issues in the first pillar of Basel II, as highlighted by an article in the ECB Bulletin (ECB, 2005b):

1. Operational risk is included.
2. To compute credit risk, a bank needs to choose one of three recommended methods: standardised approach, foundation internal ratings-based (IRB) approach and advanced IRB approach.
3. To compute operational risk, three ways are introduced: basic indicator approach, standardised approach and advanced measurement approach.

To enhance solvency, the minimum capital requirement is calculated as:

$$\text{Capital requirement} = \text{capital ratio} \times (\text{credit risk} + \text{market risk} + \text{operational risk})$$

where the capital ratio is set at 8 per cent. Note that Basel II assumes that the correlation across individual assets is ignored. That is, the overall capital requirement is calculated based on the risk of its individual assets. This characteristic is known as 'portfolio invariant'.

As the metrics of market risk were covered in the previous introduction to VaR, Basel's methods of evaluating credit risk and operational risk are described in the following subsections.

Standardised approach

This approach has been used since the 1988 Accord. It is used to set a minimum capital requirement (called regulated capital or solvency) against credit risk exposure. It is calculated according to the following formula:

$$\text{Regulated capital} = 8\% \times \text{risk-weighted assets} = 8\% \times \Sigma wA$$

That is, a bank needs to hold at least 8 per cent capital against the risk-weighted assets (RWAs), which are just weighted values of all drawn corporate assets and off-balance sheet positions.

When a weight is considered for each obligor (borrower), it is chosen from a list suggested by the Basel Committee. The obligors are divided into three categories[5] – sovereigns, banks and corporates – where banks are subdivided into retail and wholesale. While Basel I distinguished the weights given to the OECD and non-OECD, Basel II recommends using a credit rating that is provided by an external credit assessment institution (ECAI), such as Standard & Poor's, Moody's or Fitch, and thus several classes of weights are assigned to various obligors. For example, the weights given to most SMEs that are not rated by ECAI are treated as 100 per cent.

Smaller banks, such as newly established e-banks might choose the standardised approach to determine their solvency. However, a limited range of collateral (such as real estate, eligible securities or guarantees, gold and cash) can be taken as the regulatory capital, provided that the collateral is properly evaluated and managed.

Internal ratings-based approach

The IRB approach, whether foundation or advanced, is recommended by the Basel Committee as a method to model credit risk across all types of banks. It is supported by the asset pricing theory and the assumption that the likelihood of an obligor being unable to repay its debt is determined by the difference between the value of its assets and the nominal value of its debt. By the start of 2007, Basel II requires banks to adopt the IRB approach in their estimation of credit risk.

In Figure 10.8, the expected loss (EL) of a lending institute is the average level of credit losses it can reasonably expect to experience in a year. This is the amount that Basel II assumes that a bank needs to include in the cost of its business. However, a bank may experience losses that exceed its expectation. To prepare for this unexpected loss (UL), a bank also needs to reserve a buffer, which, if insufficient, will make the bank insolvent. However, keeping too much capital for an unlikely event

Figure 10.8 Loss versus time (left); value-at-risk distribution (right)

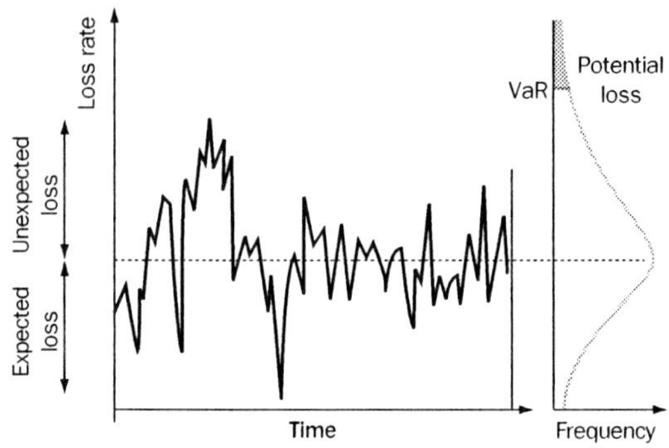

(i.e. UL) is not economically efficient because the bank will be deprived of profitable investment opportunities. A bank must therefore leverage between potential losses and rewards when it is making a decision concerning investment (i.e. holding less capital).

The IRB approach is proposed by the Basel Accord to determine the capital level at which a bank should rest. As the right side of Figure 10.7 represents the probability distribution of losses, a bank should not prepare for the very extreme case, i.e. those cases represented by the shaded area on top of the graph. Note that the graph of the probability distribution is drawn on a reverse fashion and the top area represents the probability of having more losses. The shaded area represents the PD and the extreme case is marked by VaR.

Note that the position of VaR depends on how the bank considers what should be the extreme case. It is common that those cases having only 0.05 probability of occurring are extreme cases. In statistics terminology, this is 95 per cent confidence level and the VaR position is determined by this confidence level. Obviously, the lower the confidence level, the larger the PD and the smaller the VaR will be.

In the Basel Commitee's model, the EL of a portfolio is determined by the following formula:

$$EL = PD \times LGD \times EAD$$

where:

PD = probability of default (i.e. the likelihood of a loss)

LGD = loss-given default (i.e. percentage of exposure)

EAD = exposure at default (i.e. the estimated amount at risk)

Under the foundation IRB requirements, banks are required to calculate their own (internal) PD on their obligors and bank supervisors are required to estimate the LGD and EAD by considering credit categories provided by regulators. For banks that choose the advanced IRB approach, they must provide their own estimates of all three values, using their own loan performance data. The quality of the data collected and the procedures used to estimate PD and LGD determines whether a bank is qualified to adopt the advanced approach.

There are other references for the estimation of PD. The Basel Committee also suggests that banks collect and store substantial historical data on obligor defaults, rating decisions, rating histories, rating migration, information used to assign the ratings, the party/model that assigned the ratings, PD estimate histories, key obligor characteristics and facility information. The data collected can provide an audit trail to check compliance with rating criteria and enhance the credit rating system.

Using the IRB approach, banks are left with less capital charge. It is partly due to an even wider range of collateral being accepted by the Accord to be equivalent to the regulatory capital (if their legal status, proceeds and cost of recovery are compliant). But they must prove to the regulatory authority that they have adequate systems and data so that they are capable of computing LGD and EAD. If not, they are advised to use the standardised approach instead.

Recall that Basel's minimum capital requirement takes three types of risk into consideration: credit risk, market risk and operational risk. Although operational risk does not align with the main theme of this chapter, we need to mention operational risk below to complete the description of capital requirements.

Operational risk

The Basel Committee suggests three approaches to compute operational risk: basic indicator approach, standardised approach and advanced measurement approach. The implementation of these approaches needs several years of historical data. Figure 10.9 compares the complexity of the three.

Under the basic indicator approach, the operational risk is estimated as a percentage (alpha factor) of a single indicator; for example, the banks' average gross income over the previous three years. In many case, the capital requirement is expressed as:

$$\text{Capital requirement} = \alpha \times (\text{average gross income})$$

Figure 10.9 Comparing three approaches for measuring operational risk

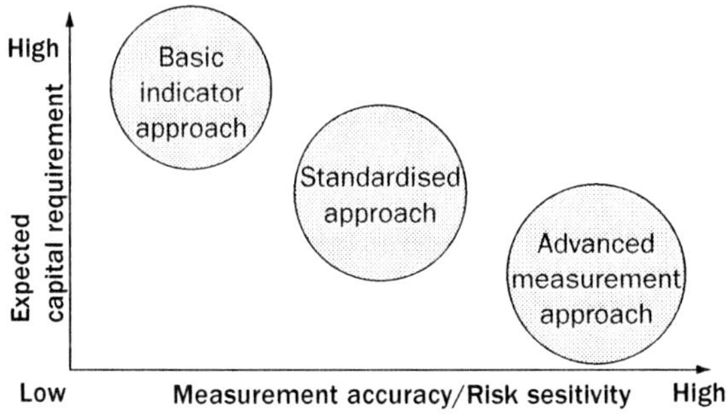

Source: BearingPoint (2004)

The alpha factor is determined by the Basel Committee (α = 15 per cent). This approach is considered too crude for international businesses.

If the standardised approach is used to calculate protection against operational risk, the capital charge is the sum of percentages of a set of indicators. The indicators are annual gross return (G) of eight standardised units, each of which is assigned a factor (beta factor), as shown in see Table 10.3. Mathematically speaking, the capital requirement is determined by the following formula:

$$\text{Capital requirement} = \Sigma \max\{\beta G; 0\}$$

G is usually the average gross income over the previous three years. This method is also known as 'business line approach'.

Table 10.3 Beta factors recommended by Basel II

Business line	Beta factor (%)
Corporate finance	18
Trading and sales	18
Retail banking	12
Commercial banking	15
Payment and settlement	18
Agency services	15
Asset management	12
Retail brokerage	12

The third of the recommended approaches, the advanced measurement approach (AMA), is for a bank that is not satisfied with the standardised approach. To do so, the bank should be qualified according to paragraphs 626–636 in Basel's Third Consultative Paper (April 2003). In theory, the bank should establish a sufficiently detailed and 'granular' model[6] that can record information on all main drivers of operational risks. An independent unit for operational risk management should be codifying principles and procedures for the management and control of operational risks. Banks choosing this approach might need to keep a capital reserve smaller in size than those trying the other options. Basel II does not prescribe any methodology to calculate the capital requirement under AMA. The banking industry is left to design AMA methods for themselves. However, Walsh (2003) hints that the industry has shown interest in adopting the so-called 'loss distribution method'.

Case: How Flexcube supports the Basel II framework (Capco, 2005; Reveleus, year unknown)

The Analytical Applications Suite in i-flex's Reveleus Business Analytics consists of three packages – Enhancing Customer Relationships, Performance Measurement and Risk Management – where the latter is able to handle credit risk for corporate and retail banks as well as ALM.

The Corporate Credit Risk Analytics module supports Basel's standardised and foundation IRB approach for credit risk management in the following aspects:

- *Standardised approach*: Credit risk mitigation with analytics that handle collateral (collateral tracking by comparing recovery data for loss accounts with latest collateral values), guarantees, credit derivatives and netting (credit limits are monitored against netting exposure).
- *Foundation IRB approach*: Computations of PD, LGD and ED.

The Retail Credit Risk Analytics module is designed to manage a wide retail credit portfolio with the priority of understanding the behaviour of portfolio credit risk. It includes a study of credit portfolio concentration along customer demographics, accounts, collateral attributes, historical default behaviour, as well as current credit portfolio delinquency analysis. The latter monitors customers' exposure to delinquent accounts and marginal delinquency exposures.

Combining scenario generation and what-if analysis, the ALM module can identify an optimal strategy to reset existing risk exposure.

In June 2005, i-flex acquired Capco and adopted Capco's Operational Risk Tool Suite (ORTOS) in its Reveleus Risk Analytics to create an enterprise risk management suite. First created by Dresdner Bank, Austria, which was acquired by Capco in December 2003, the ORTOS satisfies the basic, standardised and AMA methods as required by Basel II. For banks that choose the AMA, ORTOS supports the processes of data collation, self assessment, monitoring of risk indicators, tracing of issues and action plans and calculation of economic capital with the 'loss data' and 'scenario-based self assessment' methods.

Enterprise risk management

Taking risk management as a strategic issue, a financial services institute should have a single, integrated and centralised view on all kinds of risks (financial and non-financial risks) to which the enterprise is exposed. Thus, enterprise risk management should, in theory, provide a framework that encompasses all financial and non-financial risks. The ERM approach seems to have aligned with the movement of system integration (which, from time to time, is approved by the majority if the idea of decentralisation is found to be unattractive to them).

The goal of ERM is elusive, as Deloitte (DTT, 2004b) has commented. No one seems to know how risk management can be integrated and what special benefits ERM actually delivers. It is extremely complicated, if not unrealistic, to formulate a risk management policy which takes all kinds of risk into consideration. Today, if ERM is implemented as a corporate strategy or an information system, its meaning must have been largely compromised. For example, Deloitte only takes the integration of market and credit risk as a proxy for risk consolidation in its ERM survey.

In practice, ERM focuses more on quantifiable risks and provides integrated measures of risk at several levels of an enterprise. For example, the Algorithmics ERM Suite is composed of six applications, which respectively deal with credit risk, capital, operation risk, collateral, market risk and asset risk. Other ERM frameworks may only offer a partial solution by integrating the management processes of, say, liquidity or ALM risk and operational risk combined. The COSO ERM framework is one of the most famous.

COSO enterprise risk management integrated framework

In 2004, COSO engaged with PricewaterhouseCoopers (COSO, 2004) in producing an ERM integrated framework, which defines ERM as the process of providing reasonable assurance regarding the achievement of corporate objectives. The corporate objectives can be viewed in the context of four categories: strategic, operations, reporting and compliance.

The COSO framework has three dimensions, as shown in the ERM cube in Figure 10.10. Risk management measures can be deployed at different levels (entity-level, division, business unit and subsidiary) of an organisation, if they are decided after proper event identification and risk assessment processes. The framework also outlines the following eight components:

1. *Internal environment*: To set up an environment with risk management philosophy, risk appetite, integrity and ethical values.
2. *Objective setting*: To align with the organisation's mission and be consistent with the risk appetite.
3. *Event identification*: To identify internal and external events that affect the organisation's objectives and to distinguish between risks and opportunities.

Figure 10.10 The COSO enterprise risk management cube

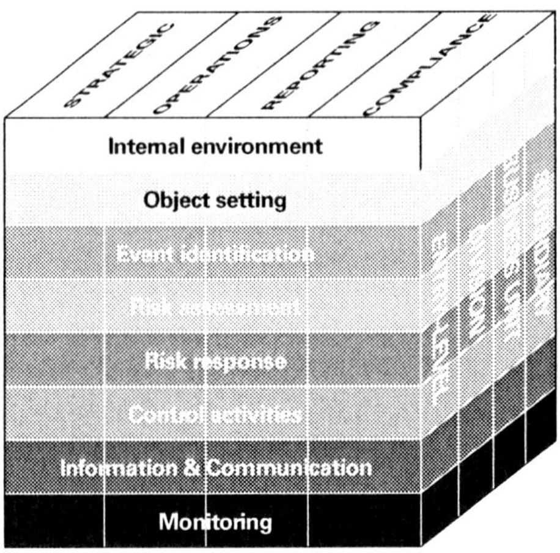

Source: COSO (2004)

4. *Risk assessment*: To analyse the likelihood and impact of each type of risk.
5. *Risk response*: Response, such as avoiding, accepting, reducing or sharing is selected in alignment with the organisation's risk tolerance and risk appetite.
6. *Control activities*: To establish and implement policies and procedures with respect to the response selected.
7. *Information and communication*: To identify, capture and communicate relevant information for people to perform as stated in risk response procedures.
8. *Monitoring*: To monitor the entire ERM practice and make modifications if necessary.

Although the eight components in the COSO ERM framework look like a guideline for operational risk management, ERM is applied to the corporate strategy that is concerned with risk, return and growth of the organisation. In other words, not only is ERM capable of reducing an organisation's risk exposure, it should also be responsible for raising the organisation's risk exposure if it is too low. With an ERM system in place, a financial institution should be able to operate in a safe internal environment, where operational risks are under control and to produce profits by assuming a calculated level of financial risk.

Thus, the concept of ERM should cover possible risks from all dimensions – financial risks, operational risks and even political, legal and reputational risks. It opposes the 'silo approach' of risk management that lets individual functions solve their own problems. A sophisticated ERM system would incorporate risk management into other business processes and decisions so that the dynamic relationship between risk and value throughout the enterprise could be optimised to meet its strategic aim.

Technical framework for enterprise risk management

Architecturally speaking, an ERM solution can roughly be divided into three layers (Figure 10.10). The storage layer might centralise data captured from related functions in the enterprise (for operational risk management) and financial transactions (for financial risk management). For example, an ERM solution that offers some protection against financial risks might have the following databases:

- *Operational risk*: such as loss event database;
- *Credit risk*: such as retail investments; and
- *Market risk*: such as market price history.

Metavante (2004) indicates that the ERM framework of some organisations may need to import data from a variety of external sources. All data in this layer should thus be pre-processed by extraction, transformation and loading (ETL) tools so that they can give a consolidated and integrated view to applications at a higher level. The technical infrastructure of the system must provide the necessary connectivity so that risk data can be delivered to the organisation at various levels, which range from entity to subsidiary.

Whatever resides in the middle application layer depends on the risk portfolio of the organisation and the expertise available. It is common to have several analytical engines to construct various risk models and to assess related risk exposures. For example, these applications can monitor and estimate financial parameters, such as PD, LGD, EAD and the like, and provide tools for statistical analysis, stochastic projection or Monte Carlo simulation.

ERM solutions should provide some means to integrate parts of the risks (e.g. credit risk and market risk) in the selected risk portfolio. Risk integration may occur at the data level – during data clean-up and consolidation – or at the application level where a holistic risk management policy may be implemented. For example, the overall portfolio risk can be reduced by diversification among assets' returns that are not correlated or by hedging with a dozen risk factors (DTT, 2004b).

Figure 10.11 also depicts a business process layer on which those applications could be activated if any financial parameter reaches an unacceptable magnitude. Those applications, usually regulatory compliant, can provide an automated or semi-automated response to any discrepancy detected, as guided by predefined risk management policies. Those responses may include alerts to respective financial managers, activation of business continuity plans and preparation for disclosure and documentation. Sophisticated ERM solutions are able to manage real-time risk allocation and transfer across the entire investment portfolio so as to get the best for the organisation out of the given environment. In the case of a loss event, some solutions offer an optimisation procedure to allow the organisation to make the best choice of action in response to the event.

Figure 10.11 A general architecture of enterprise risk management

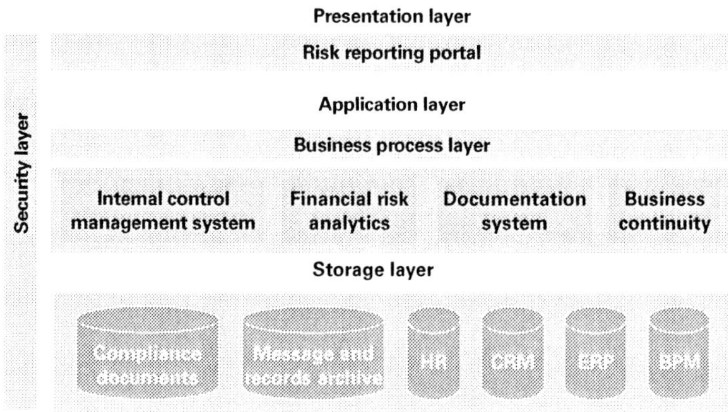

BPM: business performance management; CRM: customer relationship management; ERP: enterprise resource planning; HR: human resource

Although the market for ERM systems is still in its infancy, software vendors have already been competing strenuously with technological innovations and mergers and acquisitions. For example, the aforementioned acquisition of Capco by i-flex (in 2005) demonstrates how eager i-flex is to enhance its ERM suite by integrating the operational risk tool ORTOS with Reveleus Risk Analytics. In the same year, Fitch acquired Algorithmics and Moody's took over KMV.

Management issues in enterprise risk management

Whether financial services institutions adopt an ERM approach or a silo approach, they still need to assess and prioritise risks to select an optimised risk portfolio to suit their risk mitigation policies. Management of an ERM system differs in how risk management is raised to the enterprise level.

Thus, ERM is a *policy* issue more than an ICT *application* issue. In its executive summary of the COSO ERM framework, PWC (2004) mentions six objectives:

1. Aligning risk appetite and strategy.
2. Enhancing risk response decisions.
3. Reducing operational surprises and losses.

4. Identifying and managing multiple and cross-enterprise risks.
5. Seizing opportunities.
6. Improving deployment of capital.

Unlike the traditional view of risk management, this ERM approach also aims to seize opportunities and improve capital deployment. Thus, the success of these objectives requires not just innovative technology but the renewed mindset of risk managers. Both line managers and executives must have the knowledge to oversee all ERM processes. Metavante (2004) even suggests modifying the organisational structure to create the proper infrastructure for ERM to be effective.

The specialty guide produced by the Society of Actuaries (Bowen et al., 2005) divides ERM processes into four themes: risk control, strategic risk management, catastrophic risk management and risk management culture. The authors describe the role of the management in each of these themes:

- *Risk control*: The theme includes processes of identifying, monitoring, limiting, avoiding, offsetting and transferring risks. A senior manager is responsible for the management of each prioritised risk.
- *Strategic risk management*: Those processes that reflect risk and risk capital decided by the organisational strategy. These processes are applied to all management levels – to all functions throughout the organisation. The line of command – which involves at least the management, board of directors, risk officers and internal auditors – in relation to risk management is clearly defined.
- *Catastrophic risk management*: Those preparing for extreme events must be flexible enough to prepare for something unexpected. The management is ready to take decisive and timely action as planned at time of those events.
- *Risk management culture*: To create an ERM culture in which management across the organisation is aware of the risk tolerance, risk governance process and the return for risk expectations. To foster the risk culture, management should support activities like training, communicating and compensation to risk smart behaviour.

In addition, management needs to develop a technology management strategy to provide leadership in the investments, development and management of the ICT system that supports the ERM objectives.

However, many organisations remain sceptical about the promises of ERM. Deloitte found (DTT, 2004c) that 60 per cent of the participants in their survey said changing culture was the greatest challenge to implementing ERM. Some organisations still linger on their 'silo' view of risk management and value the risk management efforts from the perspectives of low-level business units. As there are no quantitative metrics that can be applied to measure all kinds of risks in the organisation, different risks cannot be compared on the same grounds. Thus, any attempt to manage risks from an enterprise angle is deemed to be incomplete and non-integrated, and the objectives of ERM can only be partially achieved. For the time being, those with a positive view of ERM may build an infrastructure that assesses and controls a few areas of risks, in compliance with regulations, such as SOX and Basel II, and gives a solid foundation for the future enhancements of ERM.

Conclusion

Together with the last two chapters, this chapter completes the discussion on risks and regulatory compliance – the two issues that demand commitment from the management of financial services institutions in the new millennium. ICT is a two-edged sword: it has opened up new opportunities as well as risks, and the financial services industry has to take both or none. There are numerous regulations, directives, guidelines and rules being proposed to the industry. As compliance with these regulations might require a huge cost that many institutions cannot afford, over-regulation is now being seen as a major threat to business growth prospects (Millar, 2005).

This chapter began with an introduction to the three major types of financial risk – credit, liquidity and market risks – which are managed in a totally different way from those for operational risk. It also described metrics and assessment methods that have been developed specifically for financial risks and the calculation of capital requirement under the instructions of Basel II.

Although the development of risk management methodologies, technologies, and regulations is not particularly aimed at the financial institutions that conduct business online, they and the traditional institutions are threatened by the same risk and are under the same jurisdiction of various laws and regulations. As effects of some laws and regulations (in particular, SOX and Basel II) have not been observed yet, the entire financial services industry is speculating how this safer but more restrictive business environment will impact on the industry. However, foreseeing more competition in the increasingly globalised marketplace, the financial services industry will be investing more in their online businesses and replacing some of their traditional operations. Very soon, every institution will adopt electronic businesses, and they will probably utilise technologies described in earlier chapters.

Questions for discussion

1 The chapter has introduced many quantitative methods to assess risk. What role should qualitative methods play, especially in the e-finance arena?

2. Do you think a bank needs to implement the advanced IRB or AMA approach to minimise its regulatory capital requirement?

3. Is ERM just another buzzword, after BPR, ERP and Y2K?

Notes

1. These betas have very low statistical significance in correlating the variation in the market and that of the subject company.
2. A transition matrix is made up of probabilities of transition. Normally it is a square matrix and the sum of each row is 100 per cent. The last row in Figure 10.5 is missing because it represents probabilities (no chance) of changing from a default status to others.
3. CRMPG was established by 12 large international commercial and investment banks in 1999, under the endorsement by Chairman Greenspan, Chairman Levitt, and Secretary Rubin.
4. The Basel Committee was first established to regulate the banking industry in the G10 countries. But it was later accepted in more than 100 countries and its Accord was applied to all banks in these countries.
5. The class of sovereigns includes governments and central banks while corporates include insurance companies. The class of banks is further divided into two Options (1 and 2) according to the recommendations by supervisors and ECAI.
6. The following seven regulatory loss categories should be considered: internal fraud, external fraud, employment practice and workplace safety, clients/products/business practices, damage to physical assets, business disruption and system failures; and execution/delivery/process management.

Post script

I spent exactly one year in writing this book. It was five years after the e-commerce bubble and we saw more and more financial institutions moving their business – partly or wholly – onto the Internet. As more ICT solutions are becoming available, we can only expect electronic financial services operations to replace their bricks-and-mortar counterparts. E-financial services is a new market where a few organisations might benefit by just being early entrants, but the last to enter will surely suffer a great loss.

The book is written to fill the gap between technical manuals and management discourse. New developments of ICT in relation to information systems available to the financial services industry were introduced in Chapters 1 and 2. Deployment of ICT for digitisation in individual sectors in the industry – banking, payment, insurance, stockbrokerage and fundraising – were discussed in Chapters 3 to 7. The last three chapters focused on security management, compliance and financial risk management respectively, addressing management concerns on these subjects whether their financial services are delivered on- and offline.

Discussions in these chapters are meant to provide knowledge of the current developments and applications of ICT as well as risk management, all of which are essential to the effective management of an e-financial services institution.

Appendix: European Financial Services Action Plan

The European Commission is now proceeding in its endeavour to integrate financial systems in its member states. The President of the European Central Bank, Trichet (2005), asserts the importance of giving advice on shaping the legislative and regulatory framework of the integrated financial system. The EC has been working for many years to achieve a high degree of regulatory and supervisory convergence across its members. One of the milestone achievements is the project led by Baron Alexandre Lamfalussy, the former president of the European Monetary Institute.

Having studied the European securities infrastructure with an objective to enhance the flexibility of its regulatory framework, Lamfalussy and his team (the so-called 'Committee of Wise Men') made a series of recommendations to reform securities legislation in the EC. Lying at the centre of the Lamfalussy approach is a regulatory reform that is divided into the following four levels (Committee of Wise Men, 2001: 6)

- *Level 1: Framework principles* – the EC adopts a formal proposal for Directive/Regulation after a full consultation process. The European Parliament and Council reach agreement on the framework principles and definition of implementing powers as stated in the Directive/Regulation.
- *Level 2: Implementing details* – set up two new committees – European Securities Committee (ESC) and Committee of European Securities Regulators (CESR)[1] and agree on working methods and mandates. The EC consults the ESC and requests advice from the CESR on technical implementation measures. The CESR prepares advice in consultation with market participants, end-users and consumers. The advice is to be examined and adopted by the EC.

- *Level 3: Strengthened cooperation* – the CESR works on joint interpretation recommendations, consistent guidelines and common standards for administrative regulations, peer review and compares regulatory practices to ensure consistent implementation and application.
- *Level 4: Enforcement* – the EC checks member state compliance with EU legislation and takes legal action against those member states suspected of breach of Community Law.

The framework is now being extended from securities to banking, insurance and investment funds sectors. Its largest influence is found on the Financial Services Action Plan (FSAP), another ambitious endeavour to create a single financial market in Europe. First drafted in 1999, the regulatory framework set by FSAP has since been under several rounds of reviews and revisions. Lamfalussy (Committee of Wise Men, 2001: 88) criticised the contemporary FSAP framework as too slow, too rigid, containing too much ambiguity, resulting in inconsistent implementation and over-reliant on primary legislation for determining detailed rules.

The process of integrating the European financial markets is not easy. The FSAP Securities Expert Group initiative released a paper in 2004 to reassure the continuation and extension of the Lamfalussy process. However, the Group worried more about whether a new regulatory environment will deliver the desired economic benefits, or impose restrictions that are unfocused, unnecessary, or disproportionate to their regulatory aim. For example, the Group asserted that (Securities Expert Group, 2004):

- Regulation needs justification in order to avoid over-regulation – i.e. underlying policy-making must be evidence-based and subject to regulatory impact analysis.[2]
- Regulation should take into account the impact of regulations on Europe's international competitiveness.
- Regulation should not inhibit innovation (such as securitisation) and its quick dissemination.

At the corporate level, the Group stressed that regulations applying to listed companies should include:

- *Trade execution venues*: National regulators and supervisory authorities should cooperate with the CESR to ensure effectiveness and robust real-time trading in secondary markets

- *Corporate governance*: The Group agreed that corporate governance codes across Europe show a high level of convergence. The Group did not recommend a single code of corporate governance for the EU but suggested (Securities Expert Group, 2004) flexible guidelines, such as:
  - a definition of 'corporate governance';
  - internal elements of corporate governance, including disclosure, shareholder rights and responsibilities and boards of directors;
  - interaction of external elements (auditors, financial analysts, investment banks); and
  - greater compliance with corporate governance criteria.

  Member states are allowed to follow these guidelines in a way such that the diversity of operational methods and organisational models can be taken into account.

- *Accounting standards*: International Accounting Standards (IAS) should be enforced through the EU (and other countries). The IAS are developed and maintained by the International Accounting Standards Board (IASB) as an instrument to help eliminate barriers to cross-border securities trading. IAS were later renamed International Financial Reporting Standards (IFRS). The EU issued a regulation requiring all listed companies in the EU to adopt IFRS by the beginning of 2005. To comply with the regulation, all these companies needed to review their accounting practices and improve their audit trails and information indexing on their data repositories.
- *Disclosure of corporate information*: Dissemination of corporate information (including price-sensitive and periodic announcements) is necessary, electronic financial disclosure mechanisms are able to combat market abuse practices.

The enactment of the Financial Services and Markets Act 2000 (FSMA) made the Financial Services Authority (FSA) the sole regulator of the UK financial services sector. The FSA was given the statutory powers to promote and enforce the following 'regulatory objectives' stated in the FSMA:

1. *Market confidence*: To maintain market confidence in the financial system.
2. *Public awareness*: To promote public awareness and understanding of the financial system.

3. *Protection of customers*: To enhance consumer protection, while having regard to the general principle that consumers should take responsibility for their decisions.
4. *Reduction of financial crime*: Such as money laundering, fraud and insider dealing.

Together with the HM Treasury and the Bank of England, FSA is the authority to implement FSAP in the UK.

FSA adopts a risk-based regulatory approach and divides financial institutions into four categories – A, B, C and D – where firms in the A category have high risk and need close and continuous supervision (FSA, 2000). FSA does not pursue every rule breach but examines cases according to their seriousness and whether the cases fit into FSA's statutory objectives. Detailed directives are compiled in the Handbook published by FSA (*http://www.fsa.gov.uk/handbook*), which has also taken other regulations (such as Basel II) into consideration.

Notes

1. CESR is the European version of the US SEC.
2. The aim of the impact analysis should be (1) to set out the identified problem clearly and the objectives of any solution; and (2) to assess, to the extent possible, the impact of different solutions to the identified problem in terms of their impact on the various stakeholders involved and thus judge the subsidiarity and proportionality of each solution before taking final decisions on a policy approach (Securities Expert Group, 2004).

Glossary

4Cs of commercial lending/credit: *Capacity*, *character*, *capital*, and *collateral* are four factors considered in lending decision. Capacity is the relation of current income to current expenses. Character is the history of credit repayments. Capital refers to savings and other accumulations that could be used in the event the borrower's income was reduced. Collateral is the security pledged for the loan that would be available to satisfy any outstanding debt should the borrower be unable to make any further payments.

Abandonment (referring to options): The choice of not exercising or offsetting an option before its expiration.

Alternative trading system (ATS): Electronic system that brings together potential buyers and sellers of securities. ATSs include call markets, matching systems, crossing networks and ECNs.

Anti-dilution: If a company issues new shares after angel financing and the price of the new shares is lower than the price that the investor has paid, the investor may suffer a loss.

Application programming interface (API): The interface (calling conventions) by which an application can access the operating system or other low-level utilities.

Asset/liability management (ALM): Pertinent to the management of a business by formulating, implementing, monitoring and revising strategies related to assets and liabilities in an attempt to achieve financial objectives for a given set of risk tolerances and constraints.

Assignment (referring to options): The preparation of a notification to a broker to certify if one of its clients has options written that were exercised.

Automated clearing house (ACH): An electronic network that transfers and clears funds between banking institutions on behalf of merchants and their customers.

Automotive aftermarket: The part of the automotive industry that is concerned with the manufacturing, re-manufacturing, distribution and retailing of replacement parts or upgrades for vehicles not made by the original manufacturers. It also includes tools, equipment, accessories, chemicals and all services needed during the lifetime of a vehicle.

Banks Automated Clearing System (BACS): An electronic payments method in the UK that is primarily used for large volumes of transactions such as payroll and regular B2B client and customer payments.

Bank GIRO (UK): A system operated by the clearing banks in which a document instructs a bank branch to credit a sum of money to a specified account at that branch.

Bill consolidator: A bill service provider that consolidates bills from other bill service providers or billers and delivers them for presentment to the customer service provider.

Book building: The process by which an underwriter determines a price at which to offer an IPO, by considering demand from institutional investors.

Botnet armies: A number of computers being used to forward transmissions to other computers so as to deny the service of the latter. Users of those computers being drafted to do so are often unaware of the situation.

Business intelligence: It consolidates and analyses raw business data and turns it into conclusive, actionable information. It enables companies to tap into disparate sources of customer, operational and market data and then use this information to gain a competitive edge. It provides companies with the intelligence needed to spot trends, enhance relationships, reduce financial risk and create new sales opportunities. (IBM, year unknown)

Catastrophe equity put (CEPut): An option contract that gives the insurer the right to sell a given number of shares to a specific counterpart for a fixed price. This option can be exercised only after the occurrence of a catastrophe of an agreed-upon magnitude.

Catastrophe swap: A bilateral agreement that creates reciprocal reinsurance between two insuring entities.

Central counterparty (CCP): An organisation that acts as a formal counterparty in all transactions. It novates and guarantees trades or positions at or after time of trade and through settlement.

Central securities depository (CSD): An entity that holds and administers securities and enables securities transactions to be processed by book entry.

Certificate authority: An organisation that, on request, can verify the identity of a party and issue a digital certificate for that party to use. The digital certificate contains the public key for its holder to use in encryption and decryption.

Cession: Insurance that is reinsured. The insurer is referred to as the ceding company or cedent.

Cheque truncation: Stopping the tracking of a cheque. In the USA, if a client does not opt for cheque truncation, the cheque they are sending will eventually be returned. This facilitates the client tracking the cheque. If cheque truncation is agreed, only an image, copy, or a line item statement will be returned from the bank.

Clearing: (1) The transfer and confirmation of information between the payer (sending financial institution) and payee (receiving financial institution). (2) The process of transmitting, reconciling, and, in some cases, confirming payment orders or security transfer instructions prior to settlement, possibly including the netting of instructions and the establishment of final positions for settlement (ECB, year unknown).

Common object request broker architecture (CORBA): A standard adopted by OMG as a framework to provide common ORB services and interfaces to support portable clients and services.

Community of practice (CoP): A group of self-governing people whose practice is aligned with strategic imperatives and are challenged to create shareholder value by generating knowledge and increasing capabilities (Saint-Onge, 2003).

Compliance risk: Associated with the failure to comply with legislation or internal procedures to prove compliance. Failure to comply risks exposure to prosecution, judicial review, employment tribunals, increased government inspection, liability to enforce contracts.

Contract: A specification of the runtime environment for the components to activate. It includes security, concurrency, lifecycle management, transaction, deployment and other services.

Control objectives: COBIT defines a control objective as a statement of the desired result or purpose to be achieved by implementing control procedures in a particular IT activity.

Corporate events (referring to securities): Events that affect a security regardless of any action taken by the holder.

Corporate governance: The framework of accountability to users, stakeholders and the wider community, within which organisations take decisions, and lead and control their functions, to achieve their objectives (Audit Commission, 2005).

Credit insurance: Insurance against financial losses sustained through the failure due to commercial reasons of policyholders' clients to pay for goods or services supplied to them.

Credit risk: (1) Potential that a borrower or counterparty will fail to meet its obligations in accordance with agreed terms. (2) Risk due to uncertainty in a client's ability to meet its obligations. (3) The change in net asset value due to changes in the perceived ability of counterparties to meet their contractual obligations (Pyle, 1997).

Creditworthiness: The probability with which a borrower will be able to generate the necessary profits so that they can meet the requirement to pay.

Cross-border e-banking: The provision of transactional online banking products or services by a bank in one country to residents of another country.

Crossing network: A system matching buy and sell orders at a derived price.

Custodian: A bank or other institution that keeps and administers securities and other financial assets on behalf of others. It may also provide other services such as clearance and settlement, cash management, foreign exchange and securities lending.

Customer service provider (CSP): An agent of the customer that provides an interface directly to customers, businesses, or others for bill presentment. CSP enrols customers, enables presentment and provides customer care: particularly in the B2C space.

Data controller: A natural or legal person, public authority, agency or any other body that determines the purposes and means of the processing of personal data (EU Data Protection Directive 95/46/EC).

Data mining: The process of discovering meaningful new correlations, patterns and trends by sifting through large amounts of data stored in repositories.

Data subject: The person who is the subject of the personal and sensitive data.

Data type definition (DTD): The portion in an XML document where the building blocks (document structure, legal elements, etc.) of the document are defined.

Decision support system (DSS): A system that can assist or replace the decision maker by combining current and historical facts, numerical data and statistics from both inside and outside the organisation and by converting these data into information useful in decision making.

Delivery system: A system to force convergence between cash and futures prices as the delivery period is near.

Demutualisation: A process by which a mutual company becomes a stock company. In the financial market there is a trend of demutualisation of stock exchanges, i.e. one by one stock exchanges in different places transform themselves into for-profit shareholder-owned enterprises.

Denial of service attack: An attack that can bring down a system. Methods include flooding the server with traffic so that it cannot handle other business.

Digital certificate: A digital identity document binding a public–private key pair to a specific person or organisation.

Discount brokers: Brokers who charge a reduced commission and do not provide investment advice.

Domain name: A familiar, easy-to-remember name for computers on the Internet. It is mapped to a series of numbers (the IP address) that serve as routing address on the Internet.

Dynamic financial analysis (DFA): The class of structural simulation models of financial institution operations, focusing on certain hazard and financial risks and designed to generate financial pro forma projections.

E-billing: The process of sending an invoice over the Internet to a customer or client to indicate that an amount is due and owing.

E-commerce: Business transactions that take place in whole or in part through an electronic medium over an electronic network (e.g. the Internet).

Electronic bill presentment and payment (EBPP): A process to present bills to a customer online, via either e-mail or a notice in an e-banking account. After presentment, the customer may pay the bill online when convenient. The payment is deducted electronically from the customer's account.

Electronic communication network (*ECN*): A regulated type of agency broker that facilitates continuous matching of customer buy and sell orders while providing those orders with direct electronic access to the National Market System (Nasdaq).

Electronic data interchange (*EDI*): The computer-to-computer exchange of business data in a publicly published and globally standardised format. EDI is the transfer of structured business data, by agreed message standards, from one computer application to another by electronic means and with a minimum of human intervention.

Electronic invoice presentment and payment (EIPP): The process by which companies present invoices and make payments to one another through the Internet.

EJB container: The runtime environment of those enterprise bean components that support the business logic of the J2EE architecture, for example, services for transaction management, security and multi-threading.

EMV: An industry-wide smartcard specification developed by Europay, Mastercard and Visa to enable interoperability of smartcards and card terminals for finance sector.

Enterprise application integration (EAI): The technology to integrate applications and enterprise data sources so that they can easily share business processes and data.

Enterprise information integration (EII): The process of aggregating data from multiple back-end sources into a single database and enabling a single query to access it in real-time.

Enterprise risk management (ERM): A process effected by an entity's board of directors, management and other personnel and applied in strategic settings across the enterprise. It is designed to identify potential events that may affect the entity, to manage risk to be within its risk appetite and to provide reasonable assurance regarding the achievement of entity objectives (COSO, 2004).

E-payment: The process of transmitting the amount specified on a bill to the biller by electronic means.

Exercise (referring to options): The options owner chooses either to call (take delivery of) or put (sell) the underlying asset at the option's strike price.

Exposure: The term refers to units for measuring the size of an insurance portfolio, such as the number of policies, number of property locations, aggregated coverage amounts, or other alternative measures (see *http://www.actuary.org/pdf/casualty/catmonograph_june01.pdf*).

Fair value: An accounting term that refers to the amount at which an asset may be bought or sold in a current transaction between willing parties, i.e. other than in a forced or liquidation sale.

Fill-and-kill (*FAK*) *orders*: Orders are those that are valid until the first transaction is made or, if the order is to be executed in several subsequent transactions, until the first transactions are made. An FAK is executed immediately after placing and may be executed in part. The unfulfilled portion of the order then becomes void.

Financial engineering: The use and creation of financial instruments for the purpose of managing financial risks.

Financial supply chain: A financial supply chain enables financial collaboration within the enterprise and its business network using defined corporate policies and shared services to handle all customer- and supply chain-related financial processes.

FIX engine: The application that manages the activities within a so-called 'FIX session'. Activities include formatting and parsing FIX messages, managing message-level encryption, managing/validating counterpart connections and managing message gap recovery. At the end of the FIX session, messages may be propagated to other management systems.

Float time: The time between the moment one writes a cheque and when the money is withdrawn from the account.

Full-service brokers: Services offered by stockbrokers are traditionally divided into three segments: advisory, discretionary (to privileged customers only, service includes equity portfolio management) and execution-only. Full-service brokers offer all main types of service and charge expensive commissions. They often take control of the investment activities of their clients.

Gap analysis: A common method to measure exposure to interest rate risk, by comparing total quantity of an institution's rate-sensitive assets and rate-sensitive liabilities for each of a number of different future time periods.

Give-up: The process in which a trader acts on behalf of another trader. For example, Broker A asks Broker B to buy some stocks on behalf of A's client. Such a transaction is a 'give-up' transaction on A; i.e. A is the buyer but is not involved in the trading.

Haircut: The amount of a collateral margin by which the value of collateral exceeds the loan it secures.

Hedge accounting: An accounting method whereby the hedged item and the hedging instrument are accounted for on a consistent basis with movements in value matched together within reserves.

Hedge ratio: The ratio between the size of a position needed in a hedge instrument and the size of the position being hedged. This ratio is determined by delta.

Historical simulation: An approach to calculate the hypothetical change in value of a portfolio in the light of actual historical movements in risk factors.

Identity: The information of a person or a group, consisting of traits, attributes and preferences upon which personalised services may be granted.

Identity lifecycle management: The processes used to create and delete accounts, manage account and entitlement changes and track policy compliance.

Inherent risk: Risk to an entity in the absence of any actions management might take to alter either the risk's likelihood or severity.

IT governance: The responsibility of the board of directors and executive management to ensure that the organisation's IT sustains and extends the organisation's strategies and objectives.

Java message service (JMS): Sun's standard API for message queuing system. It allows application components based on the J2EE platform to create, receive and read messages.

Key performance indicators (KPIs): Events, results or activities which when measured with suitable metrics can provide some insight into how 'well' the business is performing.

Liability insurance: The insurance gives policyholders a protection from financial responsibility for injuries to others or for damage to other people's property.

Limit orders: Orders to buy or sell a quantity of securities at a specified or better price.

Liquidity risk: The potential that an institution will be unable to meet its obligations as they come due because of an inability to liquidate assets or obtain adequate funding.

Margin calls: A clearinghouse's request to its clearing member to deposit cash or marginable securities to satisfy requirements for the purchase or short sale of securities, or to cover an adverse price movement.

Market risk: (1) Risk of loss in on and off balance sheet positions arising from movements in market prices. (2) The change in net asset value due to changes in underlying economic factors, such as interest rates, exchange rates and equity and commodity prices (Pyle, 1997).

Mark-to-market (MtM): The MtM value of a transaction is the sum of the present values of all of the future cash flows due to be paid (generally signed negative) or received (generally signed positive) during the remaining lifetime of the transaction.

Message: A request, report and/or event that contains information needed to coordinate communication between different applications.

Middleware: Software that resides between the client and server applications. It provides an interface between these applications irrespective of their vendors. It also manages message transfer between clients and servers so that clients need not know which specific server contains the desired data. In a more complex architecture, middleware provides for interoperability among applications.

Monte Carlo method: A simulation method used to test the value of a portfolio with a large sample of randomly chosen combinations of factors, based on the probabilities determined by historical data.

Netting: An agreed offsetting of positions or obligations by trading partners. Netting reduces a large number of individual positions or obligations to a smaller number of obligations or positions. Netting may take several forms, which have varying degrees of legal enforceability in the event of the default of one of the parties (Giovannini Group, 2003).

Non-repudiation: A cryptographic method which prevents an individual or entity from denying having performed a particular action, in particular, change of data.

Notice of execution (NOE): A notice of the trade details provided by a broker/dealer to its customer when a trade is executed on the customer's behalf.

Novation: A process through which the original obligation between a buyer and seller is discharged through the substitution of the CCP as seller to buyer and buyer to seller, creating two new contracts.

Object: In computer science, an object is regarded as an abstraction of a thing with definite boundaries and meaning for the problem at hand.

Object request broker (ORB): A mechanism by which a client can transparently make requests and receive responses.

Offsetting (referring to options): A method to reverse the original transaction in order to exit the trade, for example, someone may need to sell a call with the same strike price and expiration if they bought a call earlier.

Open account: The supplier agrees to ship the goods, or provides the services, before getting paid; i.e., the supplier is exposed to the buyer's credit risk.

Operational risk: (1) The risk of direct or indirect loss resulting from inadequate or failed internal processes, people and systems or from external events. (2) The risk of loss resulting from inadequate or failed processes, people and systems or from external events (The New Basel Capital Accord, 2003).

Over-the-counter (OTC): Stocks are traded by brokers/dealers who negotiate directly with one another over computer networks and by phone. They are not traded on a formal exchange such as the NYSE because the companies involved are small and unable to meet listing requirements of the exchanges.

Packet: A message (data) travelling on the Internet is broken up into small fragments called 'packets', each of which travels along different paths to reach the destination. At the destination, these packets are merged to give the original message.

Password synchronisation: A network infrastructure that enables users to maintain a uniform password on multiple logic accounts. Once a user changes their password, the change is acknowledged in every system.

Payment engine: An application on a merchant's server that handles payment process. It stores all business logic of payment and originates communications with other entities (e.g. financial institutions).

Payment gateway: Software and hardware interfacing merchants and acquirer (e.g. credit card authorisation) networks. It can also be referred to a value-added service provider that accepts and processes credit card transactions from consumers before channelling the transaction information to the merchant.

Payment-versus-payment (PVP): In foreign exchange transactions, the currency sold is only delivered when the currency purchased is received. This means that both sides of the settlement instruction will be settled, or neither side will be settled.

Portal: An easily mastered website that connects corporate resources relative to a particular job function. There are portals for customers, employees, suppliers, etc.

Posting: Registering a trade (e.g. add, change, delete) in one of the accounts opened in the member's structure within a clearinghouse.

Property and casualty (*P&C*) *insurance*: Insurance to protect against loss or damage to property resulting from hazards, such as fire, theft and natural disasters, such as vehicle and homeowner's insurance.

Real-time gross settlement system (RTGS): The system enables clearing and settlement of each transaction to occur continuously during the processing day.

Repurchase agreement (Repo): A borrower sells securities to a lender with the agreement to repurchase securities of the same type and quantity at a prearranged later date.

Residual risk: Risk that remains after management responds to the risk.

Resource manager: Software that provides access to a set of shared resources. A resource manager participates in transactions that are externally controlled and coordinated by a transaction manager. It is typically in different address space or on a different machine from the clients that access it.

Securitisation: (1) The process of aggregating similar instruments, such as credit portfolios or catastrophe risks and transferring them to the capital markets by a negotiable security. (2) The practice of structuring and selling negotiable investments in order to spread a risk, which is normally taken by a single lender or syndicate, over a broad group of investors (Donaldson, 1986).

Security management: The process of managing a defined level of security concerning information and IT services.

Self-registration: A function that allows new users to register themselves at logon.

Service: An implementation of a well-defined business functionality that operates independent of the state of any other service defined within the system. A service has a well-defined set of interfaces and operates through a predefined contract between the client of the service and the service itself.

Service-oriented architecture (SOA): An architecture solution based on a collection of network services to accomplish business functions.

Settlement: (1) The actual transfer of funds between the payer's financial institution and the payee's financial institution. (2) A process that discharges obligations in respect of funds or securities transfers between two or more parties (Giovannini Group, 2003).

Simple Object Access Protocol (SOAP): Set of standard rules for formatting an XML message so that it can be interpreted by different web services.

Solvency: The status when liabilities are less than assets.

Specialist's display book: An electronic workstation that keeps track of all limit orders and incoming market orders.

Spread: The difference between the bid price and the ask price. This is how a specialist makes money in the NYSE.

Strategic risk: Long-term adverse impacts from poor decision making or poor implementation, such as risk damage to the reputation of a company, loss of public confidence and possible government intervention.

Stress test: A way of revaluing a portfolio using a different set of assumptions. It is applied to understand the sensitivity of the portfolio to changes in various risk factors.

Systemic risk: (1) The risk of a failure firm triggering the failure of another firm. (2) A firm's failure leads to a liquidity crunch as informational asymmetries and concerns about asset values and counterparty solvency cause participants to suspend normal trading.

Taxonomy: An XBRL taxonomy is an XML schema-compliant file that contains XBRL elements, that are defined by XBRL-specific attributes.

Term life: Policies that provide life insurance coverage for a specified period of time. They differ from whole life policies that cover the entire life of the insured.

Term sheet: A legal contract between an investor and a venture company describing the conditions under which money is provided.

Threat profile: According to CERT, a threat profile is a structured representation of the range of threat scenarios for various sources of threats, such as system problems and human actors using network or physical access.

Transaction manager: It provides the services and management functions required to support transaction demarcation, transactional resource management, synchronisation and transaction context propagation.

Value-at-risk (VaR): A measure of risk based on a probability of loss and a specific time horizon in which this loss can be expected to occur.

Virtual private network (VPN): By using encryption in the lower protocol layers, an insecure network (e.g. the Internet) can be converted to provide a secure connection. VPNs are generally cheaper than real private networks using private lines but rely on having the same encryption system at both ends. The encryption may be performed by firewall software or possibly by routers.

Web application: An application that runs on the Web. In the J2EE environment, it is an application that operates within a servlet container that provides the runtime environment for the web application.

Web container: The runtime environment of applications as servlets, JSPs, etc. that provides services to web-specific services, for example, the generation of dynamic and static content for web browser-based clients. It is usually found in the J2EE architecture or a web server.

XML schema: An alternative to DTD, an XML schema is written in XML.

Zero-day attack: An exploit, worm or a virus that attacks a system on the same day the vulnerability of the system is made public.

Bibliography

ABN AMRO (year unknown) 'Success Story: Basell Polyolefins', ABN AMRO White Paper; available at: *http://www.workingcapital.abnamro.com/resources/includes/Attachments/Basell_Case_Study.pdf* (Last accessed: 6 December 2005).

Accenture (2005) 'Risk & regulation management: Basel II services'; available at: *http://www.accenture.com/xd/xd.asp?it=enweb&xd=industries%5Cfinancial%5Cbanking%5Ccapabilities%5Cfsi_basel2.xml* (Last accessed: 6 December 2005).

AcuTech (2002) 'The HAZOP method'; available at: *http://www.acusafe.com/Hazard_Analysis/HAZOP_Technique.pdf* (Last accessed: 3 December 2005).

Al-Attar, A. (2002) 'Data mining – beyond algorithms'; available at: *http://www.intellicrafters.com/algorithms.pdf* (Last accessed: 6 December 2005).

Alberts, C., Dorofee, A., Stevens, J. and Woody, C. (2003) *Introduction to the OCTAVE Approach*. Pittsburgh, PA: Carnegie Mellon Software Engineering Institution; available at: *http://www.cert.org/octave/approach_intro.pdf* (Last accessed: 6 December 2005).

Algorithmics (2001) *The Benefits of Enterprise Credit Risk Management*. Algorithmics Incorporated; available at: *http://www.algorithmics.com/research/advertorials/2001CreditRiskAdvrt.pdf* (Last accessed: 6 December 2005).

Allen, F. (2002) 'E-finance: an introduction', *Journal of Financial Services Research*, 22(1,2): 5.

Altman, E., Resti, A. and Sironi, A. (2003) 'Default recovery rates in credit risk modeling: a review of the literature and empirical evidence'; available at: *http://pages.stern.nyu.edu/~ealtman/Review1.pdf* (Last accessed: 6 December 2005).

American Academy of Actuaries (2001) 'Insurance industry catastrophe management practices', Public policy monograph; available at: *http://www.actuary.org/pdf/casualty/catmonograph_june01.pdf* (Last accessed: 6 December 2005).

Anand, S. (2003) 'Crystal gazing: issues in bank consolidations', *The Financial Express*, December; available at: *http://www.financialexpress.com/fe_full_story.php?content_id=49335* (Last accessed: 6 December 2005).

Andersen, K. V. and Bjorn-Andersen, N. (2001) 'Globalization and e-commerce: growth and impacts in Denmark', *Globalization of e-commerce*; available at: *hltp://www.crito.uci.edu/GIT/publications/pdf/denmarkGEC.pdf* (Last accessed: 6 December 2005).

Andersen, K. V., Bjorn-Andersen, N. and Dedrick, J. (2003) 'Governance initiatives creating a demand-driven e-commerce approach: the case of Denmark', *Information Society*, 19(1): 95.

Anderson, J. (2005) 'Nasdaq to acquire electronic stock trader', *News.com*, 23 April; available at: *http://news.com.com/Nasdaq+to+acquire+electronic+stock+trader/2100-1030_3-5681859.html* (Last accessed: 6 December 2005).

Andreeff, A., Binmoeller, L.C., Boboch, E.M., Cerda, O., Chakravorti, S., Ciesielski, T. and Green, E. (2003) 'Electronic bill presentment and payment: is it just a click away?' *Business Credit*, 105(9): 22–36.

Anonymous (2000) 'Data protection', *Freshfields Bruckhaus Deringer*, August; available at: *http://www.freshfields.com/practice/ipit/publications/22367.pdf* (Last accessed: 8 December 2005).

Anonymous (2002) 'Back from the brink', *Voice&data Online*; available at: *http://www.voiceanddata.com.au/vd/feature_article/item_052002b.asp* (Last accessed: 5 December 2005).

Anonymous (2004) 'Payments pressure', *The Banker*, October; available at: *http://www.thebanker.com/news/fullstory.php/aid/2216/Payments_pressure.html* (Last accessed: 6 December 2005).

Anthes, G. H. (2004) 'ETrade bests the clock', *Computerworld*, 27 September; available at: *http://www.computerworld.com/managementtopics/ebusiness/story/0,10801,96136,00.html* (Last accessed: 2 December 2005).

Aragonés, J. R., Blanco, C. and Dowd, K. (2001) 'Incorporating stress tests into market risk modeling', *Derivatives Quarterly* 7(3), Spring; available at: *http://www.fea.com/resources/pdf/a_stresstest.pdf* (Last accessed: 6 December 2005).

Arbor Networks (2005a) 'Sarbanes-Oxley/Cobit and Peakflow X', *New Release*, 25 July; available at: *http://www.arbornetworks.com/news_detail.php?id=458* (Last accessed: 3 December 2005).

Arbor Networks (2005b) 'Sarbanes-Oxley/Cobit and Peakflow X', *Compliance Brief*; available at: *http://www.arbornetworks.com/downloads/SOX_CobiT_Compliance_Brief.pdf* (Last accessed: 3 December 2005).

Arbor Networks (2005c) 'Peakflow X', *Data Sheet*; available at: *http://www.arbornetworks.com/downloads/Arbor_Peakflow_X_Data_Sheet.pdf* (Last accessed: 6 December 2005).

Asian Development Bank (2001) 'Strengthening the banking supervision and liquidity risk management system of the People's Bank of China' available at: *http://www.adb.org/Documents/Reports/TAR3098/TA3098_PRC_Final_Report.pdf* (Last accessed: 6 December 2005).

Atkinson, W. (2004) 'The supply chain's missing link', *Collections & Credit Risk*, 9(2), pp. 36–42.

Atwell, S. (1998) 'Case study: effective use of FIX via the Internet'; available at: *http://www.fixprotocol.org/documents/641/sinny0998.ppt* (Last accessed: 6 December 2005).

Audit Commission (2005) 'Corporate governance inspection', *Local Government Consultation*, July; available at: *http://www.audit-commission.gov.uk/Products/NATIONAL-REPORT/3344117A-F738-4053-B808-5969F53B2993/CorporateGovernanceInspection.pdf* (Last accessed: 12 December 2005).

Babbel, D. F. and Santomero, A. M. (1996) 'Risk management by insurers: an analysis of the process', *Wharton School Working Papers*, University of Pennsylvania; available at: *http://fic.wharton.upenn.edu/fic/papers/96/9616.pdf* (Last accessed: 6 December 2005).

Bace, R. and Mell, P. (2001) 'Intrusion detection system', *NIST Special Publication*; available at: *http://csrc.nist.gov/publications/nistpubs/800-31/sp800-31.pdf*. (Last accessed: 6 December 2005).

Bakhru, A. and Brown, A. (2005) 'Online broking strategies: surviving the downturn at Merrill Lynch, Charles Schwab, and E*Trade' in Grant, R.M. (ed.) *Cases in Contemporary Strategy Analysis*, 5th edn. London: Blackwell Publishing.

Bank of Japan (2003) 'Business continuity planning at financial institutions', July; available at: *http://www.boj.or.jp/en/set/03/data/fsk0307a.pdf* (Last accessed: 6 December 2005).

Banque de France (2002) 'Developments in France's banking system since the late 1960s', *Annual Report Commission Bancaire 2003*, Study 3; available at: *http://www.banque-france.fr/gb/supervi/telechar/cbreport/2002/study3.pdf* (Last accessed: 6 December 2005).

Bartlett, A., Nicol, S, Schechter, A. and Zanocco, G. (2000) 'Ecommerce and competition – charities', *Master Projects*, December, London Business School; available at: *http://www.fundraising.co.uk/library/research_papers/londonbusinesschool_200012.pdf* (Last accessed: 6 December 2005).

BBDO Consulting (2004) 'European market for retail payment service providers – The customers' perspective', Presentation at Strategy Forum, April 2004, Rome; available at: *http://www.eurogiro.com/members/docs/Strategy%20Forum%202004/02%20-%20European%20market%20for%20retail%20payment%20service%20providers.pdf* (Last accessed: 6 December 2005).

BEA (2004) 'Why upgrade to BEA WebLogic server 8.1', dev2dev article, 19 January; available at: *http://dev2dev.bea.com/pub/a/2004/01/wls_why_upgrade.html* (Last accessed: 10 December 2005).

BearingPoint (2004) 'Many roads lead to Basel. Let BearingPoint be your navigator!', *Poster*, September; available at: *http://www.bearingpoint.com/portal/binary/com.epicentric.contentmanagement.servlet.ContentDeliveryServlet/published/pdfs/public/Poster_Basel_II_engl_2005.pdf* (Last accessed: 6 December 2005).

Benhamou, E. and Serval, T. (1999) 'On the competition between ECNs, stock markets and market makers', *EC-Web 2000*; available at: *http://www.egyptse.com/download/research_papers/educational_brochures/competition_ECNs_stock_markets_market_makers.pdf* (Last accessed: 7 December 2005).

Best-Devereux, I. (2003) 'WIR reinsurance technology interview' *World Insurance Report*, No. 712, 25 April; available at: *http://www.ereinsure.com/press/eReinsure-PR-4-25-03.pdf* (Last accessed: 7 December 2005).

BIS (1990) 'Report of the Committee on Interbank Netting Schemes of the Central Banks of the Group of Ten Countries', Basel: Bank for International Settlements; available at: *http://www.bis.org/publ/cpss04.pdf* (Last accessed: 7 December 2005).

BIS (1994) 'A discussion paper on public disclosure of market and credit risks by financial intermediaries', *Fisher Report*, September, Basel: Bank for International Settlements.

BIS (1998) 'Risk management for electronic banking and electronic money activities', *Basel Committee Publications*, 35: March; available at: *http://www.bis.org/publ/bcbs35.pdf* (Last accessed: 7 December 2005).

BIS (2000) 'Principles for the management of credit risk', Basel: Bank for International Settlements, Risk Management Group; available at: *http://www.bis.org/publ/bcbs75.pdf* (Last accessed: 7 December 2005).

BIS (2001) 'Risk management principles for electronic banking', Basel Committee on Banking Supervision White Paper, Basel: Bank for International Settlements; available at: *http://www.bis.org/publ/bcbs82.pdf* (Last accessed: 1 December 2005).

BIS (2003a) 'Payment systems in the Netherlands', *CPSS Red Book*; available at: *http://www.bis.org/cpss/paysys/NetherlandsComp.pdf* (Last accessed: 7 December 2005).

BIS (2003b) 'Risk management principles for electronic banking', Basel: Bank for International Settlements, Electronic Banking Group; available at: *http://www.bis.org/publ/bcbs98.pdf* (Last accessed: 7 December 2005).

BIS (2003c) 'Management and supervision of cross-border electronic banking activities', *Basel Committee on Banking Supervision White Paper*, Basel: Bank for International Settlements, Electronic Banking Group; available at: *http://www.bis.org/publ/bcbs99.pdf* (Last accessed: 7 December 2005).

BIS (2004) 'Survey of developments in electronic money and internet and mobile payments', Basel: Bank for International Settlements, Committee on Payment and Settlement Systems; available at: *http://www.bis.org/publ/cpss62.pdf* (Last accessed: 7 December 2005).

BITS (2003) 'BITS framework for managing technology risk for IT service provider relationships'; available at: http://*www.bitsinfo.org/downloads/Publications%20Page/bits2003framework.pdf* (Last accessed: 7 December 2005).

BITS (2004a) 'Kalculator: BITS key risk measurement tool for information security operational risks'; available at: *http://www.bitsinfo.org/downloads/Publications%20Page/BITS%20Kalculator/bitskalcnarrative.pdf* (Last accessed: 7 December 2005).

BITS (2004b) 'BITS IS Service Provider Expectation Matrix'; available at: *http://www.bitsinfo.org/downloads/Publications%20Page/bitsxmatrix2004.xls* (Last accessed: 7 December 2005).

Black, F. and Scholes, M. (1973) 'The pricing of options and corporate liabilities', *Journal of Political Economy* 81: 637–59.

Blanco, L. (2002) 'Audit trails in an e-commerce environment', *Information Systems Control Journal* 5; available at: *http://www.isaca.org/Template.cfm?Section=Home&CONTENTID=17108&TEMPLATE=/ContentManagement/ContentDisplay.cfm* (Last accessed: 7 December 2005).

BNY Brokerage (year unknown) 'DEx – The new paradigm in executive management'; available at: *http://www.bnybrokerage.com/exmgmt_DEx.asp* (Last accessed: 7 December 2005).

Bolkestein, F. (2003) 'Corporate governance in Europe', Address to Conference on Corporate Governance at Clifford Chance; available at: *http://www.paris-europlace.net/eu/doc61543.htm* (Last accessed: 7 December 2005).

Bond, A. and Stone, M. (2004) 'How the automotive insurance claims experience affects customer retention', *Journal of Financial Services Marketing*, 9(2): 160–71.

Boucher, K. (1999) 'Application servers on the front lines', *Software Magazine*, December; available at: *http://www.softwaremag.com/L.cfm?Doc=archive/1999dec/AppServers.html* (Last accessed: 7 December 2005).

Bowen, J., Cassel, R., Collins, C., Dickson, K., Fleet, M., Ingram, D., Meyers, S., Mueller, H., Samaniego, Z., Siberón, J., Wille, S. and Yu, M. (2005) *Enterprise Risk Management Specialty Guide*. Schaumburg, IL: ERM Working Group, Society of Actuaries; available at: *http://library.soa.org/library-pdf/SPG0508ERM.pdf* (Last accessed: 7 December 2005).

Bradley, D. and Josang, A. (2003) 'Mesmerize – an open framework for enterprise security management', *Proceedings of Conferences in Research and Practice in Information Technology* 32; available at: *http://www.crpit.com/confpapers/CRPITV32Bradley.pdf* (Last accessed: 7 December 2005).

Brandt, A (2004) 'Privacy watch: two passwords double your privacy', *PC World*, September, also available at: *http://www.pcworld.com/howto/article/0,aid,116989,00.asp* (Last accessed: 7 December 2005).

Bray, M (2004) 'Application programming interface'; available at: *http://www.sei.cmu.edu/str/descriptions/api.html* (Last accessed: 7 December 2005).

Brownlow, D (2004) 'In a spin over money laundering', *Financial World*, February; available at: *http://www.huntswood.com/_uploads/In_a_spin_over_money_laundering_Feb_04.pdf* (Last accessed: 9 December 2005).

BSA (2003) 'Information security governance: toward a framework for action', Business Software Alliance White Paper; available at: *http://www.globaltechsummit.net/press/ISGPaper-2003.pdf* (Last accessed: 7 December 2005).

Cadbury, A. (1992) 'Report of the Committee on the financial aspects of corporate governance'; available at: *http://www.ecgi.org/codes/documents/cadbury.pdf* (Last accessed: 7 December 2005).

Capco (2005) 'I-flex to acquire Capco's operational risk product'; available at: *http://www.capco.com/uploadedFiles/Press/Press_Releases/2005/PR_June_21.pdf* (Last accessed: 4 December 2005).

Caplehorn, R (2004) 'PayPal: Fast, easy, secure payments', Presentation at European Central Bank e-payments conference; available at:

http://www.ecb.int/events/pdf/conferences/epayments2004/041110_eConf_Capleborn.pdf (Last accessed: 7 December 2005).

Celent (2002) 'Commercial lending market overview: The calm before the storm'; available at: *http://www.celent.com/PressReleases/20021021/CommercialLending.htm* (Last accessed: 7 December 2005).

Centers for Medicare & Medicaid Services (2005) 'Security standards: organizational, policies and procedures and documentation requirements', *HIPAA Security Series* 2(5); available at: *http://www.hipaadvisory.com/Action/Security/CMS_Series/Requirements.pdf* (Last accessed: 8 December 2005).

CERT (2003) 'OCTAVE overview', Presentation at Carnegie Mellon Software Engineering Institute; available at: *http://www.cert.org./archive/pdf/octave_Alt_Exec_Session.pdf* (Last accessed: 7 December 2005).

CGI (2005) 'IT governance and managed services'; available at: *http://www.cgi.com/cgi/pdf/cgi_whpr_59_gov_manag_serv_e.pdf* (Last accessed: 7 December 2005).

Chan, S. and Lepeak, S. (2004) 'IT and Sarbanes-Oxley', *CMA Management*, June/July; available at: *http://www.managementmag.com/index.cfm/ci_id/1941/la_id/1* (Last accessed: 7 December 2005).

Chan, Y. L. and Chan, H. Y. (1998) 'Java smart cards', *Surprise 98 Report*; available at: *http://www.iis.ee.ic.ac.uk/~frank/surp98/report/ylc3/report2.html* (Last accessed on 7 December 2005).

Chanel-Reynaud, G. and Chabert, D. (2005) 'The organisation of securities clearing and settlement infrastructures in Europe', *Clearing and Settlement of Financial Markets: Europe and Beyond,* London; available at: *http://www.cass.city.ac.uk/conferences/clearingandsettlement/reynaud_chabert.pdf* (Last accessed: 7 December 2005).

Chtaneva, A. (2001) 'Investing online: concerns about the evolving use of the Internet as an investment tool in the secondary market context'; available at: *http://www.lex-electronica.org/articles/v7-1/Chtaneva.pdf* (Last accessed: 7 December 2005).

Cin/technology (year unknown) 'Proven online technology for offering and trading financial products', White Paper at *http://www.cintechnology.com/documents/brochure/eng/cintec.pdf* (Last accessed: 7 December 2005).

Cisco (2002) 'Internetworking technology handbook', *Cisco Systems Documentation*; available at: *http://www.cisco.com/univercd/cc/td/doc/cisintwk/ito_doc/index.htm* (Last accessed: 7 December 2005).

C. J. & Tuck Consulting (year unknown) 'Accounts receivable check conversion', at: *http://www.cashflownow.org/more/arc.html* (Last accessed: 1 December 2005).

Clarke, R. (1997) 'Regulating financial services in the marketspace: the public's interests', *Proceedings of Conferences on Electronic Commerce: Regulating Financial Services in the Marketspace*, Sydney, February, also available at: *http://www.anu.edu.au/people/Roger.Clarke/EC/ASC97.html* (Last accessed: 7 December 2005).

Clearnet (2002) 'A model you can bank on', White Paper; available at: *http://www.clearnetsa.com/information/files/A_model_you_can_bank_on_vd%E9f.pdf* (Last accessed: 7 December 2005).

Clearnet (2004) 'Clearing 21 and peripheral systems', White Paper, Release 2.0; available at: *http://www.clearnetsa.com/information/files/Clearing%2021_LCHClearnet_FINAL.pdf* (Last accessed: 7 December 2005).

Clemons, E. K., Hitt, L. M., Gu, B., Thatcher, M. E. and Weber, B. W. (2001) 'Impacts of the Internet on financial services: a quantitative analysis of transparency, differential pricing and disintermediation', ver. 2, *Federal Reserve Bank of New York Research Papers*; available at: *http://www.ny.frb.org/newsevents/events/research/2001/Clemons.pdf* (Last accessed: 7 December 2005).

COBIT (2000) *COBIT Framework*, 3rd edn; available at: *https://audit.byu.edu/website/tools/COBIT/PDFS/Framewrk.pdf* (Last accessed: 7 December 2005).

Cohen, L. (year unknown) 'Online donations. The time has come.' Heartbeat Digital White Papers; available at: *http://www.heartbeatdigital.com/intellibeat/pdf/online_donate.pdf* (Last accessed: 2 December 2005).

Coleman, D. W. and Bowman, C. F. (2004) 'Extreme availability with IBM WebSphere and DB2', *WebSphere Advisor*, Week 51; available at: *http://zones.advisor.com/doc/15076* (Last accessed: 7 December 2005).

Committee of Wise Men (2001) *Final Report of the Committee of Wise Men on the Regulation of European Securities Markets*; available at: *http://europa.eu.int/comm/internal_market/securities/docs/lamfalussy/wisemen/final-report-wise-men_en.pdf* (Last accessed: 7 December 2005).

Complinet (year unknown) 'Anti-money laundering solutions', AML brochure available at: *http://www.complinet.com/file_store/pdf/brochures/AML_brochure.pdf* (Last accessed: 7 December 2005).

Cooley, C., Smeder, P. and Zahratka, A. (2000) 'CATEX', *Case UVA-F-129*, University of Virginia; available at: *http://faculty.darden.edu/gbus885-00/Documents/catex.pdf* (Last accessed: 7 December 2005).

Cornell Equity Research (1997) 'Ameritrade Holding Corporation', 28 November; available at: *http://parkercenter.johnson.cornell.edu/*

docs/other_research/1997_fall/amtd_1.pdf (Last accessed: 7 December 2005).

COSO (1992) 'Internal control – integrated framework', American Institute of Certified Public Accountants (AICPA) Publication; executive summary available at: *http://www.coso.org/publications/executive_summary_integrated_framework.htm* (Last accessed: 8 December 2005).

COSO (2004) 'Enterprise risk management – integrated framework executive summary'; available at: *http://www.coso.org/Publications/ERM/COSO_ERM_ExecutiveSummary.pdf* (Last accessed: 7 December 2005).

Coudert Bros LLP (2004) 'The European Union's Data Protection Directive and its effect on employers', White Paper; available at: *http://www.coudert.com/news/client_advisory/041123_727_eudata_cb.pdf* (Last accessed: 7 December 2005).

Coughlan, G., Kolb, K. and Emery, S. (2003) 'HEAT technical document: A consistent framework for assessing hedge effectiveness under IAS39 and FAS133', JP Morgan White Paper; available at: *http://www.labmorgan.com/cm/BlobServer?blobtable=Document&blobcol=urlblob&blobkey=name&blobheader=application/pdf&blobwhere=jpmorgan/investbk/heat_techdoc_2Apr03.pdf* (Last accessed: 7 December 2005).

Craig, D. (2004) 'High-tech systems help make the agent an underwriting', *Insurance Journal* 17; available at: *http://www.insurancejournal.com/magazines/west/2004/05/17/features/42620.htm* (Last accessed: 7 December 2005).

CRMPG (1999) 'Improving counterparty risk management practices', Counterparty Risk Management Policy Group, House Committee on Financial Services; available at: *http://financialservices.house.gov/banking/62499crm.pdf* (Last accessed: 3 December 2005).

CSK (2003) 'EBA/STEP2 solution'; available at: *http://www.csksoftware.com/main/pressnews/download/intern/documents/fact_sheets/FS_eba-step2_bulk-payment_eng_10-03.pdf* (Last accessed: 7 December 2005).

D'Arcy, S. P. (2001) 'Enterprise risk management', *Journal of Risk Management of Korea* 12(1), also available at: *http://www.business.uiuc.edu/~s-darcy/papers/erm.pdf* (Last accessed: 7 December 2005).

Darlington, A., Grout, S, and Whitworth, J. (2001) 'How safe is safe enough? an introduction to risk management', Presentation to The Staple Inn Actuarial Society; available at: *http://www.sias.org.uk/papers/risk2001.pdf* (Last accessed: 7 December 2005).

Datamonitor (2002) 'Business continuity planning and disaster recovery solutions – achieving continuous availability', Datamonitor White Paper; available at: *http://www.sybase.com/content/1024633/BCPDRv1.22May02.pdf* (Last accessed: 7 December 2005).

Datamonitor (2003) 'Readying the banks for Basel II', Datamonitor White Paper; available at: *ftp://ftp.software.ibm.com/software/data/pubs/tech-consult/basel-datamon.pdf* (Last accessed: 7 December 2005).

Datamonitor (2004a) 'Claims automation in US P&C insurance', *A Datamonitor report.*

Datamonitor (2004b) 'Single sign-on – enterprise access made secure and easy', Computer Associates White Paper; available at: *http://www3.ca.com/Files/IndustryAnalystReports/ca_sso_whitepaper.pdf* (Last accessed: 7 December 2005).

Dawson, R. (2005) 'How collaborative technologies are transforming financial services', Strategic White Paper, Collaboration in Financial Services Europe Conference, June; available at: *http://www.abtgroup.com/Collaboration_in_Financial_Services_White_Paper_2005.pdf* (Last accessed: 7 December 2005).

Degryse, H. and Achter, M. V. (2002) 'Alternative trading systems and liquidity', in Balling, M., Lierman, F., and Mullineux, A. (eds) *Technology and Finance: Challenges for Financial Markets, Business Strategies and Policymakers*, Chapter 10; London: Routledge, or at: *http://www.econ.kuleuven.be/ew/academic/macrofin/papers/working/final%20version%20including%20SUERF%20reference.pdf* (Last accessed: 7 December 2005).

Donaldson, J. A. (1986) *ACT – Companion to Treasury Management*, London: The Association of Corporate Treasurers.

DSPA (year unknown) 'Insurance sales compensation', DSPA software brochure; available at: *http://www.dspasoftware.com/dspa/product/fasat-brochure.pdf* (Last accessed: 2 December 2005).

DTT (2003) 'Business ethics and compliance in the Sarbanes-Oxley era', Deloitte & Touche; available at: *http://www.deloitte.com/dtt/cda/doc/content/ethicsCompliance_f.pdf* (Last accessed: 3 December 2005).

DTT (2003a) 'Anti-money laundering compliance survey', Deloitte & Touche; available at: *http://www.deloitte.com/dtt/cda/doc/content/dtt_financialservices_AMLComplianceSurvey_101003.pdf* (Last accessed: 7 December 2005).

DTT (2004a) 'Global security survey', Deloitte & Touche; available at: *http://www.deloitte.com/dtt/cda/doc/content/dtt_financialservices_SecuritySurvey2004_051704.pdf* (Last accessed: 7 December 2005).

DTT (2004b) 'Assessing the value of enterprise risk management', Deloitte & Touche; available at: *http://www.deloitte.com/dtt/cda/doc/content/us_fsi_erm_oct2004%283%29.pdf* (Last accessed: 7 December 2005).

DTT (2004c) '2004 Global risk management survey', Deloitte; available at: *http://www.deloitte.com/dtt/cda/doc/content/2004%20Global%20Risk%20Management%20Survey%281%29.pdf* (Last accessed: 7 December 2005).

DTT (2005a) 'Financial reporting brief', Deloitte, July; available at: *http://www.deloitte.com/dtt/cda/doc/content/dtt_ie_JulyFRB05.pdf* (Last accessed: 7 December 2005).

DTT (2005b) 'Global security survey', Deloitte & Touche; available at: *http://www.deloitte.com/dtt/cda/doc/content/dtt_financialservices_2005GlobalSecuritySurvey_2005-07-21.pdf* (Last accessed: 7 December 2005).

Dumm, R. E. and Hoyt, R. E. (2003) 'Insurance distribution channels: markets in transition', *Journal of Insurance Regulation* 22(1): 27–47; also available at: *http://www.iisonline.org/pdf/Insurance%20Distribution%20Channels%20(JIR%20submission).pdf* (Last accessed: 9 December 2005).

Earl, M. (2001) 'Knowledge management strategies: Toward a taxonomy', *Journal of Management Information Systems* 18(1): 215.

EBA (2002) 'A possible legal framework for the single payment area in the internal market', Working Document by the European Commission; available at: *http://europa.eu.int/comm/internal_market/payments/docs/framework/framework-workingdoc-contrib/eba_en.pdf* (Last accessed: 7 December 2005).

EBA (2003) 'STEP2 Presentation'; available at: *http://www.oenb.at/de/img/eba_roadshow_tcm14-4540.pdf* (Last accessed: 10 December 2005).

ECB (2004) 'E-payments without frontiers', European Central Bank Issues Paper for the ECB Conference 10 November; available at: *http://www.ecb.int/pub/pdf/other/epaymentsconference-issues2004en.pdf* (Last accessed: 7 December 2005).

ECB (2005a) 'Payment systems business continuity', European Central Bank Issues Paper, May; available at: *http://www.ecb.int/ecb/pdf/cons/paysysbusinesscontinuity/paysysbusinesscontinuity.pdf* (Last accessed: 7 December 2005).

ECB (2005b) 'The New Basel Capital Accord: main features and implications', *Monthly Bulletin*, January, pp. 51–60; available at: *http://www.ecb.int/pub/pdf/other/ecb_mb0105_basel_2en.pdf* (Last accessed: 7 December 2005).

ECB (year unknown) 'All glossary entries'; available at: *http://www.ecb.int/home/glossary/html/glossc.en.html* (Last accessed: 12 December 2005).

EIU (2001) 'Insurance on the Internet', Presentation at the Casualty Loss Reserve seminar; available at: *http://www.casact.org/coneduc/clrs/2001/handouts/wagner1.pdf* (Last accessed: 7 December 2005).

EIU (2004) 'The 2004 e-readiness rankings', Economist Intelligence Unit White Paper; available at: *http://graphics.eiu.com/files/ad_pdfs/ERR2004.pdf* (Last accessed: 7 December 2005).

EIU (2005) 'The role of IT in compliance', An EIU report sponsored by VERTIAS; available at: *http://graphics.eiu.com/files/ad_pdfs/VERITAS_COMPLIANCE_3.pdf* (Last accessed: 8 December 2005).

EIU and PricewaterhouseCoopers (2001) 'E-insurance: Creating a competitive advantage', Executive Briefing; available at: *http://www.pwcglobal.com/fr/pwc_pdf/pwc_e-insurance_report_exec_briefing.pdf* (Last accessed: 8 December 2005).

Epner, S. (2004) 'Surviving fundraising on the Internet', *Nonprofit World* 22(2): 17–19.

Ernst & Young (2004) 'Global information security survey 2004', Assurance and advisory business services; available at: *http://www.ey.com/global/download.nsf/International/2004_Global_Information_Security_Survey/$file/2004_Global_Information_Security_Survey_2004.pdf* (Last accessed: 8 December 2005).

euractiv.com (2005) 'Money laundering rules: thwarting terrorists or threatening liberties?' 25 February; available at: *http://www.euractiv.com/Article?tcmuri=tcm:29-136024-16&type=News* (Last accessed: 3 December 2005).

Euronext (2001) 'Euronext the year 2000', Annual Report; available at: *http://www.euronext.com/file/view/0,4245,1626_53424_351259523,00.pdf* (Last accessed: 8 December 2005).

Fadlalla, A. and Wickramasinghe, N. (2004) 'An integrative framework for HIPAA-compliant I*IQ healthcare information systems', *International Journal of Health Care Quality Assurance* 17(2–3): 65–74.

Fairchild, A. M. (2003) 'Value positions for financial institutions in electronic bill presentment and payment (EBPP)', *Proceedings of the 36th Hawaii International Conference on System Sciences (HICSS'03); available at: http://csdl.computer.org/comp/proceedings/hicss/2003/1874/07/187470196a.pdf* (Last accessed: 8 December 2005).

FATF (2003) 'The forty recommendations', 20 June; available at: *http://www.fatf-gafi.org/document/28/0,2340,en_32250379_32236930_33658140_1_1_1_1,00.html* (Last accessed: 8 December 2005).

Federal Reserve System (2002) 'The future of retail electronic payments systems: industry interviews and analysis', *Staff Study* 175; available at: *http://www.federalreserve.gov/pubs/staffstudies/2000-present/ss175.pdf* (Last accessed: 1 December 2005).

Federal Reserve System (2004) 'The 2004 Federal Reserve Payments Study', Payment Research Report, December; available at: *http://www.epaynetwork.com/infofiles/FRB_Payment_Research_Report_120604.pdf* (Last accessed: 8 December 2005).

Fehle, F. and Tsyplakov, S. (2005) 'Dynamic risk management: theory and evidence', *Journal of Financial Economics* 7(1), October, pp. 3–47; also available at: *http://dmsweb.moore.sc.edu/tsyplakov/papers/Fehle_Tsyplakov.pdf* (Last accessed: 8 December 2005).

Fettig, D. (2004) 'Federal Reserve studies confirm electronic payments exceed check payments for the first time', Announcement, 6 December; available at: *http://www.federalreserve.gov/BoardDocs/Press/other/2004/20041206/default.htm* (Last accessed: 8 December 2005).

FileNet (2005) 'FileNet compliance framework'; available at: *http://www.filenet.com/English/Products/Compliance/* (Last accessed: 8 December 2005).

Finacle (2004) 'Finacle at ABN-AMRO Bank', Case Study; available at: *http://www.infosys.com/finacle/pdf/abnamro.pdf.* (Members only; accessed on 8 December 2005).

FASAT (year unknown) 'Insurance sales compensation', Brochure; available at: *http://www.dspasoftware.com/dspa/product/fasat-brochure.pdf* (Last accessed: 8 December 2005).

FSA (2000) 'Building the new regulator', *Progress Report 1*; available at: *http://www.fsa.gov.uk/pubs/policy/bnr_progress1.pdf* (Last accessed: 8 December 2005).

FSA (2004) 'Countering financial crime risks in information security'; available at: *http://www.fsa.gov.uk/pubs/other/fcrime_sector.pdf* (Last accessed: 8 December 2005).

FSTC (year unknown) 'FSTC Projects', Executive Summary; available at: *http://fstc.org/projects/web-services/index.cfm* (Last accessed: 17 January 2006).

Fuji (2004) 'Risk management system', Annual Report, Fuji Fire & Marine Insurance Co., Ltd.; available at: *http://www.fujikasai.co.jp/2_kabu/pdf_annual/2004risk.pdf* (Last accessed: 8 December 2005).

Furst, K. and Nolle, D. E. (2004) 'Technological innovation in retail payments: key developments and implications for banks', *Journal of Financial Transformation* 12: December; available at: *http://www*

.occ.treas.gov/netbank/OCCFurstNolleJFT.pdf (Last accessed: 8 December 2005).

Galvão, G (2001) 'Countering money laundering: The FATF, the European Union and the Portuguese experience, past and current developments', Work Product on the 117th International Seminar, UNAFEI; available at: *http://www.unafei.or.jp/english/pdf/PDF_rms/no58/58-22.pdf* (Last accessed: 5 December 2005).

Garzone, J. (2005) 'Why are they asking for so much collateral?' *Risk Management* 52(8): 28–32.

Giovannini Group (2003) 'Second report on EU clearing and settlement arrangements', Brussels, April; available at: *http://www.finextra.com/Finextra-downloads//featuredocs/EU_clearing_and_settlement_arrangements.pdf* (Last accessed: 12 December 2005).

Glaessner, T., Kellermann, T. and McNevin, V. (2002) 'Electronic security: risk mitigation in financial transactions public policy issues', The World Bank, June; available at: *http://wbln0018.worldbank.org/html/FinancialSectorWeb.nsf/(attachmentweb)/E-security-RiskMitigationInFinancialTransactionsv4/$FILE/E-security-Risk+Mitigation+In+Financial+Transactions+v+4.0.pdf* (Last accessed: 5 December 2005).

Godeffroy, J.-M. (2000) 'TARGET and the coexistence of different large-value payment systems in economic and monetary union in Europe', Papers presented at a workshop on payment systems at CEMLA, Mexico City, May; the paper collection is available at: *http://www.bis.org/publ/cpss41.pdf* (Last accessed: 8 December 2005).

Gordon, C. and Setteducati, D. (2004) 'Things are happening in automated underwriting', *NAVA OUTLOOK* 13(2): 6–7; available at: *http://www.navanet.org/res/outlook/MarApr2004.pdf* (Last accessed: 8 December 2005).

Gorvett, R. W. (1999) 'Insurance securitization: the development of a new asset class', Discussion Paper Program, Casualty Actuarial Society; available at: *http://www.casact.org/pubs/dpp/dpp99/99dpp133.pdf* (Last accessed: 8 December 2005).

Grant Thornton LLP (2003) 'SEC adopts internal control rules', *SOXalert* 1(1), June; available at: *http://www.grantthornton.com/downloads/SOXalert_603_96767.pdf* (Last accessed: 8 December 2005).

Greenspan, A. (1999) 'Remarks before the World Bank Conference on recent trends in reserves management', Washington, DC; available at: *http://www.federalreserve.gov/boarddocs/speeches/1999/19990429.htm* (Last accessed: 8 December 2005).

Gribble, J. and McGing, S. (2000). 'Insurance: Online or On the line?' The Institute of Actuaries of Australia; available at: *http://www.actuaries.asn.au/PublicSite/pdf/sessionals/sessional_05-2000_InsuranceOnline_or_OnTheLine.PDF* (Last accessed: 8 December 2005).

Hagerty, J. (2005) 'Regulatory compliance: an $80 billion opportunity', *CIO Magazine*; available at: *http://www2.cio.com/analyst/report3316.html* (Last accessed: 8 December 2005).

Haimila, S. (2003) 'CRM serves as strategic centerpiece', *KM World*, 1 February; available at: *http://www.kmworld.com/Articles/ReadArticle.aspx?ArticleID=9441* (Last accessed: 8 December 2005).

HAL Knowledge Solutions (2005) 'IT complexity confounds financial sector compliance', *Press Release*, 15 June; available at: *http://www.ebcvg.com/press.php?id=1196* (Last accessed: 8 December 2005).

Hansen, F. (2003) 'Global e-commerce growth', *Business Credit* 105(9): 58.

Hashimi, S. (2003) 'Service-oriented architecture explained', *O'Reilly windows devcenter.com,* 18 August; available at: *http://www.ondotnet.com/pub/a/dotnet/2003/08/18/soa_explained.html* (Last accessed: 8 December 2005).

Hirtle, B. and Metli, C. (2004) 'The evolution of US bank branch networks: growth, consolidation, and strategy', *Current Issues in Economics and Finance* 10(8): 1–7.

Hitachi Data Systems (2003) 'Hitachi storage at work AOK', White Paper; available at: *http://www.hds.com/pdf/cs_aok_english.pdf#view=FitH&pagemode=none* (Last accessed: 9 December 2005).

Hochmuth, P. (2001) 'Be your own MAN', *NetworkWorld*, 10 September; available at: *http://www.networkworld.com/news/2001/0910gigman.html?net* (Last accessed: 9 December 2005).

Hong, K.-S., Chi, Y.-P., Chao, L.R. and Tang, J.-H. (2003) 'An integrated system theory of information security management', *Information Management & Computer Security* 11(5): 243–8.

HP (2004a) 'HP OpenBank.NET', Technical White Paper; available at: *http://h71028.www7.hp.com/enterprise/downloads/HP%20OpenBank.NET_WHite%20Paper_3_6-28-04%20040628.pdf* (Last accessed: 9 December 2005).

HP (2004b) 'HP Cisco data replication solutions'; available at: *http://www.cisco.com/warp/public/756/partnership/hp/solutions/resources/pdf/hp_cisco_drsoln_brief_070204.pdf* (Last accessed: 9 December 2005).

HP (2004c) 'HP real time financial services for retail banking'; available at: *http://h71028.www7.hp.com/ERC/downloads/RTFS_WP_final.pdf_2.13.pdf* (Last accessed: 10 December 2005).

HP (2005a) 'Management for the adaptive enterprise', HP White Paper; available at: *http://h71028.www7.hp.com/enterprise/downloads/5981-2191EN_LO_RES.pdf* (Last accessed: 3 December 2005).

HP (2005b) 'HP SOA Manager: an overview'; available at: *http://devresource.hp.com/drc/resources/lcm4ws_overview/index.jsp* (Last accessed: 3 December 2005).

HP (year unknown) 'HP's OpenPayments meets today's demands', *Advertorial*; available at: *http://h71028.www7.hp.com/enterprise/downloads/HP%20Open%20Payments%20Advertorial%20.pdf* (Last accessed: 10 December 2005).

Humphreys, T. (ed.) (2003) 'The newly revised Part 2 of BS 7799', *XiSEC Consultants*, Ver 6; available at: *http://www.xisec.com/The%20Newly%20Revised%20Part%202%20of%20BS%207799ver6.pdf* (Last accessed: 9 December 2005).

Hurwit & Associates (2004) 'The taxation of unrelated business income', *Nonprofit Law Resource Library*; available at: *http://www.hurwitassociates.com/l_unrelated_income.html#4* (Last accessed: 5 December 2005).

Hyle, R. R. (2002) 'Manulife Financial/AgoraINS', *TechDecisions for Insurance*, June; available at: *http://www.technologydecisions.com/backissue/0602/6_19_02_4.asp* (Last accessed: 9 December 2005).

Hyle, R. R. (2004) 'Rearming for reinsurance', *TechDecisions for Insurance*, April; available at: *http://www.technologydecisions.com/backissue/0404/april04_cover_story.asp* (Last accessed: 9 December 2005).

IAA (2001) 'Positioning statement'; available at: *http://siebre.auto.sohu.com/siebre/file/Acord%20and%20IAA.pdf* (Last accessed: 15 April 2005).

IBM (2003) 'Banking data warehouse and the Basel II Capital Accord', IBM White Paper; available at: *http://www-1.ibm.com/industries/financialservices/doc/content/bin/bdw_baselII_rev102003.pdf* (Last accessed: 9 December 2005).

IBM (2004a) 'IBM announces new software and services to help companies adapt information–technology infrastructures to changing businesses', *Business Integration Journal*, 28 April; available at: *http://www.bijonline.com/News.asp?NewsID=1203* (Last accessed: 5 December 2005).

IBM (2004b) 'Insurance application architecture (IAA)', IBM White Paper; available at: *http://www-1.ibm.com/industries/financialservices/doc/content/bin/fss_iaa_gim_06-29-04.pdf* (Last accessed: 15 April 2005).

IBM (year unknown) 'On demand business'; available at: *http://www-5.ibm.com/e-business/uk/glossary/?tactic=305AX03W*. Accessed on 12 December 2005).

i-flex, HP and Intel (2002) 'Net-generation, back-office banking solution', *Solution blueprint*; available at: *www.hpintelco.net/pdf/solutions/financial/iflex_bp.pdf* (Last accessed: 8 December 2005).

Intel (2003) 'Real-time limit and compliance checking', *Solution Architects*; available at: *http://www.intel.com/business/bss/solutions/blueprints/pdf/misys_eagleye.pdf* (Last accessed: 9 December 2005).

Ironside, D. (2003) 'How ri3k Asia utilizes XML ACORD to provide a framework for the admin of all classes of reinsurance risk through one electronic channel', Presentation to ACORD Seminar, Tokyo, February; available at: *http://www.acord.org/global/japan_presentations/Ironside_EN.ppt* (Last accessed: 6 December 2005).

Irsfeld, M. (2005) 'SOX is working, but can we reign in the costs?' *Compliance Pipeline* 14 April; available at: *http://www.compliancepipeline.com/160900658* (Last accessed: 9 December 2005).

ISACA (1999) 'Materiality concepts for auditing information systems', IS Auditing Guideline, Document G6; available at: *http://www.isaca.org/ContentManagement/ContentDisplay.cfm?ContentID=18549* (Last accessed: 9 December 2005).

ISACA (2003) 'Internet banking', IS Auditing Guideline, Document G24; available at: *http://www.isaca.org/ContentManagement/ContentDisplay.cfm?ContentID=18637* (Last accessed: 9 December 2005).

ISACA (2005) 'COBIT case study: Charles Schwab'; available at: *http://www.isaca.org/Template.cfm?Section=Home&CONTENTID=22042&TEMPLATE=/ContentManagement/ContentDisplay.cfm* (Last accessed: 3 December 2005).

ISDA (1999) 'Collateral review', ISDA; available at: *http://www.isda.org/press/pdf/colrev99.pdf* (Last accessed: 9 December 2005).

ITGI (2000) 'COBIT: an overview', Presentation by IT Governance Institute, July; available at: *www.soa.fau.edu/friedberg/Cobitovr.ppt* (Last accessed: 12 December 2005).

JCRS (2002) 'ACORD XML for P&C Case Study', P&C Case Study; available at: *http://jcrs.com/case_study_JCRS_proc_redesign.pdf* (Last accessed: 9 December 2005).

Jendrey, S (2005) 'Best practices: outsourcing and SOX compliance'; available at: *http://www.itcinstitute.com/display.aspx?id=122* (Last accessed: 3 December 2005).

Johnson, J., Boucher, K. and Hicks, M. (2001) 'Project manager's guide to middleware'; available at: *http://www.findarticles.com/p/articles/mi_m0SMG/is_4_21/ai_78436107* (Last accessed: 5 December 2005).

Josefowicz, M. (2004) 'The insurance industry mines the value of web-based solutions', *Insurance NetworkingNews*; available at: *http://www.insurancenetworking.com/supplements/2004webbased/insurance.cfm* (Last accessed: 9 December 2005).

JP Morgan (1997) 'CreditMetrics – technical document'; available at: *http://www.gloriamundi.org/picsresources/CMTD1.pdf* (Last accessed: 9 December 2005).

JP Morgan (2005) 'E-payment migration gaining ground', Industry issue report; available at: *http://www.jpmorgan.com/cm/cs?pagename=Chase/Href&urlname=jpmorgan/cash/newsletter/winter2005/epayment_migration* (Last accessed: 9 December 2005).

Kasun, N. (2003) 'Electronic commerce (electronic payments)', Presentation; available at: *http://www.ucsc.cmb.ac.lk/People/tnk/ecom/ecom6.pdf* (Last accessed: 9 December 2005).

Keeling, D. I. (2002) 'Smart-card technology: business and consumer aspects within a European perspective', Papers, Euromart 2002; available at: *http://www.hispec.org.uk/public_documents/7_4SmartCardTechConsumerIssuesFull.pdf* (Last accessed: 9 December 2005).

Kelly, K. S. (1998) *Effective Fund-raising Management*. NJ: Lawrence Erlbaum.

Kelly, K. S. (2001) 'Public relations & fund raising revisited', Presentation; available at: *http://www.quantanpm.nl/downloads/atlanta_docs/59.pdf* (Last accessed: 2 December 2005).

Kimble, C., Hildreth, P. and Wright, P. (2001) 'Communities of practice: going virtual, knowledge management and business model innovation', Chapter XIII, pp. 220–34; available at: *http://www-users.cs.york.ac.uk/~kimble/research/13kimble.pdf* (Last accessed: 9 December 2005).

King, D. (2001) 'Three Rs of web-based fund-raising: virtual donations for libraries', *New Library World*, 102(7/8): 265–8.

Koscielny, M. (2005) 'Fair Isaac automates Auto Club Group's underwriting process with powerful business rules', *DM Review*, October; available at: *http://www.dmreview.com/article_sub.cfm?articleId=1038116* (Last accessed: 9 December 2005).

KPMG (2000) 'Spotlight on liquidity risk management', KPMG White Paper; available at: *http://kpmg.com/Rut2000_prod/Documents/4/LiquidityRiskManagement.pdf* (Last accessed: 9 December 2005).

Kronseder, C. (2003) 'Measuring liquidity risk', *GTNews*; available at: *http://www.sensalis.com/Publikationen/Measuring%20Liquidity%20Risk.pdf* (Last accessed: 9 December 2005).

Kumar S. P. and Swarup, S. (2001) 'Business intelligence and insurance', Wipro White Paper; available at: *http://www.wipro.co.in/resources/whitepapers/bidw_biinsurance.pdf* (Last accessed: 9 December 2005).

Kyle, A. S. (1985) 'Continuous auctions and insider trading', *Econometrica* 53(6): 1315–35.

Lange, C. (2005) 'Electronic payment', *ECOMOD*; available at: *http://www.wi-inf.uni-essen.de/FGFrank/ecomod/index.php?lang=en&&optionId=Rev_1.4* (Last accessed: 9 December 2005).

Lave, J. and Wenger, E. (1991) *Situated Learning. Legitimate Peripheral Participation*. Cambridge: Cambridge University Press.

Leech, T. (2004) 'Distilling SOX 302, 404 & 906', *Compliance Week*, 25 May; available at: *http://www.net4solutions.com/clients/CARDdecisions/website/CARDWebDownloads.nsf/vwAllDocsFlat/AB5073439CA57BDD85256E9F006746B8/$FILE/DistillingSOXCW.pdf* (Last accessed: 9 December 2005).

LIFFE (2004) 'EURONEXT.LIFFE market solutions at work'; available at: *http://www.liffemarketsolutions.com/clients/studies/euronextliffe.pdf* (Last accessed: 9 December 2005).

Light, D. (2004) 'Property/casualty claims and technology: options and impact', *Building an Edge* 5(9), 9 September; available at: *http://www-1.ibm.com/industries/financialservices/doc/content/bin/bae_sept_2004.pdf* (Last accessed: 9 December 2005).

Lilischkis, S. (2002) 'Insurance and pension funding services', *e-Business Sector Report No. 5*, The European e-Business Market Watch, August; available at: *http://www.ifvw.de/dokumente/public/SR_No5_Insurance.pdf* (Last accessed: 9 December 2005).

Lipis, L. (2004) 'Checkmate', *Finextra*, 22 November; available at: *http://www.finextra.com/fullfeature.asp?id=526* (Last accessed: 9 December 2005).

Lipton, R. and Ostrovsky, R. (1998) 'Micro-payments via efficient coin-flipping', *2nd Financial Cryptograpy Conf. (FC'98)* or *Lecture Notes in Computer Science*, vol 1465.

Litan, A (2003) 'The big payoff of Web billing and online customer service', *Gartner Report*, April.

LogicaCMG (year unknown) 'Quantum billing – to boldly go where no biller has gone before'; available at: *http://logicacmg.com/de/constants/publications/thought_pieces.asp?display=detail&id=36&page=10&sec=0&exp=0&lan=1* (Last accessed: 11 December 2005).

Looney, C. A. and Chatterjee, D. (2002) 'Web-enabled transformation of the brokerage industry', *Communications of the ACM* 45(8): 75–81.

Looney, C. A., Jessup, L. M. and Valacich, J. S. (2004) 'Emerging business models for mobile brokerage services', *Communications of the ACM* 47(6): 71–7.

Lynn, B. and Northey, J. (2002) 'FIXML and FpML – Background, comparison, integration and interoperability opportunities', FIX protocol.org presentation; available at: *http://www.fixprotocol.org/documents/656/FIXML_and_FpML_20020402_rev5.ppt* (Last accessed: 9 December 2005).

Malik, A. (2003) 'XML standards for financial services'; *O'reilly xml.com*; available at: *http://www.xml.com/pub/a/2003/03/26/financial.html* (Last accessed: 9 December 2005).

Mantas (2003) 'Understanding behavior detection technology: emerging approaches to dealing with three major consumer protection threats', White Paper Report; available at: *http://www.mantas.com/GlobalAssets/PDF/WhitePapers/BehaviorDetection.pdf* (Last accessed: 9 December 2005).

Mantas (2005) 'Mantas anti-money laundering', *http://www.mantas.com/Products/RegulatoryCompliance/AntiMoneyLaundering.html* (Last accessed: 3 December 2005).

Marlin, S. (2005)'HSBC, SAS building advanced card-fraud-detection system', Security Pipeline, 21 July; available at: *http://nwc.securitypipeline.com/166401679* (Last accessed: 6 December 2005).

McCormick, A. and Litchfield, C. (2004) 'State of Mississippi and Bank of America's PayMode', *NASACT 2004 Annual Conference*; available at: *http://www.nasact.org/onlineresources/downloads/2004_NASACT/H/c7_litchfield-mccormick.pdf* (Last accessed: 9 December 2005).

McCue, A. (2004) 'Employees are main IT security threat', *CIO jury*, Silicon.com, 8 November; available at: *http://comment.silicon.com/ciojury/0,3800003161,39125719,00.htm* (Last accessed: 9 December 2005).

McDowall, B. (2002) 'e-Banking risks – What are they? How should they be managed?' *IT-Director.com*; available at: *http://it-director.com/article.php?articleid=9686* (Last accessed: 9 December 2005).

McEntee, E. C. (2005) 'Introduction', *Buyers Guide*; available at: *http://www.nacha.org/OtherResources/Buyers2005/BuyersGuide2005_Letter.pdf* (Last accessed: 9 December 2005).

McKendrick, J. (2004) 'ACORD XML approaches critical mass', *Insurance NetworkingNews*, 3 May; available at: *http://www.insurancenetworking.com/protected/article.cfm?articleId=2457&searchTerm=Hartford* (Last accessed: 9 December 2005).

Mercer, E. (1998) 'How can we use the Internet for fundraising?' *The Nonprofit FAQ, Idealist.org*, 27 October; available at: *http://www.nonprofits.org/npofaq/0/1511.html* (Last accessed: 9 December 2005).

Merton, R. C. (1974) 'On the pricing of corporate debt: the risk structure of interest rates', *Journal of Finance* 29: 449–70.

Metavante (2004) 'The role of technology in comprehensive risk management', *Metavante Thought Leadership*; available at: *http://www.metavante.com/mvnt/get?m=21595* (Last accessed: 9 December 2005).

Micromuse (2004) 'Achieving ITIL service management success via a proven service oriented architecture', White Paper; available at: *http://www.micromuse.com/downloads/pdf_lit/wps/Achieving_ITIL_Service_Management_Success.pdf* (Last accessed: 9 December 2005).

Microsoft (2003a) 'PayHound upgrades payment services platform to improve security and make better use of web services', *Evidence*, 5 December; available at: *http://www.microsoft.com/resources/casestudies/CaseStudy.asp?CaseStudyID=14163* (Last accessed: 6 December 2005).

Microsoft (2003b) 'Allstate connects with countrywide producer network in seven months using Microsoft Visual Studio .NET and the .NET framework', *Evidence*, 13 November; available at: *http://www.microsoft.com/resources/casestudies/CaseStudy.asp?CaseStudyID=13648* (Last accessed: 6 December 2005).

Microsoft (2003c) 'Nasdaq cuts development time in half, boosts throughput and support for complex logic', *Evidence*, 20 October; available at: *http://www.microsoft.com/resources/casestudies/CaseStudy.asp?CaseStudyID=14483* (Last accessed: 6 December 2005).

Microsoft (2004) 'Innovation in insurance: reshaping life insurance compensation', Microsoft White Paper; available at: *http://download.microsoft.com/download/0/a/c/0ac6ccc1-993b-488c-bb61-524efca5d669/DSPA.pdf* (Last accessed: 9 December 2005).

Microsoft (2005) 'Service management functions: security management'; available at: *http://www.microsoft.com/technet/itsolutions/cits/mo/smf/mofsmsmf.mspx#ECAA* (Last accessed: 3 December 2005).

Millar, D. (2005) 'Making the best of regulatory overload', *Global Risk Regulator Newsletter*, April; available at: *http://www.globalriskregulator.com/archive/April2005-19.html* (Last accessed: 9 December 2005).

Miller, L. (2002) 'Charities hope 9/11 inspires "e-philanthropy"', *USA Today*, 18 March; available at: *http://www.usatoday.com/tech/news/2002/03/19/online-fundraising.htm* (Last accessed: 9 December 2005).

MIS 100 (2003) 'HSBC Holdings', *MIS Web*; available at: *http://www.misweb.com/mis100viewprofile.asp?by=rank&rgid=7&pid=1049&year=2003* (Last accessed: 9 December 2005).

Moore, B., Fisher-Smith, J., Hudson, T., Novillo, J. and Sigl, R. (2001) 'e-Commerce payment solutions implementation and integration – Using IBM WebSphere Payment Manager', *IBM Redbook*; available at: *http://www.redbooks.ibm.com/redbooks/pdfs/sg246177.pdf* (Last accessed: 9 December 2005).

Moreno, A. (2001) 'Enhancing knowledge exchange through communities of practices at the Inter-American Development Bank', *Aslib Proceedings* 53(8): 296.

Morgan Stanley (2002) 'Quantitative and qualitative disclosures about market risk', Paper; available at: *http://www.morganstanley.com/ar2002/images/financials/Download_3.pdf* (Last accessed: 9 December 2005).

Mühlberger, M. (2005) 'Digital economy and structural change', *Deutsche Bank Research*, 11 January, No.47; available at: *http://www.dbresearch.com/PROD/DBR_INTERNET_EN-PROD/PROD0000000000183368.pdf* (Last accessed: 9 December 2005).

Muranaga, J (1999) 'Dynamics of market liquidity of Japanese stocks: An analysis of tick-by-tick data of the Tokyo Stock Exchange', BIS paper; available at: *http://www.bis.org/publ/cgfs11muran.pdf* (Last accessed: 3 December 2005).

Murphy, N. B. (2004) 'The future of banking in America – The effect on US banking of payment system changes', *FDIC Banking Review* 16(2): 67–87; available at: *http://www.fdic.gov/bank/analytical/banking/2004nov/article3/br16n1art3.pdf* (Last accessed: 9 December 2005).

NACHA (2004) 'eCheck facts'; at *http://www.nacha.org/conferences/E-cheque_2004/e-cheque_2004.htm* (Last accessed: 9 December 2005).

Nayak, S. (2003) 'Basel II: implications for financial service providers', Patni White Paper; available at: *http://www.patni.com/downloads/tp_basel%20II.pdf* (Last accessed: 9 December 2005).

netNumina (2002) 'Leading global investment bank – under NDA global compliance system', Case Study; available at: *http://www.netnumina.com/Papers/cs/Global_Compliance.pdf* (Last accessed: 9 December 2005).

NFPA (2004) 'NFPA 16000 Standard on Disaster/Emergency Management and Business Continuity Programs 2004 Edition', White Paper; available at: *http://www.nfpa.org/PDF/nfpa1600.pdf?src=nfpa* (Last accessed: 9 December 2005).

Nier, E. (2004) 'Banking crises and transparency', EFA 2004 Maastricht Meetings Paper, No. 4805; available at: *http://www.atl-res.com/finance/financeconference/nier.pdf*.

Northey, J. (2002) 'FIXML ready for launch', *FIXGlobal*; available at: *http://www.fixglobal.com/back_issues/Q2/AMERICAS/FIXML%20ready%20for%20launch.pdf* (Last accessed: 5 December 2005).

O'Connor, C. (2001) 'Surfing for investment banking', *Traders Magazine*, 1 March, p. 1.

O'Donnell, A. (2003) 'Manulife replaces legacy channel management apps with DSPA solution', *Insurance & Technology*, 18 June; available at: *http://www.insurancetech.com/resources/infrastructure/showArticle.jhtml?articleID=14705509* (Last accessed: 9 December 2005).

O'Mahony, D, Peirce, M, Tewari, H. and Peirce, M. A. (2001) *Electronic Payment Systems for E-Commerce*, 2/e, Artech House Computer Science Library.

OECD (2002) *Guidelines for the Security of Information Systems and Networks: Towards a Culture of Security;* available at: *http://www.oecd.org/dataoecd/16/22/15582260.pdf* (Last accessed: 9 December 2005).

Omgeo (2004) 'Omgeo central trader manager', *Question & answer document for broker/dealer*; available at: *http://www.omgeo.com/documents/Broker-DealerQA.pdf* (Last accessed: 9 December 2005).

Oracle (2001) 'Oracle iPayment concepts and procedures', Oracle White Paper, January; available at: *http://download-west.oracle.com/appsnet/iby115ug.pdf* (Last accessed: 9 December 2005).

Oracle (2002a) 'Oracle claims for general insurance', Oracle White Paper, 22 October; available at: *http://www.oracle.com/industries/financial_services/claims_whtpr_v1.pdf* (Last accessed: 9 December 2005).

Oracle (2002b) 'Financial services-EMEA', Presentation on Analyst Day, 18 April; available at: *http://www.oracle.com/corporate/analystportal/finserv.pdf* (Last accessed: 9 December 2005).

Oracle (2005) 'Oracle's compliance architecture: a roadmap to sustainable compliance and governance best practices', Oracle White Paper, June; available at: *http://www.oracle.com/solutions/corporate_governance/wp_sustainablecompliance_june2005.pdf* (Last accessed: 9 December 2005).

Pabrai, U. O. A. (2005) 'The COBIT security baseline', *Certification Magazine*, July; available at: *http://www.certmag.com/articles/templates/cmag_department_sec.asp?articleid=1239&zoneid=44* (Last accessed: 9 December 2005).

Pareek, D. (year unknown) 'Myths – STP in financial services', *Themanager.org Publications*; available at: *http://www.themanager.org/Resources/STP.htm* (Last accessed: 9 December 2005).

PeopleSoft (2003) 'Creating a customer-centric insurance enterprise', PeopleSoft White Paper Series, February; available at: *http://www.peoplesoft.com/media/en/pdf/crm_insurance_wp.pdf* (Last accessed: 9 December 2005).

Perumal, V. and Shanmugam, B. (2004) 'Internet banking: boon or bane?' *Journal of Internet Banking and Commerce*, December, 9(3); available at: *http://www.arraydev.com/commerce/JIBC/2004-12/Perumal.HTM* (Last accessed: 9 December 2005).

Popelyukhin, A. S. (2001) 'Let me see: visualizing actuarial information', *CAS Forum*, Winter; available at: *http://www.casact.org/pubs/forum/01wforum/01wf399.pdf* (Last accessed: 9 December 2005).

Porada, W. (unknown) 'The changing face of risk management', Misys White Paper; available at: *http://www.misysbanking.com/files/file5298.pdf* (Last accessed: 9 December 2005).

Price, A. (2002) 'Anti-money laundering – reconsidering the risks', *Monitor*, 1, Ernst & Young; available at: *http://www.ey.com/global/download.nsf/Isle_of_Man/MonitorMonLaun/$file/MoneyLuand.pdf* (Last accessed: 9 December 2005).

PWC (2004) 'Enterprise risk management – integrated framework: executive summary', PricewaterhouseCoopers LLP, September; available at: *http://www.pwcglobal.com/extweb/manissue.nsf/docid/11FE433C2B151E5285256D580059C547/$FILE/Exec.Summ.web.pdf* (Last accessed: 9 December 2005).

Pyle, D. H. (1997) 'Bank risk management: theory', Research Program in Finance Working Paper RPF-272, UC Berkeley; available at: *http://www.haas.berkeley.edu/finance/WP/rpf272.pdf* (Last accessed: 9 December 2005).

Quigley, J. H. (2005) 'Deloitte CEO: Regulation will strengthen reporting confidence', *Financial Executive*, March; available at: *http://www.deloitte.com/dtt/cda/doc/content/us_corpgov_FinExecMar2005DeloitteCEO_article.pdf* (Last accessed: 9 December 2005).

Quillian, J. (2005) 'A weakening foundation', *Stock Market Forecast & Comments*, 18 July; available at: *http://quillian.net/archives/f071805.htm* (Last accessed: 9 December 2005).

Rai, U. K. (2001) 'Realising XML benefits in life insurance', Wipro White Paper; available at: *http://www.wipro.com/pdf_files/Wipro_XML_in_Insurance.pdf* (Last accessed: 9 December 2005).

Ramsaran, C. (2003) 'NetBank's new niche: small business special section', *Bank Systems & Technology*; available at: *http://www.banktech.com/utils/printableArticle.jhtml?doc_id=14700530* (Last accessed: 9 December 2005).

O'Grady, S. (2004) 'SOA meets compliance: compliance oriented architecture', *RedMonk Study*, 12 August; available at: *http://www.redmonk.com/public/COA_Final.pdf.* (Last accessed 9 December 2005).

Reveleus (year unknown) 'Reveleus corporate credit risk analytics', White Paper; available at: *http://www.reveleus.com/PDFs/Corporate%20Credit%20Risk%20Analytics.pdf* (Last accessed: 4 December 2005).

ri3k (year unknown) 'ri3k solutions'; at *http://www.ri3k.com/website/solutions.html* (Last accessed: 7 December 2005).

Rockbridge Associates, Inc (2004) 'National technology readiness survey', Summary Report, 3 February; available at: *http://www.smith.umd.edu/ntrs/NTRS_2004.pdf* (Last accessed: 9 December 2005).

Rommel, J. (1999) 'Why Java is ready for enterprise applications', *Java World*, 23 December; available at: *http://archives.cnn.com/1999/TECH/computing/12/23/java.ent.idg/* (Last accessed: 9 December 2005).

Saint-Onge, H. and Wallace, D. (2003) *Leveraging Communities of Practice for Strategic Advantage*, Boston: Butterworth-Heinemann.

Saraoglu, H. and Ascioglu, N. A. (2004) 'Disclosure of information on order execution practices of market centers: How can investors utilize it?' *Financial Services Review* 13(2): 151–65; available at: *http://www.findarticles.com/p/articles/mi_qa3743/is_200407/ai_n9411422* (Last accessed: 8 December 2005).

Sanders, S (2004) 'Converting customers to EBPP – Part II: Getting down to business', *Phone+*, October; available at: *http://www.phoneplusmag.com/articles/4a1feat04.html* (Last accessed: 2 December 2005).

SAS (year unknown) 'IIB bank qualifies for Basel II', *Success Stories;* available at: *http://www.sas.com/success/iib.html* (Last accessed: 6 December 2005).

Scanlan, D. (2004) 'Ironing out the kinks in the financial supply chain', *Asian Trade Finance Yearbook 2004*; available at: *http://corp.bankofamerica.com/public/products/pdf/trade/wcm_ar_iron.pdf* (Last accessed: 2 December 2005).

Shamos, M. (2004) 'Automated clearing and settlement systems', *Electronic Payment Systems Lecture 3*, Institute for eCommerce, Spring; available at: *http://euro.ecom.cmu.edu/program/courses/tcr763/2004/Slides/509,25,CHIPS Operation.*

Schuler, M. (2002) 'Integration of the European market for e-finance – evidence from online brokerage', *Discussion Paper No. 02–24*,

European Commission; available at: *http://opus.zbw-kiel.de/volltexte/2003/873/pdf/dp0224.pdf* (Last accessed: 6 December 2005).

Schwiderski-Grosche, S. (2003) 'Electronic and mobile payment systems'; available at: *http://www.fuchsberger.net/msc/teaching/opt5/archive/2002-03/slides/paymentsystems.pdf* (Last accessed: 9 December 2005).

SEC (2005) 'Form 8-K'; at *http://www.sec.gov/answers/form8k.htm* (Last accessed: 3 December 2005).

Securities Expert Group (2004) 'Financial services action plan: progress and prospects'; available at: *http://www.europeansecuritisation.com/pubs/FSAP_Stocktaking_Report.pdf* (Last accessed: 9 December 2005).

SelectX (2004) 'Rules-based underwriting systems, concise version', Report for Sapiens International; available at: *http://www.sapiens.com/en/ftp/selectx_report.pdf* (Last accessed: 9 December 2005).

Sem, A. (2004) 'Electronic bill presentment & payment (EBPP) in Europe', *Eurogiro News*, 4 November; available at: *http://www.eurogiro.com/News/200411-04.pdf* (Last accessed: 9 December 2005).

Siegel, F. (2004) *E-Payment in Europe – a payment scheme's perspective*, Presentation, Frankfurt, November 10; available at: *http://www.ecb.int/events/pdf/conferences/epayments2004/041110_eConf_Siegel.pdf* (Last accessed: 9 December 2005).

Sigma (2000) 'The impact of e-business on the insurance industry: Pressure to adapt – chance to reinvent', *Sigma*, Swiss Re, No. 5; available at: *http://www.swissre.com/INTERNET/pwsfilpr.nsf/vwFilebyIDKEYLu/MBAR-4VFJQ3/$FILE/sigma5_2000_e.pdf* (Last accessed: 9 December 2005).

Singer, M. (2002) 'Sun follows the money trail', CIO Update; available at: *http://www.cioupdate.com/news/article.php/1497001* (Last accessed: 9 December 2005).

Singh, N. (2001) *Electronic Commerce: Economics and Strategy*, book draft; available at: *http://econ.ucsc.edu/~boxjenk/* (Last accessed: 9 December 2005).

Skyview Partners, LLC (2004) 'What is COBIT security and when might you need to apply it?'; available at: *http://www.skyviewpartners.com/java-skyviewp/pdf/COBIT_Security.pdf* (Last accessed: 9 December 2005).

Sliwa, C. (2004) 'Web services: managing the building blocks', *Computerworld*, 16 August; available at: *http://www.computerworld.com/developmenttopics/development/story/0,10801,95207,00.html* (Last accessed: 5 December 2005).

Smith, H. W. (1993) 'The maturity of corporate giving and its long-term consequences', *Nonprofit Management & Leadership* 4(2): 215–28.

Société Générale (2004) 'A phase of maturity and rationalization for Société Générale's Internet banking services', *EFMA Newsletter*, 33(191), September-October; available at: *http://www.efma.com/pdf/Report191.pdf* (Last accessed: 2 December 2005).

Solution Sheet NCR Corporation and Sun (year unknown) available at: *http://www.sun.com/executives/iforce/midsize/pdf/Sun-NCR-final.pdf.*

Somasundaram, M. and Eappen, B. K. (2002) 'Architectures for insurance applications', *Technology Review #2002–06*, TATA Consultancy Services, November; available at:*http://www.tcs.com/0_whitepapers/htdocs/AIP_text.pdf* (Last accessed: 9 December 2005).

Standard & Poor's (2004) 'Transition without tears: a five-point plan for IFRS disclosure', Standard & Poor's, Reprinted from *RatingsDirect*, December; available at: *http://www.treasurers.org/technical/papers/resources/sp_transitiondec04.pdf* (Last accessed: 9 December 2005).

Star Systems (2005) 'Electronic payments in America: today and tomorrow', Star Systems White Paper, January; available at: *http://www.star.com/pdf/ElectronicPayments.pdf.* (Last accessed 5 April 2005).

Steeley, O. (2001) 'Guaranteed transactions, the quest for the "holy grail"', *Electronic Payment Systems Observatory Newsletter* 10: 4–7, November; available at: *epso.jrc.es/newsletter/vol10/docs/ePSO-N10.rtf* (Last accessed: 10 December 2005).

Stein, M. and Kenyon, J. (2004) 'A decade of online fundraising', *Nonprofit Quarterly,* Winter; available at: *http://www.nonprofitquarterly.org/files/578-204.pdf* (Last accessed: 9 December 2005).

Stickney, C. P. (1996) *Financial Reporting and Statement Analysis*, 3/e, Forth Worth: The Dryden Press, p. 511.

Stoneburner, G. T., Goguen, A. and Feringa, A. (2002) 'Risk management guide for information technology systems', *NIST Special Publication 800-30*; available at: *http://csrc.nist.gov/publications/nistpubs/800-30/sp800-30.pdf* (Last accessed: 9 December 2005).

Storage Technology Corporation (2003) 'Case Study: AOK Baden-Wuerttemberg', StorageTek Case Study; available at: *http://www.stortek.com/pdfs/AOK_Baden_Wuer_11Dec.pdf* (Last accessed: 9 December 2005).

Sullivan, R. (2003) 'Liberty Alliance really about more than just single sign-on', *American Banker*, 11 July; available at: *http://www.phaos.com/about/AmerBank_Phaos.pdf* (Last accessed: 9 December 2005).

Sun (2004) 'The role of identity management in Gramm-Leach-Bliley compliance', A Business White Paper, September; available at: *http://www.sun.com/software/products/identity/wp_identity_mgmt_gramm_leach_bliley.pdf* (Last accessed: 9 December 2005).

SunGard (2003) 'GLBA security standards: safeguarding your customer data for compliance and regulatory audit', *Executive Brief Series;* available at: *http://www.availability.sungard.com/NR/rdonlyres/16A78A24-2E37-4B29-BB02-7378D4FCF73C/0/SunGardExecutiveBriefGLBA.pdf* (Last accessed: 9 December 2005).

Swiss Re (2004) 'The impact of IFRS on the insurance industry', *Sigma*, 7; available at: *http://www.swissre.com/INTERNET/pwsfilpr.nsf/vwFilebyIDKEYLu/MPDL-67JEGX/$FILE/sigma7_2004_e.pdf* (Last accessed: 9 December 2005).

SWX (2005) 'Clearing & settlement model', at: *http://www.virt-x.com/clearing/model.html* (Last accessed: 9 December 2005).

Sybase (2002) 'Winning strategies for finance', White Paper; available at: *http://192.138.151.105/pdynamo/sybasesite/Financial_A4_12pp_FINAL.pdf* (Last accessed: 9 December 2005).

Tallman, D. (2003) 'Financial institutions and the safe harbor agreement: securing cross-border financial data flows', *Law and Policy in International Business*, Spring; available at: *http://www.findarticles.com/p/articles/mi_qa3791/is_200304/ai_n9192493* (Last accessed: 9 December 2005).

TATA (2004) 'Canada's capital markets leapfrog to T+1', Case study, TATA consultancy services; available at: *http://www.uk-tcs.com/docs/CaseStudy-CDS-1204.pdf* (Last accessed: 15 Decembr 2005).

Thomas, D. (2005) 'HSBC banking on anti-fraud plan', *Computing*, 20 July; available at: *http://www.computing.co.uk/computing/news/2140141/hsbc-banking-anti-fraud-plan* (Last accessed: 6 December 2005).

Thomson Financial (2003) 'Thomson ONE banker', Brochure; available at:*http://thomson.com/cms/assets/pdfs/financial/ib_group/T1B_brochure_US.pdf* (Last accessed: 9 December 2005).

Trichet, J.-C. (2005) 'European financial integration and the management of inflation expectations by the European Central Bank', Remarks on the Conference 'The euro: one currency, one financial market', New York; available at: *http://www.bis.org/review/r050421b.pdf* (Last accessed: 9 December 2005).

Tsai, M. (2004) 'Online sellers widen payment options', *Wall Street Journal* (Eastern edn) 7 July, New York, p. 1.

Tyacke, S. (2005) 'The National Archives' Data Protection Policy Statement', *National Archives*, 7 January; available at: *http://www.nationalarchives.gov.uk/legal/pdf/policy04.pdf* (Last accessed: 9 December 2005).

US Department of Commerce (2005) 'Quarterly retail e-commerce sales: 2nd quarter 2005', *US Census Bureau News*, 19 August; available at: *http://www.census.gov/mrts/www/data/pdf/05Q2.pdf* (Last accessed: 9 December 2005).

Vaidya, G. (2003) 'Making a difference with CRM and data mining', Presentation; available at: *http://www.ficci.com/ficci/media-room/speeches-presentations/2003/sep/session5-g-vaidya.ppt* (Last accessed: 9 December 2005).

Vartanian, T. P., Ledig, R. H. and Fajfar, M. (2004) 'Legal and business implications of the future and electronic payments', Electronic Banking Law and Commerce Report, Glasser LegalWorks, April; available at: *http://www.ffhsj.com/reprints/040401_vartath.pdf* (Last accessed: 9 December 2005).

Wallace-Wells, D. (2005) 'The givers using the web to promote tsunami relief', *Slate*, 6 January; available at: *http://slate.msn.com/id/2111952/* (Last accessed: 9 December 2005).

Walsh, P. (2003) 'Operational risk and the new Basel Accord', Hyperion White Paper, October; available at: *http://www.hyperion.com/downloads/solutions/BaselII_Opl_Risk_WP.pdf* (Last accessed: 9 December 2005).

Well, R. (2001) 'TradeCard, FCIB Documentary Services Group', *Presentation*; available at: *http://www.barrettwells.co.uk/TradeCardFCIB%20Stras10129.ppt* (Last accessed: 9 December 2005).

Wenger, E. (1998) *Communities of Practice. Learning, Meaning and Identity*, Cambridge: Cambridge University Press.

Williams, A. (2005) 'IT security management technology', Gartner Presentation, 28 April; available at: *http://www.gartner.com/teleconferences/attributes/attr_121823_115.pdf* (Last accessed: 9 December 2005).

Woodbury, C. (2004) 'What is COBIT security and when might you need to apply it?' Sky View White Paper; available at: *http://www.skyviewpartners.com/java-skyviewp/pdf/COBIT_Security.pdf* (Last accessed: 3 December 2005).

Wraith, J. (2001) 'Leveraging XML for STP', Presentation at Conference on Wall Street, NY; available at: *http://lighthouse-partners.com/xml/presentations/James%20Wraith.ppt* (Last accessed: 9 December 2005).

Wung, K. (2004) 'SQP SEM and business analytics', Presentation at SAP SEC Strategic enterprise management; available at: *http://www.kmis.or.kr/3_sig/sem_data/sem(feb04).pdf* (Last accessed: 2 December 2005).

Zeichner Risk Analytics, LLC (2004) *Risk Assessment* 2(133), 19 July; available at: *http://www.zra.com/zra/071904-F.pdf* (Last accessed: 9 December 2005).

ZipLip (2005) 'ZipLip HIPAA security rules matrix'; available at: *http://www.ziplip.com/docs/support/ZipLipHIPAASecurityRulesMatrix.pdf* (Last accessed: 8 December 2005).

Index

Printed in the United Kingdom
by Lightning Source UK Ltd.
109749UKS00001B/10